The Substance of Things Hoped For

Samuel DeWitt Proctor

THE

SUBSTANCE *of* THINGS

HOPED FOR

A Memoir of
African-American Faith

Judson Press
Valley Forge

The Substance of Things Hoped For:
A Memoir of African-American Faith

Paperback version published in 1999 by Judson Press, Valley Forge, PA
19482-0851

Originally published in hardcover by G. P. Putnam's Sons, 200
Madison Avenue, New York, NY 10016. This edition is reprinted by
arrangement with G. P. Putnam's Sons, a member of Penguin Putnam
Inc.

Library of Congress Cataloging-in-Publication Data
Proctor, Samuel D.
   The substance of things hoped for : a memoir of African-American faith /
Samuel DeWitt Proctor.
      p. cm.
Originally published: New York : G.P. Putnam's Sons, c1995.
ISBN 0-8170-1325-3 (pbk. : alk. paper)
1. Proctor, Samuel D. 2. Afro-American clergy—Biography. 3.
Afro-American Baptists—Biography. 4. Baptists—United States—Biography.
5. Baptists—United States—Clergy—Biography.
I. Title.
[BX6455.P76A3 1995]
286.1092—dc21   98-54388

Printed in the U.S.A.
06 05 04 03
10 9 8 7 6 5 4 3 2

To my wife, and the mother of our four sons,
Bessie Louise

Now faith is the substance of things hoped for, the evidence of things not seen.

Hebrews 11:1

Acknowledgments

WITH DEEPEST APPRECIATION I ACKNOWLEDGE THE encouragement and assistance of the following persons, who read my manuscript in its early stages and made invaluable suggestions: Stephanie Porter Freeman, Margaret Knispel, Dr. William Turner, Dr. Charles Booth, Dr. Jean Dorgan, and Reverend Sherry Austin. I owe an especially heavy debt to Charlayne Hunter Gault for patient, skilled, and sacrificial contributions to this effort.

The project was born in the minds of my literary agents, Barbara Lowenstein and Madeleine Morel, and nurtured by the faithful and talented assistance of Josleen Wilson, an accomplished writer in her own right. My editor, Laura Yorke, guided me from beginning to end, and she and the other Putnam professionals were zealous in their care for the finished product.

My wife, Bessie, and my sons, Herbert, Timothy, Samuel, and Steven, as always, were burdened with the tedium of laboring over every sentence at the initial stages. All this came to pass with the loyal and unstinting devotion of my secretary for twenty years, Lorraine Smoller.

However, while my thanks to those named above remains boundless, responsibility for the final outcome is mine alone, by the grace of God.

SAMUEL DEWITT PROCTOR
Somerset, New Jersey
1995

Contents

Foreword

I WAS HONORED TO BE ASKED TO WRITE THIS FOREWORD.
If you've never heard Samuel Proctor speak, you're in for a treat
here. This remarkable, wise, and beautiful spirit has graced us
with a thoughtful overview of the history of African Americans
in our country since the 1600s, an inspiring portrait of his own
call to the ministry and his struggles and successes, and a vision
of how "the substance of things hoped for" can be achieved. I
was moved by this book, as I always am by Sam Proctor. His writings and sermons ground me with his realism and awe me with
his infinite optimism and faith. And he never fails to make me
laugh.

Samuel Proctor has spent his life as a professor and college and university president, a public servant and adviser to presidential administrations and candidates (including Hubert Humphrey), a preacher and counselor, and a thinker and community leader in good political times and bad. He followed Adam Clayton Powell, Jr., as minister of the Abyssinian Baptist Church of Harlem and is equally at home in black and white churches, small and large, around the country and the world.

Sam tells us how he never absorbed the racist environment in which he grew up and has always chosen to believe unfailingly in God and the "moral order of the universe." He internalized his parents' and grandparents' definition of him, not the definition of him pronounced by many southern whites in the first half of this century. Like so many black children, Sam was blessed with loving and affirming family and neighbors and teachers, whose message was clear: You are important; let no man or woman look down on you and you must not look down on any other man or woman. He learned to share their vision of a world where committed persons do what their talents, interests, and opportunities lead them to do, forgetting about recognition and rewards, ignoring who is the "first," working hard and giving back.

In this wonderful book, Sam talks about the crises in our communities, leads us through the causes and consequences of what is happening to us as a people, and shows us paths we might take out of our wildernesses of drugs, poverty, and violence.

Those who are born to privilege, he states unequivocally, have the responsibility to help those who are not. He has devoted his life to this belief and encourages us all to follow where he has led. He has counseled, mentored, and inspired thousands of young people, always lovingly spurring them on. He has been a friend and adviser to many names which will ring through history, including Martin Luther King, Jr., Medgar Evers, and Jesse Jackson, and many more who will not be recorded in history but who are today doctors, lawyers, teachers, successful business people, and ministers instead of drug addicts and criminals.

Serving in the Kennedy, Johnson, and Carter administrations, he worked in the Peace Corps when it was changing the world and the Office of Economic Opportunity when it was changing our country. He saw and still sees government not as the enemy but as the recourse, the means to drive a wedge and then a stake into racial and economic inequities. Government, in the hands of honorable, wise, and compassionate men and women, has always addressed many of the evils of the world, and can again. It can also stoop to represent the basest, most selfish instincts of our darker side.

I share Sam's horror when, as we see countless children, families, and communities in crisis, we also see some members of the United States Congress propose radical, indiscriminate, unfair, and anti-child provisions which, if they become law, would leave millions more children destitute, hungry, and homeless.

As our society struggles to find solutions to the horrors of poverty and violence, Sam Proctor preaches the unity of mankind in which he has always put his faith. He is equally critical of white racism and black separatism. The African cultural advocates and black separatists who want to turn their backs on America ignore the struggles of four centuries of our forebears who have fought to make this their America as well. We have earned a place at the table. The answer to many of our problems is not to leave the table, but to put in all the leaves necessary to accommodate those who still stand outside looking in. And the leaves, Sam stresses again and again, are fitted in place by education and unity. Most scathing of all is Sam's indictment of blacks who blame blacks for the problems and pain we still face, who join right-wing, thinly veiled racists who say every child born in America today starts out with an equal chance. He has utter contempt for so-called conservative, well-known blacks who are "either stupidly ahistorical . . . or mendacious parasites," who use "obscure language to say virtually that blacks caused their own problems and deserve to suffer."

Sam also discusses a terrible myth among blacks that blacks who succeed are not black enough, that they are giving in to and joining in "white" society. Sam writes, "When young people put achievement out of reach for themselves and pretend to prefer ignorance, noise, drugs, and sex . . . it is a kind of suicide, or in the case of a generation of young people, genocide." He's seen angry reactions to his success from black adults and black young people. When he was a youth, he says, he expected prejudice from whites. But now it is heartbreaking to see it in blacks. And he is concerned about people who criticize his commitment to reach out to all people, to try "to make any new communication a positive one."

As Sam talks about our people and government, he naturally turns to ethics and religion. The impact of religion on human existence, and particularly on the black experience in this country, is beyond measure. And is it a coincidence that now, as violence and drugs and gangs seem to be replacing family and community and faith among our young people, we see a turning away from moral values and from God? In case after case, Sam Proctor shows us God-fearing and God-loving people who have overcome the most grinding poverty and degradation, staying together as a family and rising above their environment and bitterness. And he offers, too, the tragic stories of children born into "homes," if you could call them that, where parents have abandoned hope, and, I believe, not coincidentally, abandoned God.

My father was a minister and I was raised in a family that worshiped God in how they lived as well as how they prayed. I can't imagine what my life would have been like without that foundation of faith in God's presence.

Some people believe in God but seldom see the inside of a church or synagogue. I believe a religious congregation, a home church, plays an important role in children's lives. While it cannot replace the love and support children receive from their fam-

ilies, religious congregations can act as an extended family, helping children find the faith and hope they need to remain strong
and find their way. In the face of the pervasive breakdown of family values and bonds today, religious congregations have to be a
positive support system and the moral locomotive rather than
the moral caboose for fair opportunity for every child.

We each need to find the way to peace in our heart and soul,
and bedrock values on which to ground our life. The quality of
one's life depends so much on one's interior climate, and that
is where religion and a relationship with God make such a difference. While I won't say that you can't succeed without it, so
many young people without faith are, as Sam writes, "giving up
on any concentrated, sustained hard effort."

Sam characterizes two kinds of people: "Those propelled by
their faith that we can make it here [are] making it come to
pass." Without faith, "those for whom racist intransigence [is]
too rigid and endemic, poverty too burdensome, political indifference too powerful and resources too shallow [are] wallowing
in the muck and mire."

In this book Sam sounds the warning that "the crisis is upon
us." Violence and hopelessness spiral together. Families disin-
tegrate or never existed to begin with. Drugs and prisons are the
future for so many of our children. Children who should be
dreaming of careers and homes and families of their own are
planning what to wear at their funerals.

Pride and self-respect, Sam declares, "derive from the spiritual
core within," and there is a need within every man and woman
"for a strong religious faith and a worldview that holds things together. If you believe that there is a purpose and a power available to each of us, you have an inexhaustible source of evergreen
inspiration." Amen.

I believe, as Sam writes, that "we must reach back and find ways
to help others" who are "mired in poverty, alcoholism, violence,
and immorality . . . or the whole American nation may sink. This

is the new tenet of our faith." We must reach out most of all to children and commit to mentoring and healing. And we must understand that the solutions lie in family, education, wise public policy, and a return to moral values that are lived and not just preached.

Here Sam offers ideas for a new kind of school, a National Youth Academy, and new ways in which our society can give a hand up to the last and the least. He calls upon us to address "questions of [our] purpose and destiny" and sort out our own individual "place in the scheme of things." He presents us with the vision of a "new human paradigm" of love and respect for each other in a world without poverty, hunger, and hatred, and offers an achievable dream of a community and a nation committed to realizing *The Substance of Things Hoped For.*

Thank you, Sam, as always, for your wisdom.

MARIAN WRIGHT EDELMAN
President, Children's Defense Fund
May 1995

Prologue

MOST AMERICANS KNOW ONLY THOSE AFRICAN AMERICANS who appear on the 11 o'clock news—super-rich entertainers and car hijackers; phenomenal sports figures and rapists; a four-star general and a subway murderer; a poet laureate and a drug dealer.

But the main flow of life among African Americans occurs largely unnoticed: the millions who fill ghetto churches, whose children overrun the hundred and five historically black colleges and swell the ranks of minorities in the land grant universities, who maintain good credit, pay taxes on good incomes and investment returns, and maintain homes with order, love, and deep devotion.

Racial separation hides from public view the African Americans who have remained true to the resolve of those who marched out of slavery standing tall, who sought education immediately, who kept their hope alive and created the bedrock of the African-American middle class. They have refused refuge in otherworldly cults, ignored separatist movements, and rejected all pernicious theories about their genetic inferiority. They continue to fill the buses, subways, and superhighways, finding their way to banks, schools, factories, construction sites, hospitals, and stores, where they serve the public and pump up the economy.

A persistent faith propels them—faith in God, faith in their own worth and dignity, and faith in the idea that America's 250 million diverse peoples can cohere in a true community that gives space to ethnic preferences, but gives loyalty to the basic values of equality, compassion, freedom, and justice. Through the long, winding trail of political fortunes, with a disciplined transcendence over movements and individuals who would impede their progress, they have survived every challenge and still press forward toward helping America fulfill a unique and unprecedented role in the history of humankind.

Yet there never was a time when the future of black Americans has seemed so cloaked in contradictions and so wrapped in ambiguity as it does today. On the one hand, so many blacks have overcome the burden of discrimination, the drag of poverty and poor education, and seem to be finding a place for themselves in this society. On the other, highly visible, young black failures are seen on the news every night, handcuffed and stuffed into police cars. These powerful images project a frightful future where angry, alienated blacks seem to live in perpetual chaos. Many Americans buy into the notion that the spiral of racism and violence is swirling furiously downward and cannot be reversed.

This downdraught in race matters has culminated in a volcanic political eruption, and a chorus of politicians has won approval by chanting the refrain of black failure. They magnify data on crime, welfare, and dependence, and minimize such images as two black Rhodes scholars from New Jersey, ten black women in Congress, and a black governor elected in Virginia. It has become acceptable for civic and intellectual leaders to deprecate all blacks in cocktail party repartee, around oak boardroom tables, and more subtly in television talk-show interviews.

In the face of such lingering racism, black people pulse with pride, rushing to their churches, their asylum of hope and their fortress of faith. There, ushers are in place, choirs sway in rhythmic consent, and the pastor, healing priest at one moment and clarion prophet the next, is their incarnation of the spirit of transcendence. And there they are assured, week after week, in an unbroken refrain, that their dry bones of despair can live.

Like millions of other black Americans, I am heir to the faith that was born the day twenty frightened black captives were unloaded at Jamestown in 1619. Their slow, courageous journey from the Dutch slave boat to the present, in the face of unrelenting oppression, is the story of their faith; and therein I believe lies the clue to the answer to today's dilemma.

Faith put steel in their spines to endure physical bondage, and zeal in their souls to prevail against evil; it illumined their minds to keep the vision of a better day, and inspired their hearts to learn and embrace the great human conversation. Faith gave them a sense of eternity, a mystical transcendence that transposed their pain into song and their agony into a durable, resilient quest for complete humanity, the substance of things hoped for.

Despite the pall of suspicion and fear that hangs in the air today, I believe that enough idealism and faith remain among all of us to generate a soaring national quest for a new kind of a human paradigm in which all the diverse peoples of America can participate. I think of it as potentially the first real community in the world. I believe in this vision because of my own family's experience up from slavery.

My father's mother and my mother's grandfather were born enslaved. As a child, I could not fathom how my grandmother, a dignified, intelligent woman of impeccable character, could ever have been someone's property. To me, she seemed the zenith of human completeness. She was still living when I became a college president and I can remember how she congratulated me with cautious restraint in her voice, and with challenge and high expectation shining in her eyes.

My parents raised their six children in the rigidly divided South during the Great Depression. For most of our lives my sister and brothers and I rode in separate cars on trains, ate in separate dining rooms and used separate bathrooms, all designed to diminish our sense of worth. At times I felt ready to give up, but in the long run nothing really penetrated my shield of faith.

This faith was like the air we breathed throughout my youth, and it has followed me throughout my days. It is a habit of the heart that constrained us to focus on the stars rather than the canopy of darkness. All of us went to college and three of us hold graduate degrees. My sister became a schoolteacher, and my four brothers became, respectively, an Air Force Bandmaster, a dentist, a postal clerk, and an ophthalmologist. My own professional life began at age ten with a shoe-shine box at the gate of the Norfolk Naval Base. I ended up a professor at Rutgers University, and pastor of the Abyssinian Baptist Church in Harlem.

My wife, Bessie, saw a similar passage in her own family. Her father graduated from the pharmacy school of Shaw University, a small, black Baptist school in North Carolina, and opened a pharmacy for black physicians and their black patients in Virginia. Her brother, Maurice Tate, graduated from the Philadelphia College of Pharmacy, and in the 1950s became the pharmacist who attended President Eisenhower at Walter Reed Hospital in Washington, D.C. Today, our son Timothy is vice president and associate general counsel of Glaxo, the world's largest pharmaceutical company.

The Substance of Things Hoped For chronicles my own family history against the larger history of the black struggle for equality in America—from slavery through the Reconstruction, from urban migration and the Great Depression through the monumental victories of the NAACP; from the tedious Eisenhower era to the King oasis and the Great Society, from Nixon neglect and Reagan-Bush hostility all the way to the Clinton debut. Looked at in perspective it is like a series of doors opening and closing. In between, however, real progress leaks through.

Make no mistake, none of these were easy journeys. Every generation of black Americans has been forced to overcome new hardships. Yet I believe the faith that brought our forebears out of the midnight of slavery into the daybreak of Emancipation is still powerful enough today to respond to the despair of alienated young blacks.

As a people we still have tremendous societal deficits to overcome, particularly among marginalized youth without hope, but I believe the glass is more than half full. As I write, millions of black people are leading productive, principled lives; forty blacks are in the Congress; a black woman is in the Senate; Riverside Church has a black pastor; five black Americans serve in the presidential cabinet; one has been chairman of the Joint Chiefs of Staff; another heads the Ford Foundation, the world's largest philanthropy; a black woman is America's poet laureate; one has directed the National Science Foundation; another directs the Centers for Disease Control; and another has headed the TIAA, the largest pension fund in the world.

Their achievements prove that we are more than composites of others' definitions of us, more than a reflection of dismal government reports and negative data in sociology textbooks, and more than the sum of our deprivations and deficits. We are created in the image of God, with the same human equipment as the Queen of England, the same intellectual potential of all others, evenly distributed on the same normal curve. Differences in outcomes derive from differences in opportunities.

We are at a pivotal moment in a long and grievous struggle. In 1865, freed slaves faced their emancipation secure in the belief that their cause was just. I believe that ultimately their experience may be a prophetic precursor to this new human paradigm in the world, one that underlines the absolute equality of all persons. This new paradigm is the fruit of high religion, and the concomitant of true democracy. It will foster the maximum cultivation of all human potential, and celebrate justice, fairness, and compassion. Evidence that such a model of responsible and decent humanity might come into being is shadowy, but the faith that piloted the emancipated slaves remains the substance of things hoped for, and the evidence of things not seen.

The Substance of Things Hoped For

CHAPTER ONE

The Crucible of Faith

IT'S SAID THAT ONCE FREDERICK DOUGLASS WAS GIVING A speech in upstate New York and Harriet Tubman, the inimitable captain of the Underground Railroad, was in the audience. During the speech, as Douglass's zeal appeared to be flagging, she stood up and shouted, "Frederick, Frederick, is God dead?"

Whenever I see our faith waning today, I think of that desperate, inspiring call to arms. And I also think of my grandmother and her own unflagging belief that God was not dead. When I was a boy, my father's mother lived with us, and I would find myself absentmindedly gazing at her, wondering how she had felt being a little slave girl. I had seen images of slaves in the movies and in a few books: they always wore shabby clothes and spoke in crude and halting words; they couldn't read or write, and cowered in a pitiful broken-down manner.

None of this jibed with the image my grandmother presented. She was highly refined and poised. Her speech was perfect, her spelling and penmanship flawless, and her expectations of her children and grandchildren demanding. Grandma had a frightening piety about her. She was never tentative or ambiguous about anything. Her own early suffering had generated strength, just as the wood from trees able to survive at the frigid timberline in the Alps made the sweetest-sounding violins.

Grandma's intrepid confidence rested on a single uncomplicated notion: God created all people; any inequalities among us were due to unequal opportunity. From her we learned that hatred and vindictiveness were always destructive. "No use fretting or crying," she would say. "If you do your part, God will do the rest."

If we listened patiently, Grandma told us stories about her childhood. She was born around 1855 on a small tobacco plantation situated on the James River, a region now completely enveloped by Richmond, Virginia. On the day she was born, without rights and with a general consensus that she was an inferior being, she was named Hattie Ann Virginia Fisher, after the family who owned her. This family was not very rich or influential, which may explain why, compared to most planters, they had a somewhat benevolent attitude toward their slaves. Hattie Ann was never whipped or separated from her family as other slaves were. However, she was worked hard. Enslaved children were usually treated like farmyard animals, doing whatever came to hand and eating cornmeal and scraps of fatback at a common table. Because the plantation was near the river, Hattie Ann's father may have been able to supplement his family's meager fare with fish and small game.

Like all enslaved children, Hattie Ann imitated the work done by grown folks and, even as a small child, learned to sew well.

Her skill with a needle earned her a job in the "big" house. When she was around seven or eight years old, the Fishers entrusted their youngest children into her care. "When the Episcopal priest came around to teach the white children," she told us, "I was allowed to sit in the circle and learn right along with them." Hattie Ann was the only slave on the Fisher place who was permitted to learn to read. Although rare, her experience was not unique. Historical records show that from time to time some planters defied law and custom and taught a few slaves to read. Literacy meant that an enslaved person could perform more sophisticated tasks.

However, the vast majority of slaves were denied any access to education as part of a well-documented conspiracy to forge a racial stereotype: namely, that blacks were less intelligent than whites and fundamentally unable to learn. Slaveholders' worst nightmare was the image of enslaved blacks carrying oil-soaked torches, waving bread knives and meat cleavers, and wildly rushing the big house where white women and children slept. To protect themselves, they denied blacks privacy, time, literacy, and teachers who might stir them to action.

Apart from forestalling rebellion, there was a more subtle reason to withhold education. Bible-reading Christians had a basic conflict between their religious beliefs and their brutal ownership of other human beings. To resolve their hypocrisy, they concluded that Africans were some sort of retarded offspring of *Homo sapiens* and, therefore, not quite human. To support this fiction, slave owners put out the lamps at night, snatched books from questioning hands, separated blacks from their tribal groups, and created around them a cultural vacuum. This extremely effective practice of first denying education then saying the victim cannot learn continues to compound all other problems facing us today.

Slave owners had reason to worry. Behind the docile masks pulsed nerves strung tight with the desire for freedom. These were the "hands" who were up at the crack of dawn, as the dew still glistened on the grass, mumbling to each other in hushed tones while they fed the chickens and the pigs, led the cows to pasture, filled the dog's water pail, started the fire in the oven, and put the skillets and flatirons on the stove top. All day long they acted out their charade, pretending stoic compliance while seething with indignation; humming songs of transcendence, while silently massaging their pain and waiting for twilight's sweet relief.

For nearly three hundred years, enslaved houseworkers had been listening to their owners' prayers and Bible readings. They heard how Joseph survived his brothers' selling him into slavery. They heard how praying Daniel walked out of the lions' den alive, and how the Hebrew boys emerged from the fiery furnace unscorched. Bit by bit they memorized these stories. They would sneak among the unlighted slave quarters in the quiet hours of the night, risking their lives to pass these stories along to the other slaves and give hope to drooping spirits. They edified one another with prayers and made chants about freedom, reciting rhythmically the mighty acts of Moses, Joshua, Elijah, and Daniel.

From these epics of deliverance, they were able to interpret their own inexplicable situation and give themselves reasons to stay alive. From the Bible came a vision that one day, somehow, they too would be free. And by repeating the narratives over and over again, slaves began to fashion the faith hypothesis that would see them through every conceivable scheme of dehumanization. You might say that they found their source of faith in the very religion their owners had violated.

In Hattie Ann's youth this new faith was the single source of relief. Every Sunday morning she was saturated with the pure, undiluted, spirit-filled worship of the small makeshift plantation church, where God seemed to lean into the church-house windows.

Then early one morning word spread from the big house to

the slave quarters and likely all the way down to the riverbank where ten-year-old Hattie Ann was picking berries with the little children: freedom had come. I can only imagine how she must have felt—excited, but also frightened. Where would she go now? How would her family survive?

Emancipation was like being born naked in a wintry world. Clothed in rags, their color a badge of shame and inferiority, freed slaves had no means of sustaining themselves. Most could not read or write, and possessed no worldly goods.

They were at the chaotic crossroads predicted by the distinguished French nobleman, Alexis de Tocqueville, during a visit to the United States in 1831. De Tocqueville knew that eventually the large slave population would become free, just as the slaves of South America and the Caribbean islands had already become free. When that happened, he said, the government would have to seize one of several options: ship slaves back to Africa or deposit them among the islands of the Caribbean; tempt them to violence and then kill them; deny them jobs, food, and shelter, and force them out of sight into the mountains and caves of the Appalachians; or compel fair-skinned slaves to meld with poor whites and Native Americans, and leave the rest to vanish slowly like flying fish or other unprotected mutants. De Tocqueville never realized that millions of slaves just like Hattie Ann had another option securely hidden in their minds and souls.

The spiritual resilience derived from their faith allowed most enslaved African Americans to come through their degrading experience whole, without losing their humanity. When the hour was upon them, they set out to create something entirely novel in the history of the world: In America, they dreamed of being free, side by side with their former masters. Their dream had been nurtured with prayer and watered with the briny tears shed by generations.

In their passion, they chose to redeem their race from centuries of dehumanization and make holy the ground on which their parents and ancestors suffered and died. With nothing but faith, they *imagined* the future. They fixed their trust in God and began the journey up the road to equality.

Itinerant black preachers tramped dusty backroads throughout the South, telling Bible stories, and stomping hope into the hearts of the people. The principal thrust came, however, with the founding of a chain of secondary schools and colleges across the South, beckoning the newly freed slaves to begin immediately to enter the life of learning. Booker T. Washington, born enslaved in the rough mining regions of West Virginia, walked from the Blue Ridge Mountains to the Chesapeake Bay, seeking admission to Hampton Institute, a school founded for Indians and freed blacks by Union Army General Samuel Armstrong. Throughout the South, other ex-slaves were also crowding into mission schools, ready and eager to learn. Within forty-five years after Emancipation, 259 of these black schools were established. In almost every instance, blacks themselves had started a school and appealed to missionary teachers for help, and those teachers responded by coming in droves from the Northeast. Virginia Union University, my own alma mater, was founded in 1865 in Mr. Lumpkin's jail for uncontrollable slaves, where dank cell blocks were converted into classrooms and bloodied whipping posts into lecterns.

After Emancipation, Hattie Ann and her family continued to work on the Fisher plantation. When she reached eighteen, the Fishers hired a coach and driver to carry her the eighty miles down the dirt road running alongside the James River all the way to "General Armstrong's school."

Hattie Ann had never been off the plantation and certainly didn't know what to expect at Hampton, but she didn't have much time to worry about it. Once there, she fell immediately under the scrupulous discipline of those puritanical New England school "marms" who followed behind their hard-working students as they scrubbed floors and washed windows, testing each immaculate surface with white-gloved fingertips. These teachers were determined to put new minds and hearts into the physical bodies that had outlasted slavery. Along with the domestic chores, Hattie Ann studied mathematics, chemistry, botany, art, music, anatomy, algebra, geometry, and the Bible. She became a superb seamstress. Hampton men followed a similar curriculum, and also learned carpentry, masonry, plumbing, and tailoring. Booker T. Washington, one of the oldest fellows in the school, stayed on to teach after he graduated, and his powerful presence emanated throughout the school.

Hattie Ann was not afraid of being brainwashed or made "white" by her teachers; she stood hopefully and willingly at the portals of her fuller emancipation, the freedom of the mind.

Most impressive of all was the lofty expectation of these white New England teachers and the black teachers they trained. As a young man, I was fortunate to have one myself—Dr. Joshua Baker Simpson, who taught Latin and Greek at Virginia Union in the early 1940s. He read and wrote those ancient languages with the ease of English and thought we should all do likewise.

Dr. Simpson had finished Colby College in Maine in 1895. He was old, but energetic, always standing at attention. Every move he made was precise. He wore a collar and tie every day of the week, all day long. In his class, you could not cross your legs or assume any relaxed posture. No excuse was sufficient for being absent or late. My soul, I never met such a demanding, unyielding creature in my life.

I recall that one day Lorenzo Shephard, the son of a prominent Philadelphia pastor, shook his fountain pen to cause the ink to flow, and a mere drop fell onto the floor. Dr. Simpson stood up, lit up his light green eyes, tightened his thin lips, reddened his mulatto cheeks, and barked: "Mr. Shephard, where do you think you are? Please, go to the janitor's closet, come back with hot water, soap, and a scrub brush, and clean that ink up

7

from my classroom floor." As Shephard scrubbed, the lesson proceeded and not a soul giggled—we were all scared stiff!

Dr. Simpson was my first big academic challenge. Clearly, he was not preparing us for any lightweight assignment, nor for any subordinate tasks in life. Dr. Simpson was a child of that larger faith. He believed that black people were complete and equal. In every sinew of his body he believed that we could do whatever anyone could do, and that we should be held accountable to the highest standards. His photograph is on my desk at Rutgers now, fifty-two years later. He watches over my shoulder like my grandmother.

EVEN AS HATTIE ANN DEDICATED HERSELF TO THE FUTURE, powerful forces were getting ready to reject her claim to equality. In one of the strangest alliances in history, the Ku Klux Klan and the Supreme Court of the United States joined hands to thwart black progress. The Supreme Court had already emasculated the Fifteenth Amendment, which had granted black males the right to vote. Then in 1876, in a squabble over electoral votes in the Hayes–Tilden election, Congress granted the presidency to Hayes if his supporters agreed to end Reconstruction.

The backlash was already in motion when Hattie Ann graduated from Hampton in 1882. She was no longer a rickety little slave girl. Gone was the child who had sat up nights painstakingly looking for words she recognized in the master's Bible, gone the ragged little body who spent endless hours hemming with delicate stitches a lady's fine handkerchief. In her place stood an educated and refined woman, her painful past and hopeful present joined. At this bright moment I doubt that she realized that the open door of Reconstruction had already clanged shut. And if she did, it wouldn't have mattered. Forward was the only way to go.

While she had been studying at Hampton, Hattie Ann's family had moved off the Fisher plantation and settled in Norfolk.

The new graduate joined them there and found a job teaching little children in a segregated schoolhouse. Recently, my sister discovered among her archives a picture of Hattie's father taken in Norfolk around this time. He is wearing a fancy black suit with a vest, a watch chain draped across the front, and a breakback collar with a bow tie. One hand holds a brand-new hat, and the other is shoved casually into his pocket. He looked like the future belonged to him.

The fragments we put together about the family's early life in Norfolk suggest that soon after her graduation Hattie Ann met a fair-skinned mulatto named George Proctor, who had been enslaved in North Carolina. George was an itinerant musician and I think he came through town and caught sight of the cute little schoolteacher and that was it. Hattie Ann and George got married and started having babies—eight children, each born two years apart. George worked as a barber. It's clear from old photographs of the little wooden houses they lived in that he was not especially prosperous. Then young, handsome George suddenly died, probably from tuberculosis. And Hattie Ann was left to support and care for her eight young children alone.

The miracle of it all was that this skinny, itty-bitty woman kept them all in school. Hattie Ann supported her whole family on a black schoolteacher's pay, which was considerably less than white teachers were paid. Whatever her dreams, this was the job she would have for most of her life. All of Hattie Ann's children finished high school and all had some education beyond that. All of them knew music and played instruments well. My daddy played the piano, violin, and clarinet. One sister played the violin and a brother the trombone. All played in public concerts with various orchestras and bands.

Hattie Ann managed to defend her children and her home against all manner of intrusion. One famous family story concerns the night she set her house on fire when she threw an oil lamp at a burglar. The house burned down and the family lost everything. Grandma wasted no time looking back, she simply started over again.

We know a few more details about my mother's side of the family. Her grandfather, Zechariah Hughes, had been born enslaved in Gloucester County, Virginia, in 1849. *His* father purchased his family's freedom and changed their slave name, "Walker," to "Hughes," in recognition of the white man who had taught him to read. Zechariah grew up to become a preacher. As he preached, he also worked around the oyster beds of the York River. In 1878, he moved his entire congregation from Gloucester to Norfolk County and eventually built two churches that he served the rest of his life. He was an enterprising man who had eleven children by two successive wives. He made sure that all were educated, and all became achievers—ministers, businessmen, choir leaders, and teachers.

All of this happened at a time when blacks were being lynched for every and any trumped-up reason. In 1896, the disastrous *Plessy v. Ferguson* decision gave states the right to legalize racial segregation, and racial separation laws were immediately nailed up everywhere—in courthouses, trolley cars, universities, libraries, theaters, businesses, hospitals, factories, and even public beaches.

When I think about my grandparents making the giant step from slavery to freedom, I realize that none of my own achievements can ever live up to their legacy. Even though everything in the law and the society claimed they were inferior, through all the long days and long years of being beaten back, they held their heads high and made their mark. The lesson that I learned early from observing and listening, and trying to construct my own philosophy and pattern of life, was very simple. It was a way of seeing the stars, rather than the canopy of darkness.

WHEN MY WIFE AND I WERE VERY YOUNG AND ONLY RECENTLY married, we used to spend our vacations at her mother's home in the old colonial town of Fredericksburg, Virginia. Nothing very exciting happened there, but next door lived an old woman who had a large fragrant flower called a night-blooming cereus growing in her front yard. When other flowers were dormant, after the last rays of sunlight dimmed and the rhythms of photosynthesis ceased, the cereus spread open its petals and effused its perfume. It seemed indifferent to the void. Unnoticed and unapplauded, it performed for its own sake and gave up its beauty without admiration. Around midnight on summer nights, when we were sitting out on our porch trying to catch a late night breeze, the old woman would call us quietly to come over and see her lovely flower blooming in the dark.

When the lights went out in the 1890s, when the political currents swirled against black progress and the nation draped itself in antiblack sentiment, hope still bloomed within the black community. We had learned that the key to the future was education. Somehow we believed that we, too, could bloom, darkness notwithstanding.

CHAPTER TWO

Come Sunday!

My mama, Velma Gladys, was born in 1893, the daughter of Annie Gary and William Hughes, who was a choirmaster and a deacon in his father's church. When Velma was about twenty years old, she married Herbert Proctor, one of Hattie Ann's boys. They were students together at Norfolk Mission College, just as Velma's own parents had been when they met and married. On the eve of the First World War, Herbert canceled his plans for a dental career and got a job at the Norfolk Navy Yard. Soon he and Velma had two little babies, Herbert, Jr., and Annie.

In the winter of 1916, both babies were struck by whooping cough and died within days of each other. My parents never got over their deaths. For all of their lives they spoke of our little brother and sister who had died in infancy, and we all spent hours wondering what they would have looked like and been like.

It always impressed me that in addition to shouldering that grief, my father left the house every morning to work in a world of insults and humiliation, and my mother sang and prayed her way through long days of incessant labor at home, at the stove, the sewing machine, the wash tub and the ironing board.

Daddy and Mamma were children-oriented. They lived for us. Daddy left early every morning for the Navy Yard, where he seemed to take pride in earning a decent livelihood for his family. He was always upbeat and forward-looking. Our home, a nine-room frame structure in a long row of identical houses in Huntersville, the black center of Norfolk, was taken over by my parents from my mother's father when he became terminally ill.

There were six of us—first my sister Harriet, who was born in 1917, and then my older brother Vernon in 1919. I arrived in 1921. Three more boys came after me and all of us grew up in our grandfather's house at 918 Fremont Street. My mother's brothers and sisters lived nearby and were always in and out of our house. Their children were like our brothers and sisters, and we all had our eyes on the stars.

We lived behind a high wall of racial limits. I remember riding the ferry with my father between Norfolk and Portsmouth. No signs were posted to tell us which side was the "colored" side, but Daddy told me that our side was *always* the one reached by crossing through a heavy stream of traffic entering the ferry, clogging the area in the middle. Still fresh in my memory is the sight of a huge basket of freshly laundered linen, skillfully balanced on the head of a smiling, round-faced black woman ducking and dodging her way between teams of frightened, braying horses and loud, chain-driven trucks, as she struggled to cross the center of the ferry to reach the "colored" side.

Every day we lived with reminders of what our place was—what not to say, where it was safe to be, and how to make life a little smoother. To get a little raise in pay, or a slight promotion, we pretended to be "inferior." Any gesture that bespoke our desire for equality was saved for the black church. Speaking out elsewhere brought severe and final retribution. Some did, of course, and were willing to pay the price.

Church and family were like a seamless garment cloaked about us. Hymn-singing, praying, and Bible reading and quoting were as close as breathing and nearer than hands and feet. We never sat down to eat anything—a bowl of oatmeal, a piece of buttered spoonbread, a chicken leg—without bowing our heads and mumbling a fast prayer. When I wonder about the substance of things hoped for, I look within and remember the source of our hope for the future. The answer always was, in Duke Ellington's words, "Come Sunday!" Shoes were shined, music practiced, and the Golden Text memorized; the fish were frying in deep grease, the dog was fed and watered, the old Buick was wiped down and cleaned out, the rolls were in the oven, and every radio was tuned to the "Wings Over Jordan" choir led by Glenn T. Settles in Cleveland, singing, *Shine on me, shine on me. Let the light from the lighthouse shine on me.* It was church time, and faith would be rekindled.

Our whole family was active in church life. My aunts and uncles sang in choirs and played the organ in several churches. Four of my uncles were pastors and two of the largest churches in Norfolk were those founded by my great-grandfather Zechariah Hughes.

Our father never sent us to Sunday school. He took us with him—all six of us—shoes gleaming, trousers ironed, hair trimmed (by him!), and the Sunday lesson learned by heart. Most families in our neighborhood welcomed Sunday in the same way.

Everyone was identified by the church he or she attended.

"Did you know that Mr. Crocker died?"

"Which Mr. Crocker?"

"The one who goes to St. John's Church."

If you attended no church at all, it was like having no identity at all. Church was a social hour, a time to compare clothes, exchange news, share a sad note, celebrate a new job, look for a partner in romance, exchange recipes, learn about bargains, or pick up the name of a better doctor, tailor, or automobile mechanic.

In the Sunday school orchestra, my daddy played the violin, Vernon played the tuba, and I played the clarinet. Our churches sang with a rhythm and bounce. People often made up their own songs, adding verses as the Spirit led them, and the new verses became a permanent part of the song. Like their songs, their prayers were also memorized and repeated.

Church was also preaching time. I was generally bored by the worship service, although I was intrigued by the pastor. When I was a child, preachers wore long frock coats, high collars, and striped trousers. Week after week, they told the same familiar stories, giving content to our faith and rhythm to our emotions. People, anticipating every word, signaled the best points with verbal and, sometimes, bodily responses. Nowhere else could a group of people move from moaning and groaning to clapping and shouting for joy in so short a time. It was the same wherever black migrants gathered together and built churches up North and out West. These large urban churches, surrounded by mortuaries, cafés, blacksmiths, dry cleaners, barbershops, small stores, and professional offices, became the citadels of black American culture.

THE PEOPLE WHO MATTERED MOST TO US IN OUR YOUTH believed in the simplest virtues of honesty, sobriety, thrift, kindness, charity, and mutual respect. They abhorred dishonesty, boasting, unkindness, disloyalty, and sloth. Although such virtues bear no ethnic label, we learned them as patented human behavior from steady, predictable, devoted black Christians.

We learned Bible lessons from Grandma, who also taught us poems and hymns in her religiously correct English. She constantly policed our speech and grammar, correcting every split infinitive, every pronoun out of agreement with its antecedent, and every mispronounced word. I was perplexed that a woman as smart as my grandma could ever have been enslaved.

When I was still too young for school, Grandma took me along to her classroom at the Cumberland Street School where I sat in awe watching her teach. Believe me, no one acted up in Mrs. Proctor's classroom. All of her friends and colleagues seemed to share the same secret: they had a mission and a destiny to meet. They spoke to us children in the subjunctive mood—not what is, but what *may be,* when our faith flowered into reality.

When I was old enough for school, my days brimmed with activities—rehearsals, contests, games, and programs of all kinds. For the most part, my classmates and I were insulated from harsh, daily racial insults. And we had an answer for the ugly incidents we did have to endure: they would not last. Our teachers kept our eyes pinned on the future, and our faith stayed alive, pulsing within us.

I remember sitting in an English literature class in a segregated school, using tattered textbooks with the names, addresses, and telephone numbers of the white students who had worn them out and scribbled all over the pages. We were in an old building, scantily built for the "colored," with outdoor toilets, no lunchroom, no gymnasium, and no music or art or physical education teacher.

I recall our tall, thin Miss Edith Green, teaching us a poem by Alfred Tennyson which described a tiny flower that managed to grow through a granite wall and bloom on the other side. That poem has lived with me through these long decades, a more powerful memory than the images of that "colored" elementary school.

It was not always easy being one of the Proctor boys. The old folks pointed me out as Reverend Hughes' great-grandson, which meant that my behavior had to be irreproachable. Even worse, many of my teachers had been students of Grandma's. So I also had to live up to Hattie Ann Proctor's formidable reputation. It was incredible how we learned to handle the paradox of being compelled to hold our heads high with expectation and hope, while the social landscape was etched with denial and rejection.

AS CHILDREN WE WERE UNAWARE OF THE FULL IMPACT OF the Great Depression. We never felt severely impoverished, and our parents imposed a strong sense of security around us, just as their parents had done for them. There was never enough of what we wanted, but always enough of what we needed. We learned early to discriminate between approved ways of getting by and disapproved ones.

My brother Vernon and I were lucky enough to have a morning paper route which we had inherited from an older friend who had gone off to college. On Sundays, the papers were so thick and heavy that we had to stack them at the corner of Lexington and Church streets, then break them down into smaller bundles and deliver them a few at a time. No one bothered the main pile because a popular bootlegger called "Bear" operated his joint near that corner. Early one Sunday morning, as we were separating our bundles, we heard loud sirens wailing and two police motorcycles screeched to a stop on our corner, followed by a big LaSalle limousine. Two white men got out of the car and unloaded about ten gallon-jugs of corn whisky. Then another limousine pulled up. Bear came out of his joint and handed the well-dressed passenger a large roll of money.

Then *another* car—this one a big Ford convertible carrying four plainclothes police—slowly cruised up, and escorted the second limousine as it drove away. Bear surely looked like a hero to us—a black man defying law and custom, handling big money, and collaborating with crooked white police.

We could not get home fast enough to tell Daddy what we had seen. He told us that Bear was a boyhood friend of his, but he had not been reared in a Christian home. Bear had dropped out of school and chose to hustle and scheme for a living. No matter how poor Christians were, Daddy said, they would never steal or sell whisky for a living.

My daddy made it perfectly clear that there were two kinds of people: those who tried to live with moral accountability and those who did not. Over and over in my childhood my parents talked about and *demonstrated* the distinction between the behavior of church people—those who reflected a self-affirming approach to life—and the behavior of the unchurched.

Some people, of course, were borderline. One very warmhearted, generous woman in our neighborhood was the local numbers writer. Two or three times a year she was arrested and fined, then continued her business afterward. Although she lived in the midst of ardent church people, her whole lifestyle was something apart from the church. She smoked cigarettes in public, drank beer on her porch, and shouted profanity at her five children. Church people cringed at all of that. It saddened us boys because one of her sons was a friend of ours. He was embarrassed by his mother's behavior, but he was always getting into fights to defend her against one insult or another.

VERNON AND I USED TO LIE IN BED AT NIGHT TALKING ABOUT what we wanted to be when we grew up. Vernon said he wanted to lead a Broadway theater orchestra, although he had never seen one except in the movies. I wanted to be a lawyer, although

I had never actually seen a black lawyer anywhere at all. But Vernon and I already knew how to live on the substance of things hoped for. Our dreams took wings and soared beyond that little segregated dusty bottom in Virginia. Nothing—no ugly names, backdoor entrances, or raggedy, used schoolbooks—could stifle our faith.

Blacks living in other segregated communities around the country also made the best of their situation. They turned to each other and their neighbors and began to embroider the simple functions of life with a style and tempo that suited their taste and nourished their hope. In effect, they were creating a new black American culture that allowed them to survive with sanity in a hostile environment.

As we were growing up, that culture reverberated everywhere. Freedom's muse was joyous, profound, and often hilarious. We would dance a parody of our poverty, and sing a travesty of our pain. In our town, Saturday nights at Ashburn's barbershop, at the corner of Chapel and Anderson streets, was show time. Street messiahs, comedians, harmonica players, and poets performed routines for an audience of thirty or forty clients waiting on the five barbers.

ALTHOUGH BARRED FROM THE "LEGITIMATE" STAGE, WE also found creative ways to contribute to the larger white community. My father sang in the all-black Norfolk Philharmonic Glee Club, which comprised Pullman porters, bellhops, barbers, postmen, teachers, and even physicians, lawyers, and dentists. The Glee Club practiced every Wednesday night, and once a year they gave a concert in the city hall auditorium for a white audience. For that one night only, black families were permitted to attend and to sit in the rear of the auditorium. My mother always brought all six of us. Even though the whole society was rigidly segregated and lynchings were reported in the paper every week, the Glee Club closed each concert singing:

> Dawn is breaking and a new day is born . . .
> The world is singing the song of the dawn.

In reality, there was no new day. There was only the perennial belief that a new day would be born. Toward that end, church continued to provide the spiritual ballast needed for life's journey.

Before the Emancipation, slaveholders tried to convince blacks that God *wanted* them to be enslaved. In *Deep Like Rivers,* Thomas Webber recaptured the sinister words originally spoken to slaves by the Right Reverend William Meade, Episcopal bishop of Virginia:

> Take care that you do not fret or murmur or grumble at your condition, for this will not only make your life uneasy, but it will greatly offend Almighty God. Consider that it is not yourselves; it is not the people that you belong to; it is not the men that have brought you to it; but it is the will of God, who hath by his wise providence made you servants, because, no doubt, he knew that condition would be best for you in the world and help you better towards heaven. . . .

When blacks heard such things, they sucked their teeth, glanced at their fingernails, gazed into the deep distance, and slowly strolled away. It was not even worth a laugh. They knew their Bible.

We never accepted the self-negating religion offered by the slave masters. Our legacy flowed from preachers like Bishop Lucius Holsey, one of the founders of the Colored (now Christian) Methodist Episcopal Church, who was himself the son of an enslaved woman and a slave owner; Bishop Holsey's wife had been held in slavery by a Methodist bishop. Holsey made a direct assault on Meade's words:

> Every man is made by the same hand. . . . Neither can racial distinctions, color, climate or geographical situation of birth and growth make any difference in the characteristics of his real manhood. . . . What, therefore, is possible for one man is possible for all men under the same conditions and circumstances.

Everyone we met at our church was looking up. They were educated, neat, polite, prompt, and serious. Incidentally, my Sunday school teachers were also my public school teachers. All week long they shouted at us in the name of algebra and Shakespeare, and on Sundays, with a little more perfume, more makeup, nicer clothes and higher heels for the women, and a blue suit for Mr. Newsome, they shouted at us in the name of Moses and Jesus.

Most of our churches blended religious instruction with education in citizenship and cultural history. Unfortunately, however, some preachers leeched on the poor and promised extravagant blessings in return for all their meager earnings.

One of our neighbors, whom we called Miss Lillian, appeared to be a balanced, competent person, the mother of several lovely, bright children who went to school with us. She ran a small grocery store that was a hang-out for us kids. Miss Lillian hardly made any profit, but the store provided a kind of stage for her.

Every afternoon, the excitement started when she began to talk about Jesus. She would get up from her chair and go into a foot-clogging, holy dance, and then tilt her head back, with her steel-gray eyes fixed on blank space, and begin speaking "in tongues" until she foamed at the mouth and passed out, often gashing her head on any object in her path as she fell. Within seconds, she was back in her chair, waving her hands placidly, saying softly, "Thank you, Jesus, thank you, Jesus."

Miss Lillian belonged to a church headed by a Cape Verdean charismatic preacher from New Bedford, Massachusetts. He came to town monthly, working with a local pastor and worshiping in a large tent. He baptized believers by the hundreds, keeping his congregants shouting and dancing for hours on end. We always rushed to Church Street, our main drag, to see his welcoming parade march in to the tunes of a mediocre brass band. Crowds gathered to watch the tall, dark-skinned honor guards, wearing brass-buttoned jackets and high leather boots, sporting badges, whistles, and whisking batons to keep back the crowds. Then along came the visiting chief minister, seated in the back seat of a white, four-door Packard convertible with the top down. He wore a pink satin suit, with manicured fingernails an inch long, and his curly hair down to his shoulders. Diamond rings flashed on eight of his fingers and two very rotund sisters sat on either side of him, fanning the Tidewater humidity away from his chubby face. The "divine one" smiled graciously, waving his open hands in a kind of blessing, as his admirers trotted alongside the slowly gliding Packard.

At night he sat on a gold-papered throne as crowds of devotees marched past the rostrum and kneeled before him, dropping five-, ten-, and twenty-dollar bills in bushel baskets held by the uniformed guards. He preached brief, teasing sermons without ever using a whole sentence. They were simply empty words about God's blessings and the joy of heaven that fell like dew on the hearer's ears. Then the brass band marched in and the preacher encouraged the faithful to fill up those bushel baskets with "quiet money," as he called paper bills. The baskets ran over. You couldn't ask for more exciting entertainment.

The preacher regularly visited eight to ten cities, with more than one church in some towns. He wasn't the only one. Many smooth charismatic preachers used the same patented procedure to break free from organized denominations. They were supervised only by the "Holy Spirit." And uneducated, innocent, frustrated black people who couldn't imagine participating in the American system were their prey. There were many white "bishops" who fleeced their uneducated believers in the same way.

Interestingly, white and black Christians followed the same Jesus who taught love and inclusiveness, but they never worshiped together. Black people hardly gave a thought to this peculiar contradiction. The black church met such a critical need, and was so independent of white control, that no one considered a merger of black and white churches.

In fact, the chasm between the white and black church was unbridgeable: any gesture that signified equality was unacceptable to whites; and any gesture that implied black inferiority was unacceptable to blacks. Rather than transcend the taboos of the secular society, the churches, both black and white, simply reflected things as they were.

Although customs varied from one congregation to another, black people had carved out a distinctive style of biblical interpretation and worship. White people spent most of their time preparing for heaven; although blacks did not reject a vision of heaven, they emphasized that a better day would come, here on earth. Whites emphasized God's holiness and judgment; blacks saw God as the liberator of the oppressed. Whites asked, "What if you should die unsaved?" Blacks believed that God would help them to bear their daily burdens. Whites said that they wanted to be ready when Jesus came again; blacks that God would make a way out of no way.

IN OUR TOWN, AS IN BLACK COMMUNITIES ACROSS THE country, preachers were thumping on pulpits proclaiming that deliverance would eventually come to the faithful. In every black lodge hall in America, the brothers and sisters were drilled in voting and home ownership, and in every segregated school-house, black teachers held up photographs of C. C. Spauling, founder of the prosperous black life insurance company in Durham, N.C.; Mary McLeod Bethune, who built Bethune-Cook-man College from an abandoned freight car; W. E. B. DuBois, the black Harvard Ph.D. who founded the NAACP; Booker T. Washington, who built Tuskegee Institute; and George Washington Carver, the black Iowa-trained Tuskegee scientist.

The NAACP was bringing cases before the Supreme Court, and John L. Lewis and the United Mine Workers were fighting to get blacks, who had been shut out of the AFL, included in the new CIO labor camps.

But even then not all of us were running on the same track. The patience of some black intellectuals ran out. Some gave up and turned toward the American Communist Party, which made a big pitch for the black vote. Eighty-six percent of all blacks were still living in the South, most in rural areas where they barely survived on sharecropping. The party assumed that stagnant poverty and cultural isolation made blacks ripe for revolution. The swelling ranks of segregated trade unions in the United States added more impact to their argument.

In the midst of this, Marcus Garvey appeared, a Jamaican with a passion for black liberation and a dramatic plan to repatriate blacks to Africa. He had a poorly financed steamship line, an untrained "African Legion," composed of American blacks, which he said would run a new African state.

Garvey's whole movement had a lot of flair that was especially appealing to urban people who didn't have much education. He emphasized the beauty and promise of blackness, but most blacks knew that blackness without intellect, blackness without money, blackness without character or discipline, was just blackness without content.

The Communist Party's vision of class war and Garvey's vision of a new beginning in Africa failed to enchant large numbers of blacks. When Garvey urged American blacks to resettle in Africa in 1933, he discovered that our faith was like a rock, impenetrable; like a tree, deeply rooted. Despite the toughness of the times, no one was interested in abandoning the struggle here. Most blacks wanted solid, irreversible success here in a *changed* America, not a new start somewhere else.

Looking back now, it is clear to me that two strata of blacks in America had become solidly entrenched. Those who had been shut out still lived on subsistence wages, in cheap tenements or rural shacks along unpaved backroads, far removed from any talk of black destiny. By contrast, those who had made it through the open door of Reconstruction felt that their faith was being validated; they were leading lodges and churches, some had professional careers, and they were in the forefront of organizations dedicated to black education and black liberation.

When Franklin D. Roosevelt began to remake America's future, these heirs of the mission schools were ready, and theirs was the dominant black voice. They saw the worm turning.

CHAPTER THREE

The Turning of the Worm

▪▪

1935–1945

ONE DAY IN THE FALL OF 1935, I WENT TO SCHOOL AND learned that our vivacious and self-assured biology teacher had been fired. She, along with four other black schoolteachers, had sued the city of Norfolk for equal pay with white teachers. We were suddenly thrust into the churning vortex of history.

The salaries of black teachers were 30 percent less than those of white teachers with the same training and experience. In many instances, black teachers were actually better educated than whites. While they were universally denied admission to graduate schools in the South, many black teachers had received state-funded grants to attend graduate schools in the North. (Southern states would pay any amount of money to keep them out of their universities—an example of how irrational racism had become.)

Thus, during the summer terms, the campuses of New York, Columbia, Indiana, Temple, Boston, Michigan State, and Penn State universities were dotted with well-dressed, serious black teachers from the thirteen southern states. Our biology teacher had been among them. Her graduate teaching degree gave her the credentials to become a plaintiff for the NAACP legal suit.

Even as children, we knew that there was a huge wall "out there" that no black person could go over or around, regardless of qualifications. It's difficult to describe our feelings about the "respectable" white Christians who sang in church choirs, served as deacons, trustees, and elders in downtown churches, who joined the Boy Scouts, and sat on city councils, court benches, and in the Congress, yet felt no shame in endorsing this wholesale racial discrimination. It's equally hard to describe our own absolute, unwavering loyalty to, and belief in, the principles of American democracy.

Our teacher's suit was filed by NAACP attorneys. It eventually ended up before the United States Supreme Court and our teacher won. The case dragged on for about three years, and in the meantime, all of the plaintiffs were employed elsewhere. At our Booker T. Washington High School, even though we had only a faint notion of the sweeping implications of that victory, we were jubilant. We were so proud of our teacher. She was a beautiful, lively woman with a sense of humor. She lived on the next street from ours, and anytime she caught us teenage boys staring at her as she walked down the street or the hallway at school she gave us a slow, sly wink and a sassy smile. We thrived on such ego inflation.

Now, she had leaped out of her role as our favorite teacher and become a celebrity. Her name, Alene Black, was in all of the black weekly papers and she was talked about in every black church, conference, or assembly. We were all aware that because of her, and other black teachers mounting similar lawsuits, blatant injustice was being beaten back for once.

Our leaders had always recognized the leverage of the Supreme Court. They knew that Supreme Court decisions in 1875, 1883, and 1896 had canceled the gains made during Reconstruction. When President Hoover appointed the avowed racist John J. Parker to the Supreme Court in 1930, we children, and adults, too, prayed hard for help to defeat those senators who voted for him. After the presidential election of 1932, we prayed that President Roosevelt's newly revised Supreme Court would be our deliverer. The Court was only waiting for the right lawyers to bring the right cases.

Thurgood Marshall and the other civil rights lawyers became our heroes. We read about them trying cases across the South where they were denied drinking water and access to restrooms and lunch counters. From where we stood, it took real courage to file a complaint in a federal court against a whole city, county, or state. These were the days when a black person couldn't expect any police protection, even if his life depended on it.

Dr. Benjamin E. Mays, the distinguished president of Morehouse College, was riding on a train from Atlanta to New York. In order to eat dinner he had to sit behind a curtain which had been installed to hide black diners from the white diners. Dr. Mays protested and filed suit. The curtain, the last vestige of legal separation, came down even while much prejudice remained unprotested.

In our dining room at home we had a huge Arcola stove, with registers cut into the ceiling to conduct some of the heat to upstairs bedrooms. Every night we would gather in that dining room for warmth and enjoy listening to our radio, tuning in to Fibber McGee and Molly, Jack Benny and Rochester (Eddie Anderson), Edgar Bergen and Charlie McCarthy, Amos and Andy and the Mystic Knights of the Sea (even though, ironically, that was a program in which white comedians imitated and stereotyped black life). Almost always, blacks were parodied, made to appear ignorant, superstitious, easily frightened and deceived, and childish. They were never taken seriously. But even then certain sweet victories swelled our hearts with pride.

Every time heavyweight champion Joe Louis fought, our community was quiet as a morgue—until Joe floored another opponent, and a sudden burst of shouts and screams shattered our end of town. His victories were reason enough to wear a wide grin to work the next morning. And when Jesse Owens startled Hitler by winning four gold medals at the 1936 Olympic games in Berlin, black communities rocked with rapture.

When the Daughters of the American Revolution, descendants of the nation's earliest defenders, barred Marian Anderson from singing in their auditorium in 1939, decent people everywhere felt disgraced. Mrs. Eleanor Roosevelt, an aristocrat by anybody's standards, along with other concerned persons, arranged for Miss Anderson to sing outdoors in front of the Lincoln Memorial. Harold I. Ickes, Secretary of the Interior, set the date. More than fifty thousand people turned up for that concert on Easter Sunday, many thousands more than would ever have attended a concert in an auditorium. Blacks everywhere breathed in the fresh air of vindication.

As I approached high school graduation in 1937, other tiny apertures began to appear in the thick wall of segregation. Just before daybreak one Sunday morning my father hustled us out of bed and rushed us to our church, which was located at the far edge of our section of town. Flames were cracking and leaping across the church roof, enveloping its distinctive colonial spire. Everyone in the neighborhood gathered around, helplessly staring as the fire engulfed the whole building. Among them was Dr. Sparks White Melton, the venerable pastor of the nearby all-white Freemason Street Baptist Church. I can still see his striped pajama sleeves sticking out of his overcoat as he stood there in the predawn darkness, tears streaming down his face. Our church was in ashes and we were bereft. But Dr. Melton spoke up and invited our pastor to bring his congregation to worship in Freemason Street's auditorium, where Sunday school was held for the white children. We were welcome to stay, he said, until our church was rebuilt. His offer seems a small thing by today's standards, but at that time and place, when the two races did literally *nothing* together voluntarily, it was radical.

Today, I look back through the corridor of these long-ago events and see the doors trying to creak open on their rusty hinges. Dr. Melton's congregation comprised businessmen, government supervisors, and city administrators. These white people employed blacks in menial jobs, but they never acknowledged their total personhood. I remember my father writing letters and filling out tax forms for his white supervisors and co-workers who didn't know how to write such items, sometimes even writing an obituary for a deceased white worker.

Nothing required Dr. Melton to get out of his warm bed to stand with us as we wept over our church fire. He violated the mores of his own society when he invited us into his church. His action was indelibly recorded in my mind—I knew that God was moving.

Alexis de Tocqueville said that white people would never accept blacks as equals, unless black people radically changed in their education and culture. He assumed that blacks wouldn't and couldn't change. He never even speculated that white people might change. But my own faith package always included that prospect, too. In my limited life's experience I had already seen that not all white people were programmed for bigotry. Even in the South, where racism was a way of life, they were capable of change.

I remember Mrs. Annie Griswold, proprietor of the big drugstore near the beach in Ocean View, a suburb of Norfolk. I worked for her the summer after I graduated from high school, delivering prescriptions and cases of Rheingold beer to the vacationers renting the waterfront cottages. That was the nearest I was allowed to get to the beach where white youths lounged and played on miles of soft sand. As they watched me walking down the boardwalk in my white apron delivering beer to a party of drunken naval officers holed up in a tacky beach motel with six teenage prostitutes, they never dreamed I was working for my college tuition.

My main job was to keep ice and syrup on the soda fountain, clean up the floor when a drunk dropped his beer or vomited, and make sandwiches when the waitresses were too busy. I made nine dollars a week while the white soda jerk, who was a high school drop-out, made fourteen dollars. I had plenty of cause to see the world as unfair.

On my last day of work that summer, Mrs. Griswold told me to go in the back and find a cardboard beer box with my name on it. The box was packed to the brim with Lifebuoy soap, Gillette blades, Colgate toothpaste, Mum deodorant, Lucky Strike cigarettes (though I didn't smoke), writing paper, a pen and bottles of ink, Bayer aspirins, cough syrup, Mennen talcum powder, and, of all things, a dozen Trojan contraceptives. That last item was embarrassing because my conservative church rearing didn't even allow talk about such things. I'm certain that Mrs. Griswold didn't think I was promiscuous at age fifteen, but if I did stray she didn't want my schooling to be halted by having to stop and become a teenage father.

In her own way, Annie Griswold was breaking through that thick wall of racial separation that kept me off Ocean View beach, and showing me that she was happy that I was headed for college. Her gesture fueled my hope that the future was worth a gamble.

In my freshman summer of 1938, I worked as an elevator operator at Ames and Brownley, a fashionable department store in downtown Norfolk. When traffic was slow, I would close down my elevator, get a duster, and help the black maids clean off the counters and mop the floors. Here, affluent women came early, had lunch, and toyed with the merchandise all day. As they walked in the marble corridors of that glittering store, they seemed separated from the larger society. They talked to the clerks, and some of the more motherly ones paused at the elevators and talked with us. Many of them knew I was in college and they gave me little gifts and words of encouragement. On the surface, at least, they gave no sign of hatred or contempt.

On my last day there before going back to school, Mr. Proescher, the vice president, darted into the back room where the "colored" help ate lunch and received their daily assignments. He addressed Harry, the contemptuous white shipping clerk who was boss of all the "colored."

"Leave Proctor's card on the clock after he leaves for school."

Harry said, "For what?"

Mr. Proescher planted himself in the middle of that junky room, cluttered with broken merchandise and empty cardboard boxes. Twelve curious, tired black faces stared at him as he looked Harry in the eye. "So he can come in here and make some time whenever he comes home from college," he said, "even if it's only a half hour or a Saturday afternoon."

"Doing what?" scoffed Harry.

"Doing any damn thing he wants to. He's smart enough to find something we need to have done."

The chorus of colored porters ducked their heads and enjoyed a sniggle of triumph. This white man had broken through the barrier of racial etiquette and dressed down another white man in our presence; just like Annie Griswold, he was applauding the ambitions of a young black man trying to make something of himself.

True, some famous white voices were also sounding a clarion call for change at this time—Ralph McGill, Mrs. Eleanor Roosevelt, Walter Reuther, Eugene Carson Blake, John L. Lewis, and Branch Rickey to name a few—but to me, these small, personal episodes, like intermittent Morse code tappings, really signaled that change was coming. Each one helped keep my faith alive.

MY FIRST TWO YEARS OF COLLEGE AT VIRGINIA STATE IN Petersburg were turbulent. Money was a big problem. Three of us siblings needed college money at the same time; I had skipped three grades and finished high school with my brother Vernon, and our sister Harriet was still in college. I had to find ways to help pay my tuition.

In addition to my savings, I had earned a music scholarship with my clarinet audition of Schubert's "Serenade." I was also lucky to get a National Youth Administration job assisting the band director. I learned to play the alto sax and got a job with our college dance orchestra, called the Virginia State Trojans. We had more money in our pockets than most faculty members.

I tried hard to behave like my idea of a jazz musician; collecting cute girls, dancing, and fraternity capers crowded my agenda. I had no energy left for serious matters. College was a kind of smorgasbord—no one guided you through the menu, you just took whatever you wanted. The trouble was, I didn't know what I wanted. I was bored with books and lost in daydreaming, spinning through my days at school, but going nowhere.

It's curious how black folk have a life within and among themselves which has no reference to white people. On campus, we lived in a kind of social cocoon, since all the students and teachers were black. We imagined a world that suited our whims, a world without the presence or control of whites, where we chose our own heroes, and reeled in a fantasy future. Like my brother Vernon, I even dreamed of directing my own pit orchestra on Broadway, which was a long way from reality.

Then, we were compelled to attend our black colleges in the South. Now, integration in education at every level is irreversible as a social goal. But what was intended to be a disadvantage, we converted into a solid benefit.

My college professors had managed to escape the limitations imposed by segregated schools with poor facilities and makeshift resources, and to succeed in obtaining graduate degrees in practically every field from highly reputed institutions. One can only imagine the personal sacrifices those black scholars and their families must have made to achieve such academic laurels at that time.

My professors believed in the future. They were committed to service and never stopped to question whether they would be personally rewarded. I can see my history professor, Dr. Luther P. Jackson, wearing his one blue suit, his arms filled with papers, hurriedly walking toward his beat-up old Plymouth, getting ready to set off for some small town in rural Virginia to organize a voter registration drive. When he wasn't registering voters, he was bringing young black men together to form glee clubs. He worked constantly and never looked back.

My own uncle, Dr. Tommy Carter, was a French professor at Virginia State. When he was a student at the University of Michigan, he paid for his room and board by living in the attic of a fraternity house and serving meals to the white undergraduates. He used to send me beautiful shirts, shoes, and jackets that the white fraternity boys had discarded. When the members of his campus French Club went out to dinner to practice their conversational French, Tommy wasn't allowed to go because the restaurants in Ann Arbor barred blacks. None of this stopped him.

Tommy Carter headed the French department at Virginia State for twenty-five years, then served as a Peace Corps administrator in French West Africa (Senegal) and Morocco; and *then* became an official in the U.S. Information Administration and a higher education program officer in the United States Office of Education!

I had always been troubled by the chasm between our home, where learning was emphasized, and other homes where it was neglected; and the conspicuous contrast between those who were literate and had good jobs, and those who were not and worked as hands. That divide seemed permanent and untraversable.

It was dawning on me that black people in America were actually living in a three-tiered society. At the very bottom, some could hardly read; they had children out of wedlock, never attended church, moved constantly, and a few even bought stolen goods, drank, and fought in the streets. These were people who had a weak beginning, and believed their future held only poverty and marginality.

Above them was a wide, deep layer of black people who believed they had a place in society and that sooner or later they would enter fully into the American system. My parents and their friends were among these hard-working, self-reliant, and compassionate black people. They headed the lodges; led the Sunday schools; presided over the social clubs; owned homes; educated their children, lived with modesty and sobriety, and could be counted on to support every good cause. They represented the large center of black society—government workers, Pullman porters, postmen, artisans, building contractors, shopkeepers, ice and vegetable merchants, nurses and longshoremen, hotel waiters and barbers, insurance and real estate salespeople, teachers and entrepreneurs.

And then, as I entered college, I learned that there was yet another stratum—those who had been trained in the professions and at the Ph.D. level, as well as a handful of artists, like Marian Anderson, who had soared above most humans of whatever origin. They set a fast pace for the rest of us.

Some of my professors were part of this last group. From childhood these men and women, often descended from free blacks, had been nurtured by caring, intelligent parents. They were overwhelmingly mulatto, and by virtue of their partial white ancestry, or the powerful mythology of light-skin supremacy, their own communities placed favors on them and held high expectations for them. As children they had enjoyed early initiation into academics; later, they had been able to enter the best colleges because of their privileges and their advanced academic performance. If white universities had been allowed to hire them, no black college could have competed for their services.

All of my professors, whatever their background, were visibly impatient with the low academic aspirations of many black students, and indignant that some of us thought ourselves inferior. They didn't want to turn us into white people, but they wanted to pour new content into the color black, to destroy stereotypes and to kill rumors about our indelible inferiority.

WHEN I WAS YOUNG, BLACKS DIDN'T HAVE MANY CAREER options. Large law firms, big industrial giants, state and federal governments and universities excluded blacks, regardless of qualifications. Certainly, blacks never had jobs that supervised whites.

Within the black community the career that was always open with unlimited access was the ministry. Role models like Howard Thurman, Mordecai Johnson, Benjamin Mays, and Adam Clayton Powell, Sr., were widely known.

The role of the minister as social advocate had always gripped my imagination. Yet whenever the idea of being a minister crossed my mind, I felt a strange revulsion. For one thing, many black ministers at that time went at it without proper training; they simply declared that they were "called." Many ministers were given to gaudy dress, unbridled egotism, and self-aggrandizement; they exploited women willing to do anything to be close to the "pastor." Of course, similar behavior occurred among judges, lawyers, teachers, and even presidents of the

United States, but it turned me off when I saw preachers behaving in such contrast to the One whose life displayed simplicity and humility.

I also thought that the institutional church, with its dogma and display of riches, was often unfaithful to the person of Christ in the gospels. I didn't know about the various kinds of literature in the Bible or about the many different ways writers expressed religious ideas.

Despite my confusion, I was haunted by the notion of becoming a minister. I read the life of Jesus over and over in the gospels. When my great-uncle, Reverend Everard Hughes, came home on vacations, I talked with him for hours on end. He had graduated from the Oberlin Graduate School of Theology and worked with very enlightened churches. Our conversations helped open my view of the ministry.

Meanwhile, months passed at college without my gaining any clear direction in school. Then I faced my own Gethsemane. This is what happened:

I had been sixteen years old when I entered Virginia State. Like everyone else, I joined a fraternity. I loved my fraternity and felt close to my brothers. But all fraternities tolerated a few thugs who loved to engage in excessively brutal behavior at initiation. They would drink themselves into oblivion and proceed to beat on the pledges with long, oak paddles that had the leverage of baseball bats. I mean they floored them with fifty to sixty strong strokes to the buttocks.

After surviving my own initiation, I complained to my fraternity brothers about their behavior, but they ignored me. I threatened to report them, and they threatened to kill me. Even my uncle, Dr. Tommy Carter, told me to keep my mouth shut. He thought I had become too obsessive about it.

I sought advice from Dr. Harry Roberts, a professor of sociology who was also a Methodist minister. He listened patiently to my troubles and said I was on the right track.

I tried to launch a campaign among new members of all the fraternities to report these activities to the dean of students. Many agreed to speak up, but when the agreed-on day came to present the case to the dean, no one showed up.

Somewhere during that time I broke the peer rules against religious practice and slipped off campus to visit a local church. There, a short preacher with a sharp West Indian accent seemed to know that I was coming. His text that morning was from Joshua 1:9 (King James Version):

> Be strong and of a good courage; be not afraid, neither be thou dismayed; for the Lord thy God is with thee withersoever thou goest.

His words were aimed straight at me. After the sermon, I went forward and talked to him. Baptists practice believer's baptism, meaning that you're supposed to accept Christ on your own. As a boy I had accepted Jesus Christ several times as my Lord, but every time baptism day came, to my parents' dismay and consternation, I discovered at the last minute that I just wasn't ready. Now, I felt something unseen working in me. Within a week or so, I was baptized with about twenty small children between the ages of nine and twelve.

Then, I reported the fraternities to the dean. When the Greek letter organizations found out what I had done, I was ostracized by everyone on campus. For the last six weeks of the school year I lived alone, like a leper. I went to classes during the day, and at night I prayed by myself. I looked within for help and found those old faith propositions that I remembered from church:

> I can do all things through Christ who strengtheneth me.

> The Lord is my strength and my salvation; whom shall I fear?

I will lift up mine eyes unto the hills whence cometh
my help.

When I went home for summer vacation that year, I fumbled
around trying to sort out my future. War preparations had
begun, and for the first time President Roosevelt had opened the
door for young blacks to enter government-sponsored training
programs. Instead of returning to college, I decided to take the
examination for the Naval Apprentice School in Norfolk, and in
September of 1939, I went to work for the Navy as a shipfitter's
apprentice.

I rode to the Norfolk Navy Yard every day with my daddy and
five of his buddies, who were all a part of the civilian workforce,
laughing to some of the funniest stories I had ever heard and
soaking up globs of homespun philosophy and folklore. Being
one of the "men" helped me see the bigger picture. It was strange
how these educated black men could talk about race with a cool
objectivity that seemed to save their energy for the immediate
tasks of life.

Since this was an official government program, I expected to
be accepted by the other shipfitters and apprentices in our shop.
One day I took a break from my workbench and walked over to
the water fountain; it had two faucets, one for a right-handed person, and the other for a left-handed person. I leaned my shoulder against the wall and turned on the fountain with my right
hand. Before my lips touched the water, I heard a voice shout
from halfway across the building: "Hey, boy! That ain't your
faucet. You drink out of the one on the left."

I called back, "But I'm right-handed."

"You're colored, ain't you? Coloreds use the left faucet." Hot-
faced, I lifted my head without drinking, and walked away from
the fountain. What small, sinister mind thought up the idea of
having two faucets, so that every black person who came for a
drink would be reminded that he was unworthy to share any-

thing, even basic water, with whites? However, I too had been trained to conserve my energy and temper for significant battles. Like other black youths of my generation, I had learned never to absorb, to accept, to internalize unworthiness; I rejected the rejection that was aimed at us constantly.

The ministry seemed to be following me. I became friendly with the Rev. D. C. Rice, the new young pastor of Bank Street Baptist Church, whose engaging sermons spoke realistically about Christian living while preserving the awesome mystery and majesty of God. Reverend Rice shared several hours with me each week helping me to get a better view of the ministry. I wanted to be just like him. The broader issue of black destiny in America began to loom large before me, and building parts for battleships no longer seemed challenging.

I was absolutely convinced that I had to become an agent of that persistent faith that kept our people inching forward, living on the substance of things hoped for. I wanted to find an answer to the dilemma of black progress in America, an answer to world hunger and poverty, an answer to colonialism and imperialism.

One day I was at my workbench making a small steel cabinet with a combination lock for the captain's private papers aboard ship. My job was to punch dots on the steel sheet. It was a tedious, mindless job. I was partway through the process when I had one of those flashes of insight, like Moses at the burning bush or Isaiah in the Temple. The truth did not come in segments; rather, like falling in love, it descended in one luminous, existential moment. Suddenly I knew that I would make any sacrifice, pay any price, endure any inconvenience to go back to school and prepare for the ministry. I had to find a place to serve that would nurture the faith of my people, challenge the pervasive injustice, and complete the task of those who died, laboring in the quarries where the rocks were hard indeed.

I put down my hammer and puncher and took off my apron. Then I headed for the Labor Board to resign. Out in the yard, a man named Booker, a friend of my father, drove by in one of those huge, indestructible Navy trucks. He stopped abruptly and cut off the deafening sound of the huge diesel motor.

"Proctor, where are you going?"

"To the Labor Board to resign," I answered.

"Are you crazy? We fought hard to open up that school to colored boys. You can't quit."

"Mr. Booker, I believe I'm called to preach, and I want to get ready for school."

"You don't need to go to school to be a preacher. We have a fellow cooking in the commissary right now who's a preacher, and another one working in the coal yard. They never went to any school."

"But I want to do it differently," I said. "I want to go to college and to the seminary. I want to give it my best and be ready for any opportunity that comes."

He shook his head in disbelief and moved on, the truck's noisy chain drive erasing our conversation.

That fall, as soon as all my friends left town and returned to college, I announced to the church and my family that I was giving my life to the ministry and asked for their prayers. I knew I couldn't go back to my old crowd at Virginia State who were already laughing at the idea of me studying for the ministry. So, in the fall of 1940, I enrolled at Virginia Union, a black Baptist school known for training ministers.

In my new college I immediately organized a school band, which technically made me a college "bandmaster." One day I received a smudgy, ink-smeared letter addressed to "All Colored College Bandmasters," inviting me to join a pool of musicians to be trained as a "Colored Army Bandmaster" in Fort Bragg, North Carolina.

Well, my brother Vernon, who played piano, tuba, and the bass violin, was fresh out of Alabama State College with a music major and about to be drafted. I sent the grimy letter on to him and told him to hurry and go to Fort Bragg. Thirty years later he retired as an Air Force Bandmaster after a most fruitful career. Today he lies in eternal rest in Arlington National Cemetery.

VIRGINIA UNION WAS THE CENTER OF BLACK LIFE OF Richmond. Although the school had little money and modest facilities, the campus throbbed with intellectual excitement. The big questions in philosophy, theology, political science, sociology, and economics were grist for our mill. Chapel was compulsory, and every Monday, Wednesday, and Friday we heard outstanding black speakers from every section of the country, as well as a number of liberal-minded white intellectuals.

In the summers, I was back working as an elevator operator at Ames and Brownley. As part of the store's decoration, we wore maroon uniforms with eight brass buttons down the front, a round hat with gold braid, and black leather gloves. I would stand next to my gleaming elevator car chanting, "Going up?" One day, as I made my announcement, a jovial black porter passed by saying, "Go the hell on up, Reverend; don't nobody want to go up with you!" Standing in front of my car about to board was Dr. Sparks White Melton, the same white pastor who had cried with us the night our church burned down. "Are you a reverend?" Dr. Melton asked, looking at me with surprise.

I told him that I was still in college at Virginia Union. He asked me to let him know when I was ready for the seminary.

A year or so later, I saw him again. This time I rode him up to the sixth floor Tea Room, a racially exclusive dining room used for the Business Men's Bible class. While Dr. Melton conducted the Bible class, he could see me parked at my elevator, listening attentively. When he heard later that I was graduating from college, he arranged a full tuition scholarship for me at Crozer Theological Seminary on whose trustee board he sat. He also sent me a box of books that I have used for over fifty years.

While fully a party to the racial policy that excluded me from that Tea Room, Dr. Melton eroded the whole system by helping me to go to Crozer. I'm sure he never dreamed that one day I would be invited to preach to his white congregation in Norfolk after he was silent in death, or that I would become a teacher and a trustee of that same Crozer, and even invited to be considered for its presidency.

I ENTERED THE SEMINARY IN CHESTER, PENNSYLVANIA, IN September of 1942. On my first day I learned that I was the only black student there. In fact, I was the only black anything there! There was not a black janitor, cook, yardman, or even a black cat or dog. I was it! That afternoon, I sneaked off campus and rode a bus into a black neighborhood. I walked around awhile and ended up getting a haircut from a black barber.

When I returned to campus, the entire student body was assembled in front of the dining hall. I walked a long fifty yards up from the road, with every eye aimed at me. Then a huge redhead from Fuquay-Varina, North Carolina, stepped out and laid a big freckled hand on my shoulder.

"Hi ya doing, fella," he said. "I see you have a fresh haircut."

I admitted I had found a barbershop downtown, leaving out the "colored."

He squinted his green eyes, poked his finger in my chest and barked: "Listen, I'm the barber here. I cut all the hair on this campus. And I'm gonna cut your hair, too! If I catch you going downtown again, I'm gonna whip your ass. Heah me?" I mumbled in agreement, but it took several days for me to absorb fully that a North Carolina white boy was going to be my barber.

I took in a lot of new information in the space of twenty-four hours. During the orientation session that evening, we learned about class schedules, bills, mail, meals, and jobs. Because of the war, students carried out all campus services themselves. The faculty chairman of the student employment committee finally made all the assignments but mine. I raised my hand and reminded him that I needed an assignment.

"I'm sorry, Mr. Proctor, I forgot. Mrs. Moitz wants to see you in the kitchen."

Sitting in the front row, I instantly aged ten years. I could not believe that the *only* black student was selected for the *only* kitchen job. When I went down to Mrs. Moitz, a refugee from Hitler's invasion of Hungary, she was embarrassed. "You're the only colored boy and they sent you to me?" she said, shaking her head in disbelief. No ethical, theological, or sociological studies could match old-fashioned prejudice.

My first thought was to give up on these white theologians and go home. But another part of my mind told me to stay right where I was and be the best kitchen help they ever had—and finish my academic work with honors.

All day long I did well in classes and enjoyed the fellowship of my classmates. At about 9 P.M. every night, I descended to the kitchen to my assigned job where I spent the quiet hours of the night by myself, singing, praying, conjugating Greek verbs, and memorizing names, dates, and places while I washed dishes, scrubbed pots, and mopped the floor. I felt burdened at times, and sometimes tears flowed freely. White people seemed to think I was without feeling, like a robot. And they were scholars of Jesus, who was so filled with compassion. It hurt—not the job itself, but how it had come to me. Throughout those days of doubt and confusion, of wandering and searching, I found safe harbor at the home of a local Baptist pastor named J. Pius Barbour. Dr. Barbour and his family always had a space for me at their table, and he always had time to sit with me for hours and debate the issues confronting me. Dr. Barbour was a scholarly person with a penchant for such dialogue, and he understood my problem, having been a Crozer alumnus himself. (I would not be the only Crozer student he helped. Some years later Martin

Luther King, Jr., and many more after him, also sought and received his counsel.)

During my studies at Crozer, another learning experience came to me from outside of the classroom. I worked in the summer of 1944 as a driver for a wealthy, blind real estate man. Every morning I drove him into town from his Delaware County summer estate, parking his big Oldsmobile in the empty lot behind his office building, then walking on to school. At the end of the day, I returned and drove him back to the country. During that summer I lived at the estate with him and his wife, and every night we ate dinner together. We all behaved courteously and, while not warm friends, we got along peaceably enough, veiling our distinctly divergent social views.

The following spring I helped him again off and on; one afternoon I was waiting with the car in front of his building when he came charging down the steps alone, waving his white cane wildly over his head. He shouted to me at the top of his lungs, "Thank God, that son of a bitch is dead!"

To me and my people, Franklin Roosevelt was like a messiah, and all of our hope was pinned on him. Alone in my room that night I had a long soliloquy with myself. My blind employer thought that Social Security, helping the poor, and other Roosevelt initiatives were a formula for disaster. To me, on the contrary, they looked like the partial fulfillment of our major faith proposition. I had no idea that our country was so deeply divided between those who favored government intervention in behalf of the poor and those who did not.

Incidentally, my dormitory at Crozer had been a Union Army hospital for wounded Confederate soldiers during the Civil War. I could still see the hole in the door to my room through which food had been passed to a wounded Confederate soldier. Often, while reflecting on a racial issue, I would recall that a soldier fighting to keep my people enslaved had used that very room. Now, it was my room, and I was using it to learn how to harvest enough spiritual energy to achieve our full freedom.

I wasn't sure how it would happen, but I believed that God had a special claim on us. Black people, just like me, had always had a special ability to look beyond the hate and see something bright shining.

THE SEMINARY WAS SO RADICAL IN ITS APPROACH TO THE Bible that it actually ruined the religious beliefs of some of my classmates. We were shocked to discover that Bible study included learning the history and geography of the Near East and the land of the Tigris and Euphrates rivers; we also studied the various religions of Egypt, Assyria, Babylonia, and Persia, and examined their influences on Judaism.

We were learning that God was much greater than the oversimplified view of creation coming from the mind of a fourth century B.C.E. scribe. But many of my classmates still held on to a literal view of creation from Genesis. They had trouble accepting that God had not sat behind a cloud somewhere and dictated the Bible word for word, in English! Some gasped as one professor after another challenged them to revise their belief systems and to embrace a bigger God idea that allowed truth from the sciences to inform religion. For me, however, listening to religious scholars who respected scientific data was a relief. Hearing them was like walking through a verdant forest with a mild breeze, birds chirping from every direction, and a crystal stream of clear water singing and dancing on solid, ancient rocks. I loved it.

My seminary took the plastic off the Bible, and made it a living book with a message infinitely stronger than I had ever dreamed possible. My professors taught that certain books of the Bible reflected different types of literature; some were written like poems or long parables to make a serious point. The teachers showed us how Bible stories had been revised by various writers at different times, and taught us how to look at biblical events

47

in a larger context. Indeed, by giving a deeper interpretation of the Bible, the Crozer theologians showed us how religion could have social and ethical application in the modern world.

My seminary training helped me to see how orthodox, fundamentalist Christianity, with its credulous literalism about the Bible, ended up as a religion unrelated to the travails of humans living in the real world. It was a religion that found reasons in the Bible to accept slavery and the subjugation of women; a religion that ignored Jesus, its Lord, and became comfortable with the rich; a religion that subjugated and exploited all of the darker skinned people of the world for the comfort of the whites; a religion that quietly endorsed militarism and bloodshed everywhere. In the hands of the fundamentalists, Christianity had become an embarrassment to Jesus.

It had always bothered me that Christianity had become an antiquated religion, rather than a living one. While religion in the black churches always addressed issues of freedom and justice, in terms of the basic theological agenda it was stifling and narrow-minded. It too was filled with anti-science sentiments that were never discussed openly. Strongly wed to a literal understanding of the Bible, it was also fundamentalist, but benignly so.

I am so thankful that my seminary delivered me from such views while leaving my faith in God and the centrality of Jesus firmly in place. Intellectually and spiritually I had a bath, a new awakening. What I learned about philosophy and ethics freed me to step out of history, to examine all of my assumptions, and to reenter society with greater clarity and understanding. I came out of the seminary with a God more powerful, more worthy of praise than I had when I entered. I came out with a Bible far more relevant to our spiritual quests.

BY THE TIME I ENTERED MY SENIOR YEAR IN SEMINARY, I had become a committed "inquirer." I wanted clear, honest answers to the ponderous questions hurled at me by history, nature, and society. But it should not surprise anyone to know that a theological education raises more new questions than it offers answers to old ones. During my last year I was hungry for answers.

When we heard that Dr. Edwin E. Aubrey, a professor of theology at the University of Chicago, was coming to our campus as the new president, I felt the campus ignite with excitement. Needless to say, our seminary was branded "liberal," a term which then stood for an unstinted search for truth and for a generous response to need and suffering. It's strange that "liberal" should become a bad word for Christians today. In any event, when Dr. Aubrey came, we were pushed even farther away from center in theological circles. As a naturalistic-theist he was a theologian who emphasized the order and majesty of God's creation, and saw scientific marvels, rather than supernatural miracles, as evidence of God's power. Of course, he was held suspect by orthodox Christians. Both from the point of view of putting my personal faith together, and also from the point of view of pursuing social justice, I was standing on tiptoe, eager to learn more about Dr. Aubrey's ideas.

Meanwhile, my special friendship with a young lady named Bessie Louise Tate, whom I had met at Virginia Union University, had ripened. With a world in flux and a future in great doubt, Bessie and I took a leap and decided to get married. We planned to rent a student apartment and scuffle for food money and expenses for that senior year, and trust God for the future.

In 1944, young women were only beginning to assert their notions of absolute equality with men. It was acceptable for an occasional woman to have a career in law, medicine, or politics, but it was the exception. In our circles the optimal condition for a young lady was to marry shortly after college, begin having children, and manage a well-ordered home. The success of her children and her husband were her intrinsic rewards. Divorce was never contemplated and there was no premarital sex. No couples in our circle thought of "shacking" together before marriage. Customarily, therefore, we married young, and stayed married.

Traditionally, in a very self-regarding way, everyone looked for the best mate available, and a lot of bargaining, negotiating, and compromising went on. On a small campus of a thousand or less, in a few weeks after school began, the matching was over. It is unbelievable how parochial we were; all from the same basic backgrounds, similar parents, values, religious affiliations, socioeconomic status, and aesthetic preferences. Practically, we could almost have chosen our lifetime mates in a lottery, but it was far more fun to pick and choose. And there was nothing like the electricity that was sparked when glances met and a bold stare was sustained, and a smile confirmed approval. That happened to us, fifty years ago.

About that time President Aubrey and his wife, who was active in national volunteer organizations, were looking for a married student couple to live with them to help with domestic chores and to monitor their two young children when they were away from home. The Aubreys both traveled extensively for meetings, conferences, and on speaking engagements. In exchange the couple would receive room, board, and a modest salary. We hesitated, since neither of us had much appetite for being domestic help.

Since I had been at Crozer, I had already held jobs working nights in the post office, Saturdays at Sears in the warehouse, washing Bond Bread trucks, and cleaning up the seminary kitchen every night. Work was my companion and I liked being independent. To me, this new job was just another hustle to make ends meet.

Bessie, on the other hand, came from a small, financially well-off family. Her father, a prosperous pharmacist who owned his own drugstore, did not encourage Bessie to work outside the home. Black women always had to fight for respect and, if they could, black families tried to protect their daughters from the profanity, sex jokes, and disrespectful male attention common in workplaces. She had two summer jobs for pocket change and novelties, but never was she compelled to support herself. But Bessie agreed to take the Aubrey job with me so we could be together and save some money for the next leg of my education.

Living with the Aubreys was a completely new experience for both of us. Dr. Aubrey and his wife were from upper middle class families. They loved books, opera, the symphonies and art galleries; they never listened to the radio, never knew which football team was out front, who won the World Series, or which basketball teams made the final four. They could not dance. In nine months of living in the same house with them (we had a private apartment on the third floor), I never saw her without heels, stockings, and makeup; and I never saw him without a collar and tie. Bessie and I studied them as though they were in a museum. I enjoyed talking theology with Dr. Aubrey, and Mrs. Aubrey wanted to teach my wife more about cooking than she would ever need to know.

The Aubreys had only long-distance friends—in England, Wales, Chicago, Boston, and Canada. Nobody local ever visited except for occasional faculty teas or lunches. They seemed to enjoy life, and were always warm and generous, but to us they looked like stage actors.

The real value of that experience was a sustained, close-up peep into a social class and a cultural stratum that neither of us had known before. We found out how different life was for people who did not have to be concerned with their survival, their identity, or their space and basic rights and freedom.

Looking back, our experience with the Aubreys also showed us how easily people from completely different backgrounds could find common ground simply by respecting each other's privacy and preferences, and trying to understand the interior of their lives and goals. Even though the gaps between us were formidable, we *communicated.* I learned that experiences that drag us, kicking and screaming, out of our small worlds and compel us to stand tall in another world, can stretch our minds, forge our character, and fuel our imaginations. I believe the Aubreys had the same experience. We all learned from each other.

Although Dr. Aubrey died at an early age, Bessie and I continued to correspond with his wife. I visited her in a rest home in California when she was nearly ninety years old. She wept with joy when she saw me, receiving me like a son who had shown up after a long separation. She showed me a scrapbook of news clippings of my activities she had kept for over forty years! And she cried as she leafed through it. My soul! I had no idea. Again, I saw how artificial and dehumanizing racial barriers can be. Unless we had come into her home, she would never have known a black person at close range.

By the time I graduated from Crozer in 1945, the war had ended and the country was retooling for a postwar economy and the GIs were settling in. The poor had tasted relief with jobs in defense factories. They had listened to the oratory of Roosevelt and Truman, and had seen the revulsion of the world in the face of Hitler's vile atrocities against the Jews. Black soldiers were returning from the Pacific, Germany, England, and North Africa. They had risked their lives to make a new world safe for democracy. They had seen persons of all religions and cultures, and were fed up with the racial arrangements in their own country.

The worm was turning. The intellectual and spiritual transformation that I had experienced in the seminary was an omen of the change and openness that the world would see in the next thirty years.

CHAPTER FOUR

The New Emancipation

1945–1960

I LEFT CROZER WITH A $2,500 JOHN P. CROZER FELLOWSHIP
to study social ethics at Yale University, and $1,700 saved. At the
same time, I was called to serve the Pond Street Baptist Church
in Providence, Rhode Island. So, Monday through Wednesday
I was at Yale in New Haven, and Thursday through Sunday I was
at home with my congregation and my wife in Providence.

The town was extremely generous in extending hospitality
and openness. While the black community was small, it had
strong and loyal allies among white churches and educated liberals. Our parishioners were hard-working people, but there
wasn't much money around. Bessie and I were so young that the
church leadership treated us like we were their children, with

exceptional warmth and care. We constantly felt the love and protection of the whole congregation.

We moved into a small apartment on the top floor of a three-story frame house. On the first and second floors of the house lived Mr. and Mrs. Blount, a senior family in the church. Each evening they treated us to dessert and coffee and told long stories about old times and interesting people in the black community. These talks were always laced with advice on what to do and say, and which people to trust. The Blounts' children and grandchildren were all grown up, and Bessie and I were like surrogate family for them.

I was only twenty-four years old, and among the first generation of black pastors to have access, on a large scale, to graduate study at seminaries which were lodged in large universities. As we earned doctorates in religion, social activism became as important to us as saving souls.

One night, soon after I had begun in Providence, all the black ministers and their followers met at a big rally in the black community center. "We're going to organize a movement here for fair employment practices in this state," one pastor announced, "and Reverend Proctor will lead it."

I had studied social change, but had never actually *practiced* social ethics. I was a student with no leadership experience in civil rights, but this public announcement meant that I had to take the plunge. Within a few days, I found myself raising money, bringing carloads of people with picket signs to march in front of the statehouse, and going on the radio to bring our cause to the public. As a result, the Fair Employment Practices Act was successfully passed by the Rhode Island legislature.

Social activism was only part of my job. I saw my task as an agent for change in the lives of individuals as well as an agent of social change. In an effort to revitalize what I saw as a conservative, dormant black presence, I hosted a Saturday radio show with our youth choir and wrote a weekly column in the black community paper. I solicited funds from merchants to equip a social hall in the church for neighborhood youth and recruited young people from the local community center. We started a basketball team and participated in the local church basketball league. One of our best players, a young man named Howard Blunt, grew up to become an admiral in the Navy and is today part owner of the Baltimore Orioles. Many other young people who joined the church at that time are the leading black citizens in Providence today.

As I went about my work as a young pastor, I thought that the more privileged blacks should have extended themselves to help improve the chances for those least well prepared. The poorer blacks insulated themselves from the scrutiny of the blacks who were better off as well as from the scorn of whites. Most had abdicated all accountability for their own lives. And, at the time, I thought the best way to help them was through jobs, schools, church programs, athletic leagues, and black associations. Eagerly, I threw myself into the fray.

One day Bessie and I were returning home from church, driving through a poor section of the city, when suddenly a huge fellow dressed in jeans and leather boots came bursting from the screened door of a porch front, leaped into the street, and landed right in front of our car. Behind him came another big man, brandishing an open barber's razor in the air. Rage was written all over his face, with his lips drawn tightly over his teeth, his eyes bulging and veins protruding in his neck. With one quick slash he opened a deep gash in the jaw and neck of the first man, who fell with blood squirting in volumes from his neck. We hustled him into the car and I raced to the hospital, holding a car seat pillow over his wound. He lay silent as death. At the hospital the emergency team revived him, stitched up his wound, and bandaged him like a mummy. He remained in the hospital for several days and I earnestly visited him and prayed with him.

I learned that his assailant was his brother-in-law, and their argument had begun over nothing—a telephone bill, use of a bathroom, or repayment of a five-dollar loan. One insulted the other, and within seconds they had come to the point of murder. A fraction of an inch deeper, and that brief argument would have been followed by tearful regrets, calling on Jesus, kinfolk driving up from South Carolina, singing sad songs and walking slowly to a cold grave in a strange and distant cemetery. I probably would have been called in to do the eulogy.

None of it made sense on a rational level, but they were behaving extrarationally, responding to subcultural taboos, which included: don't talk about my sister unless you say something nice; pay me my money when you say you will; don't "dis" me in front of my friends; don't act like you think you are better than I; don't use my telephone for long-distance calls without my permission; don't raise your voice at me, and more of the same. Violation is punishable by death.

This is the way people behave when their raw need for respect and status is frustrated. These two men eventually reconciled and continued to live together in the same apartment. But I knew it was only a matter of time before another trivial disagreement would explode into violence. I believed then, as I do now, that an educated mind behaves differently, is able to canvass options, and solve misunderstandings without violence.

I was bitterly disappointed to find that so many young blacks in the North had no educational aspirations. Without any nearby black colleges, and few black college graduates in sight, many northern blacks were satisfied with menial jobs. One of our biggest efforts in Providence, therefore, was to send young blacks South to school. It's no small irony that blacks who had escaped the rigid discrimination of the South had to return there to receive a college education. There was no shortage of excellent schools in the Northeast. Brown University, the elitist Ivy League school, was first choice for most of the country's brightest students. But there was no point expecting Brown to accept average black students, and watch them struggle—and collapse—trying to keep pace.

The black youth of Rhode Island needed a more "user friendly" campus. They needed to see and hear black Ph.D.s, black deans, black choral directors, black treasurers and presidents, black cheerleaders, and black assembly speakers. They needed a higher vision of our destiny, an ocean tide of celebrative black oratory to lift them out of the muck and mire of inferiority. And they found it in black colleges. Those same black colleges that sprang forth across the South following the Emancipation and raised the veil of ignorance from the faces of ex-slaves were just as indispensable in the 1940s and beyond to save black youth from the stultifying atmosphere of failure endemic in the large urban centers of the North.

We generated a flow of young black students going to colleges in the South. One played basketball for Virginia Union, did very well academically, and then returned to Providence College to finish his degree and to teach in East Providence. Later he became a college basketball referee, then a certified NCAA "television" referee for national tournaments, and finally the head of Rhode Island's parole board. He is Dr. Kenneth Walker, and his father was the ashes man who collected furnace ashes from well-to-do Providence neighborhoods.

Another student, Melvin Clanton, played football, did well academically, then returned to his Providence high school as a teacher. He recently retired as a citywide school personnel administrator. And Dr. Wesley Mayo is a dentist in Bridgeport, Connecticut.

However, most of the students we sent South never returned. Robert Ventner is now vice president of a black-owned bank in Richmond. Janice Scott is counselor to students at Howard University in Washington, D.C.

With our efforts we were beginning to see small signs of

change. We also saw the resistance. In 1947, the Baptists opened their Wisconsin assembly grounds at Green Lake with a conference on "Christian Social Concerns." The Rhode Island Baptists selected me and two white Providence pastors, John Zuber and Art Goodwin, to attend.

With very little money to spare, we drove all the way from Rhode Island to Wisconsin, planning to stop one night in Detroit, where we had reservations at the downtown Detroit YMCA. When we arrived at about 1 A.M., we were greeted by a night janitor who had one stiff leg and hobbled with a cane. He poked the cane into my chest and shouted, "Get out of here, boy. We don't take no colored in here. Now, go!" My companions turned red as carnations. This was the YMCA in Detroit, not Birmingham, Alabama! They staged a thirty-minute dialogue in complete futility. That man was a hater, and the hate was deep.

With the rise of blacks, poor whites like him saw themselves being jeopardized economically. They also saw themselves losing the only badge of preference that they had, the advantage of simply being white. With my presence, this crippled janitor's fragile status was slipping away from him.

We got the telephone number of the black YMCA on John "R" Street and were able to get a clean, quiet night's sleep. Believe me, when we arrived at the conference on Christian Social Concerns, we had a real live story to tell.

ALONG ABOUT THIS TIME, BESSIE AND I FOUND OUT WE were going to become parents. I was hurrying to complete my postgraduate studies at Yale so I could get better situated after the baby came. Added to the acute awareness of the responsibility of parenthood and the anxiety about the Ph.D. program, I worried about keeping my performance high, representing my people well, and confounding those who thought I shouldn't be there at all.

Four other African-American males and one female were also enrolled in the Yale program. We found rich and warm fellowship among ourselves, but hardly did any of us have a single close, steady white friend. In the sedate, colonial student lounge of the Yale Divinity School in 1945–46, no matter where I sat no white student sat near me. I believe they were afraid that if they fell into conversation with me they might say the wrong thing. Here they were, the cream of the academic crop, yet they felt uncomfortable talking to someone with a background different from their own. Despite their training in theology and philosophy, they seemed not to recognize how much all humans shared the same uncertainties, the same primitive needs and fears, the same estrangement, and the same sense of awe and wonder about God and the potential transcendency of life. Our alikeness far outweighed our few differences. It was pitiful, but I was immune to insults.

I did spend many hours assessing their behavior, trying to envision the churches of the nation being served by a cadre of clergy so well educated in the history and philosophy of religion—as an academic subject—but so guarded and fearful of letting go their cultural inhibitions and embracing the habits of Jesus. The special efforts of two white professors made a striking contrast to the attitude of the students. Professors Richard Neibuhr and Liston Pope took the initiative to make sure that I was fully engaged and included in every aspect of the program.

One day Dr. Luther Weigle, dean of the Divinity School, sent for me. It scared me to death. What on earth had I done? "Mr. Proctor," he began, dragging his chair close to mine, "why is it that so many of you colored fellows do so well here, when your Graduate Record Examination scores are so skewed? You are all far above average on the verbal tests and the social science tests, but your mathematics, sciences, and fine arts scores are far below other college graduates in the same majors, both regionally and nationally."

I was relieved, because I knew the answer. I looked in his eyes and spoke slowly. "Dean Weigle, we do better on verbal tests because we do a lot of debating and discussing. We are a talking people. We survive by images and analysis, analogues and metaphors, so we get to know words. We take flight in language as a buffer for our wounded psyches. The social sciences are all dealing with our past and our future; so we live with the social sciences, too.

"On the other hand, we are hardly ever considered for jobs in the natural sciences and technology. Our schools have no well-equipped laboratories and our teachers were educated without any hope of being employed in the sciences, either. Therefore, our knowledge in those areas is comparatively sparse."

I guessed that Dean Weigle was often called on to defend admitting black students to Yale and he needed answers that made sense. He needed to find a way to say, with conviction, that the tests did not predict our capacity to learn, but simply reflected the opportunities we had been allowed.

"Thank you, Mr. Proctor," he said. "You're doing fine work here at Yale." That was all, but I sensed that he felt relieved, too.

The day our first child was born, we received tragic news. Our baby had a severely damaged heart, a hole in the wall between the ventricles—interventricular septal defect. Through the malformed opening spent blood entered his heart and mixed freely with freshly oxygenated blood from the lungs, depriving the baby of adequate oxygen. Our doctor told us that we could not expect our child to live beyond his first year, or possibly two. He was what was called a "blue baby."

I desperately needed to find a way to finish my degree closer to Providence, so I could be home every night with Bessie and our baby. Boston University, where the curriculum was also dedicated largely to Christian social ethics, was ready to give me credit for my Yale work, plus a tuition scholarship. Most important, I could manage the commute between Providence and

Boston without spending a night away from home. I stretched my energies, and Bessie's patience, by crowding my days and nights to complete my doctoral courses and examinations within two years. By May of 1949, I was finished except for the dissertation. And I had learned as much about God by coping with the needs of my family as I learned in the library at Boston University.

The next step was to get a better-paying job. We hated to leave the warm and beautiful people at the Pond Street Baptist Church, but an offer from Dr. John M. Ellison, my mentor and the president of Virginia Union University, brought us back to the campus where we had met.

Once settled in, we tracked down the cardiologist that everyone was talking about, Dr. Paul Camp, a legend around Richmond and heir to a large paper manufacturing fortune, Camp Paper Mills. The word was that Camp did not treat black patients. But I was always willing to offer anyone a chance to live above his or her worst reports, so we went to see him, Bessie carrying our little Herbie in her arms. He was now four years old.

Ordinarily, we would have been looking for resentment on the faces of the receptionist and nurses, watching for any sign of reluctance to see us, glancing at other patients to see how they reacted. But Bessie and I learned to put Herbie's recovery above everything else. There we stood with all of this anxiety, but with a clear focus on our son.

Dr. Camp, his brow furrowed, held out his arms for our child and laid him gently on the examining table. Then he bent close and listened to his tiny heart. He couldn't have been more tender if he had been touching his own child. In a flash he got on the phone and made an appointment for us at Johns Hopkins in Baltimore, at that time the only hospital in the country doing "blue baby" surgery.

Herbie was so weak that he got pneumonia in the hospital before the surgery and nearly died. We had to bring him home until he recovered. It was a six-week delay, and we learned to live without time consciousness. Days and hours are not counted in this kind of situation—it is all one extended *moment*. All desire and meaning is squeezed into one flash of eternity, and all of life is defined by one event.

At last, we were able to take him back to the hospital for a "shunt" operation, in which an arm vessel was sent around the heart defect to increase the supply of oxygenated blood. Herbie survived. That was in 1950. The attention and professional savvy that Dr. Camp directed toward our son was convincing evidence that the solid wall that excluded blacks from the main flow of life in America was wavering.

The shunt operation that Herbie received gave him a lease on life, but only marginally so. He could not run, do stairs normally, or play active games with his friends. He had to limit his output to match his heart capacity. It was all a matter of waiting until he was big enough to undergo open-heart surgery.

So, while other young mothers rolled their children up and down the aisles of the supermarket, watched them romp in the grass, and splash in warm ocean waters, Bessie had to find things for Herbie to do in his tiny world that matched his strength and also supplied him with self-affirmation. My function was to manage my work at the college, while carrying a constant concern that my own efforts might be inadequate to fuel the needs of my wife and son.

Meanwhile, we were fortunate to have another child, Timothy, who seemed to have been born grown-up. He took over the care and companionship of his older brother like a life's assignment and geared his program to suit his brother's pace. It was beautiful to see the tender, gracious behavior they displayed together. We were all able to cope with our family's challenge because we had so much fun together.

An event such as we experienced involves many people. My brothers and my sister responded as though Herbie were their child. Our parents were ever so close. My wife's mother practically gave up her life in a focus on Herbie, and her eyes and the muscles in her face spoke her feelings when words were few. Our neighbors and colleagues on the faculty defined their relationship to us with Herbie as the fixed item.

All of this happened during my first year of college teaching at Virginia Union where I was assigned six courses in philosophy, ethics, sociology, and biblical literature, each requiring new and separate preparations. Four classes met on Monday, Wednesday, and Friday, and two met on Tuesday and Thursday. Fortunately, having just come from six solid years of graduate study, I was brimming with ideas and data. My ambition also helped keep the adrenaline pumping, and it seemed like fun.

Students inspired me with their serious and open class discussion, and their obvious appreciation of my efforts. I spent hours painstakingly correcting and adding salient comments to every paper submitted by every student. In between, I struggled to finish my dissertation in time for graduation in May of 1950. My students were as ecstatic as I was when I received my doctor of theology degree from Boston University and put on my scarlet gown with three black velvet bars on each arm and marched in Virginia Union's 1950 commencement procession.

I COULD FEEL CHANGE IN THE AIR. BLACK GIs WHO HAD returned home after the war left thousands of their buddies buried under small white crosses on the hillsides of Burma, in grassy plots near the Anzio beach landings in Italy, and the sun-baked military cemeteries of Tunis. They were impatient for change, and their government promised that the time had come to guarantee their full rights.

It took ten years, but the government did fulfill at least part of its promise. By 1954, the armed forces had been integrated and the NAACP had won significant cases that eliminated all legal standing for segregation. This was tantamount to a new emancipation, an inclusion that we had never before experienced.

Every time a new decision in our favor came down from the Supreme Court, we gathered around our radios to listen to the announcements. And every time we heard another one in our favor, it seemed like the Kingdom was getting closer. Churches held services of thanksgiving, affirming that the hand of God was writing in history. This direct connection between God and politics made religion a totally relevant experience for me and many others.

I was fighting on two fronts. I wanted to encourage white and black Christians to lift up and examine the issue of race in the light of their Christian commitments, and also in the light America's message of equality and freedom. I also wanted to see black people acquire the intellectual, economic, and political clout to improve their condition. The classroom and the pulpit were my obsessions, and I wanted to get better at both jobs.

I found myself being invited to speak at venues outside of of my small Baptist college. Before I knew it, I was speaking at Penn State, Bucknell, the University of New Hampshire, Duke University, and Riverside Church. Now the American Baptists had me lecturing every year at their annual Green Lake assembly. Indeed it did seem like a new emancipation was in the making.

At the same time, the move for decolonization around the world began. New winds were blowing everywhere and it had become less feasible for white Americans to be running schools, hospitals, colleges, and seminaries nine thousand miles away from home. It was time to let go. I took a bounding leap into the larger human struggle in 1953 when I was asked by the American Baptist Foreign Mission Board to join a team of clergy traveling into India and Burma to execute the transfer of institutions from American to indigenous ownership.

Our job was to consult with the American staff of the Burmese and Indian missions, and help them put in place procedures for the transition. You can imagine the sensation I created when I climbed down from the little crop-duster airplane, on a remote landing strip in India, along with three white executives. The local Baptist pastors, school heads, and health care providers were speechless. White missionaries who had been living abroad for years were unaware of the changes taking place in the United States. They were warmly hospitable, but hardly knew how to receive me.

Sometimes the visiting team all traveled together, but occasionally, in the interest of efficiency, we separated and visited some missions alone. In one isolated station in northern India, in the province of Assam, my plane landed on a narrow, grassy airstrip where a small family of missionaries waited to greet me. As I deplaned and started walking briskly toward my host, who was standing with his wife and two young children, I lifted my fist in greeting and shouted, "Don Crider, Altoona, Pennsylvania."

He beamed at me. "Wow," he said, "it's sure good to see a white face again!" I acted like I didn't hear it.

Later that night, as we chatted about ballgames and politics, Crider's little girl said, "Daddy, when Dr. Proctor got off the plane, why did you say you were glad to see a white face? Dr. Proctor's face is brown."

"I didn't say any such thing."

"But you did, didn't he, Dr. Proctor?"

Don Crider was embarrassed. "I guess it was hearing you belt out my name and hometown," he said. "You were like a friendly voice from home. All my American signals turned on."

I never looked any farther than that for an explanation. To him, living out in that wilderness station, my dark brown face represented America. To me, the incident signified that on a deep emotional level, like it or not, we blacks, even with our marginal status, were inextricably attached to this country. We were Americans. Looking at it from that point of view, the only question is whether our attachment can become realigned to reflect greater justice and fairness.

Everywhere I went in India and Burma, I was constantly required to redefine myself for local people who had never seen a black person in such a significant role. Our Baptist missionaries, themselves so far removed from modern American life, were supposed to reflect the American democratic ideal, and their behavior toward the Indian and Burmese people was supposed to display America's greatest strengths. And when I showed up, suddenly discussions turned to the black presence in America, and suddenly they were required to face up to the flaws in our society. My participation on the study team, the candid discussions that my presence evoked among Indians and Burmese people in the presence of white missionaries, were all clear omens that something new was going on in the world.

When I returned home after ten weeks in Asia, I found myself once again on the road to Green Lake, Wisconsin, to report to the Baptist Foreign Mission Board on our visits. This time I was driving with my wife. On the highway to Racine, just above Chicago, we stopped at a restaurant whose manager refused to serve us because we were not "members." We could not "join," he said, because the membership had just closed. That was in December of 1953, fully six years after my encounter with the hotel porter in Detroit on my first trip to Green Lake.

It seemed that trying to get to equality was hopeless. But these two events were only part of the story. On the one hand I confronted raw racism, face to face, on my two trips to Wisconsin. On the other, the Baptists were transferring American mission hospitals and colleges to indigenous ownership and control, and two white pastors refused to stay in a white YMCA if I could not. It was this kind of reckoning that enabled us to keep faith alive. Before giving in to cynicism and letting ourselves be overwhelmed by negative experiences, we always factored in any positive element we could lay our hands on.

If the restaurant manager had known that I was on my way to speak of world events to an audience with much greater influence than his few customers would ever have, he would have known that his world was dying. My world was coming alive, and what a squalling, noisy birth it was.

ON THE DOMESTIC FRONT, EVERY SIX MONTHS ANOTHER NAACP victory was won before the Supreme Court. The 1954 school desegregation case was the climax. On a large scale, segregating black students automatically imposed inferior status, which supported racial hatred. Further, black schools did not have the facilities, books, or any other educational tools that white schools had.

From a more intimate perspective, however, these segregated schools were ours. Black teachers, principals, choir directors, and coaches made their schools a refuge from an ugly world that constantly looked down on their pupils. They monitored behavior and supervised manners. So while everyone knew that integration would answer our aspirations, not every black person was optimistic about instantly dissolving black schools, reassigning black principals into subordinate positions such as "directors of federal programs," and shifting black children into newly integrated schools.

But it was heresy to speak against desegregation, no matter what the consequences. Sadly, the consequences proved to be disastrous. Some school districts dismantled all black schools, so that whites would not have to attend a "black" school. In such cases all black students were shifted into white schools, where they were largely unwanted and unprovided for. Then, rather than attend schools with blacks, whites fled.

It's ironic that at the time that school integration began, its enemies had no idea we would end up the victims of our major achievement. Today, forty years later, all big-city school systems are largely black and failing; whites and middle class blacks have fled to the suburbs or private schools. Indeed, effective school integration today is a myth. Instead of attending warm and dynamic schools where they are sponsored and affirmed, black students today are educationally crippled, too often abandoned in urban, drug-infested, violent, crime-ridden holding pens and dealt with like cattle. Clearly, something radically new must occur to generate a fresh start in educating masses of urban black youth.

Surprisingly, school integration's greatest success came in moderate-sized southern towns where the black population was in the minority, and thus less threatening to whites; or in towns with a solid black middle class which had high expectations for black student performance. In Prince Edward County, however, near where Virginia Union was located, the local white leadership was vehemently opposed to "race mixing." Rather than integrate, the county closed all of its public schools. Our college faculty helped to set up an alternate school for black pupils in the First Baptist Church in the small town of Farmville. One morning I looked out into our front yard and saw the ashes of a cross lying in the grass. During the night some fanatic had been sneaking around. We ignored it and went right on doing what we had been doing.

By this time I had been made president of my alma mater. Since, in the black community of the South, the pastors and college presidents are regarded as pilots and representatives of the people to the larger public, whatever I did or said was conspicuous in the community. Bessie and our two sons had become accustomed to the loss of privacy. The boys knew that I marched at the head of the line, my picture was in the papers, and that civil rights leaders visited our home and campus. They knew that because the spotlight was always on us, they bore an extra load, and that threats came with the territory. If I made a speech supporting school integration, it was echoed throughout the area. Finding a cross burning on the front lawn was no big surprise, but it was frightening. We knew the Klan was dangerous and that its activities frequently, and without warning, went far beyond burning symbols. But Bessie and I tried to minimize the fear to our boys, who were seven and ten years old. The police chief came out, offered his help, stood around chatting and generally showed concern and sympathy. Then he took me aside and said, "Brother Proctor, you know we can't protect you around the clock, so you had better take this." He handed me a heavy box and I knew what was in it before I even opened it. Inside was what looked like a brand-new .22 caliber pistol and a package of shells.

IN THE MIDST OF THE LIGHTNING AND THUNDER THAT accompanied the storm of school desegregation in our area came occasional moments of calm. Richmond, Virginia, had a strong and solid Jewish community. Generally, blacks and Jews fared well together, and blacks knew that many Jews worked for social progress and black liberation. But when racial lines were drawn, it was expected that Jews would sacrifice their black friendships and stand with the whites. In purely economic terms, it seemed too expensive to do otherwise.

One organization of Jewish women used to hold its weekly luncheon meetings in the dining room of Richmond's Byrd Hotel, where they discussed current events and planned various community services. In the fall of 1955, they invited me to deliver a series of six lectures on different world religions, including the black church. I prepared extensively and the meetings went well. The women always invited me to eat lunch with them in the hotel dining room where blacks worked, but could not dine. The black waiters beamed with delight when they saw me walk into the dining room. Those stylish, intelligent, and charming women always made me feel comfortable.

For the next five years I was their annual lecturer. Then one morning I received a casual phone call from one of the club women saying that their next meeting would be at the YWCA, rather than the Byrd Hotel. I complied and paid it no mind.

Thirty years later, on the anniversary of my first lecture, the women's club invited me to come back to Richmond from New Jersey for a celebration. Now they held their weekly meetings in the commodious, well-equipped Jewish Community Center. They were as warm and welcoming as ever. One of the original group, a woman now in her midsixties, introduced me to the audience of about forty-five people, explaining that when we were together earlier in the 1950s, they had moved their meeting from the Byrd Hotel to the YWCA because the hotel manager refused to let me continue to eat lunch with them. In all those thirty intervening years, I had never known that. These had been crucial years in the civil rights struggle when even small acts of integrity took courage and made a large impact.

As she spoke her voice trembled and her eyes flooded. She was so embarrassed to recall that once I had been barred from eating with them, and overjoyed that now we were together under a new set of rules and free to talk about it.

Today, the struggle is far from complete, but it's important to acknowledge where we've been and how encouragement came from many sources.

BACK IN 1950, I WAS INVITED TO RETURN TO CROZER Seminary to make a chapel address. One of my old professors told me about a new student, a bright, promising alumnus of Morehouse College. After lunch that day, I went over and talked with the young man in his dorm. He was Martin Luther King, Jr., the grandson of Dr. A. D. Williams, a veteran Baptist leader in Atlanta, and the son of Alberta Williams King, a Spelman alumna, and Martin Luther King, Sr., a Morehouse graduate.

Martin talked slowly, delivering every sentence with Delphian assurance and oracular finality. He encapsulated the Morehouse mission—to lead, to be up front, and to be right and effective. It was immediately clear to me that I was talking to a prodigious candidate for leadership.

He asked me which books had influenced me the most. I told him that Reinhold Niebuhr's *Moral Man and Immoral Society* and Harry E. Fosdick's *The Modern Use of the Bible* were first, and the work of Walter Rauschenbusch followed closely. He nodded approvingly, though he was eight years younger than I. He then paid closer attention, eyes to eyes, and asked me to characterize famous black church leaders as he called the roll: Joseph Jackson, president of the National Baptist Convention; Benjamin Mays, president of Morehouse College; Mordecai Johnson, president of Howard University; Vernon Johns, pastor of Dexter Avenue Baptist Church in Montgomery; John Ellison, president of Virginia Union, my predecessor; Richard McKinney, philosophy professor at Morgan State College; and Adam Powell, Jr. and Sr., pastor and pastor emeritus of the Abyssinian Baptist Church. He seemed to be measuring where he would fit into this panoply, staking out his own turf for later. That afternoon, in the middle of the day and the middle of the week, he wore a collar, tie, and three-button suit. He was a small-framed person, who walked and talked slowly with a kind of Napoleonic assurance. He looked like a major event about to happen.

Over the next few years Martin stayed in close touch and we met several times at the annual meetings of the National Baptist Convention. Whenever I visited Boston, where he was working toward his Ph.D., we would meet at the School of Theology and continue our conversations. Occasionally he would meet my train and drive me to my hotel, talking all the way. He loved to debate theology and philosophy with me. Martin was very career

oriented and fixed on the future. His goal at that time was to succeed Dr. Benjamin E. Mays as Morehouse College's president.

It was no surprise to me when he was called to preach in the
front-line, silk-stocking, Dexter Avenue Baptist Church in Montgomery, succeeding the inimitable Vernon Johns. Johns, a brilliant, radical graduate of the Oberlin School of Theology, had
a well-earned reputation for throwing caution to the winds in the
cause of freedom and justice. In a certain sense, he had prepared
the congregation at Dexter Avenue for Martin. They were solid
citizens with a preference for orderly change, but after spending a few years with Dr. Johns they were capable of taking on
more dramatic action. They were primed to speed up behind
leaders with integrity.

By then I was vice president and dean at Virginia Union, and
I often invited Martin to speak to our student body. Like an old
man, he was deliberate in everything. But when he spoke, his
rhythmic cadences, his flow of language, and his sagacious finality about big problems captivated the students. Martin dis-
armed his listeners with his simple idealism and his unapologetic
allegiance to the most sublime ideals that have echoed through
the long corridors of the centuries. He had answers, and everything he said was true.

Martin gave no quarter to compromise, to the accommodation of evil, to caprice or calumny. I often think of him now when
I read newspaper columns written by prominent black conservatives, like Dr. Walter Williams and Dr. Thomas Sowell, who are
partners with those who consistently try to keep black people
from pursuing simple fairness. With their scholarly cant they
cloud the issues and drum on themes that draw applause from
their cynical sponsors. I wonder if they are ever frightened when
they look around and notice who is applauding them.

Shortly after Martin settled in at his new church, a black citizen of Montgomery was asked to give up her seat on a bus to a
white man and move to the rear. In effect, Rosa Parks' heroic

refusal began the legend of Martin Luther King, Jr. Martin led a bus boycott that effectively eliminated segregated seating in public transportation. Many other black pastors also had talent and courage, but they didn't have Rosa Parks! She was the right person, at the right place, at the right time.

Rosa Parks was a soft-spoken Christian woman active in her church, well prepared and well versed in the policies of non-violent social change. She wore her hair combed back in a soft bun, and used no lipstick, rouge, or eye shadow. She never used profanity, drank alcohol, or chewed gum. She wore modest clothes and low-heeled shoes. She looked like a temperance advocate.

Martin, on the other hand, had the charisma of an old-fashioned Baptist preacher, with a catalogue of ideas rooted in the radical social message of the eighth century B.C.E. prophets of Judaism who spoke of justice rolling down "as waters and righteousness of a mighty stream." Most of all, he believed that love—without thought of reciprocity—had inherent power and intrinsic authenticity.

Together, Rosa Parks and Martin Luther King, Jr., became the defining moment for real social change in America. Their witness was the zenith of the long struggle for full emancipation. Some secular critics said King was naive to believe that a reservoir of white good will existed out there somewhere. They could not conceive of change without bloodshed and wholesale killing. But Martin recognized that our very existence in a free society, with its accent on equality, derived from the ultimate victory of the One who died on a Roman cross with a crown of weeds and thistles on his brow.

Martin was right. He believed that in order to achieve a moral end, our movement had to be morally correct. This attitude has always been more typical of black striving than violent acts.

Martin invited me twice to speak at Dexter Avenue for his Annual Spring Lecture Series. Other black churches had revivals, but Martin's congregation, largely comprising faculty and staff from Alabama State College, preferred more sedate activities. He often told me, bragging of course, that he had thirty-nine Ph.D.s in his congregation. And I would always reply, "And how many Christians?"

One day during the Spring Lecture Series in 1956 he had to go to Tuskegee, about thirty miles away, to arrange to buy gasoline for cars that were transporting blacks boycotting the bus line. In Montgomery, any gas station owner who sold to blacks was denied his supplies. To keep Martin company, because you never knew what might happen to a radical black man on the highway in those days, I rode along with him. An Alabama state trooper followed us every inch of the way, about a yard behind Martin's old Pontiac station wagon. We were both frightened, perspiring profusely, and silent. When we reached the edge of Tuskegee, the trooper pulled over and stopped.

We spent an hour or so in town, while Martin conferred with black gasoline station owners. Then we started back. The same trooper picked up our tail as we left town, and trailed us all the way back to Montgomery. The cop's childish game of intimidation barely registered on our Richter scale. He probably would be furious to know how small an impact his harassment made on the larger purpose.

Incidentally, not long ago I was caught in a terrible rainstorm while driving from Mobile to Atlanta. Driving frantically, hunched over the wheel, I found myself traveling on that same road between Tuskegee and Montgomery, now widened and renamed Martin L. King Jr. Highway.

Back in the mid-1950s, the table was set, but I wondered, when do we eat? We were naive in believing that legal victories alone would mean social change. Institutions like the Boy Scouts, YMCA, churches, labor unions, lodges, and fraternities—all operating under lofty creeds to serve humankind and promote good will—sought loopholes that allowed them to remain segregated and immune from court orders. Those "born again" Christians would not do it.

RICHMOND WAS A GOOD PLACE TO BE DURING THE GREAT transition because it had a large, educated black population with a polite connection with the white establishment. Life was tolerable, not stifling, even though resistance to change was firm. We did not experience the fear and violence that we learned about in the deep South.

Bessie and I had married during the war years when so much was unsettled, and Bessie still had some college credits to complete for her degree. Consequently, our home was tightly organized around her writing papers, the boys demanding attention, and my six courses which kept me buried in books. Preoccupied with Herbie's health, Bessie's final courses, and my workload, we hardly had time to reflect on larger issues.

Our lives were full of college sports events, church programs, college concerts, children's activities, and family visits. We frequently visited my wife's home in Fredericksburg and my own family in Norfolk, and it seems that I was always speaking in some church, conference, or school. Bessie was always busy packing and dressing the boys to get us ready to pile in our station wagon and hit the road. We knew every filling station, hamburger stand, and ice cream store in Virginia where blacks could be served without insult.

By 1955, I had become president of Virginia Union. That same year I had the privilege of awarding the bachelor of arts degree to a Mr. D. B. Jaycox, the oldest student on our campus— or any campus, perhaps. Mr. Jaycox had been the principal of my elementary school when I was a boy. I always thought he had second sight. I'll never forget the day when little Vanetta Morgan was leaning over the drinking fountain, with her long braids hanging all the way down her back. The sight of those braids was too tempting and, after being certain that no one was looking, I grabbed both of them and yanked hard. Before I knew it, Mr. Jaycox appeared out of the mist and whacked me across the fanny with his hickory cane.

Like many black teachers in those days, Mr. Jaycox had earned a teaching certificate, but had never graduated from college. After he retired, he came to Virginia Union at the age of seventy-five to earn what he considered the ultimate prize, his baccalaureate degree. When he stepped up to the platform, he didn't look nearly as fierce as I had remembered him, so as I handed him his diploma I brazenly reminded him of Vanetta Morgan's braids. He grinned at me. "That's why you're where you are today," he said. "I kept you straight."

He did indeed. And placing a college diploma in his hands was one of the most rewarding moments of my life.

As desegregation took hold, some hardened attitudes also began to change. Under the threat of court orders, a handful of black students had been enrolled at Duke University, and Dr. Howard Wilkerson, the chaplain of Duke University, asked me to speak in their chapel. Duke's president, however, told Dr. Wilkerson that no black would preach in that Gothic church unless it was over his dead body.

Two years later, the president unexpectedly died. Dr. Wilkerson invited me again, and while I was seated in the chapel getting ready to deliver my sermon, I leaned across and asked him where the former president was buried. "Directly under the pulpit," he whispered. Surely enough, I was literally preaching over his dead body!

In 1957, at the height of the heat and ferment about school integration, the president of Lenoir-Rhyne College in rural piedmont North Carolina invited me to give their commencement address. That took nerve on his part, and I accepted. I spoke on

Victor Hugo's phrase, "The Power of an Idea Whose Time Has Come," presenting the view that the time had come to abandon a segregated society, and for moral, intelligent, patriotic whites to take the leadership from the racists and the opportunistic politicians and stand up for a new beginning in race matters.

To my surprise, the all-white audience of students, faculty, alumni, and families stood up and applauded; I had to bow several times before they would sit down again. Afterward, as I was wending my way through the crowd milling around the campus near the auditorium, I heard a voice calling, "Dr. Proctor! Dr. Proctor!" Walking toward me was an elderly couple, wearing the marks of many winters in their wrinkled faces. They were out of breath trying to catch me. The old woman reached into a bag and took out a boxed Cross pen and pencil set and held it out to me. "We brought it to give to our grandson who is graduating today," she said, "but we'd like to give it to you instead. We can buy another one for him." I still use that pen and pencil. And I treasure that moment, granting it as much credibility as any court decision, act of Congress, or publication of any major treatise on social change. In terms of informing my heart about the future, I put as much trust in that moment as I would in a volume of speeches.

Also in 1957, Bessie and I participated in the Institute for College Administration at the Harvard Graduate School of Business. In this special program we met the best minds in the country on the subject of school management. In 1958, we joined in a retreat in Nova Scotia to study the Great Books curriculum of Saint John's College of Annapolis, Maryland, guided by its president, Dr. Weigle (the son of my dean at Yale).

I brought everything I gained at Harvard and Nova Scotia back with me and dumped it on the faculty and staff of Virginia Union. The idea was to elevate the intellectual tone of campus life and encourage challenging and stimulating discussions among the faculty. We had a great time fashioning our administration and curriculum to meet the needs of the young people coming to us.

Other movements were also spinning the political wheels of the nation, and in one way or another overlapped onto the black struggle. In 1958, at the height of the Red scare, anyone could grab headlines by becoming a virulent anticommunist. The Baptist World Alliance got the idea of sending three observers to the Soviet Union and Eastern bloc countries to look behind the Iron Curtain and see how small Baptist groups were faring under severe religious restrictions.

Anxious to show Eastern Europeans how some aspects of American life had changed, the Baptists chose me for the team. It was an honest, though less than significant, gesture and I was eager to go. In every circle we visited, questions about the status of blacks came up, even in countries like Belgium, Germany, and Switzerland where no blacks were visible and where they were not welcomed.

In Eastern Europe—in Warsaw, Riga, and Krakow—blacks were even less known, and I was proud to tell them how we had stood up and advanced in the face of rigid racial discrimination. All the Eastern Europeans knew how we had been treated, but they did not know how we had responded. I took pride in telling them that our spirits were never fully broken and that we always were able to muster the strength to protest, to march, to pray, to sing, and to go to jail to keep our movement for full freedom alive. It is a story I never tired of telling.

Under the communists, all churches and religions in Eastern Europe had been driven underground, except for one large Baptist church in Moscow. I preached there one Sunday morning with about two thousand people attending and another two thousand waiting outside. Those inside would periodically leave their seats and send in people from the outside to take their place. The sermon lasted more than three hours because every sentence had to be translated into four languages. I had to wait so long for the translations that from time to time I forgot where I was in my discourse. When I finally finished, I was exhausted. But before I could sit down, someone in the crowd stood up and asked that "the black brother from America should give another sermon."

After that, the police warned me to stop telling the Soviets that faith had enabled black people to outlive oppression. They advised me to stick to the Bible. That was curious, since the Bible—from Moses versus Pharaoh, to Elijah versus Ahab, John the Baptist versus Herod, and Jesus versus Caesar—is all about liberation.

> The Spirit of the Lord is upon Me, for He has anointed Me to preach the Gospel to the poor; . . . to announce release to the captives . . . ; to set free the [oppressed].
> Luke 4:18–20 (Berkeley Version)

We suspected that the Soviets permitted our visit in order to deflect reports that religion was stifled in Russia. But it was obvious to us that religion *was* being suppressed. We were moved to see old people coming to the service carrying huge Bibles, with lavishly designed covers, the pages inside ragged and thin with use. New Bibles had not been printed in Russia for thirty years. But the Baptists proudly took us to cemeteries and showed us new graves which bore tiny wooden crosses. In death, it seemed, people were free to declare their religious beliefs.

When I was departing from the Moscow airport, I found several wrinkled, handwritten notes that had been surreptitiously stuffed into the pockets of my trench coat. These scraps of paper were greetings to kinfolk in the United States. Where addresses were given, I gladly mailed them.

AS A COLLEGE TEACHER I WAS ALWAYS ON THE LOOKOUT for promising students. We never knew who might be sitting out

there, and we always cherished the notion that if we kept pushing, someone in the group would break free and pioneer into
new realms of opportunity and service. For example, in one of
my classes in ethics at Virginia Union I recognized a bright young
man named Douglas Wilder, although I never guessed he would
become the first black governor in America, no less in Thomas
Jefferson's and George Washington's Virginia.

One way to promote students' interests and expose them to
larger fields of endeavor was to carry them to conferences. Anytime I was invited to speak somewhere, I would load my car and
take off with five or six students. At a conference in Greenwich,
Connecticut, a woman came up to me and begged me to take
her son off the streets. She was terrified he was going to wind up
in jail.

I persuaded him to enroll in our college. John Merchant went
down with me, played basketball, waited table in the hotels, took
campus jobs, and made an outstanding record. He had a kind
of Yankee audacity about him and a never-give-up tenacity that
made him an excellent candidate to break down barriers. After
graduation John was ready to go back North, but we begged him
to take on a hazardous mission. He agreed to try. John Merchant
became the first black student to enter the University of Virginia
Law School, the state's most sacred cow. He is now attorney for
the state of Connecticut department of consumer affairs.

Today, John's mother, blind and frail, lives in a Connecticut
nursing home. I recently stopped by to see her and we recalled
her son's formidable journey thirty years earlier. I had the great
joy of telling her that John had just delivered the commencement address at his old law school—because his daughter, her
granddaughter, was in the graduating class. She wept with thanks
to God. These are the secrets that faith will yield and that hardly
ever get known.

At another conference in Cornwall, Connecticut, I needed a
haircut. I left my students and sneaked off the grounds alone to

find a quiet, authentic black barbershop, but I got lost driving around the Litchfield hills. At last, I spotted a young black hitch-hiker standing at the side of the road.

"Where ya' goin', fella?" I asked.

"To caddy at the golf course," he replied.

"If you can tell me where I can get a haircut, I'll drive you to the golf course."

"You'll have to go into Waterbury to Mr. Reid's barbershop," he said. "I'm going out of your way."

I traded him a ride to the golf course for directions to Mr. Reid's barbershop. In the next ten minutes, I really went after him. I told him he needed to get out of Connecticut and join the flow of young black men and women who refused to accept the limitations others placed on them, and who planned to scale the heights. He listened as if he had never heard anything like that before.

For the next two years we exchanged letters. He kept me abreast of his school progress and, eventually, he enrolled in our college. He went on to finish law school in New York and then moved to California. Today, my caddy, William Ormsby, is a judge in the Los Angeles County Court.

Believing that change is possible causes one to act in harmony with such faith. As you live it out, the unseen evidence begins to appear. Because you *believe*, the very believing makes it so. This is the substance of things hoped for. And when faith is opera-tional, strange things happen.

When I was a young student at Virginia Union in 1940 to 1942, an anonymous philanthropist in New Hampshire had paid my hundred-dollar tuition. I suppose the school thought if I knew my benefactor's name, I would write to him to express my thanks and respectfully ask for more! And no doubt I would have.

Sixteen years later, I was sitting in my office as president of the same school, facing a distraught premed honor student in the senior class. He was a married veteran with two children, and the bottom had dropped out of his life. He was telling me that he was stone broke, his rent was overdue, his children had been sick, and he had to give up. He already had been accepted at medical school, but he said there was no way he could go on. As we pondered the problem, the door opened and Mrs. Lytle, my ever-present assistant, came in. "Sorry to interrupt," she said, "but I think you want to take this call."

"I'm terribly busy," I said. "Can I call back?"

"I think you should take it now!"

A cracked, warbly voice came on the line. "Are you the same Samuel Proctor who went to school at Virginia Union back in 1940?"

"I am the same," I said.

"I'm the one who paid your tuition. I called to tell you that I'm satisfied that I made a wise investment. I'm pleased with your progress."

I was dazed, and I thanked him profusely. Then, God forbid, he said, "Can you find me another student that I could help? I don't have much time left and I would like to do again what I did in your case."

"Sir," I said, with an involuntary tremor in my voice, "he's sitting in front of me as we speak."

This was as close to a miracle as I have ever seen. With the infinite probability that no human could ever align random events with such precision, there must be a God somewhere! I handed the phone to my student and left the room. I have no idea what they talked about, but when he came out of my office several minutes later I was crying, Mrs. Lytle was in tears, and the student, now the fabulous Dr. Charles Cummings, a prominent Richmond specialist in internal medicine, was smiling through his tears.

This anonymous New Hampshire donor was no social theorist, no great reformer, no political activist. He was a simple Christian with a little money who looked around to canvass his options; back in 1940, he reached into the South and helped a young black student to equip himself. Now, as he faced life's sunset, he looked about again. Without anyone asking him, his heart moved, as though guided by the mysterious lodestone in a compass, and directed him, nearly twenty years later, to help another black student transcend the limitations imposed by history. This is the kind of evidence that black people always suspected existed, though ever so dormant, to justify their timeless and enduring faith.

BY 1959, THE COUNTRY HAD MADE SEVERAL JERKY BOLTS toward real racial change. The executive orders of Roosevelt and Truman, the Civil Rights Bill of Eisenhower, along with the string of Supreme Court victories won by the NAACP, had been positive indicators; now there was a kind of expectancy, a messianic hope, that someone would emerge who would dramatize change and celebrate America's true promise. Almost mystically, the rich, handsome, charismatic John Kennedy appeared.

In March of 1959, I sat next to him on the stage in a large auditorium in Indianapolis. I was there, with the forty United Negro College Fund presidents, to open our fund-raising campaign. Kennedy was there to promote his candidacy for the Democratic presidential nomination.

On my wall at home is a picture that recently surfaced of the speaker's platform that night. I am up at the podium doing my thing for the UNCF, and Kennedy, his head tipped, index finger supporting his cheekbone, is gazing hard at me.

Later that same night, Belford Lawson, a prominent Washington attorney, called my hotel room and asked if I would meet with the senator. "For what?" I asked.

"He wonders if you would take a leave from Virginia Union's presidency and work with his campaign."

I hastened to say, "Brother Lawson, let's face it. He is so young that the old folks will reject him; so rich that poor folks will deny him; and so Catholic that the Protestants will put him down. Now, if Stuart Symington is looking for me, tell him where I am."

Lawson chuckled, and that was the beginning of my relationship with John Kennedy. While the potential for a new racial arrangement was present in Kennedy's nomination, it was by no means automatic or inevitable. It would take real people doing real jobs to make it happen, and I discovered myself inescapably among them.

THE CURTAIN CAME UP ON A DECADE OF HOT REBELLION and frenetic campaigns for change. In 1960, black college presidents found themselves in the eye of the hurricane. Our students had grown up observing the slow, begrudging changes of the Roosevelt-Truman-Eisenhower eras; they were aware of the perennial appeasement of southern politicians and their constituents. All of their lives, they had seen promised, long-overdue change proceeding at a snail's pace. They resented the stagnant political and social climate, they resented the way older blacks seemed to accept the slow rate of change. They were right. Moral goodness was on their side. No one could justify the treatment that blacks had to accept—sitting in theater balconies, getting served only at the "carry out" end of lunch counters, and being offered only menial jobs at the lowest pay.

On the second Saturday of February, 1960, the black college presidents of the Central Intercollegiate Athletic Association were holding their annual meeting on the old colonial campus of Maryland State College on the quiet, isolated Delmarva peninsula. Squirrels and chipmunks darted between silent oak sentinels; thickly carpeted lawns were bordered by immaculate sidewalks and driveways. We were dining in the trustee boardroom, with its heavy draperies framing tall colonial windows, the table set with exquisite dinnerware, and well-groomed waiters standing by. We had just begun to dig into juicy filet mignons, when one of those handsome waiters pushed open the leather-padded door and said, "There's an urgent call for President Warmoth T. Gibbs."

Gibbs, president of North Carolina A & T, tiptoed out of the room like a mortician at a funeral. A few minutes later he was back, looking tense and drawn. Two hundred and fifty of his students were in jail! Within minutes, every president there had a similar call. The sit-in movement had begun.

Our students and their advisers had held clandestine meetings and had drawn up a scheme to strike a blow against Woolworth's Greensboro lunch counters while we were away in rural Maryland, eating steak and drinking Chablis, figuring out how to accommodate visiting football teams.

The students were doing what they could do best. Their parents, who had mortgages, car payments, and tuition bills to pay, were not in the best position to stage a confrontation with authorities.

With the student sit-ins, the new emancipation suddenly accelerated. Blacks never questioned the choice to pursue change by moral, nonviolent means. It was simply their way. There is no record anywhere—Have mercy!—of black nannies poisoning white babies or putting arsenic in the family's pot of greens. Blacks never talked about putrefying the town reservoir or burning down the sheriff's home while he and his family were asleep. When some frenzied groups decided to bomb buildings and burn cities, they were rejected by the larger black community. The majority of blacks intended to fulfill their liberation and, as a concomitant, to participate in America's fulfillment as well. This was the substance of their hope.

IN THIS PERIOD IN HISTORY, I SAW THE PAST BEGINNING TO fade away and a new world on the horizon. My grandmother,

Hattie Ann, lived to see it, too. At the age of ninety-six, Grandma fell seriously ill for the first time in her life and we spent many hours together talking about the past. I remember her squeezing my hand one afternoon and telling me how proud she was of my achievements. "I remember when your university was founded," she said. "It was called Richmond Theological Seminary." "My university" was founded less than one mile from the Fisher plantation where she had been enslaved.

That little slave girl has over one hundred descendants who are college-trained, many of them holding professional degrees. In less than one century, they had turned their simple belief that unrequited suffering would somehow be redeemed into a new political and social theory. Beginning with their mission, the black sojourn in America has demonstrated itself to be without precedent, still calling for a new society.

CHAPTER FIVE

The Horizon of Hope

¶¶¶

1960–1964

TWO BIG EVENTS MADE 1960 A DEFINING YEAR FOR ME. First, our son Herbert returned to Johns Hopkins Hospital in Baltimore where a miracle was performed: his surgeons, the widely known team of Drs. Taussig and Blalock, built a new wall between his ventricles, virtually giving him a rebirth.

During Herbie's first twelve years of life we had organized our lives around him, and through him we learned how special opportunities for growth were strewn along life's pathway. We made thirty-nine round trips between Richmond and Baltimore, accepting the hospitality of dear friends, the Reverend and Mrs. Thomas Davis, who served a church in Baltimore. These trips were like holiday picnics. We were so glad that Herbie's operation was a success; color came back to his fingernails, his lips and cheeks. He breathed with ease, walked steadily, and smiled incessantly.

His brother, Timothy, only ten years old, made every trip with us, grabbing every brief, sneaky minute with Herb that he could. Also on every trip was Bessie's mother, who gave up all of her other interests to share our needs. She was a fixture in our home and in our travels.

Sharing our son's early life, when his damaged heart prevented him from playing baseball, swimming, and dancing or going to birthday parties, taught us lessons no doctor's degree ever could. Everyone knew how risky his life was, but *him*. Everyone knew how much he was missing, but *him*. He sang and laughed through it all, and his brave, cheerful spirit made us thankful to be alive.

Timothy shared our special family secret: Herb's needs came first. The child with the unmerited, undeserved, unearned *deficit* laid a claim on all of us who enjoyed benefits from our birth that we did not earn or deserve. For the next forty years all of my teaching and preaching has had the same hidden agenda, namely: to show that those who enjoy a fast start, fond parents, strong bodies, quick minds, and the aroma of hope following their steps owe it to those who begin life with a physical limitation, poor education, and poverty coming in the window along with the flies, the noise, and the profanity to help them get over. Herbie got over, with an awful lot of support and love and constant prayer from the rest of us. Today, after finishing college and a master's degree in social work, he is a father of three and a veteran urban school social worker in New Jersey.

Here's a footnote to his childhood. One Sunday morning I was the guest preacher at the church in Petersburg where many of the faculty of Virginia State University worshiped. I mentioned that my son's big surgery was coming up, but he needed forty-eight pints of blood. The Red Cross in Richmond, where I had many friends, would not accept blood from black donors. However, the Red Cross mobile trailer in Petersburg would. Well, I didn't know forty-eight people in Petersburg. Even worse, I was president of Virginia Union, the arch enemy in football of Virginia State.

As the congregation stood mingling outside after church, no one mentioned donating blood. But on Monday afternoon, a whole busload of Virginia State football players showed up at the Red Cross trailer; technicians stayed late into the night drawing blood from quarterbacks, linebackers, tight ends, running backs, guards, and wide receivers—for our little Herbie, who knew it would happen for him, although none of us knew how. The prime movers were their coach, Sally Hall, and a huge bruising fullback named "Toby" Tobias, who had survived a rough upbringing in a Baltimore slum. With forty-eight pints of blood from young black ballplayers who had been recruited from the ghettos of Philadelphia, Newark, Baltimore, Washington, D.C., and Richmond, and the genius surgeons at Johns Hopkins built a new heart for Herbie.

The other big event of 1960 was the election of John Kennedy to the nation's presidency. To us on the sidelines it seemed that if a handsome, Harvard-trained Roman Catholic could be elected, anything might happen. His election was accompanied by a growing impatience with the pace of change, and there were demonstrations everywhere for desegregation and voting rights. All over the South, a vanguard of courageous people threw themselves in the face of insanely angry white mobs. They were beaten with tire irons, chains, bats, and fence posts, had dogs and fire hoses turned on them, and many died to turn this society around. They integrated schools, opened hotels and restaurants, registered new voters, and fought for fair employment. We owe an immeasurable debt to them. Most of them have never heard their names honored in public and have never seen them written anywhere.

For so long, the Senate had been captive to senior, southern politicians, and we had seen significant legislation and big ideas lying fallow. The Kennedy rhetoric was different. He was young and idealistic, and surrounded himself with people who created an air of expectancy. Kennedy had been a friendly senator and, surely enough, when his presidency began, we felt movement. The whole national conversation changed.

As Democratic chairman of the House Committee on Education and Labor, Adam Clayton Powell, Jr., was able to pilot one key piece of legislation after another through the Congress. I served on the board of directors of the National Urban League and saw firsthand how the government could increase opportunities for minorities in business and industry, if it had the will.

For example, the Kennedy innovators created a new program in the White House which they called Plans for Progress. Certain companies—among them IBM, Xerox, Mobil, Exxon, Chase Bank, AT&T, Bell Labs, Johnson & Johnson, Ford, Chrysler, General Motors, Citibank, and American Express—felt the pressure for change gaining momentum, and were convinced to start recruiting women and minorities, and allow the feds to monitor the results. Other companies followed their example. As a result of this push, corporate America began to enhance opportunity for blacks. For the first time we saw blacks moving up through the ranks and receiving serious appointments. Many of these early jobs were in personnel and human resources, but it was a start. Before Plans for Progress swung into action, any blacks you might have seen moving around at rush hour on Park Avenue wore doormen uniforms or carried messenger pouches. But by the time our son Timothy finished his law and M.B.A. degrees at Chicago in 1975, he had already spent a summer internship at Chase Bank; he then passed the New York bar and went to work, without missing a beat, as an attorney for Union Carbide on Park Avenue. The fruits of these '60s efforts were real.

I often spoke at Plans for Progress meetings where white corporate midlevel managers would gaze at me like cows looking at a new fence. They thought I was a mutation. They had never met educated, assertive blacks in a nonthreatening setting where they could ask naive questions and get straight answers.

All of my speeches followed the same pattern: I first presented the anti-thesis: Here is the kind of America we are creating—a huge underclass, an embarrassing jail population, illiteracy at 15 percent and poverty at 35 percent. Minorities are locked into low-paying jobs and minority students have low expectations. What kind of leadership is this?

Then I presented the thesis: We can change this. We can start recruiting and training bright young women and minorities. We can encourage colleges to recruit them and offer scholarships. We can get placement officers to prime them for job success.

Today, as I reflect on those awkward events, I am puzzled that I could speak so confidently about change before such uncommitted, reluctant groups. But I was convinced that I was right, and the companies bought into it.

I had spent so much time with the great social prophets of Israel and Judah and Jesus of Galilee, I really had no fear.

By the fall of 1960, I had left the presidency of Virginia Union, and moved to North Carolina A & T State University, a larger school whose students a few months earlier had spearheaded the sit-in movement. As a college president I was on call fourteen hours a day. The biggest part of my job was trying to develop a faculty and an academic program strong enough to propel black students into a demanding future. Our students usually came from disciplined, church-going families, reared by both parents, and backed up by at least two grandparents. Now, I began hawking foundations and federal offices for money to recruit a new contingent of black students coming from stagnating poverty and cultural isolation.

Even though I felt the work of the colleges was indispensable to black progress, there was so much happening in the civil rights movement that I wanted to do whatever I could to feel part of it, too. We could not leave our campuses and follow the movement, but we took any opportunity to participate. Whenever King asked me to address one of his gatherings, I would go. The campus itself was a center for student protest planning and activity. Whenever the Freedom Ride bus came rumbling through Greensboro in the middle of the night, our food service manager would haul out of bed to get meals ready and students would gladly share their beds. We tried to be ready any time, and were prepared to go anywhere to speak and organize.

While earthshaking events raged around us, I tried not to lose sight of the personal needs of individual boys and girls. Like my mother I had a habit of poking into the lives of the young people, a kind of pastoral spillover into my academic role. Because of my position, I had many opportunities to use contacts and influence to generate some new hope in individual lives. One day our public relations officer and I attended a 4-H Club conference in a poverty-stricken county in east Carolina. The boy who introduced me was dressed in a clean, starched, and neatly ironed 4-H Club uniform, and he spoke with unusual clarity. But as he turned toward me and bowed slightly, I noticed that his eyes were severely crossed. After the ceremony I learned that his family were poor people who practiced a typical rural philosophy: love the Lord and do your best; God will do the rest.

Back at my desk at A & T, I sat gazing out of the window. There had to be an ophthalmologist somewhere in Durham who would straighten out that little fellow's eyes. I called Dr. Waldo Beach, a respected scholar in Christian ethics at Duke's Divinity School, and asked him if he knew anyone who could help. He told me that among his church's congregation were a father and two sons, all three outstanding ophthalmologists. Only one more phone call, and these prominent white specialists agreed to correct the eyes of a poor black 4-H Club child—at no charge at all.

My only task was to convince his frightened and skeptical

mother that the same God whose natural order failed and let her boy be born with severely astigmatized eyes was the same God who allowed medical science to perfect the art of ophthalmology. She agreed, and the boy's eyes were operated on. He finished high school and college, completed an M.B.A. at the University of Wisconsin, worked for Quaker Oats, Gulf Oil, Johnson & Johnson, and now heads his own marketing consulting firm in Chicago. His eyes have been busy, and Bob Hughes has done well.

I had many similar encounters in the 1960s, and many trials, too. Down the road apiece from my Greensboro school was an expensive private Southern Baptist school called Wake Forest University. At that time, Wake Forest was trying to ease away from religious control in order to attract scholars unwilling to teach under the rubric of religious fundamentalism. Someone got the idea of asking me to come to Wake Forest and speak to their middle class, white student body on the issue of race relations and the rising claims of blacks on the society. For the most part, these students liked things as they were. My job that day was to show them how racial discrimination hurt everyone.

As I stood at the podium pouring out my soul, the crowd suddenly hooted. I turned just in time to see a completely naked male student race across the stage behind me. I paused, and then asked the audience if there were any other volunteers. They roared with laughter.

It might have been a fraternity prank or a racist gesture. I was immune to either insults or interruptions. I continued speaking, marshaling the strongest arguments I could find to pry open the minds of those potential leaders of the new era. When I finished, they stood applauding. But none of this was easy.

I spoke to many different audiences during these years, and the questions I heard were always the same. It's hard to imagine the measure of self-control needed to face one hostile white audience after another, looking in the faces of assorted antagonists, and pitifully ignorant, fearful hypocrites, whose agenda was to cling to their advantages and perpetuate the subordinate status of blacks. I answered their questions then as I answer them now:

"Do you believe in reverse discrimination, giving blacks preferences over others for jobs?"

Answer: Because of the long years of discrimination against blacks, and because tenure and seniority have been given to those who have enjoyed preferential treatment for generations, it's fair for qualified blacks to receive preference to correct such past abuses. How long it will take or how many cases are matters of legal judgement, but it should not be a permanent practice and we never asked for that.

"Do you believe that blacks should be granted admission to graduate and professional schools on any basis different from other students?"

Answer: Since the Emancipation, blacks have been deliberately deprived of equal educational opportunity. In many states it was illegal for blacks to be educated at all. All of my education through college was in segregated schools where the facilities and equipment were inadequate or not available. Most blacks, therefore, ended their early schooling with huge gaps in their preparation. Our scores on admissions tests often reflect this unfair disadvantage. When grade-point average, class standing, personal references, or in-depth interviews show that a black student is capable of successful performance, such evidence should take precedence over entrance exams—for the time being—as a fair corrective for the decades of unfair isolation and denial of opportunity.

"Why should this generation of whites be asked to pay for the discrimination perpetrated against blacks a long time ago?"

Answer: Just as blacks have inherited disabilities and stigmas and accrued financial, educational, and social *deficits*, so have whites accrued financial, educational, and power *benefits* while blacks were in physical bondage for eight generations and legally segregated for three more. It is fair for this generation that enjoys those unfair advantages to compensate blacks for such unfairly imposed deficits.

"What does the future hold for black people in America?"

Answer: As opportunities in education and employment improve, the quality of life among blacks will be further enhanced, as it was for the Jews, Germans, Irish, Italians, and Greeks. Our journey is harder because, unlike them, we bear the stigma that has been stamped on our color, and our previous condition as slaves. Our struggle is more tedious.

"What do blacks like you plan to do about so many blacks in prison and so many black teenage mothers on welfare?"

Answer: Blacks in prison read at the fourth-grade level and were reared without fathers. Whites in prison are the same. Whatever caused whites to end up in jail caused blacks also, and whatever corrective works for whites will work for blacks. It is a national problem, like air pollution and alcoholism, not a black or white one.

There are more young, white mothers on welfare than black. They also read at the fourth-grade level and most of them were reared in single-parent families of mothers who were also children of unwed parents. We need to work on the poor education and the family dysfunction that produces both black and white teenage mothers.

The causes of all these problems relate to ignorance and poverty, not skin color. Sadly, the questions I hear from audiences today are virtually the same. Prejudice is deep, strong, and intractable.

ALL BLACK LEADERS AND EDUCATORS IN THE 1960S WERE well aware that the causes of crime and social dependence were endemic among blacks, and caused our data always to be embarrassingly negative. But we also knew the causes behind the data, causes so deep and impenetrable that they would require serious national attention. We did what we could, and from where I was, I felt proud of the results that we generated.

The goal of black progress was clear: we wanted *in*, to become full participants and not marginalized mendicants. Ironically, two new black groups rose up to challenge the premise that blacks could eventually find a place in the mainstream of the society. First came the African culture advocates. They thought that equal participation was misconstrued to mean the "whitening" of black Americans: the abandonment of black heritage and identity, a sense of shame among blacks for being black. Consequently, they rejected the adjective "black" in favor of Afro-American. They put down black leaders who worked with white leaders, and all black organizations that cooperated with whites.

African cultural advocates believed that we should insulate ourselves from all white influences in the same way that the Amish and the Hasidic Jews had isolated themselves. They believed that we should run our own schools and ask for full political control of our communities, like an urban reservation.

Black separatists had a somewhat different agenda. They too believed that whites would forever look upon blacks as inferior, world without end, Amen. They advocated federal reparations to finance blacks wishing to relocate to a newly acquired African state, or even in a newly set-aside settlement in America, out West somewhere. It was more a mood, a feeling, than a well-thought-out strategy.

Of course, there was also a third, even smaller, group of blacks who wanted peace and tranquility at any cost. They blamed blacks for their plight, and thought we should stop "whining and bitching," as Judge Clarence Thomas puts it today. These men acted as though their own good fortunes rolled in softly on a gentle tide. Yet they enjoyed an education and job placement that would never have occurred without the steady protest and advocacy of black agitators.

Although these splinter groups attracted a great deal of attention from the media, most blacks continued to stay in touch with the larger society and maintain contact with people of good will.

A lot of black special interest groups at the time were trying to recruit our students for various campaigns and purposes. We taught them to ask relevant questions, look for the facts rather than propaganda, and opt for the position that was not self-contradictory. We honored our heritage, taught black history and black pride, and worked for a national community of diversity, compassion, and justice.

One particular student was always hanging around my office, darting in to snatch a few words with me between appointments, clinging to me like a vine. He was Jesse Jackson, bright, bold, and destined to be *somebody* in this country. Jesse had come to us as a transfer student from Illinois. He came to my attention when he turned up on our campus one day, seeking admission and financial aid. My public affairs officer came into my office, puffing and blowing, begging me to intercede with our registrar on this young man's behalf. "Dr. Proctor, please, don't let them turn that fellow away. We need him here!" I never knew exactly what Jesse had said to impress him, but it was immediate and indelible.

Jesse had spent a year at Illinois as a football recruit. That was a long way from home for a Greenville, South Carolina, boy, raised by his mother and grandmother in a modest public housing project. But he was adventurous enough to try anything. He gave up after a year and opted to come to us, with no money and ineligible for an athletic scholarship, pleading to be admitted. Even in his interviews he was so impressive that we made some very special arrangements to have him admitted. We never regretted it.

PRIOR TO THE KENNEDY YEARS HARDLY ANY BLACK PERSON ever received a telephone call from the White House. We hardly mattered at all. So one afternoon in January 1962, when my secretary buzzed me to pick up for a call from the White House operator I was stunned. There was Sargent Shriver, President Kennedy's brother-in-law, talking fast and spraying me with facts faster than I could absorb them. He was feverishly trying to get me to accept an appointment to direct the first full Peace Corps unit abroad, in Nigeria. Then President Kennedy came on, adding his persuasive charm and earnestness to the request.

The president said Nigeria was his showcase to help establish a more positive relationship with the new African states. He said it was urgent that the Peace Corps succeed there. (I did not discover until some weeks later just how urgent.) President Kennedy concluded by saying, in typical Kennedy fashion, "Dr. Proctor, your country needs you desperately."

Minutes later, the governor of North Carolina called. Kennedy had been burning up his phone lines, too. "Go, Sam. I guarantee your job when you return."

I hesitated. I knew little about Nigeria and even less about the Peace Corps. I did know that their volunteers were young, altruistic alumni of America's best colleges, and practically all of them were white. I also enjoyed my job, and felt I was on firm ground where I was, doing the work I was meant to do.

My reluctance was overcome by guilt feelings. During World War II, I had been a deferred seminary student, and dozens of my boyhood friends never returned from Anzio beach and the Pacific islands. I owed them something. More to the point, as a college administrator throughout the civil rights protests, I had done good work, but not on the front lines. I had never been shot at, beaten, thrown in a dirty jail, or chased by police dogs. I called Shriver back and told him I would go.

That night, I presented the situation to Bessie. Ordinarily, family problems and obligations would interfere with such a commitment, but Bessie knew I always weighed and debated every move endlessly. I told her I felt three powerful pistons moving me. One was the sense that America was on the threshold of something new and I thought that black people, including us, should be a living, active part of it. The president had in mind 15,000 to 20,000 young Americans helping students, many of them black Africans, in developing countries to obtain secondary educations. I had never done anything really sacrificial in my life, and this looked like it.

Next, I felt ashamed that black Americans had failed to help Africans. We made the faintest token gestures, but we had not developed a real commitment to Africa. Here was a chance.

Then, the world was changing. Two and a half billion people were about to start moving to close the gap with the rest of the world. I wanted us to be a part of that.

She listened to me and her response was immediate: "Let's do it!" she said. Bessie grasped clearly what it would take to move the whole family to Nigeria. Of course, neither of us really knew what life would be like or what the job would entail. But we were ready for the risk. After two or three hours of discussion with the boys, she had them on board. We were all excited and ready to go. For the next two weeks we had an African fit, being briefed by the state department and reading everything we could get our hands on about the Peace Corps and Nigeria.

The Peace Corps was a fully independent agency, free of the state department, AID, or the CIA. Its objectives were simple: to supply personnel in areas of critical shortages to newly developing nations, to enable Americans to learn firsthand about other cultures and ethnicities, and to allow the people of those countries to learn about Americans.

I knew that a pilot group of volunteers had already arrived in Nigeria with a temporary director, and I knew that one teacher had been sent home because of some kind of a misunderstanding. Before I could learn more, we were on our way. When President Kennedy said it was urgent, he wasn't kidding.

Once in Africa, the real facts surfaced. A young female Peace

Corps teacher attending a training session at the University of Ibadan had written a postcard to her mother back in Ohio. Her message described the filthy, crowded streets of Ibadan, with pregnant women carrying babies in their arms, and holding toddlers by the hand, the odor of urine rising from drainage ditches, and beggars clogging every crowded intersection. Before mailing the postcard, she inadvertently dropped it on the campus grounds, where it was later picked up by a Nigerian student. As fate had it, he belonged to a "nonaligned" political wing, a euphemism for leftist bias. He turned the card over to the press and it was published in every newspaper in the country as evidence that the pro-western Nigerian government had made a mistake in inviting seven hundred "capitalist" teachers into Nigeria; the Peace Corps teachers, they alleged, were part of a U.S. scheme to subvert their national autonomy and to begin a recolonization movement.

To avert a national crisis, the Nigerian government demanded that the United States immediately send a black educator to direct the huge cadre of white volunteers. If not, the Peace Corps would be evicted from the country. Bill Moyers had recommended me to Sargent Shriver, by way of a referral he had received from the president of Stetson University in Florida. I had been checked out from head to toe; I was clean, but green, for the job.

In Lagos, the degrading remnants of colonialism were everywhere. Segregation was the absolute rule. Many Americans serving in foreign posts automatically sent their children to schools in Europe. We wanted our two teenage boys to live with us in Nigeria, but when we tried to place them in the local schools, we saw that they were terribly crowded, poorly equipped, and followed a limited curriculum.

When we learned that an excellent American school had been established in Oshogbo for the children of white missionaries, we prepared for battle. Surprisingly, we met virtually no resistance at all. Through some white friends and colleagues in the States, I contacted the Foreign Mission Board of the Southern Baptist Convention. Within hours, our boys were invited to integrate the school. As a result, indigenous Africans were also invited to enroll.

Soon it became clear to me that the black struggle in America was a vanguard to rebuilding the tremendous damage colonialism had wrought in Africa. As desegregation was taking hold in the U.S., my sons were integrating a Nigerian school. The work of the Peace Corps in Africa seemed to be an extension of the faith package that we had inherited.

I had seven hundred freshly graduated white volunteers ready to learn a new language, eat a new diet, live in a strange culture, and do without supermarkets, television, libraries, buses, hot water, and, for some, electricity and indoor plumbing. Volunteers were paid fifty dollars a month, plus their living costs. Most taught in Nigeria's high schools, and a few taught in teacher training colleges. I never ceased to marvel at how these young people accepted their assignments, coped with the political skirmishes, negotiated their acceptance in the face of some bitter opposition, and maintained poise and confidence in the merit of their mission. We had so much opportunity to fail, but did not.

My family stayed in a state of curiosity and inquiry. We wanted this experience to yield a world of sophistication about Nigeria and Africa. We were less interested in African antiquity than we were in the people. Every household of a government employee came with a staff of seven servants attached to the house, whether they were needed or not. There was no question that we would keep them and pay them above the prevailing wage. Bessie is extremely gregarious and starts out trusting everyone. Her trust always begets trust, and within hours of taking up residence she had the house helpers feeling that they had known her for years. Our sons are a copy of her. From their relationships with the household staff we had a constant source of facts on Nigerian life as lived at the grass roots. The time flew by. The house ran so smoothly and with such warmth and joy that we practically forgot that we were three thousand miles from home. Our comfort level radiated outward, and we were able to give extra assurance to the volunteers who needed it. Most did not.

These volunteers were working on the front lines of world need and they loved it. Given the political climate, a big part of my job was to make sure that the Nigerians loved them back. I had a private pipeline to the Nigerians through which I could learn of their real reactions to our efforts. Many of the leaders of the independence movement in Africa had been educated by white missionary organizations in Africa and gone to black colleges in America. Fifty-five Nigerian officials were alumni of Virginia Union. One of them, a tribal chief in Oshogbo, had finished his degree at my alma mater in 1911! My own great-uncle had been his schoolmate.

Through the day-to-day living, I had the opportunity to look closely at Nigeria. I saw sick children all day long, crippled beggars, and masses of young, pregnant women with other infants on their backs. Young men had two or three wives, all of whom were bearing children constantly. Life was cheap. It was impossible for education and the economy to catch up with needs that were leaping ahead of progress.

How could Africans with the least resources be expected to reverse such a tide of woe which had been created by centuries of abuse by European colonists? When I was a schoolboy, we had to draw maps of the world. Our teachers would ask us to paint all of the French colonies blue, the Spanish yellow, the German black, the Belgian purple, the Dutch green, the Italian pink, the Portuguese orange; we left the British the color of the paper to save paint. No one ever asked why these people were so far from home, ruling someone else.

Today we are still seeing the consequences of colonialism in a sea of humanity, largely illiterate, living in poverty in countries like Somalia, Rwanda, and Uganda. Blacks cannot redress these wrongs by themselves. This was a global sin and it calls for a global cure. (Much as the depressing situation in the former Yugoslavia is the result of earlier Austro-Hungarian colonialism that today cries out for a global response.) When we look at African states that are doing well, it is obvious that they had better access to education and literacy. While we have to approach the more technical issues of infrastructure, communication, and fiscal management on a longer-term basis, the nations of the West—the former colonists—can multiply manyfold their paltry efforts at education now. This is the basic resource on which all other progress must depend.

American blacks are caught in a moral dilemma. No other people on earth can match the experience of black Americans or compare themselves to us. No one can identify completely with the metamorphosis through which we have gone. But now most of us enjoy a standard of living that is higher than 95 percent of the rest of the world's population. And we should be the chief advocates and participants for a change in the quality of life in Africa. Although we are so different from each other in so many ways, we are called together by our common social history, and our common quest for justice. It is our obligation to help Africans where we can.

MY EXPERIENCE IN NIGERIA FORCED ME TO REACH DEEP inside and probe my sense of being. Who was I, really? It is a question that every educated, upwardly mobile black person has to ask every day, but it had extra poignancy for me at this time. While I dealt with budgets, transport, housing, Nigerian politicians, and their leftist detractors, unfamiliar feelings overwhelmed me. I seemed to be hearing voices, like vibrations, and seeing visions, like mirages.

One afternoon, at Port Harcourt in eastern Nigeria, I stood

with my face to the sea and thought I could see a young African youth standing before me. The boy I envisioned had been snatched from his village and family by his own people, roped together with strangers, and marched through quiet trails at night to a waiting ship, where he was sold to slave dealers in exchange for wine, beads, and tobacco. From the very spot on which I stood, the slave traffic had flourished for centuries.

In the weeks that followed, my mind kept returning to that African youth. Every day I walked the streets of Lagos around Tinebu Square, and imagined him being chained into rows of other men and stacked like salted fish in the depths of the ship. Some captives hit their heads against nails until they died; others refused to eat and starved themselves to death, but the young man I envisioned shut down all of his human instincts and swallowed whatever was put in his mouth. After months at sea, the reeking ship finally reached shore and he was still alive. He was dragged out of the hold and sold to the highest bidder. I could see him sick and starving, unable to understand or speak to anyone, toiling in the murderously hot fields and disease-infested swamps of the Southeast. At night he dreamed of being free.

In my imagination, the African youth lived to be an old man, and despite his dreams, he never regained his freedom. But he never stopped believing that, somehow, his life had a special purpose. He might have been my own ancestor. Because of his will to survive and his faith in things unseen, I was a free person, appointed by the President of the United States to represent America in this African nation, making a small effort to indemnify the moral atrocity committed against her.

But I knew that despite my title and privileges, back in America I was not a first-class citizen. I was barred from entering some hotels, barred from eating in some restaurants, barred from using some bathrooms. When white people looked at me in America, they didn't see a doctor's degree or a director's title. They saw a black man who was, by virtue of his color, inferior.

Every now and then an ordinary exchange magnified my dilemma. One day one of our domestic helpers turned up with a fresh haircut. "Jacob," I said, "you have a neat haircut. Where did you get it?"

"My friend who comes by on the bicycle cut it."

I thought his friend was a "bookie" who came to collect bets on the soccer matches. I knew he came by to eat, because our steward was operating a clandestine family-style restaurant in his small quarters on the compound, using our food as his supply! But now I learned that the man on the bicycle was a barber, too.

"Jacob, how much does he charge you?"

"Only two shillings."

"Well, will he cut my hair, too? I have to pay six shillings downtown."

"Oh, yes," Jacob replied. "But he will charge you six shillings, too."

"Why?"

"Because you are a white man."

There were only two kinds of people in Jacob's world: his own tribal people and everyone else. I lived in a well-equipped house with a staff; a driver carried me from place to place, and I took hot baths, wore socks, and ate a varied diet. That separated me by great lengths from his people. If I were not one of them, I had to be a white man, regardless of my pigmentation.

His remark stayed with me. I didn't seem to have a place to put my foot. As a black man I lived a marginalized life in America, and in Nigeria I was a stranger. Was I in Nigeria as an American visitor, or as a child come home?

One day an associate and I were visiting one of our volunteers in Ogbomosho. She carried us out into a small rural village where we met a distinguished-looking chief with a broad smile, a twinkle in his eyes, and three deep Yoruba tribal marks in his round cheeks. This was Chief Oyrinde, my great-uncle's classmate. For more than fifty years he had been living in that small village, running a school, managing a dispensary, and serving as the local pastor. From that village he had sent a steady stream of young Yorubas to colleges and universities all over the world. When I was president of Virginia Union, we had dozens of Nigerian students coming from the same stream. They stayed away from home and family for four years, hid their loneliness and estrangement, never displayed any negative attitude toward their black American cousins, whose lifestyle was so different and whose opportunities so infinitely greater.

Chief Oyrinde greeted me like a prodigal who had come home. And I felt like a shadow before him. I was African in ancestry; but all the while I was growing into an amalgam of European metaphors and analogies, mixed in with an American worldview, he had been living here in unbroken continuity with his African heritage.

As I stood there I felt naked; my ignorance of his life story was embarrassing. All of my schooling had overlooked a close, fair examination of Africa. We saw only the National Geographic portrayals of African people, and no one like Chief Oyrinde was ever introduced to me. I ought to have had longer, deeper, closer connections to my own people. Nevertheless, with all of this ambiguity about our identity, our context here was clear and we had to live out our lives where we were.

And as precarious as my existence was in the United States, I again confirmed, as my experience in India had shown, that I was thoroughly an American. Like other black Americans, I survived on the belief that one day our society would become fair and equal. Black Americans always have been in the process of creating their own identity. We could never stop and wait until all the ambiguities of our existence cleared up. With only shaky ground to stand on, we kept moving forward.

•   •   •

BACK HOME, THE CIVIL RIGHTS MOVEMENT WAS REACHING its denouement. When George Wallace, the governor of Alabama, personally barred the enrollment of two black students in the University of Alabama, President Kennedy didn't mince any words:

> This nation was founded on the principle that all men [and women] are created equal, and that the rights of every man are diminished when the rights of one . . . are threatened.
>
> . . . It ought to be possible . . . for American students of any color to attend any public institution they select without having to be backed by troops. It ought to be possible for American consumers of any color to receive equal service in places of public accommodation, such as hotels and restaurants, and theaters and retail stores without being forced to resort to demonstrations in the street.
>
> And it ought to be possible for American citizens of any color to register and to vote in a full election without interference or fear of reprisal.
>
> It ought to be possible, in short, for every American to enjoy the privileges of being an American without regard to his race or his color.

Earlier that year Sargent Shriver asked me to leave Lagos and come back to Washington to be one of his three associate Peace Corps directors. One associate director worked with the Congress and the media; one worked with host countries on feasible programs and logistics; and one recruited volunteers, selected them for their assignments, and supervised their job performance, living conditions, and personal decorum. This last was my job, watching over sixteen thousand volunteers in thirty-eight countries.

We often asked celebrities to help sell the Peace Corps to potential recruits. On the day of the March on Washington—August 28, 1963—I was in my office, trying to get Boston Celtics' star Bill Russell to help us recruit black college seniors for the Peace Corps. While black students talked about their African roots and consciousness, 98 percent of our volunteers in Africa were white. As Bill and I talked, I looked at my watch and realized it was time for King's speech. We walked over to the Lincoln Memorial and as we approached the basin we were speechless at the sight of a virtual sea of Americans come together in one great moment of celebration and commitment. It looked like something apocalyptic. They were old, young, bearded, bald, formally dressed and barely covered, serious and somber, casual and carefree. They were white, Hispanic, black, and Native American. All of us were there. And there was order and electric control from within. When Martin began to speak, he was artful in capturing the mood and the passion of that assembly, and he articulated in sonorous, rhythmic phrases exactly what they felt. For a fleeting instant, time stood still and eternity bent low over Washington, and *the word* became flesh again.

A few days later, my leave of absence was over, and I left Washington to return to A & T. I felt as if I had a secret: the country was on tiptoe, leaning into the future. A new horizon of hope was palpable.

I had kept abreast of the news from A & T and knew that the new president of the student body and quarterback of the football team was none other than Jesse Louis Jackson. For my first five days back, my wise and efficient secretary, Doris Durham, helped me plan a tight schedule: every day from 8 to 10 A.M., Doris and I would work on the piles of mail; 10 to 12 noon, I would see staff and faculty to catch up; 1 to 3 P.M., I would meet with deans and vice presidents for the forward look; and then, between 3 and 5 each afternoon I would see anyone who wanted to see me. Jesse made an appointment for 3 P.M. on Wednesday.

But when I got to the office at 7:30 Monday morning, there he was in a blue suit, white shirt, and a striped tie. He smiled, gripped my hand like I was a prodigal returned home, and said, "I realize that I am due on Wednesday at three o'clock, but as one president to another, I thought we should talk first before anyone else." That was pure Jesse!

From the beginning, Jesse had all of the marks of an aggressive, take-charge agent of change. Not every member of A & T's board of trustees had approved of my going to Africa in the first place. Thus, I planned to make my return from Nigeria as inconspicuous as possible. Jesse didn't see it that way. He planned a major convocation, demanded that I speak, and presented me with a handsome Omega watch that I still wear thirty years later. He was aggressive and bodacious, but he matched it with intelligence and purpose. Whatever he said, or did, he was usually right and reasonable.

Later that fall I was attending a serious policy meeting of North Carolina state college presidents, hosted by Dr. William Friday, president of the University of North Carolina at Chapel Hill. While we were trading jokes and trivia during lunch, a stocky black waiter suddenly pushed open the door, waving a large white napkin. "Somebody just killed the president!" he shouted.

We looked around at each other and whispered, "Which president? Bill Friday is right here at the table."

By then, someone had gone out to the front desk and returned, saying, "It looks like President Kennedy was murdered a few minutes ago in Dallas."

We were sealed in stony silence. Each of us canvassed his mind instantly on the long- and short-term consequences of this earth-shaking trauma. The future was bent badly, but by how many degrees no one rightly knew.

My instinct told me to capture immediately any redeeming aspect of the tragic event, before anyone put another face on it for my students. I did not want a young student leader to take charge in my absence and lead the campus into a reaction that we could not live with. I rushed to a telephone and called my unfailingly trustworthy secretary and asked her to have the choir and the band excused from class. Both Air Force and Army ROTC cadets in dress uniform were to be in full formation on the front lawn at sunset. She was to notify the local media that we would be holding the first memorial service for President Kennedy on the steps of Dudley Hall.

At dusk, the front lawn of our campus was covered with young black students, encircled by all the people of Greensboro. I spoke a few words of tribute to mourn the passing of our president. As president of the student body, Jesse spoke next, calling on the students to renew their determination to bring about the change that Kennedy had begun. Everyone was silent in the deepening night as the college choir sang the Brahms *Requiem Mass.*

Only a few months earlier Kennedy had presented his Civil Rights Bill to Congress. Was this the price he paid for coming forth in our behalf? A week later, when all of the dust settled, and the echo of the last bugle had died in the wind, when the flowers had shriveled and the rhetoric had collapsed into one loud "Amen," no matter how you took it all in, John Kennedy seemed to have laid down his life that we might live.

MUCH CHANGE HAD BEEN ACHIEVED WITHOUT VIOLENCE, but now a noisy contingent of young blacks demanded action. Curiously, it was not black violence, but white violence that precipitated change. When a sleazy coward bombed a black church in Birmingham, killing four young girls, the Civil Rights Act of 1964 was passed; then, after the abuse at Selma, the Voting Rights Act of 1965 was passed.

By this time, with the country awash in controversy over civil rights and Vietnam, the issue of poverty lit up the national agenda. The talk among blacks was how Lyndon Johnson, scion of southern democratic political domination, had come around 180 degrees to carry the banner for black liberation.

Before I knew it, early in 1964, Bill Moyers and the governor of North Carolina were back on the telephone. Moyers had moved over to the White House with President Johnson, and the president wanted me to return to Washington as associate director to Sargent Shriver again. The first time I had joined the Peace Corps, I had been granted a leave of absence. I had been back on the job less than a year and was just settling in again. If I wanted to go back to Washington now, I would be forced to resign from my college presidency. That was the choice I made. As always, the whole family got into it. Our moving around never seemed to make our sons feel insecure. The whole society was already in flux. The news was flooded with images of Vietnam War protests, mobs confronting police, and Civil Rights demonstrations. By contrast, home and family, wherever we were, seemed like a fortress of stability. The two older boys always felt closer to us than to any fast peer friends, and they liked the adventure of living in new locations.

Bessie's mother was almost always with us, and her home in quiet, undisturbed, colonial Fredericksburg, Virginia, continued to be our haven for holidays and family celebrations. Moreover, our family considered going to Washington to serve the government personally prestigious, and also an omen that a more promising future was ahead for black people. The Washington appointment was clearly an approved move.

All over the country, things were really popping. I sometimes felt guilty as I worked in Washington in a safe, air-conditioned office with four secretaries and two deputies. Yet I knew the struggle was about blacks gaining more positions just like the many who had received recent presidential appointments. We seemed to have reaped the harvest before others could get in line, and we felt guilty about it. But we knew we were pioneers in a process that had to take place. Some people called us "tokens"; in fact, we were more like wedges, pushing doors open and then trying to hold them open.

I spent some time down in Mississippi with Medgar Evers, who was head of the state conference of the NAACP. Medgar lived with danger night and day, eschewing notoriety and working in quiet devotion for freedom and justice.

As we talked late into the night at a friend's home, I offered him a two-year appointment as a Peace Corps deputy in Ghana. I laid out all the benefits he could gain from the job: he could get acquainted firsthand with Africa, earn a good salary for a while to pay some bills and get ahead a little, and get a respite from white terrorism for himself and his family. When I suggested that he would return to the fight rested, refreshed, and reinvigorated, his eyes widened and he smiled. I gave him a week to think it over.

A few days later Medgar called me in Washington. He would like to go later, he said, but not right now. Things were at a boiling point in his state. The 1964 Democratic convention had failed to seat the Mississippi Freedom Democratic Party, which comprised black and white liberal Democrats who had been ostracized by the southern Democratic Party. When the chips were down, white liberals failed to support their cause and blacks felt betrayed. It was also a bad year for violence. Five black churches had been bombed in Alabama and Mississippi, and in twenty different instances white mobs had attacked blacks demonstrating for their rights. Medgar said he couldn't leave his country at that moment. But would I ask him again, maybe in a year or so?

Two years later, as he was getting out of his car one night in his own driveway, a gunman shot him to death. It was another cowardly, hateful act, but Medgar's tragic death added momentum to the movement.

Another great soul was given to us by Mississippi. Fannie Lou

Hamer was a sharecropper and a grassroots political organizer. I met her for the first time when I was working as Sargent Shriver's special assistant in the Office of Economic Opportunity. OEO was authorized by Congress, but had no appropriation for a while. Shriver ran it out of his Peace Corps office with the help of his Peace Corps staff.

We all worked twelve-hour days and had working sessions at Shriver's home in Silver Spring on weekends. One of the rewards of this era for me was to witness the dedication of some of the nation's brightest and most privileged people as they tried to change circumstances for poor Americans, whether they were Appalachian whites, or urban and rural blacks. Head Start and the Job Corps did not make the splash that some street battles created, but the long-term effects of such solid institutional efforts were the difference between a thunderstorm and a full season of steady, intermittent, generous rainfall.

At one early OEO meeting, Fannie Lou Hamer was sitting at one end of the long conference table and Sargent Shriver at the other. I sat next to Shriver and took notes about proposed projects. In the midst of a heated discussion, Fannie Lou suddenly bellowed at him, "And another thing, what do you know about poverty? You're a millionaire sitting here planning for the poor. You're like the fox in the henhouse!"

Shriver turned red as a beet, and banged on the table: "I don't have any money! My wife has the money. I bet Sam Proctor has more money than I."

I choked. I hardly had enough in my wallet to get my car out of the parking lot. Shriver jumped up and stormed out of the room. The rest of us sat frozen at the table, but Fannie Lou didn't turn a hair.

A few minutes later, I found Shriver in the men's room, splashing cold water on his face. He raged on, "Here I am fighting these right-wing congressmen and southern senators to get enough money to change the direction of this country and I have to keep defending myself because I'm married to a rich woman who cares as much about this as I do!"

Sargent Shriver is a decent, sensitive, and good-hearted person. He really didn't have a lot of money of his own. I knew that his family lost everything in the Depression and that he went to Yale on scholarships. We used to joke about how staff people on the road with him often had to buy his lunch; and once in Chicago I even had to lend him a clean shirt.

As he spoke, I realized that he and Fannie Lou were speaking at each other through a solid wall. She spoke the white-hot rhetoric of those who had been waiting for so long, living cheek-to-cheek with intractable white racists. Shriver was a Yale-trained social engineer who had only an academic acquaintance with chronic and desperate poverty. I was trying to translate Fannie Lou Hamer to him, and him to her.

"Did I insult her, Sam?" he asked.

"I don't think so," I said. "This was an open debate, and things need to get said. She did you a favor by bringing an important issue to the surface. If we expect to make any headway with this program, people need to know that you're not a rich man's son dabbling around with poor folks' miseries."

The simple fact was that we did have people like Fannie Lou Hamer who were vigilant to assure that the plain truth was spoken. Fannie Lou Hamer always looked white people straight in the eye, told the truth, and *never* blinked. There were many black men and women just like her.

CHAPTER SIX

Great Expectations

■ ■

1964–1968

WHILE I WAS IN WASHINGTON IN 1964, RUMBLING complaints poured in from black leaders around the country. Nothing Lyndon Johnson did was enough. It seemed that our hopes, demands, and new agendas were running way ahead of what liberal Democrats could deliver, both domestically and around the world.

President Johnson raised our expectations to a peak when he pushed through the Civil Rights Bill that year. Automobile horns were blowing all over Washington that day as liberals, white and black, passed each other on the streets and highways, flashing peace signs as recognition. It wasn't enough. Super-right-wing groups started dropping from trees and crawling out from under rocks. Even Barry Goldwater could not control the extreme far right. Whenever blacks progressed an inch, right-wing extremists reacted as though it were a mile. When Howard Hughes died, a note was found among his memorabilia saying that enough had been done for blacks to last them for a hundred years.

I suppose I, too, became a little cynical about my role in Washington. I felt like I was in the wrong place, walking the hallways of a federal office building, tied to an administration that had no popular mandate. I longed to be back at the ground level, where hearts and minds could be influenced.

By this time I was weary of short-term assignments and high-pressure jobs. I longed to settle into a normal position with a challenge that was close to my training and experience. Blacks who had academic credentials, experience, and a record of satisfactory job performance were in demand. Sensitive people in high places wanted blacks to receive more opportunities, and I was contacted by several. A major aircraft corporation with huge defense contracts found itself under pressure to change its hiring policies; as a result, they offered me—of all people—an attractive position. I also had several job offers from universities, foundations, and church agencies.

I chose an invitation from the National Council of Churches, a fragile assembly of mainline Protestant churches, with no authority but with a tacit commitment to promote Christian ethics in national affairs. My job as associate general secretary was to explain the goals of the council to the country and keep the churches and their congregations behind us.

Our chairman was Edwin Espy, a saintly layman who had lived a lifetime on the side of the angels. He was surrounded by serious and committed church leaders, but they failed to recognize the huge gap between themselves and the people in the pews. When white Protestants realized what their liberal clergy were up to, the money simply evaporated. The better I explained the goals of our mission—to inaugurate a just, fair, and free society with equal opportunity and a higher quality of life for all, just as Jesus talked about—the worse our fortunes became.

Our daily mail showed just how unpopular Jesus was among those Christians. They loved little Jesus in the manger and hanging on the cross, Jesus in the hymnbooks and on bumper stickers. But on Wall Street, in the Congress, in city hall, and in the boardrooms, not many really loved Jesus.

Even so, in the 1964 election, the right wing wasn't yet powerful enough to muster the popular vote, and Lyndon Johnson was elected by a landslide. Bill Moyers called *again,* and I was headed back to Shriver for the fourth time, after less than a year with the National Council of Churches. As Shriver's Northeast Regional Director, I was now working only in the Office of Economic Opportunity and not in the Peace Corps.

This time it was different. President Johnson won so impressively that I thought the residual of good will in the country was broader and deeper than I had perceived. Also, it appeared that the attitude that seemed to dominate the churches was not really representative of the country's majority. There was more good will in secular circles than could be found in evangelical Protestantism, which had made a tacit alliance with segregationists in the South and ethnic pockets in the North. It was culture-bound, not prophetic; more loyal to the status quo than to the teachings and example of Jesus.

By now it was apparent that the changes we yearned for had a better chance if they were the outcome of a broad political consensus. It seemed that the church had so completely accommodated itself to the white middle class that it had little to say. Even the black churches stepped back from the vanguard and clung to their traditional role of providing nurturing and inspiration to their flocks. They resumed their identities as stabilizing institutions, and from them would emerge, here and there, a flaming prophet of change.

Meanwhile, increasing numbers of young blacks were losing

hope. The line between blacks who still believed in the substance of things hoped for and those who had given up grew clearer, wider, and deeper.

New talk surfaced of a separate Afrocentric culture, resulting from our rejection as full citizens and our lack of a cultural reference. Young blacks who had courageously entered college under enforced court orders were tired of begging for their rights. Ostracized by other students, they changed their hairstyles and eating habits to reflect boldly the African culture that had been stolen from their people in the seventeenth century. They even changed their names. Black students grew zealous in their demands for separate dining halls, libraries, recreation centers, and curricula. Some also changed their manners and attitudes toward non-Africans and certain blacks whom they called "Negroes" or assimilationists.

One night during the mid-1960s, I attended a Sigma Pi Phi dinner at the Commodore Hotel in New York. This is a sort of superfraternity, founded in Philadelphia in the early 1900s to give black intellectuals a place to go for mutual support and stimulation. The group was composed largely of black attorneys, businessmen, judges, physicians, college professors, and clergy.

As I leaped up the steps headed for the meeting room, I looked back and saw a gathering of black men dressed in African attire filling up the hotel lobby.

I heard a voice call out, "Sam, where the hell are you going in that tuxedo?" It was an old friend of mine, wearing a richly patterned green, red, and black dashiki, open sandals, a huge gold bracelet, a beaded neckpiece, and a full, expansive Afro hairstyle.

I came back down the stairs to meet him and told him where I was headed. He screamed to his buddies, "Hey, y'all. Sam is headed upstairs to one of those 'Oreo' meetings with a bunch of big shots. Let's go with him and check it out." As it happened, they were at the hotel for a convention of the National Association of Black Educators.

*Hattie Ann's father, and
my great-grandfather, William Fisher,
after the emancipation.*

*Hattie Ann Virginia Fisher's diploma
from Hampton Normal and Agricul-
tural Institute, signed by General S.C.
Armstrong, 1882. My grandmother
has more than 100 descendants who
are college graduates.*

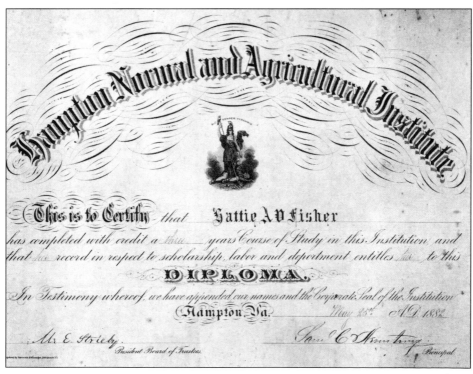

Hampton Normal and Agricultural Institute

This is to Certify that Hattie A.V. Fisher
has completed with credit a three years Course of Study in this Institution, and
that her record in respect to scholarship, labor and deportment entitles her to this

DIPLOMA.

In Testimony whereof, we have appended our names and the Corporate Seal of the Institution

Hampton Va. May 25th A.D. 1882

Mr. E. Strieby.
President Board of Trustees.

Sam'l C. Armstrong.
Principal.

My grandfather Zechariah Hughes built the house we lived in, in 1919. My brothers are, from the top, Charles, age eleven, Edgar, the youngest, age nine, and Oliver, age thirteen. Behind them are my parents, and the man on the left reading a newspaper is Pop Cherry, our star boarder.

My sister and brothers and me standing in front of my uncle's house. Clockwise from top, Harriet, eleven, me, seven, Charles, three, Oliver, five, and Vernon, nine.

Bessie, about four years old, with her brother, Maurice, age seven.

On my bike, ready to make a delivery for Griswold's Drugstore, 1937.

My sister, Harriet, at Howard University, Washington, D.C., 1938.

Bessie and I met at Virginia Union, in the winter of 1942.

Summer student conference at Huntington Mountain, Pennsylvania, 1943. Sixty foreign students gathered to study a "just and durable" peace in the midst of World War II. The event was sponsored by the Committee Friends Service. I am in the first row, second from left.

At commencement time
with a group of my Crozer
colleagues. I am on
the right.

Our first car, a used 1939 green
Chevy, parked in front of Bessie's
family home in Fredericksburg.
Bessie's widowed mother, Stella
Tate, loaned us the $450 to buy
the car, which we paid back at
$50 a month for nine
long months.

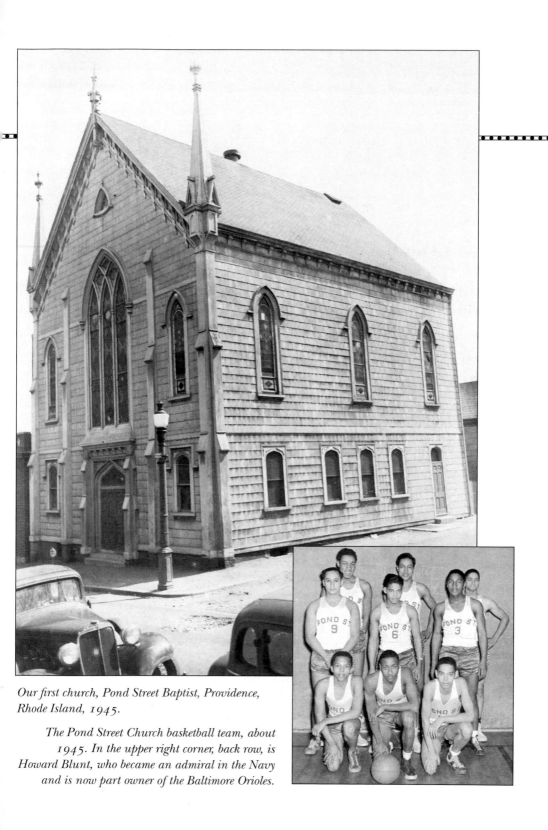

Our first church, Pond Street Baptist, Providence, Rhode Island, 1945.

The Pond Street Church basketball team, about 1945. In the upper right corner, back row, is Howard Blunt, who became an admiral in the Navy and is now part owner of the Baltimore Orioles.

Receiving the Outstanding Church Leadership Award from the Baptist State Convention, Providence, 1946.

Rhode Island State Baptist Christian Education Conference on Block Island, 1949, one of the early opportunities for integrated participation in church affairs. I am in the top row, center. Bessie is in the second row from the top, middle.

Herbie, age five, after the surgery that saved his life. Timothy, our second son, and Herbie's biggest supporter, age two.

Commencement season is my greatest joy, when, every June, I have the opportunity to meet face-to-face thousands of bright, well-educated young people staking a claim on the future. Here I am delivering a university commencement address back in June 1951.

My sister and brothers and me, with our parents, Velma and Herbert Proctor (seated), 1955. From left to right, Oliver, me, Harriet, Edgar, Vernon (in his Army Air Force uniform), and Charles. A picture of my great-grandfather Zechariah Hughes hangs on the wall.

The faculty of the American Baptist Christian Education Conference at Ocean Park, Maine, 1955. This was an early effort toward integration on a national basis. I am in the front row, seventh from right.

In Moscow in 1958, on a preaching mission at a conference of Baptist leaders. The Soviet police warned me to stop preaching that faith had enabled black Americans to outlive oppression, and to "stick to the Bible." I am in the front row, fourth from left.

Bessie, Herbie, and Tim with me at the reception for my inauguration as president of Virginia Union, 1955. Herbie was getting ready to go back to the hospital, where surgeons would rebuild his heart.

When the KKK burned a cross on our front lawn at Virginia Union in 1955, we went about our business as usual.

United Negro College Fund Kick-Off, Indianapolis, 1959. I am at the rostrum; John F. Kennedy is seated in the front row.

After the speech, with JFK and Dr. Benjamin E. Mays, president of Morehouse College. Later that night, Belford Lawson asked me to work on Kennedy's campaign for the Democratic presidential nomination.

My parents, Velma and Herbert,
attended my inauguration as president
of North Carolina A & T University,
a proud moment for all of us.

Here we are with Tim
and Herb, in September
1960. This was our
"portrait" for the North
Carolina A & T inaugu-
ration. I'm not nearly as
solemn as I look. Six
months earlier, Herbie
had undergone the heart
surgery that saved his
life. Look at that smile!
That's the way he always
was, cheerful and brave.

Peace Corps staff, Nigeria, 1962.

When I returned to North Carolina A & T after Peace Corps duty in Nigeria, the president of the student body was there to greet me. Jesse Jackson presenting me with an Omega watch, 1963.

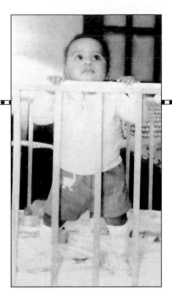

Sammy getting ready to learn to walk.

With Sargent Shriver (center) and Lewis Dowdy (right), acting president of North Carolina A & T, attending commencement exercises, 1963.

With Lyndon B. Johnson and Bill Moyers. President Johnson had officially invited me to accept the appointment as Northeast regional director of the Office of Economic Opportunity.

With Muriel Humphrey, Vice President Hubert Humphrey, and Bessie, at a State Department reception for the president of Liberia, 1968. Vice President Humphrey and I had just returned from Africa.

Sam at age three,
and Steven,
one and a half.

With Steven at our cottage on Chesapeake Bay in about 1968.

A group of Rutgers graduate students, 1976. These students entered graduate school without college degrees, but were handpicked because of their unique awareness of community. They graduated with master's degrees in education.

All of us at Abyssinian Baptist Church in Manhattan. Standing, left to right, are Tim, Sam, Herb, and Steven.

This group was challenging the curricula and teaching style of schools serving black children. They wanted more Afrocentric materials and less of a Eurocentric focus. They wanted blacks to control the governance and policy making in black schools. The details of how this program would be accountable to the statutory schoolboards were not clear, but the agitation stage had begun.

They stormed our meeting—about forty of us and about twelve of them—demanding that we justify our existence. The late Julius Thomas of the National Urban League was there. So were Kenneth Clark of City College, Justice Delaney of the New York Supreme Court, and Stephen J. Wright, then the head of the United Negro College Fund. We represented the signs of success and change, a new image, new movement toward inclusiveness and fairness. But there we were, apologizing because our advancements seemed to be a trade-off for the denial of other blacks.

In that room in the Commodore Hotel the sharply defined paradox of black life in the 1960s was clear: one group believed that America could change; the other believed she would not.

To the National Association of Black Educators, accepting status as quasi-citizens and subscribing to the culture of America was tantamount to agreeing to inferior status unworthy of any person. But by resisting the signs of change, they were, in effect, rejecting the goals established in the 1950s.

The members of the Sigma Pi Phi fraternity, whose origin dated back to the turn of the century, had already debated the issue of identity and survival. Around 1915, they concluded that blacks had only one destiny—and it did not lie on the African continent, nor on an island in the Caribbean, nor on a bleak, arid reservation in the deserts of New Mexico, Arizona, or Nevada. Their destiny was to dig in and fight for justice and respect right at the center of America. Their destiny was to engage in creating a new culture of their own, a blending of African residuals, survival strategies learned in slavery, and consciousness of their dual personalities—U.S. citizens tacitly aware that they were participating in a unique transition that would lead America to become something entirely new.

The tuxedoed gentlemen seated at the banquet tables were not childish mimics of an artificial status. They were intentional about creating their own culture. Each one of them was involved in some cause devoted to black amelioration, and many were in the foreground of change. They regarded the Afrocentrists as cop-outs who had recognized how long and how hard the real struggle would be and chose something quicker and closer.

The Afrocentrists thought the fraternity brothers had bought into the dominant culture too deeply, had sacrificed their African identity, and had moved too far—too high—from grass-roots blacks.

I felt frustrated, feeling that both sides had legitimate platforms yet, at least that night, at the Commodore, with one group dressed in tuxedos and the other in African garb, both appeared excessive. We did need agitation to make schools alert to the needs of black students for affirmation and identity. And the fraternity members were the big link between black problems and the resources needed to solve them. They were in touch with the power structure and they were sincere in their advocacy.

At some other point in history it might have been possible to bring the two sides into alignment, but not in that decade. The debate was hot and angry on both sides. Each person believed passionately in his agenda. The argument descended to the black teachers calling the fraternity members Uncle Toms and the fraternity members calling the teachers hustlers and phonies.

SHRIVER ASSIGNED ME TO NEW YORK TO RUN THE NORTHEAST regional Office of Economic Opportunity. This was the hottest spot in the country. In fact, the protests were so frequent that I often had to leave my office and hold meetings in that same Commodore, which was one block away. On any given day I would have mothers visiting who had been evicted from their apartments, tenants bringing boxes of rats to show their living conditions, students coming to protest tuition increases, artists demanding money to put on exhibits and performances, and drug addicts and alcoholics coming to demand housing.

To maintain family stability in this chaotic situation, Bessie and I had chosen to settle in a quiet community in Teaneck, New Jersey. Our two older boys were in high school, and we now had a new baby, Samuel, who had been born after our return from Africa. We had all but forgotten what it was like having a baby in the house. He demanded more attention than any of us anticipated. I always brought my problems and paperwork home and always talked over everything that was going on with Bessie and our sons. It was not our style to separate my job from the ebb and flow of family life. It was all one. So between giggles, toddler feedings, teenage dilemmas, and dramatic reports about the latest protest at the OEO, we made it one day at a time.

Our daily travails were nothing compared to the hardships endured by those being bombed, beaten, jailed, and chased by police dogs across the South. I was willing to endure any challenge in New York to do whatever I could to bring change through the OEO. At the same time, I resented the cynicism of the protestors who came to harrass me because I was an executive of the government, and to them the government was the enemy. I thought they should have known that the White House and the courts had given us the only hope we had. Corporations had to be forced to hire us and universities had to be sued to admit us. When we were admitted to schools, we went on federal programs and grants and loans. In return, federal agents who were black were being treated like the enemy. No one was prepared for the ambiguities America was passing through. There was no limit to the name calling, the labels, the slogans, and the blame placing, and it continues today.

The whole spring and summer of 1965, I was spread out over New York, New Jersey, New England, Puerto Rico, and the Virgin Islands keeping track of how OEO dollars were being spent. Reactions to OEO initiatives ranged from cynics who thought the whole program was a hoax designed to deflect attention from a class war, to those who saw it as a political pork barrel to buy the votes of the poor, or a Communist scheme to redistribute the wealth of the country. Of course there were those who saw it for what it was: an excellent approach to the needs of the poor that needed to be continued and expanded. The biggest problem was trying to involve the poor, who were inexperienced with institutional accountability, budgets, and audits, in planning and managing their own programs. Their greed and cleverness were no more sinister than the greed and cleverness at every other level of government and commerce.

By September, problems were mushrooming all over the country. I had to return to Washington as Shriver's special assistant—my fifth title with the same boss. I hardly gave it a thought. It was a continuum of the New York task, only now I had to connect with the directors of every region doing the same kind of problem solving.

So, halfway through Johnson's term I returned to Washington, and became the troubleshooter responsible for trying to remove barriers to OEO operations around the country. In one large Connecticut city, for instance, we decided to fund a tenants group that wanted to monitor housing abuses. It turned out that the chief violator they turned up was a slum landlord who contributed large sums to the Democratic Party. We were called on by certain important senators to "unfund" that particular project. We couldn't call off the tenants group if we wanted to, and we did not try.

One day Bill Moyers called from the White House and asked me to leave fast, go to the airport, and fly to Charlotte, North Carolina, with Billy Graham. We were helping a lot of poor mountain people near where he lived, and we wanted to get his support.

All through the flight down we talked church, religion, and social change. When we reached his mountaintop home, we had a delicious lunch and more conversation. It all settled down to a stalemate: Dr. Graham felt that his business was to preach the gospel and change the hearts of individuals. Changed persons would then change society.

I countered with the teachings of Jesus in chapter 25 of Matthew's gospel, in which he admonished that at the day of judgment we would all be separated into sheep and goats. One got to be a sheep by feeding the hungry, giving water to the thirsty and clothing to the naked, visiting those in prison, and taking in the stranger. The sheep entered into the Master's joy. Goats did not do such things and were consigned to a burning hell.

Reverend Graham smiled and said that I was making Jesus a "liberal." It was odd, though, that while he officially avoided political involvement, he often boasted of advising several presidents. The visit was pleasant, but he did not change his position, and neither did I.

One night Shriver and I, along with his wife, Eunice, and a couple of other staff people, went to Philadelphia to attend a rally in support of a national job training program funded by the Department of Labor and the OEO. We went up to announce a $1 million grant. On our way back to the airport a black motorcycle policeman was doing some fancy stunt riding as he escorted our car through downtown traffic. His bike hit an oil slick and he went up about ten feet into the air and landed on his back, unconscious. An ambulance came and carried him to the hospital.

We followed, and Shriver and his wife stayed by the policeman's bedside. Throughout the still hours of the night they kept a vigil until the next morning, when the injured man finally regained consciousness. I was always impressed by the simple, uncomplicated commitment to people that was reflected in Shriver's choice that night. It was the same approach he had to all of his tasks. Little wonder that he moved on to head the Special Olympics.

UNDER PRESIDENT KENNEDY, THE WHITE HOUSE AND THE departments had become flooded with Harvard and MIT types, and they had many black friends in education. They were pragmatists, reaching for whatever would work. The ultimate goal was to move black youth out of poverty in a way that would be permanent and replicable, not with benign, temporary remedies. They wanted healing, not placebos.

As we kept meeting around Washington, trading ideas, it struck us that if black colleges were strengthened, with their strategic location in southern cities and their known commitment, they could become catalysts. More strong black teachers, Ph.D.s, accountants, engineers, microbiologists, dentists, physicians, nurses, agronomists, and space explorers would enter the stream and filter into the American workforce everywhere. The idea sold easily, and the Institute for Services to Education came alive. Its goal was to strengthen the faculties and programs of 105 black colleges.

Its board of directors asked me to move over from the OEO and serve the Institute. This meant leaving our Teaneck home and relocating in the Washington area. Because this was a new, independent agency, it looked permanent, worth a real investment and a long outlook. Along with our move, a fourth baby, Steven, arrived, and a new voice was added to the household. It was exciting watching a new life connect with our close unit and fight for space and attention.

I loved the new job. Working with a team of eight faculty from each school, we developed a curriculum for thirteen colleges. For once, money was no problem. We had excellent funding from various foundations and federal agencies, with seed money coming from the Carnegie Foundation. I remember walking around Washington in March of 1966, a check for $500,000 in my pocket, looking for a bank that would give us the best deal on a start-up account.

At the same time, this period brought sadness to the family. My younger brother Charles died suddenly of a heart attack. Three months later, Bessie's mother, who had been our constant companion and the real cushion in our home for all of the shocks and bounces, passed after a long bout with cancer. A year later, my mother passed, never having gotten over Charles's untimely death.

The shock of three funerals, writing obituaries, and standing silently by gravesites forced me to accept reluctantly the intrusion and the finality of death. In the midst of the frenetic excitement of Washington and the challenge of social crises, I was suddenly called into a new kind of sobriety. Death demands a longer view of things. It seemed that death was an alarm, calling us to stand up straight and stiffen the chin for life's imponderable pressures and surprises. We made a Spartan response that seemed to be the mark of maturity. The tears were mostly inside, an empty feeling of being abandoned when our parents died. Our home was so tightly knit and family was so close that we were not left alone long enough to be overwhelmed with pain.

Even as I took stock of myself, I tooled up to get ISE going. Every educator we called on for help responded by serving on committees and granting leaves of absence to their stellar teachers so they could join us in developing new curricula. We contracted for office help with the American Council on Education, through their president, Dr. Logan Wilson, a big-minded, big-hearted Texan, who saved us thousands of dollars. He managed all of our fiscal operations from his DuPont Circle building and charged us less than one half of a secretary's salary!

It was fun watching black college teachers huddled day after day with the most renowned educators in the country, searching for creative ways of inducting young blacks into the life of the mind and the world of ideas. I recall one humanities teacher running around screaming, "I got it! I got it!"

She had run upon the idea of teaching the history of ideas by a course entitled "Jailbirds," which she had developed around people who had been jailed for their innovative thinking. The timeliness of this was great. Civil rights and liberation leaders all over the world were being thrown in jail for their ideas. And there were Socrates, Jeremiah the Prophet, Jesus, Paul the Apostle, Jan Hus, John the Baptist, John Milton, John Bunyan, John Brown—all the Johns!—Copernicus, Galileo, Nat Turner, Nkrumah, Azikewe, Mandela, and Martin L. King, Jr. The list was much longer. Jailbirds 101 and 102!

OUR FAMILY LIFE WAS ENORMOUSLY RICH AND FULFILLING. Nothing can compare with the pleasure of having seen two infant sons initiated into life by their two older brothers. They found the babies to be a happy relief from the daily tensions of coping with campus violence and the vicissitudes of large-scale social change.

Of course, Samuel and Steven never knew the ways of the old South as their older brothers did; they had landed in the midst of rapid transition.

Because I was working both as a special assistant to Sargent Shriver and as president of the Institute for Services to Education, I was denied the "daddy time" the boys needed, and Bessie had to double in brass. She kept her station wagon loaded with toys and boxes, and every floor in the house was littered with signs of life.

We both recognized the need for time away from the city, and we starting spending weekends on a small farm on the waterfront of Northumberland County in Virginia. We shared this spot with nine other families, each of which had built a modest cinder-block cottage. We added to the fun with an 18-foot boat with a 40 horsepower outboard motor. For thirteen weekends each summer we went fishing, swimming, and water-skiing with the boys, played touch football and pinochle, and told each other long drawn-out crazy stories. Then, late on Sunday nights, we went back to the serious, grinding business of making a new society.

EVEN THOUGH I WAS OUT OF GOVERNMENT BY 1967, I HAD a call from a member of Hubert Humphrey's staff, telling me that the vice president had been invited by Clark College in Atlanta to give a centennial Founders' Day address. The demonstrations, Vietnam crises, and tensions in the country required the vice president to remain on board in Washington; would I stand in for him? A White House car picked me up at the ISE office, a cap, gown, and hood in the back seat, and I wrote a speech on the flight to Atlanta. When the plane touched down, the press, police, and politicians were there waiting for Hubert Humphrey. When I climbed out of the Air Force jet, we were all surprised. "What you see is what you get," I said.

A year later President Johnson was scheduled to deliver a centennial Founders' Day speech at Johnson C. Smith University in Charlotte. At the last minute, Bill Moyers called again and I had to repeat the whole exercise.

When I returned, a White House staffer ribbed me, "So, Sam, who are you replacing next?"

"I'm going home and wait for the Pope to tell me he can't make it to Notre Dame."

When Humphrey decided on short notice to run for president in 1968, all sorts of supporters demanded his attention and his presence. Humphrey's speech writer, Van Dyke, called to ask me to write speeches for the vice president to deliver to the National Baptist Convention, the African Methodist Episcopal Zion, and the African Methodist Episcopal general conferences. He would make the speeches over the next ninety days and each would be heard live by at least ten thousand blacks and another 5 million watching on television.

That meant writing three different speeches saying the same things: things have changed under Johnson-Humphrey, but we have a long way to go. Nixon wants to go backward. We must go forward and complete the integration of education, expand job opportunity, continue the War on Poverty, remain strong militarily, strengthen new nations in decolonializing, and build in America an example of a new human community of compassion, justice, freedom, and hope.

Humphrey enjoyed giving these speeches, which I inadvertently flavored with a little Baptist pulpit rhythm and glow. He would roll along with his Minnesota staccato, and whenever an audience detected the echo of a black preacher, they raised their hands and chanted "Amen!"

I was in the audience one night at the 1968 General Conference of the African Methodist Episcopal Church. Humphrey was rolling along pretty well when suddenly a robust voice shouted out, "Preach on, brother!" The colleague next to me, who had been chuckling quietly, now fell out of his seat laughing. Humphrey looked out at the audience and said, "Where is Sam Proctor? What did you put in this speech?"

The Methodists roared. It was one of the most transparently communicative moments I have ever witnessed. Humphrey and those black Methodists were on the same wavelength. They loved him. Humphrey had always stood up for black people, even though in 1964 he had been on shaky ground, going along with the party in denying seats to the Mississippi Freedom Party. That night he could have stood there and recited the Ten Commandments to a standing ovation.

In the same year, Humphrey had to go to Africa in order to look more like a presidential candidate. He asked me to go with him. We traveled on Air Force One (which is repainted and called Air Force Two when used by the vice president). We had a great trip, stopping at Zaire, Tunis, Liberia, Zambia, the Ivory Coast, Ethiopia, and the animal preserves of Kenya. Typical of such trips we were wined and dined and superficially briefed on American relations with the host country. The embarrassing part was to see the lavish lifestyle of the ruling class everywhere we went, and the unbroken landscape of poverty and sickness in the streets where the people struggled to survive. It was heart-rending. Humphrey insisted on seeing it all. And when I saw this contrast in well-being everywhere we went, I had the feeling that Americans shared the guilt, because we were friends with those rulers.

Habib Bourguiba, head of the government in Tunis, had twelve palaces! We, meaning the U.S., gave tacit consent to his behavior, just as we gave to the Duvaliers in Haiti. When we got to Addis Ababa, the students lifted up one side of our Cadillac limousine and almost turned it over, so vehement were they in their protest of our buddyhood with the royal family of Ethiopia.

Same old story. But the world was changing fast. Throughout the trip I had a chance to discuss these observations with Supreme Court Justice Thurgood Marshall and *Jet* editor Simeon Booker, an old Latin and Greek classmate from college, who were also on the trip. All of us recognized Humphrey's motives and his unpretentious idealism, but we wondered how much change he could effect if elected. Powerful economic forces were firmly in place to stalemate any significant change.

Huge corporations were involved with mega-governmental contracts, therefore contracts had to stay in place. Hiring practices were frozen in business and government, and old-boy networks kept blacks and women in the lowest grades. Cabinet offices and corporate chairs were a revolving door, and huge Washington law firms kept deals on the table with governments, fiefdoms, and sheikdoms in every corner of the planet. Politicians were all beholden to the same money. The most salutary event of the whole trip was our arrival at the Nairobi airport in Kenya. I looked out of the window and spied among the official greeters my old friend, that big bad "Toby" Tobias, who had led his football team to the Red Cross trailer back in 1960 to donate forty-eight pints of blood for my son's heart surgery. When I stepped off the plane, he gave me a bear hug, scratching my face with his wiry tropical whiskers.

"What are you doing in Kenya?" I asked.

"Well," he said, "you recall that you and Bill Moyers let me join the Peace Corps and sent me to Iran to help the Shah develop an Olympic team. After the Olympics, Kenya asked me to work for their government developing their Olympic team. So here I am."

"It was good of you to come to meet me."

"I really came to see the sergeant," he said.

I turned to see a huge black Air Force sergeant with all sorts of stripes crawling up his sleeve and medals splattered across his chest. He rushed up to my fullback and hugged him, and tears rolled down both of those stone countenances. It turned out that as little fellows trying to survive in the slums of Baltimore, they had both wound up in a boarding school founded for black youngsters who needed an alternative home. They had been like brothers. Now the sergeant was in charge of security on Air Force Two, and the fullback was training Kenya's Olympic team. That fabulous result from the ghetto and a school for troubled boys! When your eye is trained to look for it, there is plenty of evidence that there is a faith proposition that operates, and that gets results.

MEANWHILE, THE MOVEMENT AT HOME WAS ALIVE AND well. In 1968, Whitney Young asked me to preside at the plenary sessions of the National Urban League convention in New Orleans. After opening words from politicians and local officials, I began to move the meeting forward, presenting speakers and panelists. Just then, a half-dozen young men dressed in guerrilla warfare garb suddenly appeared on the stage and grabbed the microphone from my hand. The truth was that some of the Urban League staff, including Whitney Young, were former athletes and marines. They were not about to let a half-dozen self-appointed commanders take over the convention. In a flash, Whitney, all 6 foot 3 and 240 pounds of him, reached for their leader's collar, snatched him forward, and said, "You will not interrupt this meeting. I'll give you a chance later to make a statement."

Still threatening, they backed off, and we proceeded. As promised, Whitney did give one of them the opportunity to present a statement at the end. Cogent and sincere, it bore little relationship to the reality of that moment. It was simply rage. And it was the tenor of the times: discussion and debate signified weakness, while a show of force stood for integrity.

The Urban League felt the protestors were honest in their ideals, but they believed that violence would only leave the black end of town in ashes and elect the most extreme right-wingers to Congress and the White House. Their approach was negotiation, conciliation, and persuasion.

The problem was that neither approach could bring change fast enough. All of us saw the ingredients for riots in every urban setting. In Los Angeles, for example, every black neighborhood was infested with unemployed, uneducated gang members armed to do battle somewhere with someone. Violent behavior was their shield to cover their inadequacies. In juxtaposition to them were poor white migrants from Texas and Louisiana, with their boots, their tattoos, their guitars, and their racism. The brighter of them became policemen. Every riot was the outcome of an abrasive encounter between a racist white cop and a mean, bad "brother."

But if you stepped back to get a wider perspective, it was clear that in ten short years the black condition had changed dramatically. And beneath the surface of public debate were small private gestures that never made the news.

While I was in the thicket of our work with the colleges and the White House, I had a call from a Martin England, a white Baptist missionary recently retired from service in Burma. He was now working to enroll southern pastors in the American Baptist Health and Pension Plan. He called to find out if Martin Luther King had any health or life insurance or pension plan.

"It occurred to me," he confided in his gentle way, "that Dr. King has a young family and that he lives dangerously."

Martin England would never have expressed such a concern out loud, but into my ear he spoke of life's inexorable and changing scene.

"My hunch is that Martin has been too taken up with other matters to worry much about his financial condition," I said. "But why don't you give him a call and ask him?"

For two months he tried to reach King, but could never gain admittance to the black inner circle. Martin England was a tall, thin, pale man with a balding head and dark blotches of age on his hands. Whenever he showed up, dressed frugally and driving a worn old Plymouth, the black brotherhood surrounding King with their thunderous voices and rotund physiques frightened the retired missionary into a quick exit.

But England didn't give up. He called me again and described his futile efforts. I promised to try to get him in to see King. It worked. King signed up for the plan. The efforts of this unobtrusive South Carolinian made it possible for Coretta Scott King and her children to have health coverage and a monthly income from this one source ever since. Such small and apparently insignificant gestures bury themselves in the deep reservoir of my memory, and make me immune to the cynical notion that all human decency has died.

A FEW MONTHS LATER, ON APRIL 4, 1968, A DALLAS cabdriver picked me up at Love Field. He had long, stringy blond hair, tattoos crawling up his arms, and a wet cigarette butt dangling from his lips. A pair of cheap sunglasses hid his eyes. He was trying to tell me something, but he couldn't get the words out. He began to cry and was shaking so much that he had to stop the cab to collect himself. Finally his message spilled out between sobs: Martin Luther King, Jr., had been shot to death in Memphis. I felt my heart splinter.

I was on my way to a conference with specially selected white and black teachers to devise a strategy for preparing Dallas teachers for school integration. When the news of King's death lit up the airwaves, I had to reassess whether such small efforts were worth such an enormous price. I knew how much Martin would have loved to live and see his children grow up. But I knew also his sense of destiny and that he had calculated death as a possible price. He died, really, to give impetus and sanction to every effort at building a community of justice and compassion. In order to feel some sense of continuity with him, I had to look at this conference and find legitimacy in it. I knew that making all schools work well in illuminating the minds of all children would have been called redemptive by Martin.

I clung to that belief as in one city after another, black ghettos went up in flames, ignited by hot anger in a tinderbox of broken dreams and deferred hopes. Feeding the flames were decades of police abuse, unemployment, poor education, ragged and ill-kept housing, and feelings of being unwanted everywhere.

Two months later, Robert F. Kennedy was murdered in Los Angeles. America was stretched to her limits. Every imaginable controversy divided the country: the war in Vietnam, women's rights, black rights, gay rights, abortion, school desegregation, and affirmative action.

The setting was perfect for a full swing to the conservative right. Richard Nixon got out his tuxedo and polished up his patent-leather shoes. It was a dark moment for me when Nixon defeated Hubert Humphrey. The threat was always there, in the candidacies of Strom Thurmond, George Wallace, and Barry Goldwater, that the Kennedy-Johnson initiatives would stir up a backlash. In addition, the riots, burnings, lootings, and emergence of violent rhetoric among young black rebels had eroded much of the moral beachhead held by Martin Luther King. Now, all of our friends seemed to disappear, just as they had disappeared in the early 1900s. Our agenda had become too complicated.

CHAPTER SEVEN

America's Moral Parentheses

WITH RICHARD NIXON COMING TO THE WHITE HOUSE, I'D lost my appetite for Washington. Fred Harrington, former president of the University of Wisconsin, was one of the few stalwarts of the 1960s who retained enough idealism to maintain his enthusiasm for liberal causes. In 1968, he and his able assistant, Don McNeil, invited me to join his staff at Wisconsin and to bring my ideas for improving black colleges with me.

The University of Wisconsin was spearheading a program that would involve all of the Big Ten universities. Their goal was to increase the numbers of minority scientists and professors by strengthening the curriculum and the performance of black colleges. My job was to recruit and graduate a new pool of black

Ph.D.s, which in turn would strengthen the faculties of one hundred black colleges scattered across the South. We planned to graduate a hundred new professors each year. We had financial commitments from government and private foundations for the program.

I accepted Dr. Harrington's offer of a new post, which carried the ambiguous title "University Dean for Special Programs." I landed at Madison in September of 1968, and hit a wall of resentment. Most of the small group of black undergraduates had been recruited from the ghettos of Chicago and Milwaukee to attend that milk-white school, where they felt unwanted—a tiny island in a sea of thirty thousand students of Scandinavian and German descent.

While their trip to college was a release from a depressing and impoverished situation, it seemed to me that no one had told these kids what to expect. A few were so bright and tough-minded that you could have dropped them in Siberia and they would have survived. But for many, their first day in a college class was a shock. They had no faint notion of what their high school diplomas were supposed to have guaranteed them in terms of preparing them for college. In truth, their diplomas from big city schools often amounted to no more than attendance certificates.

The challenge, and the chill—from impolite gestures, hostile glances, and overt questions about their presence—created an adversarial atmosphere. It took very little to convince them that the school was wrong, the teachers were irrelevant, the curriculum was too Eurocentric, and that the school needed to change to accommodate them. Mistakenly, they thought I had been chosen as their new representative, without their consent.

Increasing our discord, the black students wanted to create a black enclave within the university. They demanded distinct and separate programs for blacks only. I agreed that we needed an infusion of African and African-American topics throughout the curriculum, but not solely for black students.

In one effort to be recognized, these students had demanded and received part of the budget for public speakers. One speaker they invited was an ex-gang leader from Washington, D.C., who allegedly spoke for the "black cause."

The student welcoming committee greeted him with pot and coke. By speaking time, he thought he was John the Baptist. It was embarrassing to sit in the auditorium and listen to him talk about "where it was." I already knew where it was! I had been there. It was no mystery. He carried on for half an hour, wild-eyed and thick-tongued. By then, the student committee was calling for him to leave the lectern. They had to mount the platform and usher him, delusional, to the wings. It was absurd that on this campus we had no better interpreter of our complicated social crisis than this young man.

I tried hard to feel what those students felt, but every conversation I had with them revealed a wide chasm between us. The truth was that no group of students could move that huge university to meet their tastes. The students were the ones who would have to change, and many did. The others left in dribbles.

WHITE PEOPLE THOUGHT THAT BLACKS WANTED ONLY A chance to outlive the past and to get caught up with the American dream. They thought it was enough to provide a new opportunity for success. They failed to understand the estrangement and cynicism that accompanied those black students from Chicago's South Side to Madison. Blind to the anger that would follow their academic embarrassment, and unable to see how closely resentment followed charity, no white person appreciated how uncertain these students were about their future. With cooperation on both sides, they could have topped off their weak high school experience with a solid, creative freshman year. But such pragmatism was too much to expect of college planners. The enraged students made one demand after another, some of which were acceptable and incorporated. Others were beyond what a university could do, such as the demand to allow students to hire and fire teachers.

I knew I had a pivotal program in my grasp at Wisconsin, and even in that frenetic crisis, it never occurred to me that I could fail if I applied my best effort. But eventually I was compelled to reconcile myself to the facts. The university experiment was going seriously awry. Constant demonstrations interrupted class schedules, lectures, visiting speakers, and everything else. Every faculty meeting was stopped by someone imposing another new political agenda on us.

Within our family we constantly talked about defeats and victories, mountains and valleys of black fortunes, and we kept before us a barometer of America's moral presence in the world. But while our boys always lived close to public issues, they never lived near bloody street trauma, gunshots, or hand-to-hand combat. They hardly heard any public profanity.

In this atmosphere of social challenge that kept violence in the news and campuses on the alert for student eruptions, Bessie and I tried to make sure the effervescent social climate was interpreted and digestible for our sons.

Our second son, Timothy, was caught as an undergraduate in two massive student revolts—1966 to 1970—first at Yale, and then Wisconsin. He had done his freshman year at Yale, but the student crisis there caused us to take him to Wisconsin with us. In his first year there, between 1968 and 1969, he made almost a 4.0 average and was invited to join the math honors major. The next year the campus was in turmoil. Picket lines, protest marches, boycotts, and rallies made class attendance seem irrelevant.

The fact was that Timothy and many other better educated

students were unprepared for the heavy rhetoric and violent gestures that other black students felt were necessary to turn a university around. They were not certain that violent strategies had any real relevance, and felt that the consequences would be counterproductive. They felt frustrated because the mood and tempo defied reason and logic. Many young people did not make it over this terrain. Drugs and dropping out were their only answers. Others found a bulwark at home, a harbor of hope, and families stayed close to see them through.

Timothy continued to live at home. The most conspicuous concession he made to the counterculture was to buy a motorcycle, play the guitar, and grow a large 'fro.

Timothy took advantage of an early admission program to enroll in the joint M.B.A./J.D. program at the University of Chicago, without having to complete the B.A. He scored well on the admissions tests and gave his career a big leap forward. Today he has a very challenging career in corporate law.

MANY AFRICAN-AMERICAN STUDENTS BECAME SO DISILLUSIONED during this time that they began to believe that they would be wiped out if they adapted to American culture or continued to measure success by prevailing standards. They lived in limbo, stranded between fantasies about a new black homeland on the one hand, and unending, irreversible white hostility on the other.

I never felt that way. My own life had been bombarded by the same racist environment, but I had never absorbed it into my personality. I regretted so much that many students became so polarized politically that the inroads they were making into traditionally white universities were lost. I had so many secrets to tell them.

I knew I was not what white society perceived me to be, and I enjoyed proving it. During my darkest hours, I never believed that God had vanished, or that the moral order of the universe was less reliable than the physical order. I believed that justice had its own inherent validity. I believed that change would come if we continued to work at it. Believing these things, I went to church where we celebrated social change as though it were reality.

I had gone to Wisconsin to contribute to creative and systemic change. Instead, with the aborted Democratic convention in Chicago and Nixon's election, the signal went out and the student rebellion and protest gathered force. The 1968–69 student rebellion at Wisconsin was an extension of what was going on at most campuses. The moral ambiguity and confused objectives of the war in Vietnam sickened students; racism was not taken seriously by major institutions, and blacks had to take to the streets risking life and limb to secure rights guaranteed by the Constitution. The quiet power of the rich paralyzed initiatives to redress poverty and marginality.

After a year, it was clear that either the white radicals and black students would close the university, the president would be fired, or the state would call a halt to special programs. Although I remained an unrepentant optimist, over the years I had also become a realist, at least in the sense of being able to gauge the level of public resistance to change.

I left Wisconsin feeling defeated. I was forty-eight, with half of my career behind me. Fortunately, new job offers started coming in during the early weeks of 1969. Dr. John Elder, dean of the graduate school at Harvard, invited me to be an associate dean. I could spend the first year dreaming, speaking, and scheming on how Harvard could reach out to the best and brightest black doctoral candidates. On Sundays, I could preach anywhere I was invited. The Harvard job seemed like a miracle. We had gone where we were needed, and fought battles where we found them. Now my family and I needed a period of stability.

As I was getting ready to accept the job, another offer came from Dr. Mason Gross, president of Rutgers University.

"What would it take to bring you to Rutgers?" he asked. "We want you to settle down and finish your life's work with us. Would you consider an appointment as the Martin Luther King Memorial Professor in the School of Education, with full tenure?" There was no such position, until he thought it up right then.

Heaven was smiling on me. At Rutgers I could write my own courses and teach on my own schedule; in the summers I would be free to write, study, and reflect. Rutgers was situated in the most thickly settled state in the Union, in the epicenter of Boston, Philadelphia, Washington, D.C., and New York. And the appointment was out of the pathway of administration, fund raising, public relations, and budget balancing.

One problem: the Harvard letter of acceptance was in my pocket. How on earth could anyone say no to Harvard? I talked it over with Bessie and our sons. We were all so anxious to settle down after Wisconsin that it did not matter if we went to Cambridge or New Jersey. The two younger boys only wanted to be with us anywhere; and the times of change and challenge that buffeted the lives of the older boys caused them not to worry too much about me. Literally, they trusted in some abstract process that would not let us fail. I prayed a little prayer, and then called Dean Elder and turned down the Harvard appointment, with sincere thanks and deep apologies.

In March 1969, we moved to Rutgers at New Brunswick. Over the next twenty years, that old colonial Dutch Reformed institution that had become New Jersey's state university, spreading out on both sides of the Raritan River, became my home.

I came into the university with tenure, at the top of the line, having had two careers already as president of two schools and a stint with the Kennedy-Johnson crew. I also came in at a time when Rutgers was hunting for blacks who were more than merely certified, but who could bring experience and seasoning to the campus. And, yet, no matter what I was otherwise, I was still black and that meant that I had to prove *everything*.

At Rutgers I was expected to do what I had been doing for several years: help increase the flow of black academics into the graduate school so they in turn could teach and help other black students fulfill their rich potential. Improving the life chances for my people changed the tone and thrust of the school itself. In the next twenty years, over one hundred of my black students graduated with doctoral degrees. Nine are teaching in Mississippi colleges, and three are college presidents in the Northeast.

Time flew. Rutgers was good for me and good to me. It was a privilege to come to work every day, and I could not wait to get into the classroom. It offered me a chance to wrestle with ideas and get to know people who had spent their lives in the pursuit of truth. Our two youngest sons grew up in the shadow of Rutgers. One of our sons did all of his college work there, while the other three did graduate work. I saw Rutgers grow from a small, Ivy League school into a major university with fifty thousand students and fourteen schools, and with the most multicultural faculty and student body found anywhere in the nation.

All of this activity was set against a hostile panorama. In 1971, President Nixon promised the nation that he would *diminish* federal enforcement of school desegregation orders. In 1972, he crushed George McGovern at the polls.

The passive indifference of the Nixon-Agnew days were in sharp contrast to the vigor and clarity of the Johnson years. Our communities were terrorized by waves of violence and the polarization of the races. Police were given a national mandate to allay black street violence, but there was no national mandate to deal with the causes of that violence.

To me, the most shameful behavior during this period was the posture of the white churches and the mean-spirited fundamentalism that was spreading around the country. All across the South television preachers sprang up in silk suits, jewelry dangling from every appendage, and fancy hairdos, a Bible raised in one hand and the other hand gesturing wildly about "born again" religion. The following that grew up around them became diverted into a right-wing political base that opposed "race mixing" in the schools. These preacher-organizers played on the ignorance and fears of their poorly educated parochial followers who never got a chance to hear any other points of view, and they built little power bases on the issue of integration.

Some were able to organize private schools and lure white pupils away from integrating schools. They did this in the name of "morality and Christian principles," and they called their schools "Christian academies."

The country was desperate for leadership, and the need was most heavily felt in the black community. The symbolic leadership of Martin Luther King, Jr., could not be easily reassigned. Roy Wilkins, Whitney Young, Jesse Jackson, and the Black Panthers had their followings, but the rhythm and the cadence did not click. We lost our magnetic pole and became fragmented. However, it never occurred to me that we needed a single leader to drive us forward. We had many dedicated servants devoted to our cause, faithfully at their posts, in every corner of the country.

Despite the diversity of our leadership, the media continued to crave a single spokesperson. The hungry television cameras drew charlatans, opportunists, misguided ideologues, and self-serving sensationalists. Our condition lent itself to easy exploitation, and prompted glib answers to complicated problems. Seizing this opportunity, several universities hired "house conservatives" who used obscure language to insinuate that blacks caused their own problems and deserved to suffer.

To present a so-called "balanced view" the media also paraded a string of unemployed militants who made a living on ranting and raving about separation and black nationalism. Many of these later turned into Reaganites, fundamentalist preachers, local politicians, or "consultants."

The business of manufacturing a leader is tricky. If people insist on having one, they come crawling from under rocks. I believe we should have many leaders, in every field, and in every state and region of the country. There is so much talent, wisdom, and energy out there that it needn't be packaged and delivered to us by the media.

EVERY SUNDAY WAS A PREACHING DAY FOR ME, SOMEWHERE. I had taught ministers in Virginia Union's School of Theology for eleven years; as a result I had alumni scattered all over the black churches in the East, and they called on me continually. I enjoyed having reunions with them and seeing how well they were doing. As a guest speaker I also met pastors up and down the length of the Atlantic Coast and across the country to Chicago, Seattle, San Francisco, and Los Angeles. Every August I was invited to preach at the magnificent Riverside Church and at small storefront churches in Harlem. I found myself as much at home in Brooklyn's fabulous Concord Baptist pulpit as in a white congregation's clapboard church on a hillside in rural Virginia.

Despite the social upheaval of the time, my religious ideas and social concerns remained intact. But I never spoke about current events, unless I first processed the information through my own experience. No matter where I spoke or the nature of the occasion, my authority was rooted in three principal biblical sources: the monumental eighth century B.C.E. Jewish prophets (Micah, Amos, and Isaiah), the life and teachings of Jesus, and in Paul's understanding of the transforming power of Christ as the object of one's faith.

I never asked my audiences to leave their minds outside when they came into church, and I never felt obliged to preach about *everything* I read in the Bible. Some of it reflects a world that is flat, with a burning hell underneath and a jeweled heaven above.

Some of it reflects a primitive view of women, killing, slavery, and war that is far short of Jesus' teachings. Our world is much too complex for simple dogma.

I kept busy speaking across the country, and into Asia and Europe. I also spoke to employee groups at giant corporations and even at the CIA, the State Department, and the Agriculture Department. In the late 1960s and early 1970s, these audiences were almost always composed of white men. I never attacked like a junkyard dog, and never wanted to leave a room filled with angry people. I always wanted to leave it filled with people resolved to do something for change, however small. I viewed these talks as teaching opportunities. Many white college graduates were immune to informed, thoughtful dialogue about controversial topics. They seemed to have been rehearsed to find the conventional views on everything and stay pat.

The invitations to speak came from people appointed by their companies to be "human resources" administrators, equal opportunity directors, or affirmative action programmers. In the wake of the rebellions and new federal initiatives, such men were found in every major corporation. I could never tell who was genuinely committed and who was merely a hireling going through the motions, but I always appreciated the audiences. It was our only chance at some of these bright people, so I never passed up a corporate opportunity.

With Nixon in the White House and Clarence Thomas in charge of the Equal Employment Opportunities Commission, we didn't expect much, but we kept pitching. Once, while speaking to the agriculture department's super grades, in a room filled exclusively with white men, a well-dressed black man carrying a large alligator briefcase entered, wearing a sharply pressed sharkskin suit, with conspicuously matching tie and pocket handkerchief. I asked his name. He answered, then added that he was the "equal opportunity officer" for the agency. His job purportedly was to encourage the hiring of more women, blacks, and other minorities—but he was the only visible outcome of his efforts. He had used up his whole office on himself!

That's what it was like then. The approach in Washington was to hire blacks who did not support government intervention in racial matters. Benign neglect was Nixon's policy, and it took root.

When we read about Richard Nixon's values, it's enough to make you weep. Only days after Nixon's death in May of 1994, H. R. Haldeman's White House diary was published. Haldeman revealed that Nixon resented the Jewish "domination" of the media and said that Billy Graham had told him that the Bible referred to "satanic Jews."

Nixon reserved his worst comments for blacks who, he said, were the only people who had never had a great nation and were the "whole problem." He wanted to eliminate welfare because it "forced poor whites onto the same level as blacks."

The president of the United States was a Quaker who graduated from Whittier College and Duke Law School, but he did not know any black lawyers, writers, clergy, or university professors with whom he could communicate. Howard University was only ten minutes from 1600 Pennsylvania Avenue, but Nixon ignored that rich resource of scholars who had spent a lifetime studying issues that affected the whole country, and instead relied on his "Uncle Tom" sycophants and a television evangelist for information.

ONE OF MY FAVORITE PLACES TO PREACH ON SUNDAYS WAS the Abyssinian Baptist Church of Harlem. Black Baptists had established the church in lower Manhattan in 1808, when Thomas Jefferson was president, and named it in honor of some visiting Ethiopian (Abyssinian) seamen whose ship was berthed in the port of New York.

Dr. Adam Clayton Powell, Sr., who became pastor in 1908,

brought a passion for social justice and personal renewal to the church. Under his stewardship this modest-sized black church moved to Harlem in the 1920s, and became one of the largest Protestant congregations in the world, with a membership well over its current seven thousand. The church became a social service agency as well as a vital religious center.

In 1938, the pastorate passed to Dr. Powell's son, Adam Clayton Powell, Jr. By virtue of his huge personal popularity as Abyssinian's pastor, Adam was elected to the city council in 1941, at the age of thirty-two. Four years later he was elected to the United States Congress, where he served for fourteen terms. Such heavy responsibilities pulled him away from church duties, and I was often asked to fill the pulpit in Powell's absence.

Powell had reached out for me before. In 1962, when I was in Nigeria, he cabled me through the state department and asked me to head up one of the antipoverty social agencies in Harlem. His telegram sounded so urgent that everyone at the post offered regrets that I was leaving. Shriver hit the ceiling when he learned that Powell was trying to steal his staff! But that was Powell's style: he was direct and bold, and let other people do the adjusting.

Someone once said that Powell's attention span was ninety seconds, and that seemed to be the truth, because he had no patience with pedantry, literal- or closed-mindedness, perfunctory traditionalism, or superficiality. He wanted conversations to get to the point fast. He lived in a hurry and he always had an important goal in front of him.

Powell was both feared and hated by the established political machines. At the height of his congressional career in the 1950s and 1960s, he chaired the powerful Committee on Education and Labor, from which he successfully piloted sixty-seven pieces of social and economic reform legislation. Working for Sargent Shriver, I had to testify for our legislation on several occasions before Powell's committee. He and his staff were truly formidable.

Adam Powell allowed few people into his inner circle, and he required in return unquestioned loyalty and confidentiality. His private life stayed private. But his inability to trust and delegate to his aides limited his leadership. My own dealings with him were very sketchy. We first met when I was a college student and a chauffeur for the president of Virginia Union. I had to meet Adam when he arrived at Richmond's Main Street train station, a segregated facility. He did not walk through the "colored" waiting room, but strode boldly through the main lobby for whites only.

He was a gifted, spell-binding orator, who could get furious over matters of injustice. I'll never forget when he spoke in our college chapel in 1941, shortly after his election to the city council. "I can't stand conservative Negroes," he said. "They don't have a damn thing to conserve!" I have never forgotten how vehement he was when he said that.

His sermons were usually on issues of civil rights and racial pride. He has never been fully credited with the contributions he made, because he was not a collaborator, never a gregarious glad-hander, and always operated alone. His blunt straightforwardness was often taken as arrogance, but it was the result of the fact that he lived in a pressure cooker.

In 1969, he lost his seat in Congress to Charles Rangel. His health declined, and he spent most of his time in Bimini, his favorite retreat, to escape public view. In 1971, the church requested that he either resign, retire, or return. When Powell failed to respond, they declared the position of pastor vacant. Adam Powell died in April of the next year.

The church officers of the Abyssinian Baptist Church asked me to deliver his eulogy. Adam's funeral filled the two-thousand-seat sanctuary and the entire block from Seventh to Lenox on 138th Street. Most people did not even know that he was no longer pastor when he died, and I conducted the funeral as though his position and title were intact.

A few months later, I was asked to accept the pastorate. I really had not anticipated beginning a new chapter in my life at age fifty-one. Our two older sons were away in school and the two younger boys were settled in their schools in New Jersey. We could not envision moving to Manhattan and starting life all over again. But it did seem important to help Abyssinian regain her posture.

I accepted the pastorate on the condition that I would continue my work at Rutgers and share church duties with other staff ministers. We continued to live in New Jersey, and I shared the pastor's salary with an extra assistant pastor.

Bessie had made such a smooth adjustment to two new sons after thirteen years, moving from America to Africa, back to Washington, to Greensboro, to Washington again, to New York, to Washington, to Wisconsin, to New Jersey—that commuting to New York (thirty miles on the New Jersey Turnpike) three times a week was a snap. We sang and joked through the commuting like it was recess time.

It was a constant, nagging tug on me to try to replicate Adam. He was brought to the church as an infant in 1908 and had been nowhere but there until 1971. Everyone in the church grew up with him. It would have been nonsense to imitate him. Powell was larger than life, obsessed with the concerns of the last, the lowest, and the least. His political articulation set in motion a spirit of courage and commitment that became the ignition for the civil rights movement.

Still, the church was warm and cooperative, and my family and I felt appreciated. Some wanted the church to remain a political center; but when I was appointed, it was clear that I would leave political offices to others and make my contribution in other ways. My training and experience were far better applied to a teaching-preaching service than to one as a New York politician who knew nothing about New York. As always, I set my priorities and my pattern of work with God's guidance.

Soon, Abyssinian was home to us. Smiling, talkative women,

friendly and supportive officers, an appreciative handclapping, singing, and responding congregation. And the excitement of Harlem was such a consuming atmosphere that it was like a new life.

All the while that I worked at the church and the university, I felt enriched by both. Religion and education are symbiotic. Each energizes the other, and I benefited greatly from two incomparable growth opportunities.

MEANWHILE, MY COURSES AT RUTGERS DREW LARGE numbers. It took personal courage for black graduate students to withstand the wintry stares of white campuses like Rutgers, and consequently students I had recruited thought of me as a big brother. I had taught many of their parents, pastors, coaches, and former teachers, and they were always baffled that no matter how remote their hometown, I could name someone they had known back home. They crowded into my tiny office as if it were a lifeboat.

Through my door came a steady flow of black students wanting to unload their problems and frustrations. Some distrusted all blacks over forty, and thought people like me were too well off to be of any use in the struggle. My brand of optimism met a cool reception in many quarters. Here we are, I thought, with much of the worst terrain already crossed, and I can't convince my African-American graduate students that the glass is half full. I would tell them how my brothers scuffled through medical and dental school, and how my son was battling his way through law school. They shrugged off these examples and called them "bourgeois." I reminded them that presently we were not loved by those in charge, and we couldn't afford to call each other names. Certainly we couldn't afford to call all educated and successful blacks "bourgeoisie," because we had to make hard work and success attractive.

One of my less committed students came to class one evening walking a large, dirty white dog on a frayed rope pieced together from fragments. The dog was happy to be in a warm room on a cold night and most students gave it a pat or a scratch on the neck, but a few moved their chairs away from the dog and its ill-kempt master.

I got that student's message: he wasn't going to take me or the course seriously. I asked the class how many had dogs. Almost every hand went up. I asked if they felt entitled to bring their dogs to class if this student could bring his. They agreed that they did. I asked if we could all concentrate if everyone who had a dog brought it to class.

They shouted, "No."

I asked the student to tie the dog outside the door or leave the class, and told him that any similar incidents in the future would earn him an absent mark; if he missed a fourth of the sessions, the course credit would automatically be denied.

He called me a czar, a tyrant, and worse. Afterward, he told me that I was following "white" standards which did not fit blacks. I said that our experiences were indeed different, but blacks and whites shared the larger areas of human concourse and that most life behavior had no racial tag. I meant it.

One of my white students entered an elevator that I was in already, and I removed my hat. "Dr. Proctor," she said, "why in hell did you take your hat off when I got on the elevator? You're living in the Victorian age." She laughed congenially.

"If you'll get off the elevator with me for a moment, I'll tell you." At my stop, we both stepped off.

"I'm not a Victorian," I said, "but some things stay in place from one generation to another, and certain manners stand for values that I hold dear. I believe that a society that ceases to respect women is on its way out. Women bear and raise our children, they are bound to them in early infancy; they need our support and security through this process. When we forget that, the keystone of family and home is lost. When we neglect and abuse women, the family falls apart and children are less well parented, and they fill up the jails and are buried in early graves. I believe that respect for women is the linchpin of the family and the society. Therefore, when you entered the elevator, I wanted you to have automatic, immediate, unqualified assurance that if the elevator caught fire, I would help you out through the top first. If a strange man boarded and began to slap you around and tear your clothes off, he would have to kill me first. If the elevator broke down and stopped between floors, I would not leave you in here. If you fainted and slumped to the floor, I would stop everything and get you to a hospital. Now, it would take a lot of time to say all of that, so when I removed my hat, I meant all of the above."

Tears sprang to her eyes. There are some values that abide. They have no racial or ethnic label. It took a lot to convince students that equality was possible, but we had first to define the optimum human condition and call *everyone* to embrace it.

Some of my students were incredibly successful. One day a book salesman from San Francisco came by my office to introduce his company's latest publications. I interrupted his sing-song sales pitch to ask him a few basic questions about himself: "Where were you born? Are your parents living? Are you married? Where did you go to school? Did you play sports? How did you get this job? Is this your future? What would you rather be doing?"

His patience ran out. "If you must know," he said, "I want to be an orthopedic surgeon. What are you going to do about it?"

"I'm not sure yet. But you don't look like a salesman to me. Maybe we can get you off this book route and on your way to medical school. What were your grades like in science?"

He was stunned. "My grades were good, but I left college to play pro basketball. I didn't make it, so here I am."

I sent him over to our medical school to talk with Dr. Harold Logan, who could evaluate his chances for entering Rutgers.

We had so few successful black applicants for medical school that I thought it was worth a try. Dr. Logan gave him the third degree and asked other faculty to talk with him. Then he struck a deal: if the young salesman would quit his job, enter summer school right then, make top grades in microbiology and invertebrate zoology, they would let him in on probation. In the fall, he would have to pass the regular admissions tests.

Four years later, I spoke at his commencement in the Garden State Art Center. An elderly professor from the medical school came to me after the exercises and thanked me for sending that student to them. Today, Dr. Michael Charles is one of the most popular sports orthopedic specialists in the San Francisco Bay Area. There is a catalogue of people like him whom I had the pleasure of knowing as students and who kept my faith alive that we were indeed capable of erasing the stereotype, reversing the bad data, and securing justice in America. I found recruiting and graduating a steady stream of doctoral students from Rutgers a source of pure delight.

I HAD MY OWN SPIRITUAL TRAIN GOING FROM THE CLASSROOM to the church, carrying lessons back and forth between the two. And the messages were always compatible. One Sunday morning, soon after I took over at Abyssinian, the deaconesses (wives of deacons who volunteer for special functions) said that several parents had brought their babies to be dedicated to God. While Baptists baptize only those old enough to acknowledge their faith for themselves, we also commit the church to serve and care for infants.

I went into the room where parents and infants were waiting and looked over the cards with the names of the four babies and their parents and godparents. I tried to match each baby's name with the tiny, round faces and jeweled eyes gazing at me with grave suspicion from under pretty lace bonnets. I noticed that two infants had the same last names as their mothers, but different from the fathers who were present. I asked those two fathers to step outside with me. We left the deaconesses and other parents looking puzzled and confused.

Apparently there had been a tacit agreement not to challenge these unmarried fathers who showed up to stand beside the mothers of their infants. It was another concession made to a declining order of things, and a statement to the whole community that a young man could impregnate a young woman and walk off without responsibility.

I took the two men into my study. "Brothers," I said, "are you the fathers of these children?"

"Yes."

"Do you intend to marry?"

They were not sure.

"Do you want the whole church to know that you are the father?"

They did.

"Do you want me to tell the congregation that you're not married and have no plans to marry?"

They did not.

"Do you have other children, either in our church or somewhere else?"

One did.

"Are that mother and child present today?"

"I don't know."

"If they were, how would they feel seeing you here with another unmarried mother and a new baby? What should we do if you come back six months from now and stand with another unwed mother and child?"

They both looked at the floor sheepishly. It hurt me to turn them away, but how could I stand in church and approve a practice that was destroying our families and communities? It was one thing to present an infant and mother to God. It was another to ask the church to celebrate casually a father who assumed no responsibility for parenting.

I told the two men that they could sit near the front of the church with other worshipers, but the infant dedication service would take place without them. I offered to counsel them, at their convenience, about marriage, schoolwork, or whatever else they wanted to talk about.

In the same way that popular culture can have a negative influence on education, it can also creep into the church and play havoc with our basic life values. Some of us have become so compromised that the rest of us have to be doubly certain that our institutions protect our gains, and continue to prepare us for a higher quality of life.

At Abyssinian we saw life in all of its extremities. We saw people whose devotion and steadiness would put the rest of us to shame. They gave and served without thought of return. We saw single mothers rear children and send them off to college. And we also saw intelligent men and women throw away their values, their goals, and their futures to drug dealers who had no conscience at all.

One day our membership secretary, Esther McCall, noticed an unusual-looking envelope in the mail addressed "To the church pastors." There was no return address, so Esther set aside the envelope. Over the next couple of weeks, several more came in, addressed the same way. We received our share of crank mail, and Esther simply let the envelopes accumulate. The pile grew so large that she finally opened the envelopes before tossing them in the trash. Inside, she found bank cashier's checks, postal money orders, and commercial money orders made out to the church. More and more envelopes came in until the total value amounted to $48,000. We opened a special escrow account and held the money in limbo. Since the source was still unknown, we decided that eventually we would use the money for our youth sports program.

One afternoon one of our three sextons announced that a huge black Mercedes-Benz with smoked windows had pulled up out front. A man emerged from the car wearing a black leather jacket, diamonds on both hands and in one ear, gold around his neck and wrists, and expensive alligator-skin boots.

We activated our little security system: one sexton stayed out in the lobby to be free to run for help; one stayed at the telephone in the office next to mine, with the door cracked, to listen for trouble and call the police if necessary; and the biggest one sat in front of my office door, keeping track of the conversation.

The visitor spoke softly. "I'm the one who sent the money," he said. "I got it in the streets and I want to do some good."

Then he began to tremble and, wiping tears from his eyes beneath his dark glasses, he asked me how he could make a new start in life. He sounded like a drug dealer. He said that if he turned his back on his "associates," he would have to leave the city.

I told him that he would be better off leaving. Staying here he had no life anyway, and he was destroying other lives every day. We prayed together. He squeezed my hand with a kind of finality, and backed slowly out the door without even telling me his name.

Later, a relative of his called and asked us to write a letter to the parole board explaining what a benevolent and charitable person our mystery man was. The caller told us his name. But we couldn't write the letter he wanted. We could acknowledge only that he had made anonymous gifts to the church over a six-month period, but other than that we knew nothing about him. We asked the caller to stay in touch with us, or have the dealer call us, but we never heard from either of them again.

OTHERS FROM AMONG THE DISPOSSESSED CAME TO US. FOR many years it was my habit before Sunday service to enter the sanctuary and walk down the long side aisle against the wall to the deacons' room. The first time I took that walk I passed by a family seated on the aisle: three neatly dressed middle-aged women, a man who could have been brother or husband to one of them, and a young man with Down's syndrome. I couldn't guess his age. He was very stylishly dressed, and seated securely between them.

He looked up at me with shock. I was wearing a black gown with scarlet arm bars, and a scarlet paneled hood lined with my school colors. It was a colorful get-up. He fixed his gaze on my face. I think he was looking for Adam Powell, who had been 6 foot 4, weighed around 210 pounds, and was fair-complexioned with straight black hair. I was 5 foot 10, 190 pounds, ginger-colored, and had short, matted hair. He stared hard.

To reassure him, I gave him a wide smile and a soft pluck on the head. He beamed. The next Sunday when I came down the same aisle, he raised up in his seat and leaned his head toward me; I gave him a little tighter, stronger pluck. Every Sunday after that, I had to give him that little sacerdotal, ecclesiastical, liturgical pluck! It may not have meant much to anyone else, but his world was small and uneventful, and few things happened to accentuate his presence. What seemed negligible to others was highly significant to him.

The church filled the vacuum for blacks in so many ways. What was left out of their lives all week long was supplied by the church on the Lord's day. Those who did not register as important in the secular world found that they mattered greatly in God's house.

This was especially true for women. All week long, black women were on the bottom—beneath black men, white women, and white men. On weekdays they were somebody's cook, typist, nanny, file clerk, maid, housekeeper, nurse, or office helper. But on Sunday they were in charge. Hardly anything happens in the black church without the support and sponsorship of women. Finally, they are moving into the pulpit. Hallelujah!

Black women are enrolled in seminaries in strong numbers. When they are allowed to preach, their success is remarkable. Sadly, however, among Baptists, where most blacks are affiliated, some pastors still argue against women preaching.

Recently, I listened to a group of pastors talking about excluding women from the clergy because Jesus did not have women as disciples. Well, Jesus did not marry, either, so all pastors should be single and celibate, and the married ones fired. His disciples didn't have college degrees, so ministers today should go directly to ordination without stopping by the Ivy Leagues. His disciples were not salaried, and had no pensions or health benefits. That calls for some changes, too. Neither did they speak English, and all were Jews. This excludes all English-speaking pastors who are Gentiles.

It would be odd indeed for God to create men and women equally, and then reveal God's truth only to males. Historically the black church has been our great liberating agent, and it is past time to liberate its women completely.

At Abyssinian a wonderful female seminary student joined our staff, and when she graduated we decided to ordain her in our church. The church called a council of sixty ministers to examine her for ordination, but only three showed up. Since the council is only advisory among Baptists, and since we had the authority to ordain whether a council met or not, the three ministers conducted the examination and Reverend Sharon Williams was ordained. She remained to serve on our staff for a brief time, and then was called to a Brooklyn parish where she still serves successfully.

The woman I remember best from Abyssinian was not a seminary student, but a worshiper who occasionally came to church a little inebriated. One Sunday morning I was rolling on in my sermon about how Jesus had a circle of friends that we wouldn't want to be seen with—harlots, poor people, the demon possessed, and those with leprosy and lame limbs. His friends were the lost, the least, the last, and the left-out. "We prefer to have friends who are the first, the finest, and the foremost," I said. "If Jesus gave a party, you all would not even want to go!"

This lady screamed from the balcony, "That's a damn lie. I would go to Jesus' party."

"I know you would," I called back. "You would go to anybody's party!"

Yet I relied on her presence—and those like her—every Sunday morning. When our fortunes were reversed, when the backlash confused our hopes, we all needed the church more than ever to keep us on track. The church held us together and warmed our hearts. The church provided sanctuary and rest for all those who were heavy laden: "Whosoever will, come!"

SEVERAL YEARS LATER, IN APRIL OF 1984, COUNT BASIE'S widow asked me to deliver the eulogy for her husband's funeral at our church. The Count was a highly regarded member of the black community, a good neighbor in St. Albans, Queens, and a family man who had lived in the same house with the same wife for forty years. Mrs. Basie could never guess what I was thinking about. In the first place, I never believed Count Basie could die; he was bigger than life to me. And second, in a way he had helped pay my way through college.

When I had been a sixteen-year-old student at Virginia State College, twelve of my classmates and I had a little jazz band. On weekends we each made seven dollars a night playing around town and at the officers' club at Fort Lee. While I stumbled through my solos with pedantic stiffness, our pianist, seventeen-year-old Billy Taylor, sparkled with precocious virtuosity at the keyboard. I spent hours trying to learn the alto saxophone riff in Basie's "One O'Clock Jump," which was our main number.

As awkward as my playing was, "One O'Clock Jump" was good enough to keep us working and we went wild with that song three or four times a night. Now, many years later, the great Count Basie was being buried out of the church where I was pastor and I felt a deep emotional stirring.

On the day of the funeral, the church was packed with twenty-five hundred people. Mrs. Basie had asked some of her husband's old buddies to say a few words of tribute, but when they got to carrying on, things got morose. Those who had been helped by the Count when they had been down on their luck wouldn't give up the microphone. They kept on groaning and crying and calling the name of the deceased in grateful remembrance. I finally got up the nerve to point to Billy Taylor, who was sitting in the front row. Yes, the same Billy Taylor who had played in our little college jazz band. Without any hesitation, one of the finest jazz pianists in the world stood up and went over to our grand piano.

The church was packed with musicians. "Please learn a little song for our dear and beloved Count Basie," I said. "It has only three verses, one line each, and you repeat it four times." Our organist, Dr. Jewel Thompson, played the tune through once and I spoke the words.

> Woke up this morning,
> With my mind stayed on Jesus.
>
> Halleluh, Halleluh, Hallelu-u-jah!

Well, this great audience of jazz artists took hold of this little tune. With Dr. Thompson on our five-manual, 67-rank Schantz organ, Billy Taylor on the grand piano, the world's best harmonizers, improvisers, and rhythm artists sang those words to a sassy Basie beat, rocking and clapping hands, heads tilted up, eyes closed, and tears streaming down their cheeks.

Then the tall, slender balladeer Joe Williams, wearing a blue blazer and gold slacks, signifying a happy mood for a home-going celebration, floated down the aisle with his toothy smile, slapped Billy on the knee and said, "Duke's 'Come Sunday,' in E flat."

Billy swung into the song, and those unfamiliar with the *élan vital* of the black church didn't know what had hit them. They had one dramatic introduction to the kind of spiritual uplift and revitalization black people use as a respite from the degradation and disgust that life dumps on them every day. Since the earliest days of slavery, in an unbroken refrain, we have been singing the songs of Zion in a strange land.

CHAPTER EIGHT

Crisis!

▄▗▄

ONE MORNING IN A POUNDING RAINFALL I DROVE MY TWO younger sons to their schools. A heavy curtain of water was blinding us, and I planned to carry them right up to the school doors. But the youngest insisted that I stop the car and let him out before we reached his junior high. After we left him on the corner, I asked his older brother why he was so adamant about getting out in the rain.

"He didn't want the other kids to see that he had a daddy who would drive him to school," he said.

Among many blacks in the school, especially among his peers, it was assumed that your daddy, if you had one at all, was missing. The children had romanticized the absent father, along with the other deficits of poverty and school failure. The year was 1975, but it might have been today.

When I saw this attitude in my son's all-American school in a middle-class neighborhood, it wasn't hard to imagine what was happening to our children growing up in urban slums. Faced with empty hours and detached loyalties, they see themselves rejected by everyone, even their own families. It is hard to stand erect and pledge allegiance when you are hungry, poor, and overlooked. Like their ancestors, there seems to be no future for these kids. In these mean streets, alienated teenage fathers walk away from their children, teenage mothers continue to bear children, young men maul elderly women for their Social Security checks, and rob schools of typewriters and computers to get money for drugs. They have given up on the future.

These young people did not choose the chronic poverty, the total social rejection, begrudging educational opportunities offered them, and denial of a fair chance at employment. They are stranded—in the streets, in jail, and stretched out in mortuaries and morgues.

These sad facts are largely the legacy of the Reagan years, combined with leaps in technology that caused anyone who was poorly educated to lose all hope of a decent job. Then, under Bush, we drank the bitterest dregs of contempt in the appointment of Judge Clarence Thomas to the Supreme Court. This cut deeper than can easily be imagined. We knew that Bush was a conservative politician, but we never thought that he would insult black people by placing on the highest court of the land a person who had so blatantly operated for his own personal comfort at the expense of his people.

Against this backdrop of national events, life went on. During the 1980s my third son, Sammy, entered Yale University. But when he got there, he and the other black students did not feel welcome. As a result, many of them shunned school organizations that white students controlled. Sammy was a computer science and economics major, but he did not join the computer science club or the economics club. Instead, he signed up for the all-black glee club, the black chapel group, and the black social services organization.

Sammy could have gone to other colleges closer by, or to one of the black schools in the South. But he wanted what he considered the strongest academic challenge. He had heard about the cold social climate on campuses, yet he found it strange when he was largely ignored by white students and faculty. So Bessie and I tooled up again to provide the auxiliary support system that he needed to get through. We did, and he did.

Countless black families all over the country found that the euphoria of having their son or daughter admitted to Yale, Wellesley, or Mount Holyoke was soon dimmed by the reality of late-night calls and rebellion against Anglo-cultural presuppositions. Many of these young people who had been warmly affirmed at home and heralded as successes and role models in their communities found themselves numbered among the "disadvantaged," the "diverse," the "high risk" and the "equal opportunity" students. This was true even for those who had no financial aid, high SAT scores, and a strong academic average.

Their families had to function as emergency first aid counselors, helping good kids negotiate the treacherous waters of Ivy League schools during a time of transition. It was all novel and unprecedented. They were making leaps to distance themselves from the stereotype that followed blacks like a shadow from slavery into the late twentieth century.

In addition to giving support to our four sons and trying to maintain the success of black graduate students at Rutgers, I was doing my best to be the spiritual leader of Abyssinian's large urban congregation. Its huge Gothic edifice stood in stark contrast with much of its surrounding community. Housing was run down, and the neighborhood bore the scars and bruises of a defeated people.

Once the membership of the church had come from the neighborhood, but as their fortunes improved, they moved to Westchester, the Bronx, Queens, North Jersey, and Long Island. Now every Sunday, well-dressed, well-educated blacks who had moved out of the neighborhood paraded back to their shrine, bedecked in furs and jewelry and effusing exotic fragrances. It would be easy to call them snobs, or elitists, or something worse. It wasn't so obvious that most of them had grown up doing manual, farm, or domestic labor, shining shoes, hauling freight, and cleaning hotel rooms and hospital wards. They had gone to school, taken whatever jobs were available, saved money slowly, bought homes, educated their children, and stayed firm in their belief that they could make it in America.

By contrast, the people living in the surrounding ghetto were defending what little pride they had left. Despite their destitution and isolation, they wanted to claim their own standing in the world. In a sense, they looked at the church people as enemies—those *other* people. The church continued to reach out to them, though—through any means we could.

The great choir at Abyssinian was under the gifted leadership of Dr. Leon E. Thompson, music education director of the New York Philharmonic. Dr. Jewel Taylor Thompson, one of the country's finest exponents of liturgical music, was our organist. The choir performed with both the New York Philharmonic and the Boston Pops, as well as making many other special appearances. With such a magnificent choir the congregation decided to make a huge effort to purchase a spectacular new organ. The base price was $250,000.

One afternoon the church secretary buzzed me in my study and announced that a group of young men wanted to see me. They didn't have an appointment, but I told her to send them on in. About six or seven of them shouldered their way through the door, dressed in faded dungarees, leather jackets, and T-shirts with violent slogans printed across the chest.

"Sit down, gentlemen," I said.

"We don't need to get so damn comfortable," their obvious leader said. "We're here on the people's business and all we want is some answers from you."

He proceeded to chastise me for buying an expensive organ for a Harlem church in a neighborhood where 250,000 hungry blacks lived.

"Let me propose a deal," I said. "Suppose we give up the organ and instead we give you the $250,000. You can give a dollar to each of those 250,000 people. McDonald's runs ninety-nine-cent specials; and each one could get one small hamburger, one small bag of French fries, and one small Coke. Four hours later, each person will be hungry again. We won't have an organ, the money will be gone, and you'll be back in here begging. Does that make sense?"

The tight-jawed youths just stared at me. I continued, "Now, the people in this church who saved the money to buy this organ started out poor, too, but they were lucky enough to have patient and caring teachers, and parents who loved them. Even so, nobody here inherited any money and they all worked hard all of their lives. They want to keep pace with the dreams of their parents and grandparents who started with even less, but who praised God in the beauty of holiness. This organ is their testimony of thanksgiving and praise. They didn't ask anyone to buy it for them.

"More importantly, these people are *organ listeners.* They sit here every Sunday and hear that great instrument copy every sound of nature—the rolling thunder, the wind whistling through the trees, and the thrush singing a love song. The music cleanses their spirits, drives out ugly thoughts, puts wings on their prayers and wafts them heavenward. Oh, yes! The organ *works* for them! They can go out of here and find a job, do it well, get paid, and eat on time. They are not hungry. They have an organ in their lives!"

I admit, when I have an audience, it's hard to stop me.

"Now, here you are, unemployed yourselves, representing hungry people. None of you is an organ listener. So I suggest that you get out of here; go and round up the 250,000 hungry constituents that you claim to represent. And bring them over here every Sunday morning and let us make organ listeners out of them. They won't be hungry long. They will change from within; and that change will be a prelude to change without. Eventually, personal hunger will not be their concern. They will be full enough themselves to start worrying about the hunger of children in Africa and Asia and Latin America, and the hunger of the elderly poor right here. My soul! Organ listeners have strange behavior."

The young men left my study, mumbling. They left behind an indelible portrait of a community in crisis. The time had come when one approach to the future had clashed head-on with the other. Those propelled by the faith that we can make it here were making it come to pass. And those for whom racist intransigence was too rigid and endemic, poverty too burdensome, political indifference too powerful, and resources too shallow were wallowing in the muck and mire. They had run out of answers and their circle of options was narrowing.

This had been a creeping trend, but by the 1980s, it had reached a crisis level. When substantial opportunities for minorities opened up in the 1960s and '70s, and when the job market simultaneously became more demanding of literacy skills and mathematics, blacks with education seized their new opportunities and began to put a new face on America. Although large numbers were finding their way into better education, better jobs, better health, better homes, and enhanced general well-being, it turned out to be largely an individual matter, and the massive bottom failed to rise.

This social paradox has wrought havoc in the black community. Some people are now so angry that they want to turn their

backs completely on the white world. While this is basically impractical, it *feels* like action and deludes many young people into
giving up on any concentrated, sustained hard effort. Just a few
young people in this frame of mind can wreck a classroom and
poison the atmosphere of a whole school.

When people have no functional relationship to the larger society, when their options are cut off, frustration builds, and the
time is then ripe for ideologues and false messiahs to emerge
with fantasies about race, culture, and destiny. Meanwhile, illegal hustling, crime, drugs, suicide, and homicide become the
only game in town. It seems easy to target achievement-oriented
blacks as the enemy. Any black person, it follows, who is successful in any field must have sold out.

It's far from clear what would happen to us today if we assumed a cultural insularity similar to small groups like the Hasidic Jews or the Amish, for example, which—on the surface, at
least—appear to maintain separate islands in a sea of Americana.
However, their communities abound with compromises and contradictions.

The Hasidim benefit daily from values generated by the larger,
multicultural political institutions: freedom of religion, freedom
of speech, and freedom of assembly. They enjoy the Protestant
legacy of separation of church and state, without which they
could never exist here. So, while they appear to live in an insu-
lar community, the whole society blesses them.

The Amish keep their children out of public schools, and arbitrarily deny them a chance for university education. Yet that
same community depends on ophthalmologists, veterinarians,
meteorologists, physicians, dentists, engineers, pilots, judges,
and the United States Army to service their needs. It's a gross
contradiction to reject formal education and then count on its
benefits being available every day.

The idea of 25 million blacks going it alone in America is fantasy. Moreover, what moral basis have we for trying to separate

from the society in which our forebears invested so much? We cannot undo the past four hundred years and divest ourselves of all the cultural accretions we have absorbed and invented.

We African Americans do have a distinct culture of our own, comprising African residuals, strategies for surviving slavery and segregation, plus an abiding determination to live out the promise of the Declaration of Independence. Why would anyone want to erase a culture that has been so hard-won and for which such enormous sacrifices have been made? It is the honest outcome of our struggles.

To replace it, we would have to expend our meager resources to construct a new infrastructure in a separate place, new economy, and a new civics of our own. Even if we did, what guarantee do we have that we would thus escape racism?

This schism in the black community is a crisis of the first order. The Afrocentric movement causes young blacks to behave tentatively and thus lose important ground. So much attention is paid to the cosmetic aspects of living—dress, hairstyles, music, diet, art, social gestures—that the main requirements for survival—economic independence, career preparation, sound health, stable families—are often left in fragments.

I find myself searching for a metaphor exact enough to embrace all of our African roots, and at the same time accept that we are fully involved in this nation's life and destiny.

I have a Native American friend who similarly grieves over the tentative outcome of his people. They were driven from their land and forced into the mountains and deserts where no one else could survive. Without a long-term strategy, they have somehow managed to scrape by on a minimal economy and government grants. It's a haunting, dehumanizing set of facts to pass on to one's grandchildren, and the future does not promise change. What choices might they have made that would have changed the outcome? What choices do they now have?

Whatever strategy they devise to participate in America's future must also honor their past. Is it possible?

THE CRISIS IS UPON US. ON THE NIGHT OF AUGUST 30, 1994, a young black bandit broke into the home of Rosa Parks on Detroit's west side, cuffed her around, and threatened to kill her if she did not give him all of her money. He left the 80-year-old civil rights heroine badly bruised and semiconscious. He had brought to that moment the whole package of poor rearing, poor education, and poor jobs. Added to that impoverishment was a poor self-image and an inadequate response to his plight. He is part of the crisis.

The crisis comes with hopelessness. The crisis grows as frustrated blacks fall behind in school and become comfortable with failure and nihilism. Their violence and adversarial posturing are childish responses to their confusion.

Next, the crisis breeds half truths, spurious anthropology, historical hearsay, and propaganda. Finally, the crisis spirals ever upward as racists grab each opportunity to amplify all the bad news.

The news is loaded with the trial of O.J. Simpson and the collapse of leadership in the NAACP. Right-wing talk show hosts and specialists in cocktail party repartee chew on these juicy items that confirm their private hopes and expectations of black failure. The crisis is upon us.

Here is a story of the crisis. On September 7, 1994, a small-framed black child lay in a wooden casket in a black church in Chicago. His schoolfriends passed by in numb silence, looking on his corpse with awe and fear. His grandmother cried hysterically.

Little Robert "Yummy" Sandifer seemed to be doomed from the outset. His father was in prison, and his mother, the third of

171

ten children from four different fathers, was a drug addict. She was fifteen when she had her first child. Now, at age twenty-nine, she had five children besides Yummy. And forty-one arrests, mostly for prostitution.

Yummy had been arrested over and over as a child offender and had already spent time in detention centers. He cursed out adults, beat up kids bigger than he, extorted money from frightened neighbors, broke into schools to steal money, and stole cars. He died at age eleven, having already been charged with twenty-three felonies and five misdemeanors. Two weeks before his death, during a gang fight, he fired a 9 mm semiautomatic into a crowd of kids playing football and killed a fourteen-year-old girl.

The last three days of his life Yummy spent running from the police while his grandmother searched for him, vainly hoping to find him alive. He ended up at a neighbor's house, asking her to pray with him and to call his grandmother. A few hours later a member of his own gang shot him twice in the back of the head to keep him from talking to the police.

In every black community today this is what it means to be young. This boy was headed for the sixth grade; he should have been getting into space discoveries, world geography, reading good books, and playing basketball. He should have been participating in church projects to help the elderly and the blind, or rehearsing for a school play. Instead, his young life was over. He had sworn his loyalty to others who had no traction, no cleats to move them forward toward sane answers about life. He and his peers were adding to the problems of their families, the society, and the whole human enterprise.

Nothing had been done to help Yummy's mother. Nothing had been done to redirect the lives of her children. From all we can tell, all of her nine siblings and her six children are still living somewhere in the margins of our society.

We must candidly face the raw data of Yummy's brief life. We have allowed some simple values to slip from us, and we seem to accept the loss without regret. A tenet of the faith that sustained us through the bitter days of the post-Reconstruction, the Great Depression, and the humiliation of racial segregation was that oppression—no matter how severe—could never destroy our character and self-respect. Now, by constantly emphasizing the details of our past, we seem to have reversed ourselves.

Curiously, the more we focus on the horrors of slavery and the more we celebrate the significance of our African heritage, the more ground we seem to lose. The bolder we are in declaring our wish to be self-reliant, the weaker the fabric of our neighborhoods becomes. Something that ought to be going forward is instead moving in reverse. And something that ought to be reversed is gaining momentum.

One of the quietest secrets in the black community is that we expected more positive results from the infusion of black studies in our colleges and black curriculum in our schools. All the classroom walls, the bulletin boards in the offices of principals, guidance counselors, and coaches are covered with pictures of Malcolm and Mandela, DuBois and Frederick Douglass. We began this thirty years ago and we thought that it would inspire our youth to claim their dignity. But curiously, this cultural elixir has left us still waiting for results. Instead, we have many more black males in jail, many more teenage mothers, and our schools are more like detention centers.

I believe that we expected too much from consciousness elevation. Africa may be too far away in time and distance for a teenager in East Orange, New Jersey, to grasp. The excitement of the street is too close. Moreover, it may be too abstract to ask a child to live in two worlds, when everything he sees and hears, and the values that propel the society, convincingly tell him that the world he sees is the world in which he must live.

We don't have long to debate this because the Yummys are all around us. It would be wonderful if we could continue to educate our youth about the great omissions of black Americans in social studies. It would be a real contribution to acquaint them with African and African-American heroes and heroines, and simultaneously keep them in step with a knowledge of world history, Western history, and all of the disciplines that will prepare them for success right here.

But somehow, all of the details of Yummy's life need to be reversed. We must ask ourselves what went wrong on the first day of his brief visit on planet Earth. If we cannot unravel these tangled cords and reweave a new pattern for children like Yummy, we should close down all of our institutions, give away the endowments, and admit that all of our past strivings were in vain.

Yummy did not ask to be born. Surely he did not wish to be born into the safekeeping of a teenage mother with a drug habit. But this is a fact for thousands of new lives, even as we wring our hands and spout cheap, escapist rhetoric about bigger jails, the death penalty, and no parole ever for anyone.

USING DATA FROM FEDERAL GOVERNMENT SOURCES, Andrew Hacker gave us a frightening summary of the current crisis in *Two Nations, Black and White, Separate, Hostile and Unequal.* I did not want to believe that we were dragging such awful data behind us, but his figures are impossible to ignore.

In 1930, blacks were 22.4 percent of the prison population; in 1986, they were 45.3 percent. In 1990, blacks committed 53.9 percent of the murders in America, 63.9 percent of the robberies, and 24.3 percent of the rapes. One out of every five black men will be incarcerated for a part of his life! Considering that for most inmates, jail is really a crime school, these are frightening statistics indeed.

Parallel to the increase in crime, another problem grows: in 1950, 16.8 percent of black births were out of wedlock, and

17.2 percent of black households were headed by women. In 1990, both of those figures had more than tripled.

Many of these young mothers will turn out to be strong, solid winners and their children will do well. Most, however, will survive feebly on public assistance, suffer abuse by aimless, part-time lovers, escape into alcohol and drugs, endure more pregnancies, and eventually lose their grip on life entirely. Their children will reach seniority by chance, loaded with trouble. Meanwhile, the class stratification among blacks widens and resentment of other blacks toward these young mothers and their children grows.

Beneath these troubled waters are powerful, hidden undertows. Whoever reads Hacker's data on crime and irresponsible parenting should also read the statistics on jobs and education. Placed side by side, the data have a clear causal relationship.

The most stubborn barrier to progress is the insistence that negative behavior stems from race, rather than from poverty and isolation. It is a scandal in scholarship constantly to report statistics by race alone. If we eliminate race from crime statistics, and measure young criminals in the light of their reading levels, family income, education of parents, neighborhood incomes, fathers in the home, and church participation, a different picture of criminal behavior emerges. Blacks who read well, whose parents are present and employed, and who attend church regularly are not in jail. And whites who read poorly, who are unparented, who grew up poor and did not attend church are in jail. Factors that lead to crime are so readily found in ghetto communities that race is mistaken as the key. Race alone has nothing to do with crime data.

The papers are covered each day with more horror stories about street crime and drug-related offenses. When blacks are involved, race is always added as an implicit causative factor. Never mind that whites have been in the news for killing infants and women, shooting a dozen students from a Texas campus tower, killing thirty boys in Wisconsin, shooting up post offices and restaurants, and killing Brinks truck guards and putting a wife in a wood-shredding machine. These crimes are not identified by "race."

There is a crime problem, and it does involve a disproportionate number of young blacks. All sorts of political opportunists who have no programs, no vision, and no imagination are thumping and screaming about crime and aid to dependent children. This is all it takes to stir up the fears of prejudiced people, cut off debate—and, unfortunately, win elections. What will the nation do after a "sweeping" election—for which only one third of eligible voters turned out—has brought to power a conglomerate of zealots who vote against gun control, but support capital punishment, reduce benefits for welfare mothers, and support vouchers for private school tuition?

Where is a vision of schools that will educate *all* of our children, a program for rebuilding our dilapidated cities, a plan for retraining our recidivists and creating viable jobs for them, and a program for health care delivery to all of our people?

It is always difficult to embrace two apparently dichotomous aspects of one issue and see the hard truth in both. Blacks have to assume responsibility for mending and restoring our own families and institutions. No one else can do this for us. At the same time, the federal government has responsibility for monitoring justice and due process, "securing the blessings of liberty" and "forming a more perfect union." The federal government is the only agent that can take initiatives to correct past discrimination, even to correct its evil consequences where possible, and remove barriers to equal opportunity. This has nothing to do with "quotas" or promoting blacks who cannot perform over whites. It has to do with giving blacks equal opportunity to earn every social benefit, even to the extent of undoing previous, gross offenses. Some call this reverse discrimination; it is simply redressing previous discrimination.

There is an answer to the crisis. Every African-American organization in the country has some program on its agenda to try to reverse the mounting data on crime, drugs, and teenage parenting. It is possible to begin to hear more about preparing young people for success, and less about the futility of trying.

From time to time I meet with a group of early parolees from drug convictions in a downtown Methodist church in a New Jersey city. They went to jail for stealing, fraud, and fencing stolen property, mostly to get drug money. They had followed the procession of their peers into despair. They are good-looking, healthy, and intelligent young men and women, but nihilism, the belief in nothing, overtook them and dragged them under.

I tell them some of my own experiences and help them revisit their own lives and review their prospects. They sit straight up and give a hard listen. It is unreal to them that any black person could have a positive outlook on life. I always try to bring something to them that they may not get a chance to hear otherwise. I try to show them how pride and self-respect derive from the spiritual core within. I talk about the need for a strong religious faith, and a worldview that holds things together. Their own lives are vacant at the center, but they always listen.

They often ask me how I found the strength to work my way through college and graduate school, and I tell them that I had plenty of strength left over. My power never ran low. If you believe that there is a purpose and a power available to each of us, you have an inexhaustible source of evergreen inspiration.

Although we must be honest in stating the facts of the crisis, if we get lost in the "paralysis of analysis" we cannot move toward change—we've lost our cleats.

Last September, I gave an address to a beautiful audience of students at predominantly black Delaware State University at Dover. I talked to them about how academic success could change the future for both individuals and society. I told them that we had the faith and the capacity to change our situation, and change America along with us. Afterward, four young black female students came running up to me. They were wearing floppy clothes and jeweled braids and they bubbled over with enthusiasm.

"Dr. Proctor, we were just talking about you," one girl said. "Your speech helped us so much. All the kids are saying that you changed our minds on a lot of things. This year will be different for us because of what you said."

I asked, "Where are you all from?"

They were from Harlem, Passaic, East Orange, and Baltimore—four of the nation's crisis pivot points. My soul! They are on their way in spite of it. That is indeed the substance of things hoped for.

CHAPTER NINE

Racism: Black and White

WHEN I WAS A YOUNG PASTOR IN RHODE ISLAND, A prosperous mortician took me to Boston to see the Brooklyn Dodgers play against the Braves. We sat in the grandstands, the only blacks in sight—except for one. Every time Jackie Robinson came to bat, epithets sailed all around us. Thunders of "nigger," "darkie," "blackie," and worse rolled around the stadium. It was a subrational tribal cry, like something primeval being vented. We kept our cool and Jackie Robinson kept his. I don't know what it cost him to do so, but I have a pretty good idea.

When I was a boy, my brothers, sister, and I were always being reminded that "colored" people had an extra burden to bear. At home, at school, in church, at our little storefront YMCA, and in Boy Scout meetings, it was drummed into us that we had to put our best foot forward at all times to prove we were not inferior. Later, in college, we got the same constant reminders.

Some black youngsters felt a special responsibility always to be clean, polite, and respectfully quiet. As if to prove our humanity, we tried to do everything superbly well. We always had jobs and succeeded in school. If we kept chipping away at the rumor of inferiority, maybe we could push some obstacles aside.

But not all our friends and neighbors were convinced of this. They joked about us being "proper niggers." They would go downtown looking "bad." They didn't care who heard their profanity and boisterous conversations. They embarrassed us, because we wanted to be seen as having pride. It was painful to see African Americans act out what whites said about us. To us, racism was at its most destructive when it earned converts among African Americans themselves.

During the bleak days of the Depression, we kids did anything to make some change for the little extras—a movie, bakery treats, milkshakes—that our parents simply could not afford. Almost always I worked for people who thought I was inferior and expected subservience from me. Even then I could recognize the difference between the person I was at home and the person I was expected to be on these odd jobs.

When I was about twelve years old, I worked after school in a neighborhood grocery store for a man named Cohen. His son also did odd jobs in the store, but when a chicken had to be killed and plucked, that was always my job. When someone dropped a carton of eggs on the floor, I cleaned up the mess. If someone wanted fish gutted and scaled, that was my assignment. And, of course, scrubbing the floor and cleaning the toilet were late-night, closing-time chores for me. I did it all with a double consciousness. Somehow, I had to do those jobs and at the same time retain my self-respect. I tried to remember that the job didn't define who I was. I separated myself from Mr. Cohen's definition of me, and chose instead my grandma's definition of me. She had convinced me that I was God's child and inherently equal to everyone else. I can still remember the schizoid feelings of those hard days.

On school vacation days my brother and I would sometimes go to the corner of Princess Anne Road and Church Street and join up with the dozens of black women and men waiting to go out and work on the farms. It was a fun ride on a big truck. Not every foreman would allow kids to get on the truck, but many of the women carried their children with them and we simply mixed in and got on board.

In the fields we played as much as we worked. We picked just enough string beans, strawberries, tomatoes, cucumbers, or peppers to exchange for coupons to carry to the owner's commissary wagon to buy a huge bottle of RC Cola and a French apple pie for lunch and still have a dollar left over for spending money.

On these days we glimpsed life lived at the survival level, where human dignity and pride were stifled by poverty and ignorance. The farmhands lived each day from hand to mouth, following orders from poor, uneducated white foremen. They ate minced meat sandwiches and greens from a pickle jar, and the women had to go behind bushes and trees to relieve themselves. Often three generations would be working in the fields together.

My brother and I would repeat the speech patterns of the "field dialect." To a stranger it might seem that these people, mostly women, were barely human. It was not clear to us why their language was so poor and their thoughts so dull and child-like. Only much later did we realize that the only difference between them and our family and neighbors was that someone, or some thing, had intervened in our lives and opened up the future.

Without such intervention, however, it is easy to see how some African Americans never got far from slavery. For generations, abject poverty and abuse were ground into their consciousness. Feelings of inferiority set limits on their aspirations and controlled their expectations.

In this regard things have not changed very much. Recently, in one of my classes at Duke University, where I also teach, a white student asked me if it bothered me to be a "token" black on the faculty. His tone was neither hostile nor offensive. Prejudice is deep and lingers long, even among people who deny its presence.

I asked him why he assumed that my appointment had to be token. I had earned a doctoral degree from a leading graduate theological center, and had retired from a chair in a large public university with an emeritus title. I had been awarded a total of forty-six honorary degrees. Did he believe that Duke University was insincere, or that I was poorly prepared? Were *all* black appointees "tokens"? Could any blacks ever succeed legitimately?

He looked at me blankly, then asked if I felt I was being "used." He simply could not believe that it was normal for a black person to succeed. There had to be a trick involved somewhere. Many young blacks are prejudiced in the same way. If a black person advances, they believe, it must be a fluke. Because of this doubt, they anticipate—and plan—failure. When young people put achievement out of reach for themselves and pretend to prefer ignorance, noise, drugs, and sex for entertainment, they are committing a kind of suicide. Or, in the case of a generation of young people, genocide.

IN THE 1960S AND 1970S, DURING THE PEAK OF THE CIVIL rights movement, newspapers often reported that some new evidence had been discovered proving the genetic liability of African Americans. This information was always presented statistically, even though no instruments exist that can measure how self-concept, environment, and cultural isolation affect learning;

or how the historical flow, tainted by generations of legal denial of education, reflects on intelligence tests.

Recently we have been harassed by another racist theory put forth by Charles Murray in *The Bell Curve,* in which the author uses the ten to fifteen points that African Americans score lower than whites on intelligence quotient tests to demonstrate our immutable intellectual inferiority and the futility of making any effort to erase these disparities. It is incredible that any legitimate scholar could be so eager to leap to hateful conclusions from partial and inconclusive data. Who can measure the extent to which oppression affects cognitive ability? Who knows the extent to which racism affects one's self-concept and, thus, performance?

Charles Murray has spent endless hours in television and newspaper interviews saying that he barely mentions race in his "data," but he knows full well that dressing up racism in scientific clothing guarantees a best-seller.

It is frightening to observe how one writer can generate the broad interest that Murray has. Charles Lane uncovered a chain of interacting researchers, writers, and "scholars" who compose a kind of vanguard of opinion-molders in the area of race and intelligence. He identified a journal called *The Mankind Quarterly* as one hub of their activities. According to Lane, this publication's editorial board includes a number of scientists who support racist views. In the bibliography of *The Bell Curve,* five articles are listed from the *Quarterly.* Seventeen authorities cited in Murray's book have been contributors to the journal. Ten are former editors. The founder of the *Quarterly* was Henry E. Garrett of Columbia University, who provided expert testimony for the Topeka Board of Education in the 1954 *Brown v. Board of Education* case. Lane further revealed that *The Bell Curve* cites thirteen scholars who have received over $4 million in grants from the Pioneer Fund in the past twenty years. The Pioneer Fund also funds Pearson's Institute for the Study of Man, which publishes *The Mankind Quarterly.* (The Pioneer Fund was established in

1937 with the money of Wickliffe Draper, who advocated the repatriation of blacks to Africa.)

Thus, instead of relying on expert, impartial data as claimed, The Bell Curve was really a megaphone for a cacophony of racist propaganda that had circulated that year. This well-financed work that attracted so much attention is dripping with stains of racist thought and is not accountable to the world of real scholarship.

In the wake of Murray's book comes *The Tragedy of American Compassion*, written by a born-again Christian named Olasky. Olasky tells us that after being influenced by Watergate alumnus-turned-preacher Charles Colson, he began to study alternatives to "liberal" programs.

Olasky bemoans the fact that homeless people who show up at shelters for food and medicine are not given Bibles to bring them to Christ, and are not asked to clean up vacant lots in exchange for their food. He imagines that passing out Bibles and rakes to homeless people, many of whom are addicted to drugs and alcohol, can solve serious social problems resulting from generations of systemic poverty, poor education, and pervasive racism. It's amazing that some people call this Christian.

His strangely titled book, which was funded by the Heritage Foundation, was originally published by a small press, but later taken up by a larger publisher when Newt Gingrich used it to validate his "contract" to cut taxes and sharply reduce benefits programs. And it's no coincidence that the introduction to Olasky's book was written by Charles Murray! Clearly, a well-funded assault has been launched to rewrite history, ignoring the ugly causes that have delivered us to this moment.

Even top scientists, trained to be coldly impartial, have been known to corrupt their own findings, simply to get eye-catching results. Back in 1977, President Jimmy Carter established the Recombinant DNA Panel at the National Institutes of Health, which

was responsible for assessing grant applications for genetic research. Microbiology and DNA research were still relatively new
at this time. I was among six "humanists" appointed by the president to work with the panel.

One panelist was a Nobel prize winner affiliated with one of
our finest and most highly respected medical research universities. During every meeting he let us know in no uncertain terms
that he objected to our presence. He grunted, giggled, and
walked around with his head tilted back and his eyes fixed on
the ceiling. For an intellectual of his standing his behavior was
embarrassing.

It was no surprise to read later in *The Washington Post*, March
21, 1991, that he was involved in a prolonged investigation, having asked that a scientific paper bearing his name be retracted
because of evidence that it contained fraudulent data.

Almost a year later, on February 21, 1992, *The New York Times*
reported that he had "stubbornly dismissed repeated accusations that his collaborator had fabricated data" for the article
they co-authored. He suffered extensive criticism from his peers,
and colleagues threatened to resign under his leadership. Although he was not implicated in the fraud, eventually he resigned one of the most prestigious scientific posts in the country.

Such a revelation alerts us to the awesome possibility that er-
rors, whether intended or not, in reporting scientific data can
spin off pure propaganda passing for truth. And critical social
theories may flow from such propaganda.

Whatever *anyone* wants to prove about genetic traits and
African Americans would require a bona fide, pure sample. And
in America, as in the rest of the world, the mixtures are compounded many times over. Biologically speaking, most scientists
agree there is no such thing as "race." For a frame of reference,
they arbitrarily divide the human species into three categories
according to hair texture, eye shape, and skin color. The cate-

gories refer more to geographic origin than biological origin, hence the current usage of Asian, Latino, African American to designate geographic derivations.

We are all made up of millions and millions of individual characteristics, of which skin color is only one, and there there are often more similarities between individuals of different "races" than between individuals of the same "race." Even geographic origin is virtually impossible to determine. After 250 million years of *Homo sapiens* migration, and centuries of ocean-going commerce, wars, religious pilgrimages, colonization, enslavement, and resettlements, it is impossible to isolate a particular gene pool. The varieties of people found all over the globe are evidence of a human blending that defies discrete racial or geographic labels.

In 1953, I remember meeting a Negroid Palestinian soldier who was a Moslem. His duty assignment was to guard the Church of the Nativity in Bethlehem. The soldier told me that he was descended from African Moslems who fled from the Crusaders in East Africa in the thirteenth century. He spoke fluent German, which he had learned at a Lutheran mission school. His is a typical story of *Homo sapiens* on planet Earth.

In 1975, my son Sammy and I visited New Zealand. We stopped first at the Fiji Islands which, we were surprised to discover, are populated by Negroid people. The Fijians found it hilarious when I told them they couldn't possibly be from Fiji, but must have been born in Bedford-Stuyvesant in Brooklyn.

On another leg of our interminable flight to Auckland, we traveled with a large group of distinguished-looking gentlemen who had distinctly African features. It turned out they were actually from New Guinea—at least five thousand miles from the coast of East Africa. Then we visited Melbourne, where we saw dark-skinned people with light grey-green eyes and blond hair!

We see similar mixes all over the United States. On a recent visit to Shenandoah University I was met in the Charlottesville airport by a gentle white male student. On the drive to campus he told me he was a piano student from Blakesly, Virginia. Now, my grandfather had a cousin Bessie from Blakesly. His mother and cousin Bessie's mother were twins. The sisters never spoke about their paternity, but it was said they were the offspring of a black slave woman and a white father.

I asked the student who had started him on the piano. He said his first teacher was a lady everyone called Miss Bessie. When I told him that I was a third cousin to her, he looked at me in shock. "Was she black?" he asked.

Well, there is the question. Was she?

Is there any such thing as a person who is purely black? Or purely anything else? And what purpose does it serve to try to figure it out?

Those who are eager to see every individual fulfill his or her highest potential don't waste time trying to twist spurious anthropology or bogus evidence to prove pseudoscientific prevarications about race—pro or con.

By contrast, people who have a keen interest in race theories generally have some ulterior motive driving them. They propagate theories about a particular group in order to put that group to some advantage or disadvantage. For example, those working hard to prove the genetic inferiority of African Americans may wish to preserve our status and remove us from competition; they may want to exploit us economically; or maybe they simply want to stay in office by appealing to people's worst instincts. Or all three. Today, these people often use code words—like "disadvantaged," or "inner city," or "marginalized," or "underclass," or "high risk," or "poor and underserved"—that allow them to converse freely and appear fair-minded. Every one of those terms means "black." And there seems no end to it.

Some people are loudly claiming that the lower Scholastic Aptitude Test scores of black college candidates prove that they are less intelligent and unable to perform at the college level. Thousands of African-American students are currently enrolled at Harvard, Duke, Princeton, UCLA, Stanford, Rutgers, Ohio State, and other major universities. Every black college is brim-full, and community colleges dotted around the country have large black enrollments. If blacks are intellectually inferior, who are these students? Are they qualified to be on college campuses?

A close look at the college admission tests reveals these informative data: black youngsters from families earning $10,000 to $20,000 a year scored 704 on the SAT, while those whose family incomes exceeded $70,000 scored 854. Whites from families of the same incomes scored 879 and 996 respectively; Asians scored 855 and 1066. (It's worthwhile noting that over half of the Asian youth had parents who were *college educated*.)

The fact is that the SAT scores show that blacks—like whites, Asians, and Hispanics—demonstrate greater success and achieve higher scores as their family incomes rise, and at about the same pace. Even though blacks begin at lower scores, they advance at the same rate as others as their incomes increase. Better incomes reflect opportunity, discipline, intelligence, seriousness, and moral discernment. All of these factors lead to higher school achievement.

Yet it is also true that even though scores go up as income increases, black candidates still lag 150 to 200 points behind on the SATs. Even well-educated, relatively unbiased academics have trouble understanding why SAT questions are fundamentally unfair to blacks. If you compare blacks with whites of similar incomes and similar social isolation, the mystery of the scores disappears. People compelled to live in a separate community, barred from the main flow of the dominant culture, have a total exposure different from that reflected in the test. Cultural isolation has the same effect on everyone. Poor African Americans have the same problem with the SATs that Kentucky and Tennessee mountaineers would have if they took the tests. (Appalachian whites with poor educations don't usually take the

SATs, however. Blacks, by contrast, are so preoccupied with the quest for liberation that many who are poor take the SATs even though they have not received adequate preparation in high school.) The evidence is overwhelming that blacks are isolated from the larger society. Andrew Hacker's data showed that in 1992 *two of every three black children, from North to South, East to West, still attended racially segregated schools.* There is even more segregation in large urban centers of the North than in the South. In fact, when it comes to segregating children by color, only four of the southern states—Mississippi, Alabama, Texas, and Louisiana—are worse than the large northern urban centers. *Forty years* after the 1954 decision! The SAT scores clearly reveal this isolation.

THE RACE ISSUE HAS DEEP REPERCUSSIONS AMONG African Americans. Some grow to hate their identity in such an obsessive way that it paralyzes constructive responses to the ordinary challenges of life. Some go to work every day, angry that they have to negotiate for space to feel comfortable. They bob and weave to fend off remarks that sound racial, whether they are or not. They must prove that they can think in the abstract, that they tell the truth, and that they don't steal. They must guard against any gesture or behavior that inadvertently might echo the stereotype. They must be detached, avoiding those who avoid them, and sometimes even avoiding those who want to impose their "love" on them in order to prove that they are not racist. It is exhausting to be so self-conscious all day.

An African American needs a healthy ego to shadowbox all day in a world not designed for her or his occupancy. Some, especially those without strong family supports, dodge the challenge and take refuge in a fortress of alternative behaviors.

That's one scenario. There are other ways in which we internalize racism. In college, I had a brilliant African-American professor of French who spent most of our class time telling jokes about uneducated blacks. Any success we had he took to be accidental—except his own. I know several people like him who cannot accept their identity as African Americans. Their days are one long, tedious debate with everyone about nothing. They cannot accept a white person as a friend, or an African American as a peer. They are aliens everywhere.

More commonly, endemic racism causes many educated African Americans to create an upper caste of their own. They attend certain churches, belong to certain organizations, live in certain parts of town, and engage in a lifestyle that manifests a caste at the top.

You would think that after hundreds of years of trying to survive aggressive and suppressive racism, blacks would be the last people in the world to be racist themselves. In fact, some of us have proved to be as susceptible to the virus of class and color discrimination as anyone else.

No one likes poverty, falling plaster, telephones cut off, bathing in cold water, sharing a bed with two others and a bathroom with six others. But those who succeed in improving their circumstances have a tendency to turn their backs on those who cannot. This response is by no means a racial or cultural characteristic, but among African Americans it does have some unique antecedents.

For example, until very recently, blacks tended to choose fair-skinned leaders with white features, a practice which stemmed from a long history of giving special advantages to the "black" offspring of the slave masters. Even when the father was unknown, fair-skinned African Americans received special rank and status because both whites and blacks believed in the myth of white supremacy. As a result, these were among the first to receive college educations and other benefits. They formed a kind of privileged, closed circle, and favors began to aggregate around them.

This tendency became entrenched in the late nineteenth and early twentieth century. Black college students began to organize Greek letter societies in blind imitation of white undergraduates. Next, we were having exclusive debutante balls and cotillions. Certain lodges were known to favor light-complexioned members, and certain churches called only light-complexioned pastors. Some church sanctuaries had fair-skinned members seated on one side and those who were darker sat on the other.

This layering of color within the black community continued for several decades. When I was president of Virginia Union University and North Carolina A & T State University between 1955 and 1964, most black college presidents were still fair-skinned. During the civil rights movement we began to put this particular form of self-discrimination behind us.

Fortunately, most privileged blacks today involve themselves in some way in the social and economic redemption of their people. Arguably, their social distance from other African Americans, as well as their ardent participation in the culture of materialism, often causes them to line up on the side of the status quo. They are likely to resist any fundamental changes that might curtail their own comfort level. In other words, they would like to cure suffering to their people, without any pain to themselves. This culpability is as pervasive among successful African Americans as it is among whites.

We cannot start the human race all over again, with everyone at the same scratch line. Nor does everyone have the same emotional makeup or internal fortitude to succeed despite enormous deficits. Some are able to suffer and endure longer than others. Some can stand up to insults longer than others. Some are more aware and perceptive than others. Some lie awake, gazing at the night sky and see nothing but the darkness, while others watching the same sky see the stars. If racial categories never existed, some humans would fail and some succeed.

But African American have to recognize that we all have common antecedents lying back in the foggy past, admit that we have arrived at widely different places on the road—and find a way to go on from here together.

ALTHOUGH THE BLACK COMMUNITY IS CLEARLY NOT monolithic, there is a huge tendency around the country to relegate the tastes and behavior of some to the tastes and behavior of all. For example, our religion is often stereotyped on the most elemental and unsophisticated level. That is racism, and even blacks succumb to the fallacy.

Along with religious expression, the accumulation of such art forms as music, dance, and storytelling have been packaged up along with the poverty and lack of education and sold as "black culture." "Black culture" became the stereotype for all African Americans, and what began as a response to oppression became known as a racial characteristic.

It is wrong to present vulgar rap songs and filthy jokes on "black" shows and networks, implying that they universally represent black culture. They call themselves "artists of protest." In my opinion they add to our burden by reinforcing negative stereotypes that are already almost impossible to destroy.

Many young blacks believe these comedians and rappers are expressing "how it is." Is this what we want to pass on to coming generations? Is this the best we can do to express anger, frustration, sorrow, jubilance, and love? Calling this, or any other single form of music, "black culture" is racist, regardless of who's saying it.

Racial theories are not always used *against* a particular group; sometimes the victims of discrimination use questionable theories to prove that their race is unique and in some way superior. This kind of racism is defensive and protective, rather than ag-

gressive and oppressive. For example, Professor Leonard Jeffries of City College in New York has tried to enhance the image
of African Americans by arguing that we are "sun people," as opposed to "ice people." To him, the extra melanin in our skin signals genetic advantages.

I admit that it's a relief to hear someone say something positive for a change. But we need to resist the appeal. Because similar anthropology and genetics have so often been used against
us, I think most African Americans are uncomfortable with his
arguments. Most of us are not willing to have untested, unproven
race theories submitted in defense of our cause, even when put
forth by an African-American academic.

Minister Louis Farrakhan has a notion that we will be better
off if we stop trying to find equality and concord among whites,
and instead seek a locus of our own, here or abroad, and do our
own nation building. He is fantastically popular and influential,
especially among young African Americans. His physical presence, and the power of his oratory, create a hypnotic surrender
to his views. More than fifty years ago, Marcus Garvey advocated
a return to the homeland of Africa, but Minister Farrakhan
would now accept a designated space for a new nation here on
the North American continent.

Those agreeing with a separatist position believe that racism
is so endemic in America that nothing will alter the black condition. Some independent African and Caribbean states might
be a haven for African Americans who wanted to join them and
strengthen them. And there are many all-black nations available
to any black who prefers to leave.

Of course, we all need to know about our ancestral home and
its history. But creating a diaspora mentality is another matter.
Before setting off on this course, we would need much more evidence that starting a new nation, or joining an existing all-black
nation, would deliver the relief and liberation we crave. It's late

to be aiming at going it alone, especially when all of the world is seeking alliances and partnerships. I believe that escaping into an all-black mythological kingdom stalls progress.

On the extreme flip side of Dr. Jeffries and Minister Farrakhan are Dr. Thomas Sowell of the Heritage Foundation and Justice Clarence Thomas, blacks who ingratiate themselves among white conservatives by claiming that we retard our own progress by failing to take advantage of opportunities.

All of these extreme positions are in heated currency now. And the majority of blacks reject them. We take pride in participating in America, with all her faults and failures. Ultimately, most African Americans have a heavy investment here and do not plan to release this rich and powerful nation from its obligation to us. We have a mortgage on New Columbia. We have every hope and expectation of being a part of a new America in a new world.

TODAY OUR HARD-WON VICTORIES ARE BEING THREATENED by amorphous racism on the part of whites, and cynicism and a feeling of futility on the part of many blacks. But our faith is not vulnerable to vapid challenges. It resists with vigor the tide of hate rhetoric, black and white, that inflames campuses and further polarizes society.

It has not been easy for us to reject rejection. In the wake of popular movements that offer more problems than answers, we all need our faith to be edified. There can be no peace without justice, but we must pursue both without adding to the problem by engaging in inflammatory rhetoric that exacerbates an already polarized situation.

My own values require me to seek change by using Christian strategies. Jesus asked us to risk loving our enemies. Jesus taught us that it is never enough to reciprocate on a tit-for-tat basis. He said:

> If you love those who love you, what reward will you
> get? . . . And if you greet only your brothers, what are
> you doing more than others?
>
> Matthew 5:46–47 (New International Version)

Jesus taught us to seek the good in others, and this means loving those who may not want our love, and even loving those who do not seem to deserve to be loved. This is tough stuff, but it is minimum Christianity.

It is tedious to have to watch for a sign of acceptance every time you meet someone. After a lifetime of unpleasant surprises, many of us wait until we receive a clear signal that the other person is not racist. My rehearsal for such encounters came from experiences gained in those odd jobs of my youth. Some were positive and some negative, and most mixed in both elements, meaning that even in the worst situation some bright light beamed. I eventually learned to enjoy anticipating people. I used my imagination and tried to understand where they were coming from. As a result, I never felt robbed taking the initiative to foster a new relationship.

By the time I reached Crozer Seminary at the age of twenty-one, I could give some slack to just about anyone in any encounter. On my first day there many students made it their business to introduce themselves and welcome me. Their courtesy cushioned me for the others who were too bound by custom to speak to me. These students refused to sit by me in the small dining room, which accommodated only ninety boarders. After a while, rushing into that small space three times a day, trying *not* to sit by the one black student got to be complicated. After ten days or so, they started sitting next to me in dining hall and chapel. Whenever one of them was in range, I tried out bits of conversation.

After six weeks it seemed that we were all going to make it together just fine. Occasionally, we talked openly about race in class, but in our day-by-day relations we put it aside. Some might call this accommodation or social adjustment, but to me it was a plain victory.

I wish every black person and every white person could have such an experience. Such experiences taught me to take the initiative in meeting people. No matter what the response, I am always—literally always—prepared to try to make any new communication a positive one.

It's true that blacks must be alert to injustice and to racial discrimination. We must be ready to use the courts, the ballot, and the boycott to complete the campaign for justice. But we need to employ a greater strategy to overcome individual prejudices. This is a moral struggle that will not yield to marches and court decisions. It requires education and persuasion; it requires exposure of blacks to whites, and whites to blacks, in close and steady relations—at work, as neighbors, as club or church members, as doctors and patients, merchants and customers, teachers and students, and students and students. It requires talking about subjects that are neutral—healing a disease, controlling a flood, getting a truck to run, painting a house, winning a baseball game, or training a racehorse—subjects without racial content. Over time, the total package of human characteristics comes into focus.

No matter how intransigent the color caste system seems, I believe that it has improved. I have seen the change over my own lifetime, although admittedly much of the positive changes in modern race relations have affected only educated and upwardly mobile blacks. In the South, however, something is changing at a level that bears more authenticity and reality. Here I have found African-American and white mechanics joking in a car dealership, and workers gossiping and teasing with perfect ease in the banks, post offices, clothing stores, utility offices, courthouses, and restaurants. This kind of change is crucial, because forward movement so often gets stalled and frustrated at the local level. If the temperature of tolerance is right, change in housing, jobs, police behavior, and education may follow.

If it were not for the efforts of institutions and political leaders to keep racism alive, and exploit it for their own benefit, I believe it could die a natural death. On a recent Sunday in October the Washington Redskins were playing the Philadelphia Eagles. The Eagles won by a narrow margin. After the game, two players slowly walked toward the clubhouse, their helmets swinging at their sides and their arms draped across each other's shoulders. They were Heath Shuler, the defeated white rookie quarterback, and Charlie Garner, the game-winning black star runner. These two young men had been teammates at the University of Tennessee. Their personal tie was more durable than any new team alliance. Sealed in their bond, I saw the future of this country.

A FEW WEEKS AGO I WAS LECTURING TO GEORGIA'S UNITED Methodist pastors on Sea Island. At lunch I sat with a white pastor and his wife, who was a teacher's aide in an all-black school in DeKalb County. She told me that a thirteen-year-old seventh grader looked her dead in the eye one day and said, "Mrs. Stansberry, are you sure you are not black?"

"Why do you say that?" she asked.

" 'Cause you got soul!"

That was a child's way of saying that Mrs. Stansberry was close, warm, and involved. She inspired trust and this girl was not embarrassed to tell her she felt comfortable in her presence. "Soul" is a human attribute that anyone may have. "Soul" has no color.

Can These Bones Live?

BLACK AMERICANS HAVE ALWAYS BEEN FASCINATED BY biblical accounts of the Jews' exile in Babylon, which began in the sixth century B.C. and ended seventy years later. Some of the Bible's most dramatic stories derive from this one experience: Daniel in the lion's den, the three Hebrew boys in the furnace, Queen Esther and her triumph over Haman, and Ezekiel prophesying to the dry bones. In the Jewish exile slaves saw a tragedy parallel to their own plight, and the Bible comforted them, reinforcing their faith.

The books of II Samuel, II Kings, II Chronicles, Isaiah, and Ezekiel all echo with the cries of God's people.

[The Lord] will not grow tired or weary,
and his understanding no one can fathom.
He gives strength to the weary,
and increases the power of the weak.
Even youths grow tired and weary,
and young men stumble and fall;
but those who hope in the Lord
will renew their strength.
They will soar on wings like eagles;
they will run and not grow weary,
they will walk and not be faint.

Isaiah 40:28–31 (New International Version)

Last fall, I spoke at a Thanksgiving and homecoming celebration held at the former Alex Haley Farm in eastern Tennessee, sponsored by the Children's Defense Fund. I chose my text from the prophet Ezekiel, who tells of a vision in which the Lord sent him into a valley of bones that were very dry, symbolizing God's people in their despondency. "Our bones are dried up, and our hope is lost, and we are cut off." God asked Ezekiel, "Can these bones live?" Then God told the prophet to speak to the bones, saying "hear the word of the Lord," and the bones joined together. After the bones were renewed with muscles and sinew, they complained that they had no breath. The prophet beckoned to the four winds to breathe breath into their bodies, and the bones rose up like a mighty army.

We are once again living in a valley of dry bones. For these bones to live now, we must candidly face the raw facts: Every 44 minutes a black baby dies; every 7 minutes a black baby is born to a mother with late or no prenatal care; every 85 seconds a black child is born into poverty; and every 40 seconds of the school day a black child drops out. Can these bones live?

Most of us who made it into the mainstream in the 1960s and '70s viewed with contempt those blacks still mired in poverty, al-

200

coholism, violence, and immorality. They were our embarrassment. In no way did we want to be approving of that type of behavior, and somehow we succumbed to the popular theory that
they were largely to blame for their condition. Without knowing,
we were really involved in a form of racism ourselves by failing to
recognize fully the causes of the delinquency of so many blacks.

Today, we are not nearly as Darwinian in our thinking. We
know we must reach back and find ways to help others come
along, or the whole American nation may sink. This is the new
tenet of our faith. But the problem is so large and so amorphous
that people who want to help can't get a handle on it. They say
to me, "Which way is forward, Brother Sam?"

It may seem trivial, but many young blacks are even confused
about what to call themselves. Little wonder, when one hears us
joking and calling each other "niggah." What *do* we want to be
called? The major organization for our redemption is called the
National Association for the Advancement of *Colored People;* and
the organization that supports our history-making colleges is
called the United *Negro* College Fund. Two new organizations are
called One Hundred *Black* Men and One Hundred *Black*
Women. Representatives in Congress have organized a *black* cau-
cus; and new university departments are called African Studies,
Afro-American Studies, Afri-American Studies, or African-American Studies.

While the term "African American" feels least loaded with
color references these days, it, too, has its limitations. It emphasizes our past, not our future. American Indians are struggling with similar language changes, and many prefer using the
term "Native American." If we succeed in creating a new American paradigm for the world, we will all call ourselves Americans.

WE ARE IN A POSITION TO MAKE A POSITIVE LEAP FORWARD—
if we have the faith and vision to make the right choices. Even

as I write, in cities across America black leaders are debating exactly what the best response will be.

We know that we are all part of an unbroken chain of humanity and we cannot write off another human being as worthless. To discount a child like Yummy as a zero is to make zeroes of ourselves, sacks of protoplasm without the breath of God breathed on us. We would all be dry bones together in the valley of death.

There is no single answer. But I believe there *is* an answer, and it is derived from five separate efforts that need to be blended together: individual involvement, family rejuvenation, specialized teacher training for public schools, more committed church leadership, and, finally, a national program to recapture failing and lost youth. There are ways to achieve each of these monumental tasks. Those that involve individuals are quite simple; those that involve churches and state and federal governments are equally do-able, but require persuasive leadership and persistent effort. All five can and should be started now.

As a primary and overdue concern, all children need to feel safe. We need to protect them and ensure that they won't be hurt in the schools they attend, the streets they live on, and in their individual homes. Every child deserves a quality education. And every child deserves an opportunity to succeed. These initiatives must be available to everyone, regardless of race or income. If we cannot do these things first, then any other measure we adopt, no matter how intense, or how harsh, will fail to make a profound change in our society.

THOSE OF US WHO HAVE FOUND AN ADEQUATE RESPONSE TO our own aspirations need to find at least one viable handle on this crisis—and pull. Everyone can show concern, either individually or through a group.

Every stable home should offer asylum for at least one life that needs direction. At the little cottage where we spent summer weekends by the shores of the Potomac and the Chesapeake, we were a part of a community of nine or ten families. It seemed natural always for our boys to bring their friends along. We treated their friends exactly as we treated our sons. Today, we have a network of young men and women who know that we are available to them, our really extended family.

A few days ago I telephoned a writer friend of mine, a stylish, intellectual, avant-garde sort of person who shares an apartment on Manhattan's Upper East Side with her husband, who is also a writer. I could hear the noise of children in the background. "Who is that talking?" I asked. "You don't have children. Is there a party going on?"

She explained that one afternoon each week she taught creative writing to middle-school kids. "What kids?" I asked.

"Just kids. They belong to a young people's athletic organization."

I pressed on. "What organization? Where?"

"Oh, uptown."

Who would guess that a dozen explosive, high-energy preteens from African-American and Hispanic families in East Harlem would have found a friend among New York's literati? A friend who welcomed them and their noise, curiosity and kinetic action into her living room, kitchen, bathroom, and refrigerator for a weekly invasion? A friend who had the patience and fortitude to teach them to write poems and short stories? The idea of individuals reaching out is not so esoteric after all. Once it was the only way to live, to share love and substance in order to attain one's own fulfillment.

I asked her what prompted her to start the class. "I always wanted to do it, because a few terrific people gave me extra help when I was growing up. I heard about the organization from a close friend who was already working with the kids and she helped me get my program started. It's a small thing, but it's something I know how to do. I know lots of people doing a lot more."

She was right, of course. It *is* a small thing. And small things add up. In other times, this kind of simple sharing and passing along was quite common. One afternoon I was waiting with Lionel Hampton in the president's office at Howard University, where we were later to receive honorary degrees. I slipped into the men's room for a few minutes, and when I returned I saw Lionel kneeling in front of a chair, his head resting on his folded hands. I waited. When he arose, his eyes were wet with tears. "Are you all right?" I asked.

"I was just thanking God for sending someone to help me," he said. When Lionel was a boy growing up in St. Louis, a German blacksmith used to play his euphonium for the black kids who had recently swarmed into his old German neighborhood. When he noticed little Lionel showing more than casual interest, he taught him scales, fingering, and execution of his odd-looking instrument. Here was Lionel Hampton, seventy years later, a world-famous artist, remembering and giving thanks for the man who took the time to help him.

It's true that a lot of people are already working one-on-one with kids. But with so many children waiting for affirmation, we need many, many more, and they must come in huge numbers from the African-American community. You don't need a college degree or a million dollars. In our corner of Norfolk, Mr. Petty would let us sit in the driver's seat of his ice wagon and ride for hours while he dispensed his ice door-to-door; Big John Gale would let us ride on his trucks and wagons and help feed his pigs and horses; Mr. Foreman, the lawyer, would take us to his office on Saturday mornings and let us type, use his staple machine, run letters through the stamp machine, and answer his telephone. It is all so vivid in my mind, the many, many people who helped us feel good about ourselves. It's not hard to reach out. Call any school, any clubhouse, any church to volunteer for mentoring programs, reading, tutoring, or nursery care.

HOWEVER, THE CURE TO OUR CRISIS CANNOT BE FOUND with individual effort alone. If these dry bones have any chance of coming alive, the recovery must also be in the family structure itself.

Family is rehearsal for life. It is the place where mutual responsibility and accountability are first learned and practiced. Family is where soft punishments are imposed, without damage to self-esteem. Family is where we learn to receive blessings, and to return them. It's where we learn to accept forgiveness, and to give it. Family is an exercise in corporate survival—we don't steal from each other or violate each other's secrets and privacy.

Family is even more than that. There we can cry when we hurt, and show our grief without shame. Family also rejoices in our successes and we, in turn, celebrate the success of others. We carry one another in our prayers and live our days vicariously in each other's lives. In a good family no one suffers alone, and no one succeeds alone. Family is the chrysalis in which young, embryonic lives receive the germinative ingredients for living, while they are protected from the hazards and major challenges of life. In that way, a young life springs forth in beauty and strength.

Even families that are intact must look for creative ways to preserve the lives of their children. When our youngest boys reached the ages of ten and thirteen, we deliberately set about finding new ways to sustain our family connections during the time of social unrest swirling around us. We went to Sears Roebuck and bought an 18-foot boat and trailer on credit. The boat was a pretty, fern-green color, with an Evinrude 40 hp motor attached. Before putting it overboard, my two sons and I ran all over Richmond looking for a loud horn, lifejackets, an oar, a towline, an anchor, a fire extinguisher, a waterproof lamp, and a bailing bucket. A trailer had to be hooked to the car to haul the boat. That meant buying a cast-iron hitching tongue, and welding flanges on the frame of the car; we had to find a hitch with a ball to hold the trailer to the car. Every time we moved the boat, we had to connect the trailer's signal lights to the car lights.

Our preparations went on and on. We had to buy a state boat permit, and learn the safety manual for boat operators. Finally, we had to study the Virginia waterways.

I could never estimate the hours and energy my boys and I invested in our little green boat. Later, we traded up to a 21-foot fiberglass one, and then another one. Now we run a 23-foot inboard-outboard, and all four boys with their friends still enjoy being together on the water, doing nothing much, just talking and laughing and talking some more. We never owned a really fancy boat, just enough boat to enjoy the water and enter each other's lives at a point of leisure and slowed pace, and to maintain our family fellowship.

In cold weather we bowled. Until I was fifty years old, I had never been in a bowling alley, but by the time our two younger sons finished high school we had two notebooks filled with bowling scores. We would bowl twice a week, and all of us became good bowlers with averages of 160 to 180. One son became captain of the high school team and the champion of central Jersey high schools.

On cold weekend nights we had pinochle games. One could find pinochle scores on scraps of paper all over our house. This lasted for fifteen years, and it still goes on every summer.

When I was a child myself, we didn't have gang leaders interpreting life for us, offering an abbreviated code of survival that leads to jail or an early grave. We began to learn life's lessons at home from aunts, uncles, parents, and grandparents. We didn't earn this priceless beginning. We were just blessed to be born in our family's environment and not in Yummy's.

We spent countless hours around the piano trying to harmonize, making up songs, and copying the big band tunes. My daddy was a music man, and we learned to play instruments, too. We made footballs out of Quaker Oats boxes, filled with rocks and grass and wrapped in layers of discarded silk stockings. Daddy made swings, carts, and doll houses out of used fish boxes. Some of our best fun was listening to "Pop" Cherry tell us of his farmboy days near Ahoskie, North Carolina. Pop Cherry was my mother's mother's sister's widowed husband who somehow ended up living with us for twenty-five years. He was a source of endless entertainment and delight. Added up, such experiences filled any and every vacuum for us.

Part of the imperative to renew the family is that all parents should be held accountable for children to the fullest extent of their ability. No one should be riding around in a new car, pimping on public funds, and leaving his child for the rest of us to support. Both parents should work in some constructive activity to learn a skill, earn a livelihood, and break the cycle that continues to dump young Yummys on the public trust.

SOMEWHERE BETWEEN THE DEPRESSION AND THE CLOSE OF World War II, the American people lost their interest in the guaranteed full employment debate. A free economy and a democratic government, resting on a respository of moral values bequeathed in the Judaeo-Christian tradition, require a program of full employment. It is a scandal to tolerate 7 percent unemployment. How can we spend $300 billion on military defense and see the nation erode from within by perpetuating begging, selling drugs, stealing, prostitution, and depending on government subsistence, when we are fully able to devise a program of guaranteed full employment? We must have the political will and the national moral commitment to eliminate beggars, homeless persons, and unemployment. We can design a national budget that assures that no one should be a ward of the government unless she or he works at a real job doing something that needs to be done.

When a mother and child receive public funds to live on, the father needs to pay back the money to the government. If he has no job, he should be able to enroll in an honest jobs program, either in an industry subsidized by public funds, or in a public institution doing a needed function, or in training for the open job market.

Young mothers in living situations not fit for child-rearing should be allowed to share safe, clean cooperative housing with a dozen or so mothers and their young, where everyone either works to maintain the cooperative or takes a job and contributes to the expenses. Such residences would be only temporary, to help young mothers learn skills for real earning power so they can adequately care for their children.

The point is that infant children should not be penalized because of unfit parents. No father should be allowed to leave his responsibility on other citizens, and every young mother should be pointed toward education and training to elevate her life permanently. Such a program can be installed with compassion and without condemnation.

However, individual outreach and family rejuvenation are not enough. The principal intervention needed is thorough and efficient schooling, from kindergarten through high school. Schools *cannot* fail; we have no institution that can do what schools are assigned to do.

The most outrageous development of our time is that young blacks are losing the opportunity for real empowerment because they are rejecting education. I wish more people really knew how much blacks earnestly thirsted for education immediately following slavery. And I wish that more people knew how determined the slave states were to deny them learning. In Georgia, for example, the state supreme court enthusiastically endorsed laws against teaching slaves.

When the Virginia House of Delegates passed a bill to prohibit blacks from being educated, one delegate said: "We have as far as possible *closed every avenue by which light may enter their minds. If we could extinguish the capacity to see the light, our work would be completed. . . .*" (The italics are mine.) When he made this statement, my grandmother was living enslaved only a few hundred yards down the road. Fortunately, her capacity to see the light was never extinguished. In fact, her capacities grew and absorbed more and more light, as her faith in a meaningful future glowed.

Rundown schools, overcrowded classrooms, and burned-out teachers are the norm for many black children. They further lose their bearings when some black educators demand that black children be taught an exclusively Afrocentric curriculum, untainted by European influences. I agree that all students—not just black students—need to learn about African origins and African history, along with colonialism and slavery. Learning one's own roots should fill one with pride, as well as ignite one's curiosity to learn the importance of everyone's roots.

But Afrocentric learning that is narrow, chauvinistic, and propagandistic is negative and stifles intellectual growth. Shallow learning results in racism, bigotry, polarization, tribalism, war, and destruction. Whatever calls us in that direction should be avoided like the plague.

What we should care about is preparing all young minds to join in the great human conversation by learning the theories which support technology and science, and the broadest range of facts known about all the earth's people and its marvelous habitats. Black pupils need to learn about the whole planet, all of her people and her physical and chemical secrets. The deeper our knowledge, the more complete our understanding of our common origins, capacities, needs, and destiny.

Furthermore, the so-called Eurocentric learning is very eclectic, a blend of wisdom, knowledge, and religion that accrued from many cultures, including Asia, Egypt, Greece, Arabia, Italy, and North Africa. There is a large fund of knowledge, art, and music from the entire human family that should be the intellectual property of everyone. And black youth would be seriously deprived if they were denied access to that broad experience. Who would be so shortsighted as to want black pupils competing for jobs and graduate study after being denied a chance to embrace the same body of facts and knowledge that all other students enjoyed? With a broadly educated mind, young black students can fully pursue any area of interest they wish.

But the sad fact is that, currently, black students are not certain that they *do* want to learn what everyone else is learning. The consequence is that only a thin trickle of black students are prepared for tough intellectual assignments; the others are left to roam the streets and abandon the quest for learning. At the same time, educational statisticians are reducing black students to numbers and spinning depressing results into theories that blacks are slow learners, that they can run, dance, sing, make touchdowns, and sink baskets, but cannot think and reason. The mischief escalates as social theorists from *without* dampen efforts to educate young blacks, and social propagandists from *within* kill off black aspirations. The sad result will be a society divided racially, and divided again on educational lines.

One way to inspire young people to learn is through the quality and commitment of their teachers. We need to open the door wider to teaching by offering incentives to people who have the vocation and the time, but who need more training. Recently, a friend and colleague of mine in New York told me that she went to a meeting which took place in a schoolroom in a public junior high in Harlem. Classes were over for the day, but the corridors were still filled with kids playing basketball and attending special afterschool classes set up by a local youth organization. What impressed her was that the kids didn't have to be there. Nobody made them go. They preferred to be inside playing and working with adults who were interested in them. They hate the noise and filth of the streets and are afraid of the violence and danger. The problem is getting enough capable volunteer tutors or teacher aides who can be available at 3 o'clock in the afternoon to meet the supply of kids.

During my tenure at Rutgers I was able to spearhead certain community efforts through old contacts in Washington. One of my friends in the U.S. Office of Education had an idea that we could develop a new corps of dedicated teachers for tough, urban schools by recruiting people without college degrees from the community and giving them a chance to gain teacher certification. We were able to get a grant for what we called the Career Opportunities Program. We recruited students from antipoverty programs, churches, and social agencies. We subjected applicants to a rigorous, two-hour interview in which their language skills, ability for abstract thinking, and personal commitment were evaluated. Once accepted, recruits received small stipends to help with living expenses during the two-year program. When they completed their studies, they had earned a Master of Education degree and a teaching certificate.

The Rutgers faculty at first greeted the new idea with "ho-hum, just another federal give-away." But when they saw that this one, like other programs we were developing, was operating with integrity, they climbed on board.

Twenty applicants entered the program each semester for the next three years, for a total of a hundred twenty new teachers for New Jersey's secondary schools. Among those recruited the first year was Edith Jackson, who was working as an office manager for a local chamber of commerce and raising three young children on her own. After taking our program she became a social science teacher in Metuchen, New Jersey, where she was twice voted "teacher of the year." Another of our recruits was Charles Morerro, who came straight out of the Job Corps and went on to become a housing officer for Rutgers and, later, dean of students for the School of Engineering and the School of

Pharmacy. Eugene Barrington went on to finish a Ph.D. in political science at Syracuse. Charles Holmes became a high school principal in Pennington, New Jersey.

When I described our teachers' program to various educational conferences, I got all sorts of challenges concerning proper training. My answer was always the same: good teachers can be produced if they love children, if they see hope even in dirty, mean, impolite children; if they believe that all children can learn; and if they have the energy and imagination to pursue the growth of a child. These gifts may be hard to measure in advance, but they are easy to recognize in action. The key is to try.

Some people say I lean too heavily on education as the agent of change, but I saw how much education did to help produce a stable black leadership class from 1900 to 1950. When I see today the sorry condition of urban ghettos, where young people are distracted by gangs, drug dealing, and sex, there's no doubt in my mind that schooling is the crucial variable in the current crisis.

It follows that we need to train teachers to work with high-risk kids. Recently a teacher named Troy Weaver was named teacher of the year in Durham, North Carolina. Weaver teaches juvenile offenders awaiting trial for murder, car theft, armed robbery, and rape in the Durham County Youth Home. Weaver's work reflects that love that is not measured and does not wait for reciprocity.

One day one of the detainees in Durham went berserk and began cursing and tossing chairs and tables across the room. Weaver approached him and ran into a storm of profanity. "You can curse me all you want," he said, "but I still love you."

The student stopped and let Weaver walk up to him and put his arms around him. The student started to cry. "My mother never told me she loved me," he said. "She loves the pipe [crack] more than she loves me."

Weaver is thirty-three years old, married, with children. One of his adopted children is a former detainee. With more Troy Weavers, these bones can live!

THE MOVE TOWARD PRIVATE SCHOOL AND THE IDEA OF vouchers is aimed at the final destruction of public schools. Public schools will become holding pens for hopeless children, while children from higher-income families and better-educated parents will be distanced from the masses in far better schools. America built public schools as a testimony to the worth and dignity of all people. How easy it is for those looking for a quick fix to social neglect to violate the democratic ideal and the most noble aspirations of the human spirit.

Schools are as much a public responsibility as clean water, safe roads, polio vaccinations, and licensing for doctors and pharmacists. Specially trained people are needed to do what Troy Weaver can do. Yet in my lifetime I have seen no national mobilization to put a new lining in our public schools, to generate exciting and productive teaching, or to reverse the downward spiral toward a permanent underclass. But we have seen enough strong students emerge from weak schools to convince us of what could happen with a greater effort.

Three thousand colleges and universities in America are training teachers. Yet there is practically no contact between these prestigious schools of education and the public schools struggling to stay alive. If the colleges would direct their efforts toward training teachers to respond to those most in *need* of learning, we would see a revolution in urban behavior.

We need a national program to upgrade teaching and the teaching profession. This means making a career in teaching pay at least as well as carrying mail or driving a garbage truck in New York City. It means luring the best minds—not the C+ survivors—into teaching. It means keeping schools open until 5:30 all year long, except for two-week recesses in August, December, and April.

A federally supported program like that would pay for itself. Can you imagine what we have spent on Yummy's mother, her six children on welfare, and her forty-one arrests, along with the drug programs she has visited? My soul! Compare those costs to the cost of training teachers who could have kept her in school and made her a productive, tax-paying citizen.

Training teachers is only part of the answer. Instilling order and discipline is the other part. In exchange for the money we now spend on education, we get chaos. Public schools today are coping with crime, guns, gangs, and drugs. They are more like forts than schools. As a result, we are wasting millions of dollars assigned to education. Intellectual thrust cannot be created in the midst of chaos. Teaching and monitoring discipline are two separate tasks, and personnel are needed in all of our schools to maintain order so that teachers can teach until a new generation of public schools evolves.

The extra cost of improving public schools would be offset by reduced payments to teenage mothers, lower detention and court costs for young recidivists, and increased tax revenue from a larger pool of earners. Everyone wins.

When children begin with a great school experience, the line between philosophy and the prophet fades, and the space between Athens and Jerusalem narrows. When that happens, those bones are about to live!

BUT IT TAKES EVEN MORE THAN GOOD SCHOOLS TO SAVE our children. Back in the 1920s and '30s, in the rural South, black schools were pitifully understaffed, and children attended only four or five months out of a year, with frequent interruptions for farm labor. Many had to work to survive and could not afford to go to school at all. Yet a progressive, hard-driving, proud black middle class emerged in America one generation after slavery.

Fifteen-year-old George Lewis fled a rural backwater of Mississippi and ended up working in the Omaha stockyards. But George Lewis was a religious person and stayed around people of faith. He worked hard and participated in worthwhile activities. He became the chairperson of the Board of Deacons of the Abyssinian Baptist Church, and was one of the most highly regarded church leaders among African Americans in New York City. In a lifetime of work, he never earned more than five dollars an hour, but he was careful always to save a little. When he died, Deacon Lewis owned a beautiful condominium and left his church $50,000 in his will.

Deacon Lewis told me that when he was a little boy, he and his schoolmates had to walk five miles to and from their raggedy school, where one teacher taught forty pupils in four grades. On the way, they walked by the neat white schools. As they walked, white students would pass them on the road, riding in a large wagon drawn by a team of horses. They rode, although the distance to their school was half the distance that blacks walked. George said he was glad when it rained because the side canvases on the wagons were lowered and the white students couldn't spit on them as they passed by.

In the wake of such experiences it required a strong faith to retain a sense of personal worth and to aspire to do well. Obviously, not everyone could summon such faith. Others from Deacon Lewis's background ended up with fifteen descendants on welfare, and half of them in and out of jail. Like Yummy, they never had a chance.

So even though it would seem that education is a large part of the answer, it is not all. The truly educated person, in my view, is never content until a satisfactory, operational answer is found to the questions of purpose and destiny. In our early years, school is largely in control of the life of the mind and the world of ideas. But eventually we must turn our focus outward and upward to look for our own larger frame of reference. Religion brings our quest for purpose and direction to closure and our soul to ease by revealing our place in the scheme of things.

To resolve the present dilemma and move forward, we need a major intervention from the black churches. Such a renaissance is already taking place all over the country. Locally, our churches are centers of progress. They are centers for day-care, even alternative elementary and high schools, credit unions, athletic teams, family life centers, travel clubs, senior citizen residences, low-income housing, Alcoholics Anonymous chapters, Bible study, drama groups—you name it.

The local churches are doing great, but at the national level African-American churches need a wake-up call. They are still burdened with stagnant leadership bogged down in "old boy" connections. They handle money like a mom-and-pop store, with inadequate reporting and auditing; frequent losses are almost never penalized. No real accountability goes on, and everyone retires rich, like so many American presidents.

Church officers meet constantly, staying in fine hotels, attending banquets. The meetings are largely preaching marathons. The result of all this spending is negligible. Several church-sponsored colleges have closed for lack of funding, even as the national bodies have grown and collected more money.

Nationally, leadership positions in the black churches have been mostly honorific and ornamental, without real meaning. This can no longer be tolerated. With our families falling apart and our communities disintegrating into violence and resignation, we cannot afford to have millions of people attending our churches without strong leadership at the top. Groups like the National Rifle Association, with its shadowy goals and purposes, are much better organized than we.

The African-American churches represent 20 million black

Christians. If they could speak with one voice, we would hear a powerful shout. If they created only one great national television worship hour, presenting our finest preachers and choirs, we could offer the country something besides the heavily jeweled, poorly educated, bodacious, sleazy hustlers currently seen on television pilfering from the meager earnings of the elderly and the poor.

Nor would it take much to establish a first-rate publishing house and a world-class conference center. Black people have a lot to say to each other, and much of what needs to be said may not meet the criteria of the commercial publishing market. But if all of our major denominations had their church school literature printed by their own printing corporation, it would be a major enterprise. That is do-able. If a book or magazine agency were founded cooperatively, the churches could use it to publish public training material. One denomination on its own may find it a struggle, but together blacks could match what other major church publishers are doing.

Strong leadership could create a mortgage cooperative for church building. In every major city there is always a multimillion-dollar black church building project. Our own black-owned, highly successful North Carolina Mutual Insurance Company in Durham is a model of what could happen in creating a mortgage company.

For example, the millions of dollars black congregations donate to erect church buildings could be invested in their own cooperative bank. The interest earned could be used to support black colleges, scholarships, and even the development of a national, ecumenical conference site, such as an African-American theme park and vacation center. Enough African Americans are working in high-finance positions to make this one a piece of cake, but imaginative church leadership is needed.

All of this begins with the right ideas and the right people to take the initiative. Imagine what would happen if someone with

the dynamism of Marian Wright Edelman were the executive secretary of the African-American Baptists! Look at what she has
done with the Children's Defense Fund over a period of fifteen
years. She has built it from a nonentity into an instrument of
change for the welfare of all of America's children.

EVEN WITH FAMILY, SCHOOLS, AND CHURCHES DOING THEIR
best, there is still that powerful draconian determinant called
"the economy" which has operated so that the rich get richer,
and the poor remain poor. Real change will not come until the
basic economic condition of the poor changes. Unemployment
and underemployment are heavy weights for a people to carry
from one generation to another. Every conceivable human problem is aggravated by poverty.

In 1990, one of every seven white families lived in poverty, but
one of every three black families did. This figure has been the
same for the last twenty years. That same year, the median income for white families was $36,915 and for blacks $21,423.
More telling, during the twenty years of the Nixon-Reagan-Bush
administrations, median income of white Americans rose along
with inflation. The black median hardly moved. The bottom
half was weighted heavily with those earning below the poverty
line.

What about the children growing up in Yummy's neighborhood? How much money do their households have for the bare
necessities of life? Today one of every two black children lives in
poverty (44.8 percent) compared to one of every six white children. Two of every three poor black children live in central
cities.

Unfortunately, the prospect for getting on board economically is slim in today's market because of poor education and job
discrimination. The old low-wage, manual labor jobs are disap-
pearing; if you *can* find one, the pay is so miserable that you

could work fourteen hours a day, seven days a week, and not earn enough to pay the rent and put food on the table.

Andrew Hacker, in *Two Nations, Black and White, Separate, Hostile and Unequal,* says that for as long as records have been kept, unemployment for African Americans has been twice that for whites. Sadly, one of the most visible objects in America is a black male standing on a downtown street corner, poorly educated, unkempt, unemployed, with the glaze of despair on his face.

A free and democratic government supposedly has built-in correctives to make up for the uneven beginnings in life. Victims of racial discrimination and poverty are supposed to have room enough to maneuver their way into the middle and upper class. It has not worked out. The gaps between those who have and those who have not are widening. And as a result the whole nation is suffering.

The power to change lies in the hands of the Congress, the president, and the corporate community. But unless there is a surge of decency and fairness emanating from the public will, these data threaten to follow us into the twenty-first century.

Can these bones live? If those who have overcome will share one-on-one their intellectual, moral, and cultural capital with those with deep deficits, if families can recover their values of nurturing and support, if we can renovate our schools and lead all of our children into the life of the mind, if the African-American church on a national scale can muster the leadership it deserves, and if we can build jobs and fair access into the economy—these bones will live.

AS WE MOVE THESE PROCESSES ALONG, WE HAVE TO administer a stop-gap measure right now for our present crisis.

There are 1.5 million unparented children today—male and female, black, Hispanic, white, and Native American—who are

virtually without hope of ever becoming self-sufficient, responsible citizens. The opportunity for these 1.5 million young people to become healthy, intelligent, responsible adults, prepared
for wholesome family life, a fulfilling vocation, concerned citizenship, and a meaningful view of the world is the summum
bonum.

The alternative is for more and bigger jails, more wasted
human resources, more social disorder, and an outlay of $40,000
per head, per year, for costs of trials, incarceration, and probation. Our present crisis calls us to see beyond partisan politics
and make a major national correction of past failures.

Many young people are now beyond the capacity of the public schools to help. My own idea is modeled on the Peace Corps,
and would use deactivated military bases. I propose a federally
funded National Youth Academy to educate youngsters who
need a new home, surrogate parents, and an enriched educational program. These schools would be state-managed, but
would have national goals and guidelines. The magnitude of the
problem is far beyond the capacity of voluntary or small private
efforts and more critical than merely warehousing kids to get
them out of sight.

My years with the Peace Corps taught me that large organi-
zational efforts readily reach their potential when *someone at the
top says so*. The facilities to put a National Youth Academy in action are there now, idle and available. Sewer lines, power lines,
water supply lines are in place. Even a cost of $16,000 per child
would be less than half of what we spend on prisons now.

Our Peace Corps training programs taught us that teachers—
and nonteachers—can be oriented toward a new kind of professional service. The military routinely retrains accountants,
trumpet players, plumbers, and hotel waiters to man tanks and
helicopters and win wars six thousand miles from home. In 1963,
we had sixteen thousand of the brightest and best of our college
graduates teaching in thirty-eight developing countries, speak-

ing exotic languages and living on foods they could not even spell. They worked for fifty dollars a month and had to be forced to leave after two years. They found life's greatest satisfaction in serving those who needed them most.

Many well-educated, decent Americans are willing to give two or three years to the recovery and realignment of children who are otherwise destined for a crime career or an early grave. Today we have an army of underemployed teachers who would be delighted to take on this task. We also have a wave of energetic college graduates every year, eager to share their social and intellectual capital with others. We have retired military personnel who know how to create a healthy, orderly environment of high personal expectations, conducive to serious goal achievement. And we have a surplus of well-trained, but unemployed or underemployed, experts in a variety of professional specialties.

All of these individuals could come on board at the National Youth Academy, living and boarding on the campuses, sharing meals with the students, and earning modest salaries, health care benefits, and a bonus at the end of their two-year service.

What would happen at these fifty academies with an enrollment of some five thousand each? These youth academies would be neither hospitals nor prisons. Therefore, youngsters with severe physical or mental disabilities could not be cared for there; nor could those already seriously violent. But most of our youth on a collision course with failure could be served. They would be chosen on the recommendation of the courts, schools, and detention centers, with the approval of their parents or guardians.

The National Youth Academy would enlist the country's most experienced educators to design a six-year academic curriculum, beginning in the seventh grade. This format is largely an arbitrary decision, trying to keep costs within reason. However, seventh grade is when the most serious signs of asocialization begin to appear and what little parenting that exists begins to lapse.

Six years is also an adequate amount of time to establish a foundation for good habits of work, study, and behavior. The enrollee will be ready for graduation at age eighteen, ready for college or for work, but mostly ready for good citizenship and responsible adulthood.

The curriculum would include six years of serious, no-nonsense mental challenges, especially mastering math, logic, writing, and coherent thinking. Beyond the academic work, everyone would learn to swim in the first thirty days. Being able to jump into a 40-foot tank without drowning is a dramatic way to feel mastery over one's environment. Students would learn to grow flowers, sing four-part harmony, do photography, paint landscapes, breed dogs, care for an aquarium, and play sports of all kinds. Each child would get very, very good at *something*. Everyone would use computers for the whole six years. The curriculum would also include a work program that would teach *every* student to do *every* task needed to run the school, from accounting and nursing to tuning tractor motors and cutting hair. They would know how to use every tool sold by Sears!

Above all, the curriculum would include a human development program to encourage community values. These include respect for the space and rights of others, care of the environment, self-reliance and civic contributions, and responsibility for one's own actions and choices.

What about drugs? In group living, no one would have the kind of privacy needed to access drugs easily. Moreover, with a love of learning and a program of rigorous physical development, the vacuum that drugs fill would be filled already in a positive way. There would be constant vigilance to assure that the dysfunctional world these children left behind would stay behind.

This is a fiscally conservative program. Each graduate will be an earner and a taxpayer for life. Within five years, each would have repaid every dollar spent on him or her by paying income tax. And each will continue to pay taxes for a lifetime. Anyone with a net income of $100,000 today pays $31,000 in federal income taxes. Most families that I know well have such a net and more. When I was in college, the government paid me fifteen dollars a month for nine months, over four years. A total of $540 for four years! If my net income were $100,000 I would be paying more than $540 *a week* in federal taxes! Every week for the rest of my life, I would be giving the government back in taxes more than it spent on me in four years. But without that help I would not have finished college.

Consider how many times over beneficiaries have repaid in taxes what was spent on them through the GI bill. (For example, two of my brothers were educated on the GI bill; one became a dentist, the other a physician.) Consider the land grant universities, which became our state colleges and universities. In an average career, graduates pay back the cost of their education in taxes twenty times! Consider the black colleges founded by the churches in the 1860s and 1870s. They created an entire black middle class of lifetime taxpayers.

If the government started out with fifty academies, with five thousand students in each, it would cost $4 billion a year. (The Pentagon budget runs over $300 billion each year.) Over six years each student would cost a total of almost $96,000. But if we do not spend that money now, these young losers could end up costing us $40,000 each for every year of their lives, and never pay any taxes. When they finish the National Youth Academy, they will be on their way to paying $20,000 or more each year for *forty years*. That's more than eight times the investment. Now, there's a deal!

Will there be problems? Yes. There are problems in the Vatican, at West Point, Johns Hopkins Hospital, the CIA, the New York Yankees, Buckingham Palace, and IBM. But if the people in charge are well chosen, they will be *problem solvers*. Some remarkable efforts in our world have succeeded. We did get to the moon. We do perform heart transplants. And we do have 260 million people, living in fifty states, who don't carry visas and don't have a national shootout at every election. We can rescue 1.5 million young lives from destruction, just as we have saved them from poliomyelitis.

Do we have the public will to do it? I remember when Social Security and Medicare were called "communism" by those who did not need them. If we have the compassion in our hearts and the intelligence in our heads, we can generate the consensus.

This is not a project for blacks only. It is a project for every child who needs it. If African Americans are disportionately represented in the NYA, it will be because the program responds to a need that is disproportionately felt among them. Over time, the numbers will change as opportunities increase.

After twenty-five years—with three or four cohorts of National Youth Academy students entering new lives and enhancing each thread in the fabric of American life—we would begin to see a new America. Many of our college students and our most skilled tax-paying workers, college students, artists and architects, teachers, candidates for public office will be coming from the National Youth Academy.

ALL OF THE INTERVENTIONS BY CHURCHES, SCHOOLS, families, individuals, economic equality, and government are needed, and none is independent of the other. Yet one solution need not wait for the other. We all must begin where we can. Social analysts can assemble facts to show that nothing works. But whatever has led us to this predicament can be undone; the spiral can be turned in a new direction.

The litany of sins against disenfranchised blacks is long and familiar. The question facing us now is, "Where do we go from here?" The current crisis demands that we make choices that are worth living and dying for, choices deserving of our best efforts,

choices that have the best chance of steering us toward the optimum human condition: a genuine community. To my mind,
isolating ourselves from the rest of American society, or relying
only on our African heritage for a sense of identity and pride,
are not choices that will ultimately bring us into a genuine community with fairness and justice for all.

Genuine community is possible only if we accept that our destiny lies right here, with a new America in the making; a new
America that the NYA will be a part of. The success that the
middle-class black population has achieved has a direct relationship to hard work, personal pride, deep faith in a future
filled with meaning and purpose. Such success has been earned
in the face of racism and contempt for black progress. And it has
been earned because we believed in a future where we were full
participants at the center of American life.

I will tell you a story. If you should visit the Newark campus of
Rutgers University, chances are someone will tell you about the
new Free Electron Laser Laboratory that lies near Smith Hall, in
a crater ten feet deep and seventy feet long. This ten-ton miracle
of technology is directed by Dr. Earl Shaw, professor of physics.

Dr. Shaw was born on a plantation near Clarksdale, Mississippi, where his parents were sharecroppers. When Earl was six
years old, his father was shot to death. His mother followed the
urban black migration along the Illinois Central railroad to
Chicago, seeking a better life for her little boy.

Anyone who saw the young mother and child riding in the
"colored" coach on the Illinois Central, eating chicken out of a
shoe box, rocking and shaking for hours from Jackson to
Chicago, would never have dreamed that the boy would ever
grow up to be a success in these United States. According to all
known predictors, Earl should have wound up a statistic in a
criminal justice textbook, lumped in with the norms and means,
a drug-dealing, car-thieving, teenage daddy terrifying the city
and keeping his mother on her knees.

But somehow he and his mother mined that vein of faith that blacks keep hidden in their breasts, and *believed* their way through. Earl's mother worked hard enough to get him enrolled in a good school, and at age twelve he was selected for a science high school that prepared him for the University of Illinois at Urbana. Later, he earned a master's degree in laser physics from Dartmouth, and a Ph.D. in physics from the University of California at Berkeley.

After nineteen years as a researcher at AT&T's Bell Laboratories, he was wooed by Rutgers to become its premier physics researcher. Bell Labs went right along and installed a $1.4 million laser laboratory for him there. Among other mysteries, Dr. Shaw is discovering how to make invisible light ranges visible.

Statistics can't explain how six-year-old Earl moved from the edge of a Mississippi plantation, trembling with fear and grief at his father's pine-box casket, to become one of the world's top physicists.

I believe if we can transpose young Earl's faith to the common struggles being ground out in black ghettos from Los Angeles to Boston, we can turn away the crisis and a new nation will emerge. The world has anticipated such a community since the African theologian Augustine envisioned the City of God and since the founding fathers of the United States declared that it was self-evident that all persons were created equal. Although their declaration has never actually come to pass here, we have envisioned it, and our most cherished documents say that it is possible.

African Americans bring to this moment a long tradition of seeing beyond the hard facts. We have never ceased to believe in a deliverance that will come partly by our own effort and partly by the power of a metaphysical design that made a world out of nothing. We know we are not struggling alone. Like David before Goliath, we have believed in a hidden ally.

Ezekiel saw dry bones coming together and taking on sinews

and flesh. He also saw colorful, intricately designed wheels moving in the air without any visible power. The spirit of God was moving over a captive people. In slavery, African Americans made up a song about a small wheel turning inside of a larger wheel: *"The big wheel moved by faith, and the little wheel moved by the grace of God."*

CHAPTER ELEVEN

Beauty for Ashes

EVERY NOW AND THEN, A SPIRITUALLY DISCIPLINED SOUL lends his or her heart to God as a lyre, and vibrates with such ethereal strains that they echo ceaselessly through the long corridors of time. Chapters 60 through 62 of the book of Isaiah, attributed to the hand of Second Isaiah, are the most beautiful portrait of God that has survived the sifting sands of time. Listen to the King James Version:

> Arise, shine; for thy light is come, and the glory of the Lord is risen upon thee.

> For, behold, the darkness shall cover the earth, and gross darkness the people: but the Lord shall arise

upon thee, and his glory shall be seen upon thee.
(60:1–2)

The Spirit of the Lord God is upon me; because the
Lord hath anointed me to preach good tidings unto
the meek: he hath sent me to bind up the broken-
hearted, to proclaim liberty to the captives, and the
opening of the prison to them that are bound. . . .
(61:1)

To appoint unto them that mourn in Zion, to give unto
them beauty for ashes, the oil of joy for mourning, the
garment of praise for the spirit of heaviness. . . . (61:3)

As I fix my mind on the confusion and incoherence that stare
at us every day, the words "beauty for ashes," written twenty-six
hundred years ago, obsess me. All around us we see ashes that
need to be exchanged for beauty.

No one really knows how well prepared we are in America for
movement toward a new paradigm of the human family, one that
respects everyone's innate worth, that seeks to cultivate human
potential and self-esteem, and that affirms the principles of justice, freedom, and equality. We do know that such movement is
thwarted by archaic and mean class divisions and intractable
tribalism.

We know also that what we do here in America holds promise
for the rest of the whole world. There are 5 billion people on
the planet, 4 billion of whom are brown, yellow, and black. With
the twenty-first century lying before us, there must be an alternative to chronic, worldwide ethnic strife, mass starvation, corrupt and brutal governments, and the vulgar disparity in
opportunities for the flowering of human potential. These conditions are gross contradictions to the knowledge that we have
gained and to the accumulated moral and spiritual values that
are woven into the warp and woof of our culture.

While we may not have a foolproof definition of genuine community, everyone knows what noncommunity looks like. For example, there are those who continue to turn a blind eye to starvation and epidemics in the world, and all of the dread that goes before such painful deaths. Anyone who can walk away in ease from such indescribable anguish cannot talk about community.

White professors—and black professors, too—who abandon the truth in favor of their own prejudices and indulge in innuendo and fraudulent data to "prove" their case—these pseudoscholars are enemies of community.

Universities that fail to help students understand the root causes of the African-American position in America are also enemies of real community. This is what made it so dreadfully tragic when it was revealed that the president of Rutgers University—the 50,000-student state university of New Jersey, with fourteen schools on five campuses, straddling the main artery between Washington and Boston, in the most diverse and thickly populated state in the Union—said to a closed meeting of thirty-five tenured white professors on the Camden campus in November of 1994, that African-American students "did not have the genetic and hereditary background" to achieve high scores on the Scholastic Aptitude Test. His earlier conduct as an administrator had never reflected such a view, and his public speeches had always testified to fairness and equality of opportunity. But behind closed doors he made that clear statement, and not one person demurred.

Everyone in that room knew enough social and economic history to account for the lower scores of blacks on the SATs. In fact, it would defy all reason and history if black students scored higher than whites. But here, at the very heart of American education, the classic, pseudoscientific, anti-intellectual, disproven, and abandoned racist theory was alive and well.

The result of this and similar acts is that thousands of black students on college campuses all over the country are again targets of ridicule by the racist students and faculty who have found new license for their views. Black Ph.D.s, many highly distinguished in their fields, are bowed in shame and disbelief, and black alumni are horrified, being teased and questioned by their colleagues all over the country.

The president has profusely apologized, but for what? For saying what he believed? For believing it? Or for the furor it caused?

Only a few days prior to the public exposure of his speech, I had completed my task as chairperson of a Rutgers fundraising campaign to promote diversity, excellence, and community. We raised $5.4 million, and our spirits were high. Then we had to face the reality that not everyone believed, really, in genuine community.

Another impediment to real community is the control of our political institutions by those representing the wealthiest segment of society. The domination of party politics by the privileged holds the country captive to the old paradigm of the superiority of the rich. Apparently there is no way to rescue government and public policy at the present time. Even the majority of Supreme Court justices are millionaires and were millionaires before going to the bench. Imagine the President of the United States surrounded by government aides and officers who are as distant from real moral accountability as feudal lords. The indifference of people in high places is an enemy of real community, and it can only change with the political awakening of working people.

The pall of prejudice that hangs heavily on our society and seeps into the fabric of American life is an enemy of community. Only today, November 5, 1994, I heard a report, from the Centers for Disease Control in Atlanta, that cigarette smoking had increased alarmingly among young African-American women, but had decreased among young white women. Does anyone know what racial identity has to do with smoking? What can one learn by finding out how many black women smoke cigarettes as compared to whites? It is instructive, however, to know whether smoking is related to education; or whether it is a regional phenomenon relating to local customs or loyalty to the tobacco-growing economy; or the influence of advertising on smoking. Perhaps it has something to do with income, or the type of job someone has. Do more *poor* young women smoke? With this information we can do something to stem the increase in smoking. But what possible use is it to know the race of smokers?

Likewise, any data on crime, teenage pregnancy, disease, and illiteracy are always given by race, thus implying that race is more causal than other factors. This "data" treats the truth with contempt, and keeps prejudice alive. Statistical reporting by race is a barrier to community.

Those who pretend that blacks are either rapists, car thieves, and drug peddlers on the one hand, or Michael Jackson, Michael Jordan, and Magic Johnson on the other, are aliens to community.

The saddest resistance to a new human paradigm comes from the very place where it should be most enthusiastically supported, the Protestant church. A special brand of churches—usually smaller, quasi-churches on the fringes of major denominations—cluster around right-wing leaders who support nationalism, heavy defense expenditures, and Christian schools that deliberately subvert racial integration.

These people accept the view that women are subordinate based on the creation story in Genesis and the writings of Paul. They regard these stories as God's will, ignoring the rest of the sixty-six books of the Bible, which display God's many marvelous gifts to women in biology and history. Others cite special phrases in the Bible out of context to prove that races should live separately. This falls short of a thorough understanding of the Bible and a more complete view of God's creation. People with a narrow God concept see AIDS as punishment of a particular group, and ignore the many other wonderful people who suffer dreadful illnesses. They cannot see that some people used the freedom God gave them to exploit others, deny them opportunity, and impose suffering upon them. All such views misrepresent more comprehensive ideas of God and vitiate efforts at building community. Indeed, a prerequisite for the new community is having an adult concept of God that makes us immune to narrow and provincial views of people, even of ourselves.

Another barrier to a new human paradigm is the long-term dependency of the poor on public largesse. Community will be hard to achieve if an underclass of poor, uneducated African Americans and whites fails to recognize that self-reliance, accountability, and personal pride are the trademarks of a free and just society. Nothing will change significantly if the society has to provide sustenance for large numbers of people who have no hope of becoming self-supporting. Our purpose should be to protect any new life brought into the world and nurture it so that it becomes self-reliant and self-fulfilling. Consequently, we should be making every effort to eliminate the practice of young women giving birth outside of the family and without adequate support.

African Americans on the bottom have to struggle to make themselves immune to cynical, hate-filled orations that persuade them that they cannot win. Those of us who have already made a commitment to stand firm and work and sacrifice for the movement toward a genuine community have to share our faith with them. This is a matter of trust and long-term commitment. We received that commitment from our own antecedents, and it made us immune to cynicism. We must now share it likewise, to the same end. Those without hope must believe that a new human paradigm is possible and that persistence will work. If

they remain anesthetized by the ether of hate rhetoric and separatist propaganda, they will remain on the margins.

SOME OLD BARRIERS TO COMMUNITY ARE IN FACT CRUMBLING.
The state of Mississipi, once the most violent hotbed of racism,
has shown many signals of lasting change. It is a fact today that
the dean of the Law School of the University of Mississippi, for
instance, is a black legal scholar reared in a public housing project in New Orleans.

Fifteen years ago, the Mississippi State NAACP Conference invited me to speak at their annual banquet, in Yazoo City. When
I arrived at the Ramada Inn, there was a huge neon sign proclaiming, "Welcome, Dr. Proctor and the NAACP State Conference." This sign stood less than fifty miles away from the spot
where Medgar Evers, that devoted and revered leader, was shot
to death only a few years before.

On October 17, 1994, I addressed the "Parents University" in
Hattiesburg, Mississippi. This is a sophisticated PTA program intended to get parents more involved in their children's education. I was addressing citizens of a state whose very name
symbolized the old, die-hard, Jim Crow South. Yet the first thing
I saw there were black and white teachers hugging each other,
and moving like hornets to get the program rolling. Black and
white parents were all over the place, serving finger-food and
punch, hanging posters, passing out programs, and welcoming
the workshop leaders. The workshops covered every relevant
topic for school-age children. The superintendent of schools
knew all the African-American leaders by name, and all of the
faculty knew all of the parents, black and white. It was one
smooth, impressive performance. Scores of American cities,
North and South, would covet Hattiesburg's situation.

Real community is built on common needs, talents, and contributions—great and small. We need to share these as a nation.

We need to aspire to a network of relationships that will affirm all of us in our rich diversity and decency. In a global, cosmic context, we must view every other human in a way that is compatible with one worldview.

We need to appraise honestly what is essential for a good life. We are all sojourners here, and we need each other to survive. This means that we are best off if we back away from perpetual rivalries and draw closer to an intelligent, fair basis for mutual support.

We need to revisit the past and look at the practices of previous generations that led to such unmanageable inequalities—and also at those that led to progress and achievement. Any new strategy for the future must also honor the past. The new human paradigm depends on first accepting hard facts, then reclaiming the positive, productive practices that have led to success.

When Franklin Roosevelt came to the nation's leadership, he proposed the Works Progress Administration and the Public Works Administration. All of us are accustomed to driving through tunnels built by the WPA and crossing bridges with letters burned in steel indicating that they were built in the late 1930s under the WPA and the PWA. He created the Civilian Conservation Corps so that any able-bodied young man who could not find employment in the open market could count on the government giving him an assignment. In the Forestry Service and in dredging harbors and cleaning up the wilderness, there was work to be done. It was far more honorable for the government to finance earnest labor for a just reward than to give people grants that would weaken their character and create a habit of dependency.

We need to stop wringing our hands and gritting our teeth now, and put our economists, labor leaders, and legislators to work in coming up with feasible ways to scrap the Band-Aid, tentative, placebo welfare programs, and return to honest labor that builds respect and guarantees every person with a sound mind and an able body a minimum decent level of employment. Our schools in urban centers badly need able-bodied monitors in every hallway. Our parks and swimming pools need able-bodied guards for safe play and recreation. Our beaches need to be kept clean and safe. The infrastructures of Baltimore, New York City, Richmond, and all of our other older cities need to be rebuilt. Floods and blackouts occur everywhere because of the inadequacies of the infrastructure. Sewer lines, underground tunnels, electrical power lines, bridges, and roadways all need to be overhauled. There is work to be done.

Federal or state agencies can do the job themselves, or they can subsidize industries that are able and willing to perform these services on a competitive basis, using extra labor supplied by the government in order to assure guaranteed full employment. This will sound like socialism to people who have no compassion. But those who care deeply about other people will hail work programs and welcome them as an intelligent response to a chronic problem.

It doesn't mean getting rid of or even reducing free enterprise. On the contrary, the corollary to free enterprise and the other freedoms that we cherish is to establish a bottom beneath which our compassion will allow no one to fall. It is incredible that our leaders are saying that we are unable to do this when we have an average national per capita income of $34,000—when most human beings on the rest of the planet live on less than $3,400. Lord, have mercy!

And what about affirmative action? Ninety-seven percent of managerial jobs in the country are still in the hands of white males. Anyone who thinks affirmative action has been overdone should go to any airport early in the morning and see who are carrying briefcases and rushing to makes planes. Go to any office building or hotel in downtown Manhattan, and see who's riding up in the elevators. It's a myth that competent white males have been shoved out of the line and replaced by incompetent females, Hispanics, and blacks. Somewhere now and then, no doubt, there has been a less competent black in the line in front of a more competent white. But generally, competent blacks are not being considered at all. Affirmative action, by whatever name, must continue because otherwise seniority, tenure, and the old-boy network will continue the status quo in perpetuity.

The administration of welfare needs to continue at the federal level. The states are unequal in their economic sufficiency. Industrial states and states with vigorous economic activity are far more able to meet the needs of people in disadvantaged circumstance. The only agency that can achieve national parity is the federal government, not because it wishes to seize power, but because through federal taxation it has the capacity to equalize that states and counties do not have. Moreover, where is the record that shows that states are cleaner and more disciplined in handling public funds than the federal government? Where is the evidence that they care more about their people? Corruption at the state level matches anything that we've ever seen at the federal level.

The institution of slavery was a monumental moral failure, just as the slaughter and dispossession of Native Americans were. Both must be remembered, as the Holocaust in Europe must be remembered. These are indelible blots on the ledger of time, and the lessons learned must stay alive. But we also must move on. An emotional appeal to ethnic solidarity is important, but early Monday morning little African Americans and little Native Americans must step into the context of today's America, and claim the future for themselves. They need to acquire the equipment to make a living, fulfill their potential, participate in government, and take the fragments of a broken society and put them together. The sad history of ethnic conflict, religious hypocrisy, and moral collapse is the wilderness-wandering that precedes movement to a new human paradigm of genuine community.

Other prescriptions may make moving rhetoric, but when pursued to their logical conclusions, we will be standing again in the killing fields, like the Crusaders trekking from Gibraltar to the Syrian desert for hollow victories, and leaving a crimson trail of innocent blood. We are destined for something better. Blacks and Native Americans, like litmus tests, must prove to the world that we have options that we are only beginning to explore. We do not need to reinvent the wheel. We already know the price of ignorance and exclusion. We have seen the result of generations denied decent employment and we know what poverty breeds. We know what beauty and grace attend the lives of those who enjoy the proper uses of the mind and fruitful employment. Strategies based on fabricated data, systemic hatreds, and self-interests of the privileged will have to be forfeited.

Each of us, to one extent or another, is already committed to a network of community. At Christmas time I discover how vast my own is, and how it grows and grows from the center out. I have to make several greeting card lists. One is for kinfolk. Then my buddies from Norfolk, many friends for over sixty years.

My circle widens, and the lists grow, embracing college schoolmates and fraternity brothers I used to joke with about the slim prospects that a better day for us would come. Then come my seminary and graduate school friends, and my colleagues from later years. We've followed one another through the tensions of the Cold War, the Johnson gains and the civil rights struggles, the long night of Nixon-Reagan-Bush, the nagging ethnic skirmishes and the slow birth pangs of a new community. We are white, African American, Asian, and Hispanic; Catholic, Protestant, and Jew. This circle is wide and deep. Because I have been closer to this crowd, for a longer time, my bond with them is the strongest. What a blessing it has been. I have already lived in a community that I call a new human paradigm. Such a community becomes richer as the years go by.

I retired from the Abyssinian Baptist Church in 1989 and

spent the next year recovering from a triple bypass heart operation and writing the 1990 Lyman Beecher Lectures on preaching for Yale Divinity School. I spent another year at Vanderbilt, and the next as professor of Christian Ethics at United Theological Seminary in Dayton. These were inspiring experiences and splendid opportunities to be with people living, working, and preaching genuine community.

I was lecturing at Duke University one day in 1992 when I ran into Dean Campbell of the divinity school. He invited me to spend my remaining teaching time at his school. Then he reminded me that he had been a sophomore the day I preached in their famous Gothic chapel, the first black person allowed to do so. He said that he had sat there wide-eyed when the black preacher stood in the pulpit directly over the crypt of President Few, the man who had decreed that it would be over his dead body before a black would preach in that majestic sanctuary. That was thirty-five years ago. My eyes welled up at his memory, and I gladly accepted his offer. I am now at the end of my second year at Duke University Divinity School.

This semester, spring of 1995, I teach a class in preaching on social issues. It's a diverse class of six African-American students and eight whites, from all over the country, from age twenty-two to fifty-two, and from four different religious denominations. Twenty years ago, there would have been no class by that title, no racial mixture, and no African-American professor.

I teach another class called "Leadership in the Black Church in the Twenty-First Century." Of my forty students, twenty-two are white and eighteen are black. Any and every issue concerning blacks is discussed; whites are allowed to disagree with blacks, and both are encouraged to disagree with the teacher. Twenty years ago, no such course would have been offered. If it had been offered, the room would have been empty, for no whites would have taken it, and there were no blacks on campus. These classes are overtures to the opera, a movement toward the consummation of the faith of blacks. They are the substance of things hoped for.

When I get up to preach in a ghetto church in Bedford-Stuyvesant, or at Riverside on Morningside Heights, in Abyssinian or in the Princeton or Duke chapel, in a rural black church in East Carolina or in Harvard's Memorial Church, I try hard to share with my listeners a moment of trust in our common existence. We are all vessels of clay, derivative, finite creatures, but we are not here alone. And this is the faith that sustains us. When we feel impelled to search for ultimate meaning, we are sounding the alarm, ringing the chimes, striking the cymbal, and calling attention to God's investment in our condition.

AMERICA HAS NO STATE RELIGION, NO SINGLE POLITICAL party, no royal family, and no single ethnic root. That puts us in an excellent position, at just two hundred years old, to create a new model of community. As citizens of the United States we carry her passport and her Social Security card, but such contracts do not create a meaningful, viable relationship among ourselves. However, if we recognize and celebrate the majestic principles on which this nation was founded, and in doing so discover our unity in nurturing the ideals of democracy, we can set an example for the world. Other nations bond around their culture, religion, or royal family, but we are bonded by ideals of equality and justice, which are the zenith of human aspiration.

We could all simply wait to see how we make out, swallowed up by those who match greed against need. We can wait to see where a culture that pivots on hedonism, prurient entertainment, and brutal industries leads us. We can hold on and continue to indulge in politics that are polarized by Darwinian ethics versus human compassion and fairness. But we can do much better by deliberately embracing the new human paradigm.

For the first time in this century we are free to revise our national agenda without worrying about a contending military superpower. We can capture this rare moment of change through strong leadership from churches and synagogues, from universities, and voluntary associations, and from the inspired vision of our intellectual and spiritual leaders. They can point the way toward true fulfillment, the completion of the sublime intentions of the founders of this noble experiment. We needn't wait for some wild development to lead us there. By our own intentionality we can be bold in its pursuit, as when Alexander brought Occident and Orient face to face, and the thirteen colonies said "no" to George III.

The important thing is that we hold on to this rock of faith. By faith we know we can accomplish our goals with integrity. We will help America to redefine herself. This nation began with the ignominious dispossession and near obliteration of Native Americans. It compounded its shame with the disgrace of slavery. Yet this same nation is the world's last and best hope of a free and democratic society.

Where we are today demands that we make choices that are worth living and dying for, choices deserving of our best efforts, those that have the best chance of steering us toward the optimum human condition, a genuine community.

WHEN THE PROPHET ISAIAH PROMISED THE EXILES RETURNING from their captivity in Babylon that they would be given beauty for their ashes and joy for their mourning, the promise was not made in the name of some clever political maneuver or artful social theory. The prophet had been lifted out of his mundane, terrestrial existence, and dipped in a wellspring of new truth. He had been wafted as though on eagle's wings into celestial realms, where he communed with the Ancient of Days, the Eternal One.

Ashes will be turned to beauty by a power beyond our own fragile will. Black people have a long history of standing up to the impossible, and making the possible real. Likewise, we know how to stay our course and ply heavy seas of disappointment. We know how to trust the most invincible surmise that the mind can imagine and that the heart can embrace. By our faith in the substance of things hoped for and the evidence of things not seen, a new human paradigm can be achieved.

About the Author

Prior to his death in 1997, Samuel DeWitt Proctor was professor emeritus at Rutgers University and pastor emeritus of Abyssinian Baptist Church in Harlem. He earned a doctorate in theology at Boston University, became president of two colleges—Virginia Union, his alma mater, and North Carolina A & T—and served as associate director of the Peace Corps under Presidents Kennedy and Johnson. A speech writer for Hubert Humphrey's presidential campaign of 1968, he also was associate general secretary of the National Council of Churches and headed the Institute for Services to Education. More recently Proctor was Lyman Beecher Lecturer at Yale and a professor at Vanderbilt University, United Theological Seminary, and Duke University. He was author of *Samuel Proctor: My Moral Odyssey*, *The Certain Sound of the Trumpet: Crafting a Sermon of Authority*, and *"How Shall They Hear?": Effective Preaching for Vital Faith*. He was also coauthor of *We Have This Ministry: The Heart of the Pastor's Vocation* (with Gardner C. Taylor) and *Sermons from the Black Pulpit* (with William D. Watley).

	DATE DUE		

Social Media and the Law

Social media platforms like Facebook, Twitter, Pinterest, YouTube, and Flickr allow users to connect with one another and share information with the click of a mouse or a tap on a touchscreen, and have become vital tools for professionals in the news and strategic communication fields. But as rapidly as these services have grown in popularity, their legal ramifications still aren't widely understood. To what extent do communicators put themselves at risk for defamation and privacy lawsuits when they use these tools, and what rights do communicators have when other users talk about them on social networks? How can an entity maintain control of intellectual property issues—such as posting copyrighted videos and photographs—consistent with the developing law in this area? How and when can journalists and publicists use these tools to do their jobs without endangering their employers or clients?

In *Social Media and the Law*, 11 media law scholars address these questions and more, including current issues like copyright, online impersonation, anonymity, cyberbullying, terms of service, and WikiLeaks. Students and professional communicators alike need to be aware of laws relating to defamation, privacy, intellectual property, and government regulation—and this guidebook is here to help them navigate the tricky legal terrain of social media.

Daxton R. "Chip" Stewart, Ph.D., J.D., LL.M., is an associate professor at the Schieffer School of Journalism at Texas Christian University. He has more than 15 years of professional experience in news media and public relations and has been an attorney since 1998. His recent scholarship focuses on the intersection of social media and the law.

Social Media and the Law

A Guidebook for Communication Students and Professionals

Edited by
Daxton R. "Chip" Stewart

Routledge
Taylor & Francis Group

NEW YORK AND LONDON

First published 2013
by Routledge
711 Third Avenue, New York, NY 10017

Simultaneously published in the UK
by Routledge
2 Park Square, Milton Park, Abingdon, Oxon OX14 4RN

Routledge is an imprint of the Taylor & Francis Group, an informa business

Library of Congress Cataloging in Publication Data
Social media and the law : a guidebook for communication students and
professionals / Edited by Daxton R. Stewart.
      p. cm.
   Includes bibliographical references and index.
   1. Online social networks—Law and legislation—United States. I.
Stewart, Daxton R.
   KF320.A9S625 2013
   343.7309'944—dc23   2012023696

ISBN: 978–0–415–53513–7 (hbk)
ISBN: 978–0–415–53514–4 (pbk)
ISBN: 978–0–203–11291–5 (ebk)

Typeset in Bembo and Helvetica
by Swales & Willis Ltd, Exeter, Devon

Contents

Preface

Daxton R. "Chip" Stewart

Schieffer School of Journalism
Texas Christian University

A few years ago, early in the fall semester, a couple of editors for the student newspaper approached me with a question. During the summer, a TCU student had won the Miss Texas pageant, but because it was when the students were on break for the summer, we did not have a photographer present. On deadline, and without a photo in hand, the student journalists had turned to the web—and to their network of contacts and friends on Facebook. Sure enough, they found photos of the pageant—including those of our resident winner—on Facebook.

The students had a seemingly simple question any editor or newsroom lawyer should expect—can we use these photos we found on Facebook? The answer was less than obvious. My initial response was along the lines of, "I don't think so, at least not without permission, so go and ask first, but I'm honestly not sure." Copyright law, I believed, makes it pretty clear that use of a whole photo without permission goes beyond fair use, even for news purposes. But I wanted to find out for sure, so I looked online for judicial rulings on the copyright status of photos shared via social media. There were none. So I checked for law review articles. No luck there, either. The blog posts I read were as hesitant as my own advice.[1]

These kinds of questions have become more and more prevalent when I have spoken to professional journalism and public relations groups and have worked with students. New issues arise nearly every day brought on by social media use by media professionals or other citizens, issues that are uncharted terrain for the law. A man is arrested for using Twitter to broadcast police locations, discovered using a police scanner, during G-20 protests in Pittsburgh.[2] A pharmaceutical company receives a warning letter from the

FDA because it used a Facebook widget to market one of its prescription drugs.[3] A judge orders a newspaper to stop making posts on Twitter during a high-profile murder prosecution and to delete its previous posts about the trial.[4] Federal investigators issue a subpoena to Twitter for personal information of users suspected of collaborating with WikiLeaks to publish confidential U.S. documents.[5] A high school principal resigned amid allegations that she created a Facebook account under a pseudonym to monitor students.[6] An attorney shuts down her Pinterest boards after reading the terms of use and fearing liability for copyright infringement for photos she posted.[7] The Associated Press advises its staff not to retweet anything that may appear to be "expressing a personal opinion on the issues of the day."[8]

Social media have unquestionably permeated the practice of communicators such as journalists, public relations and advertising professionals. Our audience, our clients, and our colleagues expect that we, as professional communicators, become expert in using all available communication tools to do our respective jobs—and to do so in a way that dodges potential legal and ethical pitfalls.

Centuries of jurisprudence about media law provides a foundation for understanding the particular challenges we face when using social media. However, courts, lawmakers, and regulators have done little to keep up with these challenges, particularly for media professionals.

The lack of formal guidance from courts and legislators is understandable, of course. New communication tools emerge—and disappear—at a rapid pace, faster than the legal system can evolve to handle the particular issues each presents. In the year preceding the publication of this book, Pinterest rose from obscurity to become the third-most visited social media site, after Facebook and Twitter, with 17.8 million unique visitors in February 2012.[9] Though Pinterest has been in existence since March 2010, a LexisNexis search of all federal and state court decisions using the term "Pinterest" returned exactly one result—in which Pinterest was mentioned in a footnote describing social media tools in a case involving the state of New York's efforts to subpoena information from the account of a Twitter user suspected of criminal deeds in connection with Occupy Wall Street protests. As the Criminal Court of the City of New York noted, "The reality of today's world is that social media, whether it be Twitter, Facebook, Pinterest, Google+ or any other site, is the way people communicate."[10]

This footnote, of course, provides little guidance to media professionals about how the law treats social media communications. The purpose of this book is to bridge this gap, providing practical guidance for communication students and professionals as they navigate the dangers of daily use of social media tools. To what extent can we use photos users have voluntarily shared on a social media site? Who is responsible when a person's reputation is

harmed, or one's privacy is violated, through social media communications? How can social media tools be used to gather information or transmit news and commercial messages? These questions and more are addressed in this volume.

WHAT ARE SOCIAL MEDIA?

Before addressing the particular challenges social media present, it is helpful to understand exactly what social media are.

Communication scholars generally begin with the definition authored by danah boyd and Nicole Ellison in 2007 of social networking sites as "web-based services that allow individuals to (1) construct a public or semi-public profile within a bounded system, (2) articulate a list of other users with whom they share a connection, and (3) view and transverse their list of connections and those made by others within the system."[11] It is the third item—allowing users to make their social networks visible, thus permitting new connections to be made and networks to become larger—that boyd and Ellison say make social networking sites unique.

These core commonalities between social sites are visible in the most trafficked social media sites today. Whether sites are used primarily for social networking (such as Facebook and LinkedIn), for sharing videos and photos (YouTube, Flickr, Pinterest), or for sharing thoughts and ideas and other content through microblog (Twitter, Tumblr), they have at their center a transformational way of human interaction.

Social media, as such, are tools that have changed the way people communicate, as noted by Clay Shirky. "The tools that a society uses to create and maintain itself are as central to human life as a hive is to bee life," Shirky wrote in 2008, noting how social tools enable sharing and group formation in new ways.[12] The structure of the tools—individual profiles in bounded systems that can make connections public—has inexorably led to the culture of sharing and voluntariness on social networks.

But sharing and voluntariness are difficult concepts for the law, which often seeks more rigid definitions and boundaries to regulate human affairs. As such, legal definitions of social media often struggle to nail down these concepts. For example, when the Texas legislature sought to outlaw online impersonation—that is, creating a false profile online to harass or defraud another person—it chose the following definition of "commercial social networking site":

> any business, organization, or other similar entity operating a
> website that permits persons to become registered users for the

> purpose of establishing personal relationships with other users through direct or real-time communication with other users or the creation of web pages or profiles available to the public or to other users. The term does not include an electronic mail program or a message board program.[13]

Such a definition is so broad as to encompass nearly any online activity, whether publicly available or not, as long as it is not email or message boards—though even message boards, which enable discussion among strangers or friends, have a social aspect to them.

In fact, such statutory definitions have been deemed overbroad by federal courts when it comes to First Amendment concerns. For example, Louisiana's law forbidding sex offenders from using social media was struck down by a federal district court in 2012. The court noted that the term "social media" was not defined in the "Unlawful use of social media" act, though the act did mention "social networking sites, chat rooms, and peer-to-peer networks," a phrase so broad that the court expressed concerns that forbidding access to such sites was tantamount to "a near total ban on internet access."[14] As such, the law infringed some people's rights to express themselves freely, a violation of the First Amendment's mandate that the government "shall make no law . . . abridging freedom of speech, or of the press." A similar law in Nebraska[15] was also deemed overly broad because it encompassed nearly any kind of online communication.[16]

Courts have been a bit less clunky at defining social media. A federal district court in California in 2007, in a case involving MySpace, also described social networking sites in a functional way, as sites that "allow visitors to create personal profiles containing text, graphics, and videos, as well as to view profiles of their friends and other users with similar interests."[17] The court, as such, focused on what users do with social networking sites as a way of defining them. A Maryland state court in 2010 perhaps got closer to the heart of what makes social media challenging:

> Social networking sites and blogs are sophisticated tools of communication where the user voluntarily provides information that the user wants to share with others. Web sites such as Facebook and Myspace, allow the user to tightly control the dissemination of that information. The user can choose what information to provide or can choose not to provide information. The act of posting information on a social networking site, without the poster limiting access to that information, makes whatever is posted available to the world at large.[18]

This definition goes beyond function to consequences. The voluntariness aspect of social tools—users volunteer to share information with the world, perhaps with some limitations—makes them unique.

American courts have been handling disputes involving social media for almost a decade. The first reported opinion I was able to find was in 2004, involving Classmates.com, a site that allowed high school and college acquaintances to register and reconnect. An attorney in Oregon was publicly reprimanded by the state's Supreme Court by posing as a classmate who had become a teacher at their former high school and posting, "Hey all! How is it going. I am married to an incredibly beautiful woman, AND I get to hang out with high school chicks all day (and some evenings too). I have even been lucky with a few. It just doesn't get better than this."[19] Since then, courts have been handling cases involving social media in greater numbers each year. Facebook has been the subject of litigation almost since its founding, with Mark Zuckerberg battling ConnectU LLC, the operation put together by Tyler and Cameron Winklevoss and Divya Narendra, over who owned what intellectual property rights to the site. Just one case—*ConnectU v. Zuckerberg*—was the subject of an opinion in 2006.[20] The caseload has steadily grown. A LexisNexis search found 10 cases mentioning Facebook in 2007; 22 cases in 2008; 67 in 2009; 183 in 2010; with 484 cases in 2011 and an even greater rate to date in 2012.

Not all of these cases involve issues for media professionals, but many of them have, as is detailed in this book. Beyond the courts, the federal government has become increasingly aware of the impact of social tools on commerce, with regulatory agencies such the Federal Trade Commission and the Food and Drug Administration offering guidelines for making marketing communications via social networks. Professional media organizations such as the Public Relations Society of America, the Institute of Advertising Ethics, and the American Society of News Editors offered updated guidelines and best practices for professional social media use in 2011 as well.

LOOKING FORWARD

The particular challenge of a volume like this is to nail down the landscape of social media and the law at a fixed moment in time—as social tools are launching and evolving, as legislatures and regulators are trying to come up with ways to manage the impact of these tools, as professionals are trying to maximize effective use of social tools while minimizing legal risks. All of this is being done in the shadow of the developing culture of social media, one that is rooted in voluntariness, sharing, and group formation rather than legal formalities such as contracts, property, statutes, and regulations.

As such, it may very well be that Lawrence Lessig was right, that "Code is law"—that is, that the hardware and software that make up cyberspace determine its culture and use, so that management of human affairs online is best left to the code, not to legislatures and the courts.[21]

Nevertheless, courts have already handled thousands of cases that involve social media tools, with thousands more on the way. Online human affairs can be and certainly have been the subject of our laws, and those who would use social media tools should be aware of the legal obligations, duties, and expectations created by the law.

Fortunately, we are guided by precedent. While social media may be revolutionary technologies, so were the telegraph, the telephone, the radio, the television, and the Internet. We are guided by the First Amendment and centuries of jurisprudence regarding the law of communication. And the more we understand how social tools work, and how they have fundamentally transformed human interaction, the more we should be able to understand how to use them legally and responsibly.

This volume comprises 11 chapters by media law scholars examining the way the law interacts with social media in their areas of expertise. Media professionals continue to face many of the same challenges they have in the past—defamation, privacy, intellectual property, commercial speech regulations, access to government records and court proceedings—so this volume is organized around these particular challenges. Some areas touch on other aspects of communication—obscenity, cyberbullying, student speech—in which the implications of social media on the law have developed, shedding light on how courts may treat these issues for communicators in the future.

Each chapter opens with an overview of the law in that area, examining how legislatures, courts, and regulators have handled the law in the digital environment. The authors go on to examine the particular challenges that social tools present, and how professionals and the law have responded to them. Finally, each chapter concludes with a "Frequently Asked Questions" section, with answers to five practical questions that professionals and students may most often encounter. The first nine chapters of this volume focus on areas of substantive law, while the final two examine practical consequences for professionals, offering guidance on developing social media policies for strategic communication and journalism professionals.

Our hope in writing this book was not to provide a comprehensive, definitive volume on the law of social media as it pertains to media professionals—that would, of course, be impossible in this time of great upheaval to the media landscape. Instead, our goal is to provide professional communicators a foundation of knowledge with practical guidance in what we know to be the most dangerous terrain, with an eye on what is happening now and what is to come. While the law may often seem ill-suited to

adapt to technological and social change that have transformed the way people communicate, adapt it has and will continue to do.

NOTES

1   Ultimately, I addressed this in a legal research article. See Daxton R. Stewart, Can I Use This Photo I Found on Facebook? Applying Copyright Law and Fair Use Analysis to Photographs on Social Networking Sites Republished for News Reporting Purposes, 10 J. Telecommunications & High Tech. Law 93 (2012).

2   Colin Moynihan, Arrest Puts Focus on Protesters' Texting, N.Y. Times, October 9, 2009, http://www.nytimes.com/2009/10/05/nyregion/05txt.html?_r=2.

3   Katherine Hobson, FDA Dings Novartis for Facebook Widget, WSJ Health Blog, August 6, 2010, http://blogs.wsj.com/health/2010/08/06/fda-dings-novartis-for-facebook-widget/.

4   Dianna Hunt, Judge Restricts Reporting on Capital Murder Trial in Fort Worth, Fort Worth Star-Telegram, January 6, 2012, http://www.star-telegram.com/2012/01/06/3640977/judge-restricts-reporting-on-capital.html.

5   Scott Shane & John F. Burns, U.S. Subpoenas Twitter Over WikiLeaks Supporters, N.Y. Times, January 8, 2011, http://www.nytimes.com/2011/01/09/world/09wiki.html?pagewanted=all.

6   Jessica Bock, Clayton High's Principal Resigns Amid Facebook Mystery, St. Louis Post-Dispatch, May 6, 2012, http://www.stltoday.com/news/local/education/clayton-high-s-principal-resigns-amid-facebook-mystery/article_70bd065a-5912-551a-ac73-746ea58177af.html.

7   Alyson Shontell, A Lawyer Who Is Also a Photographer Just Deleted All of Her Pinterest Boards Out of Fear, Business Insider, February 28, 2012, http://articles.businessinsider.com/2012-02-28/tech/31106641_1_repinning-copyright-entire-image.

8   Mallary Jean Tenore, AP Issues Staff Guidelines on Retweets, No "Personal Opinions" Allowed or Implied, Poynter.org, November 3, 2011, http://www.poynter.org/latest-news/mediawire/152016/ap-issues-staff-guidelines-on-retweets-no-personal-opinions-allowed-or-implied/.

9   John D. Sutter, Report: Pinterest is Third Most-Visited Social Site, CNN.com, April 6, 2012, http://articles.cnn.com/2012-04-06/tech/tech_social-media_pinterest-third-social-network_1_social-networking-facebook-and-twitter-social-media?_s=PM:TECH.

10 New York v. Harris, 2012 N.Y. Misc. LEXIS 1871 at *3, note 3 (Crim. Ct. City of N.Y., N.Y. County, 2012).

11 danah m. boyd & Nicole B. Ellison, Social Network Sites: Definition, History, and Scholarship, 13 J. Computer-Mediated Communication 210, 211 (2007).

12 Clay Shirky, Here Comes Everybody 17 (2008).

13 Texas Penal Code § 33.07(f)(1) (2012)

14 Doe v. Jindal, 2012 U.S. Dist. LEXIS 19841 at *27 (M.D. La. 2012).

15 Neb. Rev. Stat. § 29-4001.01(13) (2012)

16 See Doe v. Nebraska, 734 F. Supp. 2d 882 (D. Neb. 2010).

17 LifeUniverse v. MySpace, 2007 U.S. Dist. LEXIS 43739 at *1 (C.D. Cal. 2007).

18   Independent Newspapers Inc. v. Brodie, 407 Md. 415, note 3 (Md. Ct. App. 2010).
19   In re Carpenter, 95 P.3d 203 (Oregon 2004).
20   See ConnectU LLC v. Zuckerberg, 2006 U.S. Dist. LEXIS 86118 (D. Mass, 2006); ConnectU LLC v. Zuckerberg, 522 F.3d 82 (1st Cir. 2008).
21   Lawrence Lessig, Code and Other Laws of Cyberspace 6 (1999).

CHAPTER 1

The Boundaries of Free Speech in Social Media

Jennifer Jacobs Henderson

Trinity University

ABSTRACT

Although the fundamental questions regarding free speech have changed little since the advent of social media, these new ways of connecting and communicating have left judges and legal scholars questioning the shifting boundaries of speech in social digital spaces. To better understand how laws regarding free speech are evolving to address this new medium, this chapter examines three areas of social media law where the boundaries remain contested ground: access, content, and surveillance.

At a time when more people in the United States use social media than vote, what happens in these spaces is becoming increasingly significant—shaping politics, economics, and history. If health care policies, stock market movements, and entertainment franchises are now debated on social networks rather than traditional media, understanding the boundaries of allowable speech in these spaces is essential. The amount of and ability to access digital content means that the potential for disagreement over speech has increased exponentially, and thus the number of legal challenges regarding speech has increased. From patent infringement[1] to defamation,[2] social media are a new breeding ground for legal action. Whether it is Courtney Love's potentially defamatory Twitter rants about her daughter's boyfriend,[3] her fashion designer,[4] or her former lawyer,[5] or the UK Ministry of Defence warning soldiers through a series of YouTube videos to take care using social media lest their speech fall into the wrong hands,[6] the fundamental questions raised are not so different than those posed when people with a podium and a bullhorn spoke a century ago: What kinds of speech should be allowed?

When can government intervene? How can someone protect private speech from public eyes? The distributed and participatory nature of social networks, however, have left judges analyzing complex new communication patterns as they attempt to draw the boundaries of free speech, government intervention, privacy rights, and copyright protections.

Two recent cases involving the "like" button on Facebook demonstrate the confusing legal reality of speech in a social media age. In the first case, the Hampton, Virginia, sheriff fired six employees who supported an opposing candidate during his re-election campaign. One of these workers contended in federal court that he was fired for expressing his support of the other candidate by "liking" him on Facebook. Essentially, he was being punished for expressing his protected political speech. The district court judge in this case ruled that the firing could not be linked to the employee's support of the opposition candidate because clicking the "like" button on Facebook was not equivalent to writing a message of support for the opposition candidate. The "like" button, the court found, was not expressive speech.[7]

In a second Facebook "like" suit, users are having the opposite problem— not only is their "like" being considered expressive, it is being used as an endorsement.[8] In this case, Facebook is being sued for using the profile photo and names of users who have said they "like" a product or service that pitch that same product or service to their "friends" on the site. Users bringing the suit argue that they have not given consent for such uses. Facebook argues that consent is automatically assumed when the "like" button is clicked.

Whether the simple act of clicking a "thumbs up" icon in an online social network is a statement of popularity, support, or endorsement will be debated in courts for years to come. Like all of the legal battles that arise from this space, it is both an old and a new problem. Judicial interpretation of intention behind speech is and always has been difficult. A slip of the tongue has simply morphed into a slip of the mouse.

ACCESS TO SOCIAL MEDIA

For almost a quarter of a century, public interest organizations have fought for physical access to the most basic Internet services, with scholars noting gaps in access based on race, ethnicity, income, and geographic location.[9] And, while battles against "information redlining" and "the digital divide" might seem to be a relic of another time, the core issue of access still remains. Low-income citizens still have limited access to the Internet, and by extension, to social media communities and content. Their speech in these prolific spaces is hampered even before they begin to create.

In the United States, the right to access social media sites has been addressed recently by state courts and attorneys general. For example in Louisiana, a court recently ruled that a law restricting registered sex offenders from accessing "social networking websites, chat rooms, and peer-to-peer networks," was both unconstitutionally overbroad and vague.[10] The court found that the law as written would make it a crime to access protected content such as online newspapers and had already caused several people to refrain from using the Internet at all for "fear that they may unintentionally and unknowingly violate the law."[11]

Access has also been restricted to online video games through an initiative between Attorney General Eric T. Schneiderman of New York and video game manufacturers such as Microsoft, Apple, Blizzard Entertainment, Electronic Arts, and Disney Interactive Media.[12] The goal of Operation: Game Over is to remove convicted sex offenders from online game interactions with juveniles. Based on data collected from registered sex offenders in New York, 3,500 accounts were deleted or communication privileges suspended by game companies in the first phase of the operation. While much narrower in scope, Operation: Game Over may also be challenged in court based on the blanket assumption that registered sex offenders are always engaged in criminal activities in online games.

Questions regarding freedom of access to the Internet and social media sites vary greatly around the world. Freedom House, a non-profit organization concerned with global speech and press freedoms, in its report *Freedom on the Net 2011* rated nations based on "obstacles to access," defined as "infrastructural and economic barriers to access; governmental efforts to block specific applications or technologies; and legal, regulatory and ownership controls over internet and mobile phone access providers." Countries such as Iran, Burma, Cuba, and Ethiopia were ranked highest among those who impede access to the Internet.[13]

While outrage against repressive regimes is resonating through social media spaces today, it is important to remember that governments have always attempted to control the flow of information. From the sentencing of Socrates in 339 BC to the prosecution of U.S. socialists Schenck and Debs, who spoke out against involvement in World War I,[14] to the contemporary restriction of access to 21 social media sites by India,[15] governments have sought to suppress speech they find to work against the interests of the state. At this time of unrest worldwide, it is not surprising that government authorities, fearing their loss of power, are turning to access restrictions and censorship for control.

Though the censorship and suppression of speech by government is both common and historically grounded, pressure against oppressive regimes is growing. For example, opposition parties in Russia, dissidents in China, and

insurgents in Syria are all using new technologies to secure access to social media streams. These minority voices have found international support. In May 2011, the United Nations General Assembly's Human Rights Council declared that access to the Internet was a "basic human right" and, if restricted, would be a violation of international law.[16] On United Nations World Press Day in 2012, President of the UN General Assembly Abdulaziz Al-Nasser reiterated the importance of social media in expanding these basic human rights. "Governments that try to suppress or shut-down new media platforms should rather embrace new media for the beneficial transformation of their societies," he said in a speech at UN Headquarters. "They need to create and promote a thriving environment for free media and free expression."[17]

SOCIAL MEDIA CONTENT

Media content in the second decade of the twenty-first century has been characterized as "mobile," "ubiquitous," "voyeuristic," and "mean." The most common term used to describe this period, however, has been "social." Social sounds friendly enough, but the content of social media (online participatory sharing communities) has been anything but. Today, media accounts are filled with stories of cyberbullying, brash examples of defamation, and unauthorized celebrity photos.

Speech in social media is being challenged—along traditional legal lines and in new ways. Obscenity, libel, and copyright cases related to social media are on the rise in many countries. For example, online defamation more than doubled between June 2010 and June 2011 in the U.K.[18] New laws related to activities on social network sites such as cyberbullying and cyberstalking are being implemented at an amazing rate. According to the National Conference of State Legislatures, in 2012, 48 states had anti-bullying laws and many had implemented additional protections through cyberstalking or cyberharassment legislation.[19]

Private Speech

What were once considered private matters, topics such as sex, spousal conflict, personal habits, and finance, are now broadcast 24 hours, seven days a week via television, podcasts, and on social media sites. Where in past years media attention was focused mainly on those who placed themselves in the public limelight—politicians, celebrities, athletes—people now have a near-equal opportunity to create their own public stage. While many participants in online social networks behave as if their content is private, these are not "backstage" areas where scandal and intrigue can be revealed to some and

kept from others. Instead, content posted on social networking sites such as Facebook is, more often than not, searchable, sold, and shared. For example, concerns regarding private speech were raised in early 2012 when Google announced its new Search Plus Your World feature that combs through both your personal Google+ social media content and the Internet to return results. While the information collected from your personal Google+ account is not available to others, there are still concerns that messages posted by friends and family on Google+ were never intended to be searched. At the time these messages were posted, they may have been more personal or private than the new search system now makes them.[20]

Instead of relying on the hit or miss privacy protections of many social media sites, users are beginning to take privacy into their own hands. As of 2012, 37 percent of social network users have untagged photos, 44 percent have deleted comments, and 63 percent have "unfriended" someone. In addition, 58 percent of users "restrict access" to their social media sites by setting privacy controls so "only friends can see."[21]

Many privacy cases hinge on whether the person had an expectation of privacy in the particular forum in which the utterance was made. The courts have long held there is no expectation of privacy in public. On the user-side, this is where confusion reigns. Private companies (or publicly traded ones) run these sites. A user must register and agree to terms of service. How, then, can these sites not be private?

Political Speech

Until the Arab Spring of 2011, social media were seen primarily as vehicles for personal identity construction and storytelling. When protesters in Egypt used the social network Twitter to spread messages about government crackdowns and arrests, social media were transformed into the preferred medium for free speech activities. Despite the sincere hope of many, this free and open platform for connecting distributed voices is neither entirely free nor open.

It has been decades—probably not since the Vietnam era—since we have seen direct political action arise from speech. With the rise of participatory technologies, movements of collective action are forming across countries and around the world. Since 2010, voices transmitted through social media have called for the overthrow of the ruler of Sudan, toppled the governments of Egypt and Libya, and shown the horrors of oppression in Syria. For example, Andy Carvin, a media strategist at National Public Radio, has facilitated and aggregated live blog posts and tweets of dissidents, creating a real-time, social media news service covering uprisings around the world as they happen.[22] Because of direct-to-user content such as this, which bypasses

traditional media channels often connected to government institutions, officials around the world not only respect the power of social media, they often fear it.

As calls for free speech protections spread across the world, more and more regimes that were comfortable with suppressing expression and press are being pressured to choose speech over silence. Reporters Without Borders concluded in its 2012 *Enemies of the Internet Report*, "The revolution of miroblogs and opinion aggregators and the faster dissemination of news and information that results, combined with the growing use of mobile phones to livestream video, are all increasing the possibilities of freeing information from its straightjacket."[23]

Over the course of 350 years, the idea of a free and open venue for speech has percolated. John Milton wrote: "Where there is much desire to learn, there of necessity will be much arguing, much writing, many opinions; for opinion in good men is but knowledge in the making."[24] It was 1644. John Stuart Mill's "marketplace of ideas," where the best ideas rise to the fore through free and open debate[25] resounded in 1859, and Justice Oliver Wendell Holmes, Jr. contended, "the best test of truth is the power of the thought to get itself accepted in the competition of the market" in 1919.[26] The maxim exhorted is just as applicable today. When they work well, social media encourage a wide range of often competing voices.

For almost 100 years in the United States—from 1920 at the dawn of radio to 2010 and the rise of social media—the biggest concern among free speech activists was how individual citizens could be heard. Due to the cost of production and distribution, media remained solidly in the hands of the few.[27] Beyond the states, ownership also resided in the hands of the few, though often in the hands of a few government officials.

"The marketplace theory justifies free speech as a means to an end," writes Professor Rodney Smolla, "But free speech is also an end itself, an end intimately intertwined with human autonomy and dignity."[28] In this theoretical vein, the UN's 2011 declaration regarding access to the Internet is a part of a larger report "on the promotion and protection of the right to freedom of opinion and expression" and begins by outlining the rights provided for in article 19 of the International Covenant on Civil and Political Rights. They are: "the right to hold opinions without interference," "the right to seek and receive information and the right of access to information," and "the right to impart information and ideas of all kinds."[29]

These basic rights are clearly consistent with First Amendment protections, however, even in the United States political expression in social media is being squelched. Currently, there are 17 states that have some kind of law that makes it a crime to state a falsehood in an election campaign.[30] These laws have already been put to use in silencing Twitter messages. Mark

W. Miller, a Cincinnati resident concerned with how the city was allocating funds for a new streetcar project, sent regular tweets voicing his complaints. For example, "15% of Cincinnati's Fire Dept browned out today to help pay for a streetcar boondoggle. If you think it's a waste of money, VOTE YES on 48." When charged with a crime under the Ohio law forbidding such speech as a lie, his non-profit, the Coalition Opposed to Additional Spending of Taxes, sued the Ohio Election Commission, claiming the law was unconstitutional restriction on free speech.[31]

These election laws, especially as they have been applied to social media, restrict speech that has always been afforded the highest protection under the First Amendment. In challenges involving the limitation of political speech, courts rule the law constitutional only if (1) a compelling government interest is articulated, (2) the law is narrowly tailored to meet that interest, and (3) it is the least restrictive means necessary to address the government interest.[32] This strict scrutiny test should protect political speech in social media as it does in traditional media, erecting a legal firewall between government and the opinions of the people.

Government Regulation of Media Content

A quiet debate is raging between those who believe the Wild West of the Internet Age supports free speech and democracy and those who argue that the new "vast wasteland" of hate, violence, and porn is delivered via the Internet rather than television. These rumblings are growing louder as politicians are pressured to regulate and public interest organizations are preparing to defend freedom online.

It all began when the Internet first started worrying elected officials, way back in the days of Bulletin Board Systems (BBS). In 1996, Congress, concerned about the potential for the Internet to become a "red light district,"[33] passed the Communication Decency Act (CDA), Title V of the Telecommunications Act. Section 223 of the CDA regulated access by minors to indecent material on the Internet. In June of 1997, the Supreme Court ruled on the constitutionality of the Communication Decency Act in *Reno v. ACLU.*[34] The Court unanimously agreed that Section 223 of the CDA was unconstitutional. Here, Justice Stevens writing for the Court contended that the CDA, as written, was overbroad and vague. When considering the issue of over-breadth, the Court found that the Act's use of the term "indecency" was not consistent with the First Amendment protection of all but "obscene" materials when adult audiences were considered. In addition, the Court said the CDA was a content-based restriction, which "raises special First Amendment concerns because of its obvious chilling effect on free speech."[35]

The lasting effect of *Reno* was the blanket of First Amendment protection placed on the Internet by the Supreme Court. Eight years earlier in the *Sable* decision,[36] the Court had made clear that each telecommunication medium should be considered individually when determining the breadth of First Amendment protection. In *Reno*, the Justices gave the widest possible berth to the fledgling Internet, comparing its First Amendment rights to that of traditional press such as newspapers and not broadcasters whose regulation had been upheld due to the passive nature of the audience in relation to the medium.

Obscenity is not the only purview of government speech regulation in social media. Students at public colleges and universities have also been punished for commentary placed on social media sites. A mortuary science student at the University of Minnesota posted comments on Facebook in 2009 regarding her coursework. In one post, she wrote about the cadaver she was working on: "(I get) to play, I mean dissect, Bernie today." She also wrote of her ex-boyfriend that she would like to use an embalming tool "to stab a certain someone in the throat." In response to her Facebook posts, the University of Minnesota gave her an F in the course and required her to complete an ethics class and undergo a psychiatric exam. The woman has appealed the university's decision in court saying that the actions violated her right to free speech.[37] Similarly, a nursing student at the University of Louisville was kicked out of college for violating the Honor Code and a Course Confidentiality Agreement when she posted a description of a live birth on her MySpace page. The student, in turn, brought suit against the university for a violation of her First and Fourteenth Amendment rights as well as injunctive relief and damages under the Civil Rights Act.[38] The U.S. District Court for the Western District of Kentucky found that this was not a free speech issue, but a contractual one, and that Yoder did not violate the contract of the Honor Code or the Confidentiality Agreement with her post. The court ruled that the woman must be reinstated as a student.[39]

Student-athletes at state colleges and universities have also been the target of censorship on multiple occasions. At Mississippi State, basketball coach Rick Stansbury banned the use of Twitter after student-athletes criticized his performance and the team's fans following a loss.[40] Western Kentucky University went a step further when they suspended a football player in October 2011 after he posted comments critical of fans on Twitter.[41] A student-athlete at Lehigh University was also suspended for retweeting a racial slur.[42] While none of these student-athlete cases has yet to lead to court action, the oversight and restriction of student speech by government employees could easily lead to a chilling effect on free speech across college campuses.

Courts have also considered social media an appropriate venue for punitive actions. Mark Byron, engaged in a bitter divorce and custody suit over his young son, wrote on his Facebook page, "If you are an evil, vindictive woman who wants to ruin your husband's life and take your son's father away from him completely – all you need to do is say you're scared of your husband or domestic partner and they'll take him away." Based on these comments, Domestic Relations Magistrate Paul Meyers found Byron in contempt of a protective order. To avoid a 60-day jail sentence and a $500 fine, Meyers said Byron could post an apology on his Facebook page every day by 9:00 a.m. between February 13, 2012 and March 16, 2012 when he returned to court.[43] Byron contends that the apology, which states he was placing his ex-wife in "an unfavorable light" and "attempting to mislead" his friends, is untrue.[44] Many free speech advocates found this court-compelled speech to be concerning as government-forced speech is equivalent to restricting free speech.

These cases of government intervention are illustrative of a lack of knowledge regarding social media on the part of judges as well as a tightening of free speech restrictions on expression in these venues.

Judges can lag behind the general population in their understanding of social media for many reasons. Most notably, they participate in an occupation where connections outside the courtroom are limited to protect individuals' rights to a fair trial.[45] For example, in December 2009, the Florida Judicial Ethics Advisory Committee ruled that judges should not be Facebook friends with lawyers who could try cases before them because it could appear outwardly as a conflict of interest.[46]

A lack of familiarity with the range of content present on social media sites could also explain, at least in part, why judges are quick to censor speech in these spaces. Just like novels, comic books, and motion pictures before them, social media are seen by many without direct experience as time-wasting realms of low-brow content with potentially corrupting influences. Media stories abound regarding the inane content flowing through social media—Ashton Kutcher's tweets, YouTube videos with talking fruit, and cyberbullying dominate the headlines. Fewer media accounts point to everyday uses of social media for professional networking, news, or political action. The combination of these two factors—professional ethics and biased understanding—may very well explain some of the more recent court rulings restricting free speech in social media.

SURVEILLANCE OF SOCIAL MEDIA

Surveillance of social networks and the messages created in them is increasing daily. Today, social media networks are more a fish tank than a lock box.

Government agencies, employers, site operators, and advertisers are all peeking into the aquarium of social media to see what's up. Users of social networks, just now realizing that everyone is a Peeping Tom, are beginning to close their blinds.

Government Agencies

Security agencies for governments around the world are reading, watching, and listening in social media networks. The ultimate "lurkers," these agencies are tracking conversations, looking for clues to crimes and other misdeeds. As law enforcement agents link social media to terrorist recruitment efforts and plots of violence,[47] additional oversight is inevitable. For example, the National Security Agency (NSA), a long-time surveillant of private citizen information, stated in March 2012 that it would begin storing digital information collected on U.S. citizens even when they were not under investigation. Information, once only stored for those suspected of terrorist activities and only for 18 months, would now be held for anyone caught in the net of surveillance for up to five years.[48]

Government agencies in many nations also monitor social media sites for material that is deemed inappropriate for their citizens. In 2011, India submitted 68 requests of 358 individual "offending" items to be removed from Google-owned sites. Just over 51 percent of those requests were granted.[49] Other nations are more concerned with monitoring messages that disagree with government leaders or policies. In Eritrea, for example, the government surveyed social networking sites for criticisms, then launched online attacks, including disinformation campaigns against those posting these concerns.[50]

Employers

Employers have always known that applicants selectively construct résumés to create their workplace personas. As everyone knows, social media sites are rife for identity reconstruction, where individuals can build virtual profiles that shape real world opinions about themselves. Human resources professionals are now playing Match Game with these two identities. With multiple data points of information displayed through social networking sites, those who make hiring decisions are now able to construct their own, more comprehensive, profiles of potential employees. In 2009, a study by Harris Interactive for CareerBuilder.com found that 45 percent of employers use social media to screen job candidates.[51] In 2011, a study by the U.K. Business Psychology firm OPP reported that this percentage rose to 56 percent.[52] Employer surveillance of applicants is most often conducted by

compiling publicly accessible information available to everyone through search engines such as Google or Bing. In fact, 75 percent of all human resource professionals have been instructed to search the Internet for public information on applicants.[53]

Some firms, however, have moved into more legally dangerous territory, demanding that applicants turn over the passwords to their social media accounts. These requests have become so commonplace that in March 2012, Facebook made a formal announcement to employers telling them to stop demanding the passwords of users looking for a job with their organizations and reminding employers that practice goes against Facebook's privacy policy which forbids the exchange of account password information to a third party. In April 2012, the state of Maryland became the first to prohibit employers from requesting user names and passwords for social media sites as a requirement for employment.[54] California and Illinois have similar legislation pending. The U.S. Congress has also taken note of this practice and has drafted a bill, the Social Networking Online Protection Act (SNOPA), to forbid it. SNOPA would extend protection of user names and passwords to employers, K-12 schools, and universities, outlawing the punishment of users based on refusal to comply.[55]

Surveillance on the job goes on far beyond the hiring process. While employers have the right to sift through email messages stored on their own servers, for example, the National Labor Relations Board (NLRB) has come down on the side of the employees in a series of cases involving negative messages posted on blogs and personal social media accounts. In January 2012, the NLRB issued a memo outlining more than a dozen instances in which employers went too far in punishing employees for personal speech.[56] In one case, a woman used her cell phone at work to post sexist comments made by a supervisor and her disapproval of a co-worker's firing to her Facebook page. She continued to post Facebook messages that criticized management and ignored a supervisor's warning to "not get involved in other workers' problems" even after being asked to refrain from such activity. In this case, the NLRB found that by punishing the woman for discussing wage and working conditions with fellow employees via Facebook, the employer had unlawfully terminated her employment.[57]

In many of these cases outlined in the report, as in the one above, the NLRB found social media policies that could be construed as "prohibiting discussions of wages or working conditions,"[58] a violation of Section 7 of the National Labor Relations Act. These NLRB regulations, which originally ensured face-to-face deliberations among employees and with labor union representatives regarding working conditions and salaries, are now being applied to online communications to multiple, diverse parties. What was once a whisper in the break room to a colleague is now a Twitter

or Facebook post to hundreds or thousands of "friends" or "followers." The challenge for the NLRB and other regulatory agencies is how to best balance the protection of employee rights with the potential scope and power of social media messages.

Advertisers

Social media users may be unaware that advertisers and media companies are tracking their movements online, paying close attention to keywords, hashtags, and "likes." Gone are the days of simple cookies deposited on one's computer through an Internet browser. Today, advertisers track mouse movements, widget use,[59] online purchases, GIS location data, and even your latest prescription refill. They compile this information in real time and often sell it to the highest bidder.

When users find out about these practices, they are often astonished, then appalled. For example, a *USA Today*/Gallup poll from December 2010 found that 67 percent of U.S. Internet users surveyed believed advertisers should not be able to target messages based on "your specific interests and websites you have visited,"[60] and the 2012 Digital Advertising Attitudes Report concluded that "more than one in four (27%) British and one in five (20%) American online consumers said they would stop using a product or service —such as a social networking site—if they were subjected to too much advertising."[61]

Currently, there are no government regulations limiting to the kind or amount of information that can be collected by advertisers online. Recent media attention in the United States, however, has encouraged the Federal Trade Commission, in conjunction with the nation's largest advertising associations, to support federal Do Not Track legislation. Beginning in 2009, advertisers and media companies could voluntarily offer users the "do not track" option on their sites. On February 23, 2012, the White House announced the development of a "Consumer Bill of Rights" in concert with the Digital Advertising Alliance's (DAA) self-imposed "do not track" policies.[62] The Consumer Privacy Bill of Rights would assure individuals had control over their personal information online including easy-to-use privacy settings. Through this bill, consumers would be given access to all of the information collected by companies as well as notification of how that information would be collected, used, or disclosed.[63]

Site Surveillance

Those who own, and thus control, social media sites are also key surveillants of content. For example, Facebook employs a team of "User Operations

Analysts" who act upon complaints regarding content and behavior violations and determine whether users have violated the terms of service
agreement. In many ways, these Facebook staff and those of other social
media sites are asked to determine the outcome of free speech issues usually
decided in the courtroom.

While everyone accepts the terms of social media user agreements with
little consideration for the contractual obligations set forth, each of these
agreements has restrictions on free speech. At their most basic (for an
extensive examination of terms of service agreements, see Chapter 3), user
agreements for social media sites contain two kinds of restrictions: those
courts have ruled are acceptable limits on free speech (copyright, defamation,
etc.) and restrictions that would be ruled on as violations of free speech
rights such as "hateful" or "objectionable" language. An example of this first
category, LinkedIn does not allow material that "infringes upon patents,
trademarks, trade secrets, copyright, or other proprietary rights." In the
second category of extra-legal restrictions, Facebook will not allow "hateful,
threatening, or pornographic" material or content that "contains nudity" or
"graphic violence."[64] LinkedIn reminds users that their accounts can be shut
down if they participate in "discriminatory" discussions.[65]

Moderators in online gaming communities monitor real-time in-game
chat. Offending remarks made in these chat logs can get players removed
indefinitely for speech that would otherwise be protected on the sidewalk
outside their door. Xbox LIVE has a Code of Conduct that bans "topics or
content of a sexual nature" and immediate suspension can be applied for
"severe racial remarks."[66] The online social bulletin board, Pinterest, has an
even more restrictive speech policy, banning speech with may be "racially or
ethnically offensive," or "profane," or "otherwise objectionable."[67] Pinterest
notes in its Terms of Service agreement that "we have the right, but not the
obligation, to remove User Content from the Service for any reason."[68]
YouTube, one of the most popular social media sites with more than four
billion videos viewed each day,[69] has very specific limits on expression
outlined in its Community Guidelines. YouTube will remove any videos that
violate the Community Guidelines including those that feature "pornography," "child exploitation," "bad stuff like animal abuse, drug abuse, under-
age drinking and smoking, or bomb making," "graphic or gratuitous
violence," "predatory behavior, stalking threats, harassment, intimidation,
invading privacy, revealing other people's personal information, and inciting
others to commit violent acts."[70] YouTube also reminds users on the
Community Guidelines website that videos are screened for unseemly
content 24 hours a day.

Self-Surveillance

When Facebook was a shiny new social media platform, just out of the box, users friended with abandon. High school boyfriend? Friend. College roommate? Friend. Random woman you met at a conference? Friend. Don't really recognize the person but somehow they found you online? Friend.

In recent years, however, the "friendzy" has subsided. Over the past half-decade, we have read thousands of status updates, viewed hundreds of cats playing piano videos, and given a big "thumbs up" to more news articles than we can count. Just as users learned Second Life and MySpace no longer contributed positively to their online identities, users of contemporary social media platforms have become savvier through self-surveillance.

Now, people are removing those they once considered "friends" from social networks. A recent Pew Internet and American Life survey on social media privacy found that 63 percent of those surveyed had removed someone as a friend from their social network.[71] In the process, these "unfrienders" have limited the kinds and number of voices they are willing to hear.

The power to pick and choose whom to hear was granted by the Supreme Court in the 1943 case *Martin v. City of Struthers*.[72] In this case, a city ordinance forbade the distribution of handbills door-to-door. The ordinance, challenged by the Jehovah's Witnesses who delivered literature door-to-door as part of their ministry, was found to be an unconstitutional restriction on free speech. Here, the Supreme Court ruled that individuals should have the right to listen to or turn away speech at their own door. It was unconstitutional, the court concluded, for the government to take on this role of speech gatekeeper. This decision was reaffirmed almost 60 years later in *Watchtower Bible and Tract Society v. Village of Stratton*,[73] when the Court again found door-to-door distribution of literature constitutional. Many people who found these rulings more nuisance than fundamental right as politicians, solicitors, and religious adherents rang their doorbells are now using this power to control their personal information online. Each time a person is "unfriended," it is as if a homeowner has said "no thank you. Please don't knock on my door again."

In recent years, legislatures and courts have extended the right not to listen to the Internet. For example, the CAN-SPAM Act of 2003 (Controlling the Assault of Non-Solicited Pornography and Marketing Act) banned false, misleading, or deceptive messages from being sent via email and gives email recipients an opt-out option for receiving commercial messages (spam) via email.[74] In 2011, a federal district court in California expanded the interpretation of the CAN-SPAM Act to include social media sites such as Facebook, concluding that deceptive commercial messages posted on

Facebook walls, sent as messages to "friends," or included on newsfeeds were also "electronic mail messages" and illegal under the act.[75] By opting-out of advertising on social media sites, users now have additional control over their participation in social media.

In an effort to protect young people from cyberbullying (a laudable interest), Facebook created a Network of Support that encourages users to "block bullies," "report harassment," "stick up for others," "think twice before posting," and "get help if you feel overwhelmed."[76] While this is an important initiative, some of the suggested actions clearly encourage self-censorship. For example, the Network of Support guidelines suggest, "it's also important to be aware of how your own behavior can harm others, even unintentionally. Before you post a comment or a photo that you think is funny, ask yourself [if] it could embarrass or hurt someone. If in doubt, don't post it."[77]

Users of social media are more aware than ever that their comments and photos follow them. To help reconstruct (or rescue) their digital identities, users are now self-censoring across social media. A 2012 Pew study on social media use found that 44 percent of respondents reported that they removed comments from their Facebook profile.[78] This social media spring cleaning may not be enough to scrub the past, however. Recent news stories explain that photos deleted from Facebook may linger on the Internet for months or years.[79]

The most significant new trend in self-surveillance is online reputation control, otherwise known as getting rid of past mistakes. Whether it is photos from a drunken night in Las Vegas, a sweet love note to a past boyfriend, or a heated rant in a refrigerator repair forum, past imperfections can be erased. You can now hire "cleaners" to help you lose your online memory. Just like the mafia version of cleaners from your favorite detective novel, online reputation companies such as reputation.com eliminate what's following you.

People are not the only ones trying to control their social media reputations. Businesses, non-profits, and even government agencies are doing all they can to control the front stage face of their organizations. For example, the U.S. Department of Homeland Security recently contracted with General Dynamic for $11 million to monitor social media for any information that could reflect negatively on the department, the Federal Emergency Management Agency (FEMA), or the Central Intelligence Agency (CIA).[80] Analysts in the Department of Homeland Security were instructed in a department manual to monitor policy debates in social networks related to their agency. Although agency officials say the program was never initiated, the 2011 manual still says employees should monitor discussions in social media such as Facebook and Twitter related to "policy directives, debates and implementations related to DHS."[81]

An even more egregious attempt at controlling social media content was recently made public by *USA Today*. In this circumstance, the Department of Defense was accused of creating fake Twitter and Facebook accounts and altering the Wikipedia pages of a *USA Today* journalist and editor who were investigating the department's payment of hundreds of millions of dollars to outside contractors to improve the image of the military in Iraq and Afghanistan.[82] This "attempt at intimidation"[83] may be the first of many brought to light as government agencies, businesses, and individuals scramble to control information flow and protect their reputations in social media.

The rise of social media surveillance adds another dimension of concern to the narrowing boundaries of free speech in social media. While these spaces are often praised as opening up debate, they may in fact be on the front lines of future censorship efforts by governments, employers, and the sites themselves. To ensure a breadth of discourse in social media, all users must be aware of the limits placed on them and speak up when the walls of free speech close in.

FREQUENTLY ASKED QUESTIONS

1. Can I be fired for making a Facebook post?

It depends. The National Labor Relations Board finds employee termination to be unlawful if the social media message discusses "working conditions or wages" and the firing is a punishment for discussion of these issues with co-workers. So, if you are criticizing your employer for the work environment, job expectations, or salary, you should keep your job. If you comment on the boss's pattern of dating very young women or repeatedly post material during working hours, probably not.

Your employer can set guidelines for your use of social media related to work—whether it is time spent on sites or what information you are allowed to post. This is especially true if your employer is one in which federal regulations apply to the distribution of information (such as in the financial services industry). Businesses that create new products or services are also likely to have a restrictive social media policy as leaking information regarding the newest product before the launch date can have disastrous consequences for the company's profits and image.

2. Who has the right to demand access to my social media accounts, either by making me friend them or give them my password?

So far, most private employers may request this information without consequences. The state of Maryland passed a law in 2012 that would outlaw

employers asking for private password information as a condition of employment, and other states are considering similar legislation.

Federal legislation known as SNOPA (Social Networking Online Protection Act) would make it illegal for employers or educational institutions to ask for your username, password, or other means of accessing your social media content (such as friending). You also could not be punished for refusing to turn over this information. However, as of the publication of this book, that legislation had stalled.

3. What kinds of statements on social media could get me arrested or charged with a crime?

Both website managers and law enforcement officials are concerned with what you post on social media sites. Guidelines for acceptable content are outlined on each site's Community Standards or Terms of Use pages. In general, you can have your membership in social networking sites revoked for a number of content categories that are protected under the First Amendment but not acceptable in these privately owned spaces such as hate speech, pornography, the use of humiliating or bullying language or images, and derogatory statements dealing with race, ethnicity, sexual orientation, and disabilities. Law enforcement officials are much more concerned with illegal content: terror and other national security threats, images of drug production or use, obscenity, child pornography, stalking, or physical abuse. Several courts have accepted evidence from social media sites to support other claims. For example, a woman on probation for drinking and driving had her probation revoked after evidence was submitted showing her intoxicated in a Facebook post.[84] Social media messages and images are also being used regularly in divorce and child custody cases to show infidelity or parenting ability.[85]

The most common legal concern on social media sites, though, is copyright infringement. You could be notified by either the site manager or the lawyer for a copyright holder to take down copyrighted material from social media sites.

4. How are American laws and policies about social media different than the rules in other countries?

Many countries have laws that allow for surveillance, censorship, and restriction of content on social network sites. When using social media sites in other countries it is very important to know the boundaries of speech in those nations. If you are traveling or studying abroad you should assume that you do not have the same breadth of freedom allowed in the U.S.—even on the most restrictive sites. In many countries, journalists, activists, and citizens have been arrested and jailed for comments made in social media.

5. Are social media sites private or public spaces?

To date, social network sites have been treated as private spaces rather than public ones. For example, in *Noah v. AOL Time Warner, Inc.*,[86] the court ruled that Google's search engine was not a place of public accommodation under Title II of the Civil Rights Act because it was located in a virtual rather than a physical space. Under Title II, places of public accommodation cannot discriminate on the basis of race, gender, or ethnicity, but this does not apply to online places such as Google's search engine. This means that social media websites are allowed to make their own rules, even if those rules are more restrictive or more offensive than allowed under the Constitution or U.S. law.

NOTES

1   Michael J. De La Merced, Yahoo Warns Facebook of a Potential Patent Fight, N.Y. Times, February 27, 2012, http://dealbook.nytimes.com/2012/02/27/yahoo-warns-facebook-of-a-potential-patent-fight/.

2   Ben Dowell, Rise in Defamation Cases Involving Blogs and Twitter, Guardian.co.uk, August 26, 2011, http://www.guardian.co.uk/media/2011/aug/26/defamation-cases-twitter-blogs; Hot New Hollywood Trend: Crazy Defamation Lawsuits (Analysis), Hollywood Reporter, August 23, 2011, http://www.hollywoodreporter.com/thr-esq/hot-new-hollywood-trend-crazy-226418.

3   Randy Lewis, Courtney Love "Should Be Banned from Twitter"—Frances Bean Cobain, L.A. Times, April 12, 2012, http://latimesblogs.latimes.com/music_blog/2012/04/courtney-love-twitter-frances-bean-cobain-dave-grohl.html.

4   Courtney Love Sued for Twitter Defamation, Rolling Stone, January 5, 2011, http://www.rollingstone.com/music/news/courtney-love-sued-for-twitter-defamation-20110105.

5   Courtney Love Twitter Defamation Suit Moves Forward, Hollywood Reporter, September 23, 2011, http://www.hollywoodreporter.com/thr-esq/courtney-love-twitter-defamation-case-239702.

6   UK Government Schools the Military on the Pitfalls of Social Media, The Next Web, June 14, 2011, http://thenextweb.com/uk/2011/06/14/uk-government-schools-the-military-on-the-pitfalls-of-social-media-videos/.

7   Clicking "Like" on Facebook is Not Protected Speech, Judge Rules, Associated Press, May 5, 2012, http://www.nytimes.com/2012/05/06/us/clicking-like-on-facebook-is-not-protected-speech-judge-rules.html.

8   Lawsuit Challenges Facebook "Like" Ads, ABC7News, December 20, 2011, http://abclocal.go.com/kgo/story?section=news/business&id=8474432.

9   See, e.g., Donna L. Hoffman & Thomas P. Novak, The Growing Digital Divide: Implications for an Open Research Agenda (2012), available at http:/ecommerce.vanderbuilt.edu/; Bosah Ebo, Cyberghetto or Cybertopia? Race, Class and Gender on the Internet (1998); Pippa Norris, Digital Divide: Civic Engagement, Information Poverty, and the Internet Worldwide (2001); Mary Keegan Eamon, Digital Divide in Computer Access and Use between Poor and Non-Poor Youth, 31 J. Sociology & Social Welfare 91 (2004).

10   Doe v. Jindal, 2012 U.S. Dist. LEXIS 19841 at *3 (M.D. La. 2012).

11   Id. at *23.

12   A.G. Schneiderma's "Operation: Game Over" Purges Thousands of Sex Offenders From Online Video Game Networks, Office of N.Y. Attorney General, April 5, 2012, http://www.ag.ny.gov/press-release/ag-schneidermans-operation-game-over-purges-thousands-sex-offenders-online-video-game.

13   Freedom House, Freedom on the Net 1 (2011), http://www.freedomhouse.org/images/File/FotN/MainScoreTable.pdf.

14   Schenck v. U.S., 249 U.S. 47 (1919); U.S. v. U.S. v. Debs, 249 U.S. 211 (1919).

15   Emil Protalinski, India OKs Censoring Facebook, Google, Microsoft, YouTube, ZDNet.com, January 13, 2012, http://www.zdnet.com/blog/facebook/india-oks-censoring-facebook-google-microsoft-youtube/7308.

16   United Nations General Assembly Human Rights Council, Report of the Special Rapporteur on the Promotion and Protection of the Right to Freedom of Opinion and Expression, Mr. Frank LaRue (May 16, 2011), http://www2.ohchr.org/english/bodies/hrcouncil/docs/17session/A.HRC.17.27_en.pdf.

17   UN Highlights Role of Press Freedom as Catalyst for Social and Political Change, UN News Centre, May 3, 2012, http://www.un.org/apps/news/story.asp?NewsID=41911&Cr=journalist&Cr1.

18   Dowell, supra note 2.

19   National Conference of State Legislatures, State Cyberstalking and Cyberharassment Laws (2012), http://www.ncsl.org/issues-research/telecom/cyberstalking-and-cyberharassment-laws.aspx.

20   Danny Sullivan, Google's Results Get More Personal with "Search Plus Your World," Search Engine Land, January 10, 2012, http://searchengineland.com/googles-results-get-more-personal-with-search-plus-your-world-107285.

21   Mary Madden, Privacy Management on Social Media Sites, Pew Research Center, February 24, 2012, at 2, http://pewinternet.org/Reports/2012/Privacy-management-on-social-media.aspx.

22   Phoebe Connelly, Curating the Revolution: Building a Real-Time News Feed About Egypt, Atlantic.com, February 10, 2011, http://www.theatlantic.com/technology/archive/2011/02/curating-the-revolution-building-a-real-time-news-feed-about-egypt/71041/.

23   Reporters Without Borders, Enemies of the Internet (2012), http://march12.rsf.org/en/#ccenemies.

24   John Milton, The Areopagitica (1644).

25   John Stuart Mill, On Liberty (1859).

26   Abrams v. U.S., 250 U.S. 616, 630 (1919).

27   See, e.g., Robert W. McChesney, Rich Media, Poor Democracy: Communication Politics in Dubious Times (1999); Ben Bagdikian, The Media Monopoly (1997).

28   Rodney A. Smolla, Free Speech in an Open Society 9 (1992).

29   United Nations General Assembly Human Rights Council, supra note 16 at 5.

30   Adam Liptak, Was That Twitter Blast False, or Just Honest Hyperbole?, N.Y. Times, March 5, 2012, http://www.nytimes.com/2012/03/06/us/was-that-twitter-blast-false-or-just-honest-hyperbole.html.

31   Id.

32   United States v. Carolene Products, 304 U.S. 144, note 4 (1938).

33   141 Cong. Rec. S1953 (daily ed. February 1, 1995).

34 521 U.S. at 884 (1997).

35 Id. at 871–872 (1997).

36 Sable Communications of California, Inc. v. FCC, 492 U.S. 115 (1989).

37 Sarah Brown, Student Free Speech Case Concerning Social Media Arises in Minnesota, Daily Tar Heel, February 13, 2012, http://www.dailytarheel.com/index. php/article/2012/02/student_free_speech_case_concerning_social_media_arises_ in_minnesota.

38 42 U.S.C. § 1983 (2012).

39 Yoder v. University of Louisville, 2001 U.S. Dist. LEXIS 129711 (6th Cir. 2011).

40 Trent M. Kays, Opinion: College is About Free Speech, Not Stamping Out Rights, USA Today, February 23, 2012, http://www.usatodayeducate.com/staging/ index.php/campuslife/opinion-college-is-about-free-speech-not-stamping-out-rights.

41 Ken Paulson, Free Speech Sacks Ban on College-Athlete Tweets, USA Today, April 15, 2012, http://www.usatoday.com/news/opinion/forum/story/2012-04-15/twitter-social-media-college-sports-coaches-ban/54301178/1.

42 Id.

43 Man Told to Apologize to Wife via Facebook or go to Jail, Associated Press, February 27, 2012.

44 Id.

45 Dahlia Lithwick & Graham Vyse, Tweet Justice: Should Judges Be Using Social Media?, Slate.com, April 30, 2010, http://www.slate.com/articles/news_and_ politics/jurisprudence/2010/04/tweet_justice.single.html.

46 Joshua Schwartz, For Judges on Facebook, Friendship Has Limits, N.Y. Times, December 10, 2009, http://www.nytimes.com/2009/12/11/us/11judges.html?_r=2.

47 Dina Temple-Raston, Terrorists Struggle to Gain Recruits on the Web, NPR.org, December 29, 2011, http://www.npr.org/2011/12/29/144342062/terrorists-struggle-to-gain-recruits-on-the-web.

48 Jaikumar Vijayan, Privacy Tussle Brews Over Social Media Monitoring, Computerworld, February 16, 2012, http://www.computerworld.com/s/article/ 9224331/Privacy_tussle_brews_over_social_media_monitoring.

49 Google, Transparency Report: India (2011), http://www.google.com/transparency report/governmentrequests/IN/?p=2011-06.

50 Reporters Without Borders, supra note 23.

51 Jennifer Grasz, Forty-five Percent of Employers Use Social Networking Sites to Research Job Candidates, CareerBuilder.com, August 19, 2009, http://www.career builder.com/share/aboutus/pressreleasesdetail.aspx?id=pr519&sd=8/19/2009&ed =12/31/2009&siteid=cbpr&sc_cmp1=cb_pr519_&cbRecursionCnt=1&cbsid=84 12d5b32ef54ce6854a035cf3a59d12-303995843-x3-6.

52 Emil Protalinski, 56% of Employers Check Facebook, LinkedIn, Twitter, ZDNet.com, January 16, 2012, http://www.zdnet.com/blog/facebook/56-of-employers-check-applicants-facebook-linkedin-twitter/7446.

53 Bidhan Parmar, Should You Check Facebook Before Hiring?, Washington Post, January 22, 2011, http://www.washingtonpost.com/wp-dyn/content/article/ 2011/01/22/AR2011012203193.html.

54 Kevin Rector, Maryland Becomes First State to Ban Employers from Asking for Social Media Passwords, Baltimore Sun, April 10, 2012, http://www.baltimoresun. com/news/maryland/politics/bs-md-privacy-law-20120410,0,4565780.story.

55 Michelle Maltais, SNOPA Bill Seeks To Keep Employers out of Private Social Networks, L.A. Times, April 30, 2012, http://www.latimes.com/business/technology/la-fi-tn-federal-bill-bans-employers-seeking-facebook-password-20120430,0,5347282.story.

56 Office of the General Counsel, Division of Operations-Management, National Labor Relations Board, Report of the General Counsel Concerning Social Media (January 24, 2012).

57 Id. at 18–20.

58 Id.

59 Amir Efrati, "Like" Button Follows Web Users, Wall Street J., May 18, 2011, http://online.wsj.com/article/SB10001424052748704281504576329441432995616.html.

60 Lymari Morales, U.S. Internet Users Ready to Limit Online Advertisers Tracking for Ads, Gallup.com, December 21, 2010, http://www.gallup.com/poll/145337/Internet-Users-Ready-Limit-Online-Tracking-Ads.aspx.

61 Marisa Peacock, Too Much Advertising May Turn Consumers Off, Survey Says, CMSWire, March 1, 2012, http://www.cmswire.com/cms/customer-experience/too-much-online-advertising-may-turn-consumers-off-survey-finds-014707.php.

62 White House and Advertisers Announce New Consumer Privacy Standards, Augmented Legality, February 29, 2012, www.wassom.com/white-house-and-advertisers-announce-new-consumer-privacy-standards.html.

63 Id.

64 Facebook, Statement of Rights and Responsibilities (2012), http://www.facebook.com/legal/terms.

65 LinkedIn, User Agreement (2012), http://www.linkedin.com/static?key=user_agreement.

66 Xbox LIVE, Xbox LIVE Code of Conduct (2012), http://www.xbox.com/en-US/Legal/CodeOfConduct.

67 Pinterest, Acceptable Use Policy (2012), http://pinterest.com/about/use/.

68 Pinterest, Terms of Service (2012), http://pinterest.com/about/terms/.

69 YouTube, Statistics (2012), http://www.youtube.com/t/press_statistics.

70 YouTube, YouTube Community Guidelines (2012), http://www.youtube.com/t/community_guidelines.

71 Mary Madden, Privacy Management on Social Media Sites, Pew Internet & American Life Project, February 24, 2012, http://pewinternet.org/Reports/2012/Privacy-management-on-social-media.aspx.

72 319 U.S. 141 (1943).

73 Watchtower Bible and Tract Society of New York v. Village of Stratton, 536 U.S. 150 (2006).

74 15 U.S.C. 103.

75 Facebook, Inc. v. MaxBounty, Inc., Case no. CV-10-4712-JF (N.D. Cal. 2011).

76 Facebook Safety, Facebook's Network of Support (October 19, 2010), http://www.facebook.com/note.php?note_id=161164070571050.

77 Id.

78 Madden, supra note 71.

79 Joann Pan, Deleted Facebook Photos May Still Lurk on the Internet, Mashable.com, February 6, 2012, http://mashable.com/2012/02/06/deleted-facebook-pictures-still-exist/.

80   Vijayan, supra note 48.

81   Charlie Savage, Homeland Analysts Told to Monitor Policy Debates in Social Media, N.Y. Times, February 22, 2012, http://www.nytimes.com/2012/02/23/us/house-questions-homeland-security-program-on-social-media.html.

82   Gregory Korte, Misinformation Campaign Targets USA Today Journalist, Editor, USA Today, April 19, 2012, http://www.usatoday.com/news/washington/story/2012-04-19/vanden-brook-locker-propaganda/54419654/1.

83   Id.

84   State of Connecticut v. Altajir, 33 A.3d 193 (Conn. 2012).

85   Leanne Italie, Divorce Lawyers: Facebook Tops in Online Evidence in Court, USA Today, June 29, 2010, http://www.usatoday.com/tech/news/2010-06-29-facebook-divorce_N.htm.

86   261 F. Supp. 2d 532 (E.D. Va. 2003).

CHAPTER 2

Defamation

Derigan Silver

University of Denver

ABSTRACT

Defamation is a false statement of fact that is harmful to another's reputation. Because defamation is a tort that allows individuals to sue for monetary damages, it creates a risk for journalists, other professional communicators, and average people. However, in the United States, defamation law also attempts to balance an individual's interest in maintaining his reputation with our society's commitment to freedom of expression. This chapter explains how the law applies to traditional media and online media and explores the many ways the law has adapted to—or struggled to adapt to—the new world of social media.

Since according libel protection under the First Amendment in 1964, the U.S. Supreme Court has attempted to find the "proper accommodation" between society's interest in the free dissemination of information and the state's interest in protecting an individual's reputation. However, with its roots in feudal times, the law of defamation often has trouble keeping up with both society and technology. Global networks such as the Internet have made reputation "more enduring and yet more ephemeral."[1] Reputation has become more enduring because in many ways the Internet is "forever." Information tends to lurk in the dark corners of the Internet for years and years. It is more ephemeral because maintaining one's reputation in a networked society, replete with anonymous postings that can be instantly updated from nearly anywhere in the world, is becoming no easy task. Although, as one author noted, the invention of the Internet and the spread of online speech have not required the formulation of a new area of "cyberspace tort law,"[2] Internet defamation and the advent of social media have forced courts to apply old laws to new situations.

Already called one of the most complicated areas of communication law, with many tenets that run counter to common sense, the law of defamation is even more complicated when online communication is at issue. For example, because of ambiguity in several Supreme Court decisions, lower courts are divided over whether there is or should be a different standard of review for media and non-media defendants, an issue much more likely to be raised in situations involving social media because of the ability of average citizens to widely spread information via sites such as Twitter and Facebook. In addition, since 1996, qualified "Internet service providers" have been immune from defamation suits under Section 230 of the Communication Decency Act[3] for the postings of third-party content providers.

This chapter explains both how the law for traditional media and online media are the same and explores the many ways the law has adapted to—or struggled to adapt to—the new world of social media. First, the traditional elements needed to successfully prove a libel claim and the various options available to defendants with an emphasis on the Internet and digital media are explored. Each section also explains some of the particular challenges presented by social media. The chapter concludes by discussing some emerging issues that courts are beginning to deal with and will continue to deal with as social media sites become even more prevalent.

THE LAW OF DEFAMATION

Traditional defamation law recognizes that our society considers reputation to be one of a person's most valuable possessions and an individual has an interest in preserving his good name. Defamation is a tort, or a civil wrong, that attempts to redress damages to reputation.[4] Written or printed defamation is libel, while spoken defamation is slander. Although the law used to treat libel and slander distinctly, the introduction of broadcasting blurred the distinction between the two over time. Some jurisdictions, however, still make the distinction with most considering defamation on the Internet to be libel.

Because they allow individuals to sue for reputational damages, libel and slander create financial risks for journalists, other professional communicators, and average people posting on sites such as Facebook and Twitter. However, defamation law also tries to balance an individual's interest in maintaining his reputation with our society's deep commitment to freedom of expression. In some situations, then, defamation law subordinates a person's reputational interest to freedom of expression.

Any living individual, business, non-profit corporation, or unincorporated association can sue for defamation. While government organizations cannot sue, government officials may file a suit. Dead people cannot sue for reputa-

tional damage in the United States.[5] In some states there are laws designed to protect particular products from harm by false allegations, typically known as "veggie libel laws." For example, Oprah Winfrey was sued in Texas for statements she made during a show about mad cow disease. Following a drastic drop in cattle prices after the show aired, Texas cattle ranchers sued Winfrey for violating the state's False Disparagement of Perishable Food Product Act, although the jury eventually ruled in Winfrey's favor.[6]

A person who files a defamation complaint becomes the plaintiff. The person being sued becomes the defendant. The burden of proof in defamation is typically on the plaintiff. That is, to win a defamation suit, the plaintiff must establish certain claims or satisfy individual "elements." They include:

1. publication
2. identification
3. defamation
4. fault
5. falsity
6. injury or harm.

Most plaintiffs have to satisfy all six elements of a defamation suit in order to win. Even if a plaintiff can prove all six elements, the defendant may present a defense based on the First Amendment or common law. Defamation is state common law and often varies by jurisdiction. All jurisdictions are similar in some regards, however, and it is these similarities this chapter will focus on.

Publication

Publication, in legal terms, requires at least three people—one to communicate the defamatory statement, the person being defamed, and at least one other person to hear, see, or read the defamatory statement. A false statement made directly to an individual, but no one else, cannot be the subject of a defamation claim because there has been no reputational damage. No third party thinks less of the individual because no third party received the message. Any article that appears in a printed medium or online or any story that is distributed via broadcast, cable, satellite, or the Internet is considered published. Libel can also be published in press releases, advertisements, letters, and other personal communications. Information is also considered published when it appears in a blog, a personal website, a social media website—such as Facebook or Twitter—or in an email. While no libel cases involving Twitter have made it to trial, several cases have been

settled out of court. One of the most famous involved the musician and actress Courtney Love. Love paid $430,000 to settle a libel action by a fashion designer she referred to as a "nasty lying hosebag thief."[7] As long as the communication is consumed by a third person, the information is considered published.

You are also liable for repeating—or "republishing"—defamation if the defamatory statement does not come from a "privileged" source, which is explained below. Under the common law of libel a person who repeats a libel is just as responsible for the damaged caused as the original publisher. This includes a journalist who accurately quotes a source or media organizations that publish or broadcast defamatory advertisements. However, this doctrine is limited by several factors.

First, the republication rule is typically limited to situations where the publisher controls the content. Media companies are responsible for the republication of libelous statements because their employees write, edit, select, or are otherwise responsible for the content of the communication, even if the content did not originate with the media company. Common carriers—such as telephone companies, libraries, book stores, newsstands, and others who provide content but do not edit it—are not typically liable for the defamatory content they distribute. Asking a bookstore to review the content of every book offered for sale for defamatory material would hinder the flow of information.

Second, in the United States every distribution of a libelous statement does not constitute a separate publication. Under the "single publication rule," a libel plaintiff may only sue once, eliminating the possibility of multiple suits across multiple jurisdictions for the same defamatory statement. The single publication rule also applies to text and videos on the Internet. Thus, a plaintiff may sue in only one jurisdiction even if a defamatory statement published on Facebook was accessible in every state where the defendant had a friend.

Third, under federal statutory law, operators of websites, blogs, online bulletin boards, and discussion groups are not considered publishers and are thus not liable for statements posted on their sites by third parties. This is true even if the website's operator attempts to edit or screen material for defamatory content. Section 230 of the Communication Decency Act, enacted as part of the Telecommunications Act of 1996, provides a safe harbor that protects online service providers from liability for their users' posts. Intended to encourage "interactive computer services" to restrict the flow of objectionable content Section 230 states, "No provider or user of an interactive computer service shall be treated as the publisher or speaker of any information provided by another information content provider."[8]

The law was passed in reaction to the idea that by editing material on the Internet, an ISP could be held liable under the republication rule. In *Stratton Oakmont, Inc. v. Prodigy Services Co.*,[9] a New York court held that Prodigy, an online service provider that appeared to be exercising editor control over its service by using software to screen out offensive language and a moderator to enforce content provisions, was liable for its users' posts. Thus, in an effort to encourage interactive service to make good-faith attempts to control indecency on the Internet, Congress provided Internet Service Providers (ISPs) with immunity from libel suits. After all, if policing content had made Prodigy libel for defamatory content posted by a third party, few providers would want to exercise editorial control over content. Thus, ISPs were granted immunity in order to encourage them to edit indecent material.

Section 230 attempts to distinguish between ISPs and Internet information content providers. Section 230 defines "an interactive computer service" as "an information service, system, or access software provider that provides or enables computer access by multiple users to a computer server, including specifically a service or system that provides access to the Internet and such systems operated or services offered by libraries or educational institutions."[10] The interactive computer service is protected from defamatory statements made by other information content providers, or "any person or entity that is responsible, in whole or in part, for the creation or development of information provided through the Internet or any other interactive computer service."[11] Since Section 230 was passed, courts have interpreted "interactive service providers" quite broadly. Section 230 has been applied to interactive websites, forums, listservs, and blogs. Courts have also ruled that Section 230 applies to social media sites. For example, in February 2009, a New York teenager sued four former high school classmates, their parents, and Facebook for a private Facebook group called "90 Cents Short of a Dollar." The teenager alleged the site contained defamatory statements that she "was a woman of dubious morals, dubious sexual character, having engaged in bestiality, an 'IV drug user' as well as having contracted the H.I.V. virus and AIDS."[12] In September 2009, the court dismissed the case against Facebook, ruling the site was protected under Section 230 as an "interactive computer service."[13] Section 230 has also been used to protect sites such as the now defunct JuicyCampus, even though these sites encourage anonymous gossips that are often full of vitriol.[14] In addition, Section 230 has been invoked to bar claims of invasion of privacy and other areas of law.[15]

An additional area of concern that may arise regarding publication and Internet defamation relates to statutes of limitations. All states have a statute of limitations on defamation claims, typically ranging from one to three years from the date of publication. Courts have nearly uniformly ruled that the

continuous nature of online publications does not indefinitely extend the statute of limitations for Internet libel. In 2002, for example, a New York court ruled that a defamatory statement that was posted to a website in 1996 was no longer actionable in 1998, one year after the state's statute of limitations had passed.[16] Instead, the statute of limitations for Internet material begins when the information is first published. In addition, courts have ruled that updating a website does not constitute a new publication unless the defamatory statement itself is altered or updated.[17]

Identification

Plaintiffs must establish that a published communication is about them. This requires a plaintiff to prove a defamatory statement was "of and concerning" them. That is, they must show that someone else could identify them as the subject of the defamatory statements. A plaintiff can be identified by name, picture, description, nickname, caricature, cartoon, and even a set of circumstances. Any information about the individual may identify them. Some defamation suits arise because of the naming of the wrong person. For example, reporting that Adam Smith of 123 Main St. was arresting for murder could lead to a defamation suit if the Adam Smith arrested lived at 456 First Ave. For this reason, some media lawyers recommend identifying subjects in several ways—for example by full name, including a middle name or initial if available, address, and occupation. Some commentators have argued, however, that the ability of Internet publications to reach a very large audience reduces the likelihood that a plaintiff can be identified by "mere commonality of a name or other shared attribute."[18] After all, if there are millions of Adam Smiths within the reach of the Internet, it is difficult to say your friends assumed you were *the* Adam Smith who was identified in an Internet post.

Although persons who are part of a large group are usually not able to prove identification, in some situations members of a small group may be able to prove they have been identified by reference to the group as a whole. Under the group libel rule, large groups, such as all college professors, could not sue for libel based on statements such as "All college professors are lazy and most are unqualified to teach." However, members of smaller groups might be able to sue depending on the size of the group and the language used. The smaller the group, the more likely it is that a statement identifies members of the group. While there is no definitive size or "magic number," in an oft-cited example, the Oklahoma Supreme Court ruled an article published in *True* magazine that said team "members" of a university football team used an amphetamine nasal spray to increase aggressiveness libeled all 60 members of the team. Although the article did not name any team

member by name or position, a jury awarded fullback Dennit Morris $75,000, an award held up on appeal by the Oklahoma Supreme Court.[19]

Defamatory Content

Defamation is a communication that exposes a person to hatred, ridicule, or contempt, lowers him in the esteem of others, causes the person to be shunned, or injures him in his business or profession. The New York Court of Appeals defined a defamatory statement as one which "tends to expose a person to hatred, contempt or aversion, or to induce an evil or unsavory opinion of him in the minds of a substantial number of the community, even though it may impute no moral turpitude to him."[20]

The term libel *per se* refers to statements that are defamatory on their face. This typically includes accusations of criminal conduct or activity; attacks on one's character traits or lifestyle, including claims of sexual promiscuity, sexual behaviors that deviate from accepted norms, and marital infidelity; allegations that a plaintiff has a communicable or loathsome disease; and allegations that tend to injure a person in his business, trade, profession, office, or calling. While the inclusion of statements regarding unchaste behavior or deviant sexual behavior may seem anachronistic because community mores about appropriate sexual conduct vary dramatically, statements relating to such conduct may be the subject of lawsuits, particularly when published on the Internet, which effectively distributes such statements internationally.[21]

Libel *per quod* refers to statements where the defamatory meaning of a statement results from extrinsic knowledge. Libel *per quod* is akin to libel by implication or innuendo. Libel *per quod* can be difficult for a plaintiff to prove. Typically, you cannot be held liable for statements that are defamatory because of facts you had no reason to know. In addition, as discussed below, in many jurisdictions, plaintiffs alleging libel *per quod* must prove actual monetary loss, or "special" damages. In some jurisdictions, lawsuits involving libel *per se* proof of defamation itself establishes the existence of damages. Other jurisdictions, however, have abandoned the *per se/per quod* distinction. In addition, the distinction between the two was weakened by the U.S. Supreme Court in *Gertz v. Robert Welch, Inc.*, when the Court ruled in matters of public concern all plaintiffs must prove statements are made negligently or recklessly.[22]

Fault

Fault is perhaps the most complicated area of defamation, and the element has changed dramatically over time. As Justice Byron White noted in *Gertz*

v. Robert Welch, Inc., the Supreme Court's "consistent view" before *New York Times v. Sullivan*[23] was that defamatory statements "were wholly unprotected by the First Amendment."[24] Thus, prior to 1964, a defendant was held strictly liable unless she could prove her statement was either true or privileged. [25] Under strict liability, if a defendant commits an act, even if by accident or in ignorance, they are liable for damages. Today, however, based on a series of decisions by the Supreme Court the level of fault a plaintiff must prove depends on the identity of the plaintiff, the subject matter of the defamatory statement, and the type of damages, or monetary awards, the defendant is seeking.

In *Sullivan*, the Court held that a public official could not recover damages for a defamatory falsehood relating to his official conduct unless the defendant acted with "actual malice,"[26] that is, with knowledge of the statement's falsity or reckless disregard for the truth. In addition, the Court provided added protection for defamatory speech by requiring the plaintiff prove actual malice with "convincing clarity" rather than the normal preponderance of evidence.[27] In *Curtis Publishing Co. v. Butts*,[28] the Court extended the protection afforded by the actual malice standard to "public figures."[29] The court reasoned that the distinction between public officials and public figures in 1960s America was artificial.

In *Gertz v. Welch, Inc.*,[30] the Court ruled while public officials and public figures must prove actual malice to win their libel lawsuits, private figure plaintiffs had to prove some degree of fault, at least negligence.[31] The Court, however, also made a distinction between winning a defamation suit and the ability to recover presumed and punitive damages. Because presumed and punitive damages are typically large, the Court ruled that the states could not permit their recovery unless the plaintiff could show actual malice, regardless of their status as a public official, public figure, or private individual.[32] The Court wrote presumed damages invited "juries to punish unpopular opinion rather than to compensate individuals for injury sustained by the publication of a false fact."[33] The plurality opinion in *Gertz*, it is also important to note, consistently referred to the need to protect "publishers," "broadcasters," and "the media" from juries who might award large presumed and punitive damages.[34] As discussed below, some lower courts have interpreted these statements to mean that the Constitution requires a different standard for media and non-media defendants, a move that causes concern given the ability of non-media defendants to publish information on blogs and social media sites with relative ease.

In 1976, in *Dun & Bradstreet v. Greenmoss Builders*, the Court continued to refine the law of defamation. In the case, the Court backtracked, concluding that the limitation on the recovery of presumed and punitive damages established in *Gertz* did not apply "when the defamatory statements do not

involve matters of public concern."[35] In a plurality opinion, Justice Lewis F. Powell, Jr. characterized the Court's defamation decisions as attempts to balance the state's interest in compensating individuals for injury to their reputations with First Amendment interests in protecting speech.[36] Powell wrote that *Gertz's* ban on recovery of presumed and punitive damages absent a showing of actual malice appropriately struck a balance between this strong state interest and the strong First Amendment interest in protecting speech on matters of public concern.[37] However, according to Justice Powell, there was nothing in *Gertz* that "indicated that the same balance would be struck regardless of the type of speech involved."[38] Thus, in addition to suggesting non-media defendants don't receive the same protections as media defendants in *Gertz*, the Court has also used language that has led some courts to conclude private speech by private individuals deserves little or no constitutional protection, making such libel lawsuits much easier for plaintiffs to win.

In sum, public officials and public figures must prove actual malice to win their lawsuits. Private persons must prove at least negligence to win their lawsuits and collect compensatory damages. All plaintiffs, both public and private, must prove actual malice to collect punitive damages if the subject of the report is a matter of public concern. The Supreme Court has never ruled if private figures must prove fault if the subject matter of the defamatory statement does not involve a public concern. Different jurisdictions have reached different conclusions.[39]

A public official is not simply any individual who works for the government. The Supreme Court has determined that the public official category includes "at the very least . . . those among the hierarchy of government employees who have, or appear to the public to have, substantial responsibility for or control over the conduct of governmental affairs."[40] Courts look at number of indicators to determine if a plaintiff is a public official. Courts consider if the individual controls expenditure of public money, or has the ability to set government policy or make governmental decisions, or if they have control over citizens or are responsible for health, safety, or welfare. Public officials do not have to wield great power or occupy lofty positions. For example, law enforcement personnel, even beat cops, are typically categorized as public officials. According to one scholar, school superintendents, a county medical examiner, and a director of financial aid for a public college have all been ruled public officials.[41]

In *Gertz*, the Court ruled there were several types of public figures. All-purpose public figures are individuals who "occupy positions of such pervasive power and influence that they are deemed public figures for all purposes."[42] This can include an individual with widespread fame or notoriety or individuals who occupy a position of continuing news value.

The distinction between the fault level required of public and private figures has been justified by the distinction that public figures have the resources and media access to refute defamatory content.

In *Gertz*, the Court also ruled that an individual could be a limited-purpose public figure. Limited-purpose public figures are individuals who have "thrust themselves to the forefront of particular public controversies in order to influence the resolution of the issues involved."[43] Like all-purpose public figures, limited-purpose public figures are assumed to have access to the media based on their involvement in the public controversy and can rebut false statements about themselves. When considering Internet defamation, a court might consider independent chat room discussions about the same controversy or extensive or multiple postings on a blog by a plaintiff to support a finding that an individual has thrust themselves into the controversy in an effort to affect public opinion.[44]

In contrast to public officials and public figures, a private individual is an average person who has not voluntarily injected themselves into a public controversy. Many individuals who allege a defamatory statement was made about them on a social media site would probably fall into this category of plaintiff.

Proving actual malice can be very difficult for a plaintiff. As noted above, actual malice is publishing with knowledge of falsity or reckless disregard for the truth, and plaintiffs must prove actual malice with clear and convincing evidence, a higher burden than most civil cases, which only require proof by a preponderance of the evidence, a more-likely-than-not standard. While knowledge of falsity is easily understandable—the defendant knew what they published was false—reckless disregard for the truth can be a more nuanced concept.

Reckless disregard has been described by the Supreme Court as "the purposeful avoidance of the truth,"[45] "serious doubts as to the truth of the publication,"[46] and "a high degree of awareness of probable falsity."[47] Neither ill will nor even "extreme departure from professional standards"[48] qualifies as actual malice, although along with other factors these might contribute to a finding of actual malice. Actual malice is usually either a knowingly false statement or a combination of reckless behaviors that led someone to publish a story even if there were obvious reasons to doubt its veracity. In addition to inquiring into the state of the mind of the defendant at the time of publication,[49] courts consider the source(s) that were used or not used, the nature of the story—especially whether the story was "hot news" or time-sensitive—and the inherent probability or believability of the defamatory statement.

Negligence is the fault standard most states have adopted for defamation involving a private individual and a matter of public concern. Widely used

in tort law, negligence is a failure to act as a reasonable person would in similar circumstances. In libel cases, courts sometimes use the "professional" standard rather than the reasonable person standard. For journalists, this standard asks if they failed to follow accepted professional standards and practices. When the professional standard is used, a journalist's behavior is measured against what is considered acceptable behavior within the profession. While there is no set definitive list of what practices are considered negligent, negligence by a journalist might include failure to check public records, failure to contact the subject of the defamatory statement unless a thorough investigation had already been conducted, failure to contact multiple sources or verify information from more than one source, or a failure to address a discrepancy between what a source says he told the journalist and what the journalist reported. As with actual malice, courts consider the source(s) that were used or not used, whether the story was time-sensitive, and the inherent probability or believability of the defamatory statement. Courts do not usually demand that a story is investigated exhaustively before publication, so long as a communicator contacts the subject of the defamation directly and checks all information carefully with reliable sources. In addition, many jurisdictions hold that it is not negligent to publish a wire service story without checking the facts in the story. The so-called "wire service defense," which is not really a defense, but rather is simply considered to be an absence of negligence, is recognized by numerous states because wire services are normally considered trustworthy.[50]

Falsity

A defamatory communication must be harmful to someone's reputation and false. To be protected, a defamatory statement does not have to be absolutely accurate in every aspect. Minor flaws are not actionable, so long as the statement was "substantially true." Mistakes in a statement that do not harm a plaintiff's reputation cannot be the subject of a defamation suit.

Under American law, public officials, public figures, and private persons involved in matters of public concern must prove falsity. Put another way, anytime a matter of public concern is involved the plaintiff must prove falsity. Writing for the majority in *Philadelphia Newspapers, Inc. v. Hepps*,[51] Justice Sandra Day O'Connor said *Sullivan* and its progeny reflected "two forces" that had reshaped the common law of libel: the plaintiff's status and "whether the speech at issue is of public concern."[52] The Court ruled that whenever the speech involved a matter of public concern the Constitution required that the plaintiff bear the burden of proving falsity as well as fault in a suit for libel.[53]

Because both fault and falsity deal with determining what is a matter of public concern, both elements raise some difficult questions regarding the subject matter of defamatory speech, particularly as it applies to Internet defamation. As online speech becomes more ubiquitous in our culture, it has replaced other means of communication. However, much of the speech on Facebook, Twitter, and blogs may interest a relatively small number of people, and it may be difficult to determine whether it is a matter of public or private concern. This is particularly troublesome because in some situations the conclusion that a statement is merely a matter of private concern may ultimately determine the outcome of a defamation suit. Further, it's unclear if the public nature of social media publications—unless you have protected your account, you can publish to the whole world—may cause problems. While some may argue this could serve to elevate private speech into public speech, numerous courts have ruled expression is private even when widely distributed.[54]

Complicating matters, the U.S. Supreme Court has never defined "matters of public concern" although the phrase appears in a wide variety of cases, including cases involving speech by government employees,[55] intentional infliction of emotional distress,[56] and false light invasion of privacy,[57] as well as others.[58] Recently, in *Snyder v. Phelps*, a case involving the tort of intentional infliction of emotional distress, the Court explicated the concept. After writing that the Court itself had admitted "'the boundaries of the public concern test are not well defined,'"[59] Chief Justice John Roberts nonetheless set out to articulate some principles. Roberts began by noting that speech on a matter of public concern can "'be fairly considered as relating to any matter of political, social, or other concern to the community' or when it 'is a subject of legitimate news interest; that is, a subject of general interest and of value and concern to the public.'"[60] Private speech, on the other hand, "'concerns no public issue.'"[61] Roberts said one factor that "confirmed" the credit report at issue in *Dun & Bradstreet* was private speech was that it "was sent to only five subscribers."[62] Roberts then contrasted that with the speech at issue in *Snyder v. Phelps*, which was "designed, unlike the private speech in *Dun & Bradstreet*, to reach as broad a public audience as possible."[63]

Unfortunately, adding audience size to the public interest calculus is especially problematic in today's Internet environment as it would appear to require courts to take into account how large an audience or how many "followers" a speaker might have in a forum like Facebook or Twitter. In addition, as noted above, while some users have elected to enact privacy settings on Twitter, others have not, which makes publication on Twitter in effect publication to the whole world regardless of the number of followers you have. Blogs also might become problematic forums for expression.

Would, for example, a blog post by an unknown writer be treated differently than a blog post on the widely read *Volokh Conspiracy*[64] even if the topic of both posts was similar? Finally, what does this say about email? Recently, the U.S. Court of Appeals for the First Circuit upheld a lower court's determination that an email sent to approximately 1,500 employees detailing the firing of a fellow employee for violating company policies was a matter of private concern involving a private plaintiff.[65] Surely 1,500 people is a fairly large "intended audience." And what if the expression in question goes viral? In the age of the Internet, even the most private video, picture, or Facebook post can quickly have an audience of thousands, if not millions.[66] As discussed below, this is further complicated by the fact that some courts treat media and non-media defendants differently.

Injury or Harm

In libel suits, plaintiffs must prove damages that go beyond embarrassment or being upset. Plaintiffs must show harm, sometimes called injury to reputation. Harm can be intangible: loss of reputation, standing in community, mental harm, emotional distress, etc. However, sometimes harm may include loss of income. Not all defamatory statements bring about harm, while with other statements harm to reputation may be "presumed." For states that still recognize the difference, damage may be presumed in cases of libel *per se*, but not in libel *per quod*. In some states, in cases of libel *per quod* plaintiffs must prove the special circumstances of the defamation—that the audience understood the defamatory connotation—and actual monetary loss before a plaintiff can recover for damages based on emotional distress, damage to reputation, or other intangible harm.

Thus, libel plaintiffs may sue for presumed damages or harm that loss of reputation is assumed to cause. They may also sue for compensatory damages, awards designed to compensate for proven loss of a good name or reputation (called actual damages in libel law) or awards designed to compensate for lost revenue or other monetary loss (called special damages in libel law). Finally, plaintiffs may sue for punitive damages, awards imposed to punish the plaintiff rather than compensate the defendant.

The system for calculating damages awards is complex, even before courts begin to consider harm as it applies to Internet communications.[67] Public officials and public figures can only be awarded damages if they prove actual malice. Private figures in matters of public concern must show actual malice if they wish to collect presumed or punitive damages, and at least negligence if they wish to collect compensatory damages. States vary greatly in how they approach the defamation of private individuals who are not involved in a matter of public concern. In some states they are allowed to collect

presumed and punitive damages without a showing of actual malice or are allowed to collect compensatory damages without a showing of negligence. Some jurisdictions have even ruled that defamation involving a private plaintiff and a matter of private concern are completely governed by state common law, and do not implicate the Constitution whatsoever.[68]

DEFENSES TO DEFAMATION

In a defamation suit, defendants have a number of defenses they can actively assert. It is widely recognized in American law that truth is an absolute defense to libel claims.[69] As noted above, in all cases involving a matter of public concern, the plaintiff has the burden of proving falsity. In these cases, if a plaintiff fails to prove a statement was false, the defendant will win without having to prove the statement was true. However, defendants can also use truth as a proactive defense.

The truth of a statement rests on the overall gist of a statement or story. Minor inaccuracies will not destroy a truth defense, and "substantially" true statements will be considered true for a defamation suit. In addition, the U.S. Supreme Court has ruled that intentionally changing quotes in a story does not equate to actual malice unless the changes substantially increase damage to the plaintiff's reputation or add to the defamatory meaning of the words.[70]

Opinion, Hyperbole, and Fair Comment and Criticism

Some statements are incapable of being true or false. Thus, while in 1990, in *Milkovich v. Lorain Journal Co.*[71] the U.S. Supreme Court declined to establish separate constitutional protection for opinion, the Court has ruled that some statements are not actionable in a libel suit because they are not false statements of fact.

First, exaggerated, loose, figurative language, rhetorical hyperbole and parody are all protected by the First Amendment. For example, calling a worker who crossed picket lines "a traitor to his God, his country, his family and his class" does not literally mean the worker was guilty of treason and no one would take the statement to imply it.[72]

Second, statements incapable of being proven true or false—such as imprecise evaluations like good, bad, or ugly—cannot be proven true or false. However, this does not mean there is a wholesale exemption for anything labeled "opinion" or using the phrase "in my opinion" (or IMHO for those familiar with Twitter) will automatically protect a speaker. Writing "In my opinion John Jones is a child molester" on a blog or "IMHO: John Jones is a liar when he says he doesn't know where his wife's body is" in a tweet would most certainly not be protected opinion. Furthermore, even unverifi-

able statements of opinion can lose their protection if they imply the existence of false, defamatory but undisclosed facts, or the statement is based on disclosed but false or incomplete facts, or the statement is based on an erroneous assessment of accurate information.

Statements of opinion are also protected under the common law defense of fair comment and criticism. This privilege protects non-malicious statements of opinion about matters of public interest. The opinion must be "fair," and many courts have stated this means the opinion must have a factual basis that has either been provided by the plaintiff, is generally known to the public, or is readily available to the public. Thus food critics, movie reviewers, and other commentators who might post a scathing review of a new restaurant, film, or music album are generally protected. For example, posting that a restaurant's new sauce tasted "like rotten garbage" is not an actionable statement, whereas "in my opinion the restaurant regularly uses expired food products" would be actionable because it implies a statement of fact—that the restaurant uses unsafe food in the preparation of its dishes. This is particularly important given the proliferation of websites on which individuals can share their opinions about everything from the restaurant down to the street,[73] the reliability of a plumber,[74] or the quality of a tour guide[75] to the suitability of miniature ponies as guide animals for the vision-impaired.[76]

Privileges

Some false defamatory statements of fact are still protected by law. An absolute privilege protects a speaker regardless of the speaker's accuracy or motives. In other situations, a speaker may have a qualified privilege. A qualified privilege protects a statement only when certain conditions are met that vary from jurisdiction to jurisdiction. The U.S. Constitution provides an absolute privilege from libel litigation for members of Congress when making remarks on the floor of either house.[77] Federal legislators are also protected when communicating in committee hearings, legislative reports, and other activities. Statements made beyond the legislative process, however, are not protected.[78] The official statements of executive branch officers and all comments made during judicial proceedings—whether by judges, lawyers, or witnesses—also have absolute privilege from libel litigation.

Similarly, the fair report privilege, sometimes called the reporter's privilege, is a common law qualified privilege that protects reports of official government proceedings and records if the reports are: (1) accurate; (2) fair or balanced; (3) substantially complete; and (4) not motivated by malice or ill will. Under common law, courts recognize that the public needs access to

information regarding the workings of government and reporters should be free to communicate what happens at public meetings and the contents of public documents. Thus, someone who reports a defamatory comment made in an official government proceeding or a defamatory statement from an official government document cannot be sued for libel as long as the conditions of the privilege are met. Courts in some states have said the report must be attributed to the official record or meeting for the privilege to apply, while other states have ruled the privilege can only be claimed by a member of the press. In addition, the privilege does not extend to comments made by government officials outside of official proceedings. A reporter's privilege also extends to any and all statements made during official judicial proceedings by judges, witnesses, jurors, litigants, and attorneys and any information obtained from most official court records and documents filed with a court.

Privileges for communications of mutual interest protect a communication between two individuals when those individuals have a common or shared interest. In these situations a statement is privileged if: (1) it is about something in which the speaker has an interest or duty; (2) the hearer has a corresponding interest or duty; (3) the statement is made in protection of that interest or performance of that duty; and (4) the speaker honestly believes the statement to be true. Thus an email between business partners or corporate employees that defamed a third party might be protected under this privilege. The privilege also protects members of religious organizations, fraternities, sororities, and educational institutions.

Some jurisdictions recognize a privilege known as neutral reportage. This privilege allows third parties to report statements by reliable sources even if the third party doubts the accuracy of the statement. The privilege is based on the idea that the accusation itself is newsworthy, even if the accusation might not be true. The privilege has not been widely recognized by courts and has never been recognized by the U.S. Supreme Court.[79] Those courts that have recognized the privilege typically require the charges must be: (1) newsworthy and related to a public controversy; (2) made by a responsible person or organization; (3) made against a public official or public figure; (4) accurately reported with opposing views; and (5) reported impartially.

SLAPP Lawsuits

In some situations, libel suits can be filed in an attempt to silence criticism or stifle political expression. These suits are referred to as Strategic Lawsuits Against Public Participation, or SLAPP suits, a term coined by two University of Denver professors in articles that described lawsuits to silence opposition to a developer's plan to cut trees or suits meant to stifle reports

of police brutality.[80] The purpose of a SLAPP suit is not necessarily to win damages. Rather, the goal is to discourage criticism because libel suits can be time-consuming and costly. As Professor Robert D. Richards wrote, "[T]he SLAPP filer does not have to win the lawsuit to accomplish his objective. Indeed, it is through the legal process itself—dragging the unwitting target through the churning waters of litigation—that the SLAPP filer prevails."[81] A proliferation of SLAPP suits led many states to pass anti-SLAPP laws. According to one source, 29 states have anti-SLAPP statutes designed to protect political speech and criticism by stopping SLAPP suits.[82]

In recent years SLAPP suits have become an increasingly popular way for business and professionals to silence criticism on the Internet or made via social media.[83] For example, in 2010 a woman was sued for defamation over negative comments she made on Yelp.com about her dentist,[84] while another man was sued for negative reviews of his chiropractor.[85] Other suits have come from postings on Twitter[86] or Facebook.[87] In one case that received wide media attention, Justin Kurtz, a student at Western Michigan University, was sued for $750,000 by a towing company after he created a Facebook page called "Kalamazoo Residents Against T & J Towing." T & J Towing sued after the page attracted 800 followers in just two days.[88] In addition, SLAPP suits can also be designed simply to unmask anonymous and pseudonymous posters to social networking sites, blogs, and consumer gripe sites.[89] When applied to anonymous and pseudonymous social media and blogs, these suits are sometimes called CyberSLAPP cases.

Fortunately, online commentators have several remedies for SLAPP suits. First, citizens can countersue and contend a lawsuit was filed from spite or maliciousness rather than on legitimate legal concerns. Second, defendants in states with anti-SLAPP statutes can have the cases dismissed and, in some states, can recover court costs and attorneys' fees. In addition, some anti-SLAPP statues allow defendants to recover compensatory damages if they can show a suit was filed against them in an attempt to harass, intimidate, punish, or inhibit free speech.

EMERGING ISSUES IN SOCIAL MEDIA

In addition to the many ways defamation has adapted to the Internet discussed above, there are a number of ways the law might adapt to—or struggle to adapt to—social media specifically. Because there is little case law dealing specifically with social media and defamation, there are many questions about how the law might be applied to this quickly growing means of communication.

One of the biggest issues facing non-media users of social media is the distinctions some courts have created between the constitutional protections

afforded the media and those afforded to average individuals. As noted above, in effect, lower courts are removing a wide range of speech from constitutional protections at the very time new communication technologies such as email, Facebook, Twitter, and blogs are giving non-media individuals the power to reach wider and wider audiences.

From the outset, it is important to note that the Supreme Court has never explicitly stated there should be a difference between media and non-media defendants. The confusion comes from a series of cases in which the Court appeared to be making the distinction without directly saying so and the Court's unwillingness to directly answer the question since then. While clarifying the rules about which plaintiffs would have to prove which level of fault to win their libel cases, the majority opinion in *Gertz* also introduced uncertainty as to whether the fault rules applied to all defendants. Justice Powell defined the issue in *Gertz* as "whether *a newspaper or broadcaster* that publishes defamatory falsehoods about an individual who is neither a public official nor a public figure may claim a constitutional privilege against liability for the injury inflicted by those statements."[90] In addition, when limiting presumed and punitive damages to showings of actual malice, Powell repeatedly referred to the need to protect "publishers," "broadcasters," and "the media" from juries,[91] words that led some courts to conclude that constitutional limits did not apply in cases involving non-media defendants.[92] Indeed, it was the Vermont Supreme Court's decision that *Gertz* did not apply to non-media defendants that brought *Dun & Bradstreet v. Greenmoss Builders*[93] to the Court in the first place. After acknowledging lower court confusion over the media–non-media issue and citing six state supreme court decisions to illustrate the disagreement,[94] Justice Powell's plurality opinion ignored the issue altogether, even though it would have been the perfect opportunity to settle the question.

The following year, in *Hepps*, while Justice Sandra Day O'Connor cited only "two forces" determining constitutional requirements in libel cases—the plaintiff's status and "whether the speech at issue is of public concern"[95]— her opinion served to further fuel confusion over whether defendant's status was a third force to be considered. In discussing various issues the Court was not required to address, O'Connor stated, "Nor need we consider what standards would apply if the plaintiff sues a nonmedia defendant."[96] Finally in 1990, in *Milkovich v. Lorain Journal Co.*, the Court continued to keep alive the possibility of a media–non-media distinction by declaring that provable falsity was required "at least in situations, like the present, where a media defendant is involved."[97] That statement was followed by a footnote stating, "In *Hepps* the Court reserved judgment on cases involving nonmedia defendants, and accordingly we do the same."[98]

Based on these statements, and lower courts that have definitively held them to mean non-media defendants are not entitled to the same level of protection as media defendants, private individuals posting on social media sites need to be particularly wary of what they post. Numerous lower courts have been willing to treat media and non-media defendants differently in defamation cases.[99] In late 2011, the question of whether non-media libel defendants enjoy constitutional protection drew renewed attention—especially in the online world—when the U.S. District Court for the District of Oregon held that a blogger did not qualify as a media defendant and, therefore, was not entitled to the protections of *Gertz v. Robert Welch, Inc.*[100] because the blogger was "not media."[101] Judge Marco Hernandez's ruling led to a jury verdict of $2.5 million against blogger Crystal Cox, who a jury found had libeled Obsidian Finance Group and its co-founder, Kevin Padrick, in one of her posts.[102]

Twitter has created a great deal of speculation in the legal community because of the lack of cases dealing with the medium. Like Courtney Love's suit, discussed above, many lawsuits dealing with Twitter have yet to make it in front of a court. For example, on January 24, 2011, Associated Press (AP) sportswriter Jon Krawczynski was covering a National Basketball Association (NBA) game between the Minnesota Timberwolves and the Houston Rockets when he thought he overheard a comment between referee Bill Spooner and Minnesota Coach Kurt Rambis. Krawczynski tweeted, "Ref Bill Spooner told Rambis he'd 'get it back' after a bad call. Then he made an even worse call on Rockets. That's NBA officiating folks." The referee denied making the comment and sued Krawczynski and the AP, seeking at least $75,000 in damages. The parties settled, however, after the AP agreed to pay $20,000 and Krawczynski agreed to delete the tweet.[103]

Despite this lack of case law, lawyers and scholars are currently speculating how the courts should treat social media posts such as tweets. One author, for example, has suggested social media's characteristics should lend courts to treat posts on these mediums as opinion rather than fact. Noting that courts have consistently considered the context of a statement when determining if a statement was fact or opinion, attorney William Charron argued the nature of tweets should cause courts to mitigate the otherwise libelous nature of a tweet. Charron wrote, "Twitter is a 'buyer beware' shopping mart of thoughts, making it an ideal public forum to spark imagination and further discussion. In and of itself, however, Twitter should be viewed as a dubious medium through which to spread libel."[104] Because of the speed in which one can communicate over Twitter, the medium, even more so than blogs or other online forums, "provides a context to more readily perceive and excuse seemingly defamatory statements as emotional, unguarded, and imprecise 'opinions,'" wrote Charron.[105] To support his

argument, Charron relied on numerous cases in which courts have found that blog readers expect to read informal and personal content akin to opinion rather than statements of fact. Based on this, Charron proposed a wholesale exemption for Twitter under current defamation law.

Others have suggested the unique nature of Twitter calls for new statutory or common law approaches to libel via Twitter. Legal commentator Julie Hilden, for example, wrote that current libel law is not a good fit for social media because much of it was crafted for a time when newspapers reigned supreme. According to Hilden, Twitter is unlike traditional mass media for a number of reasons. First, Twitter followers are easy to number and identify. This makes it easier for potential plaintiffs to determine who has enough followers to create a worthwhile suit, although because of Twitter's scrolling feed it might make it difficult to know just how much reputational damage was done by a tweet or subsequent retweets. Conversely, it also makes it easier to determine the effectiveness of retractions. Second, the 140-character nature of tweets makes it very difficult to apply the traditional protection for opinion supported by fact. It is difficult to describe both an opinion and the facts supporting it in 140 characters. Hilden also agreed that the shoot-from-the-hip nature of most tweets makes it likely tweets are opinion or hyperbole rather than fact. Finally, Hilden contended that the nature of tweets actually make them more like slander, even though some jurisdictions have blurred the distinction between the two torts while others have typically ruled Internet defamation is libel. Unless changes are made to libel law, Hilden predicted many, many more defamation suits based on Twitter.[106]

Another author has questioned how a retweet would be treated under the republication rule. Noting Krawczynski's tweet was retweeted by 14 people, Professor Daxton Stewart wrote lawyers were divided over the question of whether a retweet could constitute a defamatory republication. Stewart reasoned that while Twitter itself would clearly be protected under Section 230, a Twitter user who retweets the content of others is making the conscious decision to repeat content which would appear to make them acting more like classic republishers rather than classic distributors. The question under Section 230, however, would boil down to whether a retweeter was an "information content provider." According to Stewart's analysis, current case law makes it unlikely a retweeter would be held liable for a defamatory retweet, although a user might be liable for adding defamatory content to a modified retweet.[107] Similarly, while social media users who provide a link to a defamatory statement are unlikely to be liable for defamation, providing a defamatory comment with the link or using defamatory hypertext to create the link may make you liable.

An additional question regarding social media and defamation is how courts should handle damages. In 2012, a Texas jury awarded $13.78 million in damages to a Texas couple, Mark and Rhonda Lesher, for statements made by multiple individuals on Topix.com, self-described as "the world's largest community news site." The case involved 1,700 separate posts—which began after the Leshers were accused of sexual assault—that describe the couple as sexual deviants, molesters, and drug dealers.[108] Such a large award directed at multiple defendants raises numerous questions about social media and damages related to the number of negative posts, how spread out the posts are over time, and how audience reaction and the mob mentality of some social media sites should factor into damages.

Although the case raises far more questions than it answers about how juries will deal with defamation on social networks, it is clear this jury took the number and viciousness of posts to heart, and the already difficult process of determining harm is only going to be complicated by social media. It's also unclear how the privacy settings of a social media account might affect damages. It is also unclear how a jury would view the lack of a definable mass audience of sites like Twitter. Should my total number of followers, the number of followers who read the tweet, the number of followers who retweeted the defamatory statement, or the number of followers who know the plaintiff be determinative? In addition, as mentioned above, the scrolling nature of Twitter makes audience size difficult to determine. As Professor Amy Kristin Sanders noted, given the unique character of the Internet, it is more important than ever that courts carefully consider how to award damages in order to ensure that freedom of expression is protected.[109]

Despite these arguments, most likely it is far too early to determine exactly how courts are going to treat tweets, retweets, or many other forms of social media. As noted above, the law of defamation is centuries old, yet typically, little libel law is created specifically for a new medium. Although Section 230 stands out in contrast, most libel law has simply had to adapt to new technologies over time. Thus, only time will tell how defamation and social media will coexist as the courts continue to attempt to strike a balance between reputational interests and freedom of expression.

FREQUENTLY ASKED QUESTIONS

1. Can I get in trouble for posting a vicious lie about somebody on Facebook?

Yes, if the lie damages the person's reputation. Posting something on Facebook is considered "publishing." If you post a vicious lie about somebody on Facebook and as a result people think less of them, you've damaged

their reputation with a false statement of fact. You can be sued for defamation for a Facebook post, a tweet, a blog, or a video posted to the Internet.

2. If I repeat something I thought was true but turned out to be wrong on Twitter, will I be responsible for it?

It depends. Generally, anyone who repeats someone else's statements is just as responsible for the defamatory content as the original speaker. This is sometimes described as "The bearer of tales is as guilty as the teller of tales." However, simply posting a link to a defamatory statement or retweeting someone else's defamatory tweet will probably not make you liable. On the other hand, if you create your own tweet based on a false defamatory tweet, modify the original tweet in a defamatory way, or add you own defamatory statement to the tweet, you can be liable.

3. Is it libelous to record something in public and post it on YouTube?

Not if it's true. Defamation is a false statement of fact. Recording a real event can't be defamatory unless you misidentify the individuals in the video, suggest the video is something that it is not, or add some sort of false connotation to the video. For example, videotaping two people kissing in the street is not defamatory. Suggesting the two are engaging in an adulterous relationship when they are in fact happily married to each other or falsely identifying the two individuals in the video could be defamatory.

4. What should I do if somebody sues me for libel for posting an opinion on a site such as Yelp?

You should consult a lawyer who is familiar with your state's laws regarding defamation. It's possible your statement will be protected because it is constitutionally protected opinion, it is considered fair comment and criticism under common law, or because the lawsuit is actually designed to stifle your speech rather than win damages against you. Many states have anti-SLAPP statutes that are designed to protect people who are sued just to keep them quiet. If you qualify for protection under an anti-SLAPP statute, you can have the case dismissed before trial and, in some states, you can be awarded attorney fees from the plaintiff.

5. Why don't anonymous gossip sites such as JuicyCampus or CollegeACB get in trouble for libel?

In 1996, in an effort to get Internet Service Providers (ISPs) to police indecent sexual content, Congress passed a law that granted immunity to websites that contain defamatory content posted by third parties. Prior to

this law, ISPs would not edit content on their websites because doing so made them liable for the defamatory postings of third parties. In the years after the law was passed courts interpreted its protections broadly, granting blanket immunity to almost all websites that host the content of others. This allows websites like CollegeACB to host vicious, untrue, defamatory statements without having to worry about being sued.

NOTES

1 David S. Ardia, Reputation in a Networked World: Revisiting the Social Foundations of Defamation Law, 45 Harv. C.R.-C.L. L. Rev. 261, 262 (2010).
2 See Frank H. Easterbrook, Cyberspace and the Law of the Horse, U. Chi. Legal F. 207 (1996) for a discussion of the application of real space laws to cyberspace situations.
3 47 U.S.C. 230 (1996).
4 Historically, libel law was criminal law. Governments punished libelous speech to prevent breaches of the peace and prevent criticism of the government. Today, however, most libel cases in the United States are civil suits. This does not mean that criminal libel has disappeared. Although the prevailing view of criminal libel among communication law scholars in the United States is that there are only a handful of criminal libel prosecutions per year, a recent empirical study of all Wisconsin criminal libel cases from 1991 through 2007 suggests that criminal libel might be prosecuted far more often than realized. See David Pritchard, Rethinking Criminal Libel: An Empirical Study, 14 Comm. L. Pol'y 303 (2009). In addition, bloggers and tweeters who do not deal with public issues should be wary of criminal libel laws that might exist in their state. Professor Pritchard concluded that criminal libel is especially likely to be used when expression harms the reputations of private figures in cases that have nothing to do with public issues.
5 Reputation is a personal right and cannot be inherited. Friends, relatives, or associates of a person may only sue for defamation if they have been defamed personally.
6 Texas Beef Group v. Winfrey, 11 F. Supp. 2d 858 (1998), aff'd, 201 F.3d 980 (5th Cir. 2000).
7 Anthony McCartney, $430k Love Settlement Shows Tweets can be Costly, Associated Press, March 5, 2011.
8 47 U.S.C. 230 (1996).
9 1995 WL323710 (N.Y. Sup. Ct. 1995).
10 47 U.S.C. 230 (f) (2).
11 47 U.S.C. 230 (f) (3).
12 Finkel v. Facebook, No. 102578 (N.Y. Sup. Ct. filed Feb. 16, 2009), http://www.citmedialaw.org/sites/citmedialaw.org/files/2009-02-16-Finkel%20Complaint.pdf.
13 Finkel v. Facebook, No. 102578 (N.Y. Sup. Ct. filed Sept. 16, 2009)(order granting motion to dismiss), http://www.citmedialaw.org/sites/citmedialaw.org/files/2009-09-15-Finkel%20v.%20Facebook%20Order%20to%20Dismiss.pdf.
14 JuicyCampus, although infamous, was never sued for defamation, perhaps because of Section 230. The company went out of business because of an inability to

generate revenue. After spending $1 million of investor's money the site shut down in February 2009. Its founder has since gone on to write a book about online reputation management. See From Gossip Site Founder to Web Reputation Manager, Forbes.com, October 12, 2011, http://management.fortune.cnn.com/2011/10/12/from-gossip-site-founder-to-web-reputation-defender/.

15 But see Fair Housing Council of San Fernando Valley v. Roommates.com, LLC, 521 F.3d 1157 (9th Cir. 2008) (holding immunity under Section 230 did not apply to an interactive online operator whose questionnaire violated the Fair Housing Act).

16 Firth v. State, 98 N.Y.2d 365 (2002). See also, Nationwide Biweekly Administration, Inc., v. Belo Corp., 512 F.3d 137 (5th Cir. 2007).

17 Firth, 98 N.Y.2d at 371.

18 Madeleine Schachter & Joel Kurtzber, Law of Internet Speech 424 (2008).

19 Fawcett Publications, Inc. v. Morriss, 377 P.2d 42 (Okla.).

20 Nichols v. Item Publishers, Inc., 309 N.Y. 596, 600–601 (1956).

21 For example, some courts continue to hold that a false statement that an individual is gay is defamatory and some still view this characterization as defamatory per se. Other courts have held that changing moral attitudes toward homosexuality have made such rulings outdated and some recent cases have questioned whether an allegation of homosexuality should ever be construed as defamatory. For a discussion of these cases, see Matthew D. Bunker, Drew E. Shenkman, & Charles D. Tobin, Not That There's Anything Wrong with That: Imputations of Homosexuality and the Normative Structure of Defamation Law, 21 Fordham Intell. Prop. Media & Ent. L.J. 581 (2011).

22 388 U.S. 130, 347–348 (1967).

23 376 U.S. 254 (1964).

24 418 U.S. 323, 384–385 (1974) (White, J., dissenting).

25 Nat Stern, Private Concerns of Private Plaintiffs: Revisiting a Problematic Defamation Category, 65 Mo. L. Rev. 597, 599 (2000).

26 Sullivan, 376 U.S. at 279–280 (1964).

27 Id.

28 388 U.S. 130 (1967).

29 Id. at 164 (Warren, C.J., concurring).

30 418 U.S. 323 (1974).

31 Id. at 347–348.

32 Id. at 349.

33 Id.

34 See, e.g., id. at 350.

35 472 U.S. 749, 763 (1985).

36 Id. at 756–757.

37 Id.

38 Id. at 756–757.

39 See Ruth Walden & Derigan Silver, Deciphering Dun & Bradstreet: Does the First Amendment Matter in Private Figure-Private Concern Defamation Cases?, 14 Comm. L. & Pol'y 1 (2009).

40 Rosenblatt v. Baer, 383 U.S. 75, 85 (1966).

41 Bruce Stanford, Libel and Privacy § 7.2.2.2, at 260–264 (2d ed. 1999).

42 Gertz v. Robert Welch, Inc., 418 U.S. 323, 345 (1974).

43 Id.

44 See, e.g., Ellis v. Time, Inc., WL 863267 (D.D.C. 1997) (holding a plaintiff's multiple postings on CompuServe about a public controversy made him a limited-purpose public figure).

45 Harte-Hanks Communications, Inc. v. Connaughton, 491 U.S. 657, 692 (1989).

46 St. Amant v. Thompson, 390 U.S. 727, 730 (1968).

47 Garrison v. Louisiana, 379 U.S. 64, 74 (1964).

48 Harte-Hanks Communications, Inc., 491 U.S. at 664.

49 In Herbert v. Lando, 441 U.S. 153 (1979), the Supreme Court ruled that the First Amendment did not bar examining the editorial process and a reporter for *60 Minutes* could be asked how he evaluated information prior to publication of a story about a controversial retired Army officer. The Court held that the actual malice standard made it important for public officials and public figures to know both the actions and state of mind of defendants.

50 See Kyu Youm, The "Wire Service" Libel Defense, 70 Journalism Q. 682 (1993).

51 475 U.S. 767, 771 (1986).

52 Id. at 775.

53 Id. at 776.

54 See, e.g., Roffman v. Trump, 754 F. Supp. 411, 418 (E.D. Pa. 1990) (holding statements published in the *Wall Street Journal*, *Business Week*, *Fortune*, and the *New York Post* were "of no concern to the general public"); Katz v. Gladstone, 673 F. Supp. 76, 83 (D. Conn. 1987) (statements made in book reviews which appeared "in a number of periodicals" lacked "public concern").

55 See, e.g., Connick v. Myers, 461 U.S. 138 (1983); Pickering v. Bd. of Educ., 391 U.S. 563 (1968).

56 See, e.g., Snyder v. Phelps, 131 S. Ct. 1207 (2011).

57 See, e.g., Time, Inc. v. Hill, 385 U.S. 374 (1967).

58 See, e.g., Bartnicki v. Vopper, 532 U.S. 514 (2001).

59 131 S. Ct. 1207, 1216 (2011) (quoting San Diego v. Roe, 543 U.S. 77, 83 (2004)).

60 Id. (quoting Connick, 461 U.S. at 146; and San Diego v. Roe, 543 U.S. at 83–83).

61 Id. (quoting Dun & Bradstreet, 472 U.S. at 762).

62 Id.

63 Id. at 1217.

64 See http://volokh.com/ (last visited March 16, 2012).

65 Noonan v. Staples, 556 F.3d 20, 22 (1st Cir. 2009) (holding that an email sent to 1,500 Staples employees regarding the firing of a fellow employee for violating the company's travel and expense policy and code of ethics was a matter of private concern).

66 For a detailed discussion of this approach to defamation law and its potential problems, see Derigan Silver & Ruth Walden, A Dangerous Distinction: The Deconstitutionalization of Private Speech, 21 CommLaw Conspectus (2012, in press).

67 For a discussion of harm and the unique nature of defamation in American tort law, see David Anderson, Reputation, Compensation & Proof, 25 Wm. & Mary L. Rev. 747 (1984). For a discussion of the concept of harm in the context of Internet-based defamation, see Amy Kristin Sanders, Defining Defamation: Evaluating Harm in the Age of the Internet, 3 UB J. Media L. & Ethics 112 (2012).

68 See Walden & Silver, supra note 39 for a discussion of how different jurisdictions have handled the Supreme Court's decision in Dun & Bradstreet v. Greenmoss Builders.

69 There is one rather famous anomaly to this statement. In Noonan v. Staples, 561 F.3d 4, 7 (1st Cir. 2009) the U.S. Court of Appeals for the First Circuit refused to hold unconstitutional a Massachusetts law that allowed liability for true defamatory statements. It is important to note, however, the First Circuit apparently never addressed the constitutionality of the 1902 Massachusetts statute in its opinion because the defendant's attorneys never raised the issue.

70 Masson v. New Yorker Magazine Inc., 501 U.S. 496 (1991).

71 497 U.S. 1 (1990).

72 National Ass'n of Letter Carriers v. Austin, 418 U.S. 264 (1974).

73 See, e.g., http://www.yelp.com.

74 See, e.g., http://www.angieslist.com/AngiesList/.

75 See, e.g., http://www.tripadvisor.com/.

76 See, e.g., Burleson v. Toback, 391 F. Supp. 2d 401 (M.D.N.C. 2005).

77 U.S. Const., art. 1, § 6.

78 Hutchinson v. Proxmire, 443 U.S. 111 (1979).

79 Several states and the District of Columbia have accepted neutral reportage in some form, as have several U.S. Circuit Courts of Appeal. The inconsistent manner in which it has been applied, however, makes it an unreliable defense.

80 See Penelope Canan & George W. Pring, Strategic Lawsuits Against Public Participation, 35 Soc. Prob. 506 (1988); George W. Pring & Penelope Canan, SLAPPs: Getting Sued For Speaking Out (1996).

81 Robert D. Richards, A SLAPP In the Facebook: Assessing the Impact of Strategic Lawsuits Against Public Participation on Social Networks, Blogs and Consumer Gripe Sites, 21 DePaul J. Art Tech. & Intell. Prop. L 221, 231 (2011).

82 California Anti-SLAPP Project, http://www.casp.net/ (last visited May 26, 2012).

83 Richards, supra note 81 at 221–242.

84 Want to Complain Online? Look Out. You Might Be Sued, USA Today, June 9, 2010, at 8A.

85 Elinor Mills, Yelp User Faces Lawsuit Over Negative Review, CNET News, January 6, 2009, http://news.cnet.com/8301-1023_3-10133466-93.html.

86 See, e.g., Lisa Donovan, Tenant's Twitter Slam Draws Suit, Chicago Sun-Times, July 28, 2009; Dan Frosch, Venting Online, Consumers Can Land in Court, N.Y. Times, June 1, 2010, at A1.

87 Rex Hall, Jr., Western Michigan University Student Sued in Battle with Towing Company: Facebook Group Airing Complaints about T & J Towing Takes Off, Kalamazoo Gazette, April 14, 2010.

88 Id.

89 See Richards, supra note 81 at 242–253.

90 418 U.S. 323, 332 (1974) (emphasis added).

91 See, e.g., id. at 340–341.

92 See, e.g., Rowe v. Metz, 579 P.2d 83, 84 (Colo. 1978); Harley-Davidson Motorsports, Inc. v Markley, 568 P.2d 1359, 1363 (Ore. 1977); Greenmoss Builders v. Dun & Bradstreet, 461 A.2d 414, 417–418 (Vt. 1983); Denny v. Mertz, 318 N.W.2d 141, 153 (Wis. 1982).

93 472 U.S. 749 (1985).

94 Id. at 753 n.1.

95 Id. at 775.

96 Id. at 779 n.4.

97 497 U.S. 1, 19–20 (1990).

98 Id. at 20 n.6 (citation omitted).

99 For further discussion, see Walden & Silver, supra note 39; Silver & Walden, supra note 66; Rebecca Phillips, Constitutional Protections for Non-media Defendants: Should There Be a Distinction Between Larry King and You?, 33 Campbell L. Rev. 173 (2010).

100 Obsidian Finance Group LLC v. Cox, No. CV-11-57-HZ, 2011 WL 5999334 (D. Ore. November 30, 2011).

101 2011 WL 5999334, at *5.

102 Douglas Lee, Troubling Rulings Paved Way for Blogger's Libel Conviction, First Amendment Center (December 19, 2011), http://www.firstamendmentcenter. org/troubling-rulings-paved-way-for-bloggers-libel-conviction.

103 Spooner v. Associated Press, Inc. Case 0:11-cv-00642-JRT-JJK (D.C. Minn. 2011); Lauren Dugan, The AP Settles Over NBA Twitter Lawsuit, Pays $20,000 Fine, AllTwitter, December 8, 2011, http://www.mediabistro.com/alltwitter/the-ap-settles-over-nba-twitter-lawsuit-pays-20000-fine_b16514.

104 Michael Charron, Twitter: A "Caveat Emptor" Exception to Libel Law, 1 Berkley J. Ent. & Sports L. 57, 58 (2012).

105 Id. at 60.

106 Julie Hilden, Should the Law Treat Tweets the Same Way it Treats Printed Defamation? Justia.com, http://verdict.justia.com/2011/10/03/should-the-law-treat-defamatory-tweets-the-same-way-it-treats-printed-defamation (last accessed May 21, 2012).

107 Daxton R. "Chip" Stewart, When Retweets Attack: Are Twitter Users Liable for Republishing the Defamatory Tweets of Others? 90 Journ. & Mass Comm. Q (Summer 2013, in press).

108 Plaintiff's First Amended Petition, Leshers v. Does, No. 348-235791-09, http://www.citmedialaw.org/sites/citmedialaw.org/files/2009-07-28-First%20Amended%20Petition.pdf (last accessed May 21, 2012).

109 Sanders, supra note 67 at 117.

Privacy and Terms of Use

Woodrow Hartzog

Cumberland School of Law
Samford University

ABSTRACT

Privacy is one of the most important social media concepts. The doctrine surrounding privacy and social media is fraught with uncertainty despite being increasingly governed by terms of use agreements and privacy policies. What information, if any, is private on social media? Courts and lawmakers have struggled to determine whether and to what degree personal information disclosed on social media is private under traditional tort remedies and online agreements. This chapter will examine privacy law in the social media environment, including the ineffectiveness of the privacy torts and the ascent of privacy policies and terms of use agreements.

Users of social media must disclose personal information in order to receive the benefits conferred by these online communities. This personal information is extremely valuable to social media companies and other social media users. Indeed, personal information is the fuel that powers the social media engine. However, the disclosure of personal information on social media leaves users vulnerable to privacy violations. This vulnerability has raised the question of whether privacy can even exist in online social networks.

Courts have struggled in trying to determine whether and to what degree personal information disclosed on social media is private under common law, administrative regulations, and statutes. However, the weaknesses inherent in the privacy torts, regulations, and statutes might not remain a problem for very long, because privacy disputes are increasingly governed by contracts between the user and the website.

In some respects, the ascension of contract law in the area of privacy might be useful. The traditional privacy torts are not well-suited to protect

users of social media. In their place, a dubious patchwork of administrative and statutory laws ostensibly protects users from unauthorized disclosure by other users and the website itself. If clearly drafted and consistently enforced, contracts in the form of terms of use agreements and privacy policies can bring some degree of clarity to a great deal of, if not nearly all, self-disclosed online information implicating privacy. Yet this clarity can have unintended consequences for users who rarely understand or even read these dense, boilerplate agreements.

The current legal landscape of privacy, contracts, and social media is fraught with uncertainty. What information, if any, is private in online social networks? What laws protect this information? Is it reasonable for users to expect privacy in self-disclosed information? This chapter will examine privacy law in the social media environment, including the ineffectiveness of the privacy torts and the increasingly dominant role of contracts in the form of privacy policies and terms of use agreements.

PRIVACY LAW IS STRUGGLING WITH SOCIAL MEDIA

The proper legal response to the issue of social media and privacy has proven elusive because there is no fixed conceptualization of privacy.[1] Daniel Solove called privacy "a concept in disarray" that encompasses, among other things, the "freedom of thought, control over one's body, solitude in one's home, control over personal information, freedom from surveillance, protection of one's reputation, and protection from searches and interrogations."[2] The law's struggle to conceptualize privacy has often stunted its ability to adapt to rapid technological change.[3] That has been especially true with the Internet's rapid rise as courts grapple to define the contours of privacy in cyberspace.[4]

While privacy for social media users who cannot stop sharing information might seem contradictory, it is clear that users consider it important.[5] Today, people are disclosing very personal information on a wide array of websites. Commentators frequently argue that people who expose their deep secrets online do not value their privacy. Courts find they have no expectation of privacy.[6] The unprecedented sharing of private information on the Internet is leading some to herald the demise of privacy.[7]

It is far too easy, however, to conclude that because people are sharing private data online, they should expect no privacy. Many social media websites have elaborate privacy settings. Members of various online communities take considerable effort to manage the degree of exposure of their information.[8] Consider Facebook. Many individuals set their privacy settings so that only people they have designated as friends can see their information.[9] People using dating websites often set their profiles only to be visible to other members of the particular online dating community.[10] Members of

online support communities for substance abuse problems also expect exposure only to other members of the community.[11]

What happens when information leaks outside these communities? In short, privacy law has yet to figure out how to properly address the collection, use, and dissemination of personal information on social media. These practices on the Internet as a whole, which have been well-addressed by scholars,[12] leave Internet users such as those using social media vulnerable to a panoply of harms including excessive government and commercial entity surveillance, breach of confidentiality, misuse of personal information for such things as denial of employment or insurance benefits, damage to reputation, blackmail, loss of anonymity, chilled speech or association, and extreme emotional distress.[13]

Our current privacy protection regime is a patchwork of laws and remedies that are often muddled or in conflict with other laws and evolving technology. Privacy laws that limit the collection or disclosure of certain kinds of information or laws that are based on particular kinds of technology—for example, by classifying all communications into either wire, oral, or electronic communications—seem to create the most confusion.[14]

Many regulatory schemes governing privacy and social media inconsistently apply standards of "private" information or subjective tests such as one's "reasonable expectations of privacy."[15] Approaches that focus on the nature of the information are problematic because personal information is usually not seen as strictly private or public.[16] The same piece of information collected from social media can be considered sensitive in some circumstances and completely benign in others. For example, a Facebook user might post her new cell phone number to a discrete group of "friends," yet she might not want that information to be posted on her publicly available and widely read blog. Additionally, any law aimed at the suppression of a particular kind of expression is suspect under the First Amendment. These are just some of the many problems that inhibit the traditional tort-based approach to the protection of privacy.

THE GROWING IRRELEVANCE OF THE PRIVACY TORTS IN SOCIAL MEDIA

The traditional remedy for harms resulting from the publication of private information is the tort of public disclosure of embarrassing private facts, also known as "the disclosure tort." The disclosure tort generally prohibits giving publicity to a matter concerning the private life of another, if the matter publicized is of a kind that would be highly offensive to a reasonable person and is not of legitimate concern to the public.[17] The flaws in the disclosure tort, including a difficulty in deciding when expectations of privacy are

reasonable and when First Amendment concerns take precedence, have rendered it largely toothless to privacy harms occurring via social media.

The disclosure tort was extensively criticized before the Internet.[18] From its inception, the tort was troubled, and its faults became magnified over time. Joseph Elford noted in 1995 that "[t]he private facts tort is a mess. It has disappointed those who hope it would enhance individual privacy while it has exceeded all estimations of its chilling effect on speech."[19]

Several scholars claim the disclosure tort was rendered ineffective in 1989 in the case *Florida Star v. B.J.F.*[20] In this case, the U.S. Supreme Court declared that defendants cannot be punished for publishing matters of public significance without the claimant proving that punishment is necessary to advance a state interest of the highest order.[21] Andrew McClurg argued that this declaration almost guarantees defeat for plaintiffs pursuing claims based on the disclosure tort.[22] McClurg actually found that "[f]or the most part, the privacy torts as defined in the Second Restatement have functioned inadequately and fared poorly in the courts."[23]

However, the increased threat to privacy resulting from the technological destruction of any meaningful barriers to surveillance and publishing has rendered the disclosure tort nearly inert.[24] One scholar has argued that "[a]ttempts to apply traditional public disclosure jurisprudence to online social networking demonstrate the incoherence of this jurisprudence" because the disclosure tort is centered around keeping information from people and social networking is centered around disclosure and sharing of information.[25]

One of the main reasons the disclosure tort has been inconsistently applied and often unsuccessful for social media users is the amount of speculation the tort requires from judges. Judges regularly are called upon to make normative and subjective judgment pertaining to concepts like privacy, public concern, and offensiveness.[26] Critics assert that the cases often hinge on judges' imperfect estimates as to what society should expect.[27]

The tort also calls upon judges to determine what information is "private" and what information is public or at least "of public concern." Other scholars commenting on the tort have noted the practical and constitutional difficulty in defining the term "public" in order to determine whether information is worthy of privacy protections.[28] Dianne Zimmerman noted that "to distinguish private facts from 'public' information about an individual, courts often look either to the location of the action or to the nature of the subject matter. Courts using the 'location' analysis commonly state that information individuals reveal about themselves in public places is by definition not private."[29] Courts using the subject–matter analysis "rule that the subject matter is private even though the locus is not."[30] Zimmerman found that both approaches are practically unfeasible and threaten freedom of speech.

Perhaps the most significant failure of the privacy tort's application to social media is that the tort typically fails to protect self-disclosed information. Unlike Samuel Warren and Louis Brandeis, who worried in the late 1800s about tabloids publishing their private moments, the most likely publisher of personal information in the Internet age is the person herself.[31] In light of the mass adoption of social media and pervasiveness of electronically-mediated communication, Internet users have become their own worst enemy.

Online self-disclosure lies at the heart of the problem posed by social media. The rampant self-disclosure of personal information concomitant with an expectation of privacy is a problem because courts have struggled to determine whether and to what degree self-disclosed information is private.[32] Professor Lior Strahilevitz stated, "Despite the centrality of this issue, the American courts lack a coherent, consistent methodology for determining whether an individual has a reasonable expectation of privacy in a particular fact that has been shared with one or more persons."[33]

It is becoming increasingly clear that the privacy torts, particularly the disclosure tort, are ineffective in many scenarios involving social media. For practitioners, then, the main issue of concern is that of contract.

PRIVACY IN AN AGE OF CONTRACTS

Contracts have had a curious, bipolar relationship with privacy. As negotiated confidentiality agreements, contracts can be effective tools that help individuals control the flow of personal information. As standard-form contracts of adhesion, they can extract consent to practices that threaten the privacy of individuals who likely did not understand or even read the proposed terms. This schism rendering contracts as a cause of, and solution for, privacy problems has been magnified in a networked world, where individuals have more privity of contract than ever. Due to the ubiquity of terms of use agreements and privacy polices, the schism is widening. The erosion of privacy can be measured in standard-form contracts.

How did contracts come to have such a disparate impact on privacy? After all, in their famous article "The Right to Privacy," which influenced modern privacy law, Warren and Brandeis explicitly deemed contracts inadequate to protect individuals from the new privacy violations wrought by the technology of the late 1800s. Although the scholars recognized the utility of contracts, they asserted that because "modern devices afford abundant opportunities for the perpetration of [privacy harms] without any participation by the injured party, the protection granted by the law must be placed upon a broader foundation."[34] They went on to state:

> While, for instance, the state of photographic art was such that one's
> picture could seldom be taken without consciously "sitting" for the
> purpose, the law of contract or trust might afford the prudent man
> sufficient safeguards against the improper circulation of his portrait;
> But since the latest advances in photographic art have rendered it
> possible to take pictures surreptitiously, the doctrines of contract
> and of trust are inadequate to support the required protection, and
> the law of tort must be resorted to.[35]

Intimate and confidential information previously could have been contained by the injured party through trust and contracts, since those who most commonly obtained such information were dealt with at arm's length. Yet new technologies at the time, such as the Kodak handheld camera, enabled complete strangers to capture and disclose intimacies otherwise held in confidence.

Radio and television further frustrated an individual's ability to use contracts to protect their privacy. Because these technologies were one-way broadcast media, listeners and viewers were inundated with information about other people, yet the medium's audience had no discernible connection with each other. Initially, the Internet appeared to obliterate a user's ability to control collection and use of their information.[36] As personal information went viral online, the always-on convergence of text, photographs, audio, and video seemed to render contracts ineffective as a means of protecting privacy. After all, most Internet users are strangers to each other, and contracts provide no remedy against people with whom we have no connection.

Yet, the primary function of the Internet is to connect people. These connections can create a privity of contract between websites and users. Privity, an essential element for a binding contract, is defined as "The connection or relationship between two parties, each having a legally recognized interest in the same subject matter."[37] Contracts between websites and users are typically seen in the form of terms of use. These omnipresent online agreements have come to significantly govern the privacy of Internet users. With online agreements seemingly on every website, the 74 percent of Americans online each day likely enter into dozens of contracts that impact the flow of their personal information.[38] These agreements are adjudicated under standard-form contract doctrine because they are perceived as non-negotiable. This means users are regularly bound by terms they didn't read or understand—a common critique of all standard-form contracts. The mass proliferation of standard-form contracts[39] has significant consequences for information privacy on social media.

STANDARD FORM CONTRACTS AND SOCIAL MEDIA

Fundamentally, a contract is "a promise or a set of promises that the law will enforce."[40] Thus contracts exist to bind parties to promises by creating legal obligations. Some of these obligations can protect an individual's privacy. For example, confidentiality agreements prohibit the disclosure of information that at least one of the parties to a contract wishes to keep private.

Yet the enforceability of many social media agreements also might prohibit a user from denying "consent" to practices regarding the disclosure of personal information even if he or she failed to read the relevant terms. In any event, for good or bad, contracts that address privacy issues provide a degree of clarity.[41]

The traditional rule holds that in order for a contract to be valid the parties must reach a "meeting of the minds." In other words, both parties to the contract must agree to be bound by mutually understood terms.[42] In recent years, some critics have asserted that the traditional rules of contract law, "based on the ideal of two humans meeting in person to agree to terms, have been modified almost to the point of non-existence."[43]

As evidence, these critics cite the fact that courts do not consider the actual state of mind of the parties, but rather what they objectively conveyed to each other when forming the contract—known as "the objective theory of contract."[44] The emergence of online agreements has only hastened this evolution to objectivity by flooding the market with contracts.

Online contracts have traditionally been categorized as "browsewrap" or "clickwrap" agreements, although that distinction can be blurred at times.[45] "A clickwrap agreement is electronically transmitted and requires clicking on a button indicating an assent prior to downloading software or accessing a web site."[46] Browsewrap agreements dictate that additional "browsing" past the homepage constitutes acceptance of the contract, regardless of whether the user knows it or not.[47] The most important kinds of browsewrap and clickwrap contracts for the purposes of this chapter are terms of use agreements.

Wayne Barnes asserted that:

> [t]hrough a few clicks of the mouse, consumers are agreeing in record numbers to unfavorable, one-sided terms in adhesion contracts. These include many of the standard favorite terms of businesses, such as arbitration clauses, damage limitations, and warranty disclaimers. But, in the online and software contract context, it also increasingly includes new creations such as spyware clauses and severe license restrictions.[48]

Some of the most problematic areas of online contracting are the noticeable presentation of offers and formation of assent. "Courts presented with the issue [of online agreements] apply traditional principles of contract law and focus on whether the plaintiff had reasonable notice of and manifested assent to the online agreement."[49] Specifically regarding browse-wrap agreements, courts "have held that 'the validity of a browsewrap turns on whether a website user has actual or constructive knowledge of a site's terms and conditions prior to using the site.'"[50] Thus, in order to be bound, parties need not have a "meeting of the minds." Rather, a "reasonable communication" of the terms will suffice.[51]

The reasonable communication requirement is a combination "of reasonable notice of the contractual nature of the offered terms and the opportunity to review those terms[,]" which serves as a "proxy for the offeree's clear manifestation of assent."[52] A reasonable communication of terms gives rise to what is commonly referred to as the offeree's "duty to read."[53] In other words, if the terms of a contract are reasonably communicated, the offeree cannot then absolve herself from liability for failing to read them, because she had a legal duty to do so.

The notice requirement is fulfilled differently for clickwrap and browsewrap agreements.[54] While notice for clickwrap agreements can be satisfied by prohibiting a user through code from proceeding without first having the opportunity to review the contract, notice in browsewrap agreements "is given through conspicuous display of the contract."[55]

Mutual assent to a contract is typically manifested in the process of offer and acceptance.[56] Both offer and acceptance are categorized by an outward manifestation of intent to be bound.[57] Related to the requirement of assent, traditional contract doctrine also imposes on the parties a "duty to read."[58] Edith Warkentine noted that the practical result of this duty is that "if a party objectively manifests assent to be bound to a contract (for example, by signing a written contract document), a court will almost automatically find assent to all terms contained in the writing."[59] Thus, parties will find little relief in defenses like "I didn't read it" or "I didn't understand it."[60]

Yet, notwithstanding all of the academic attention paid to the problems with terms of use,[61] courts seem to be struggling less than scholars regarding their enforceability. A recent survey of online boilerplate cases concluded that:

> [a]n offeree who "signs" an agreement by hitting the "I accept" button is bound to its terms just as much as will someone who signs a paper contract. Repeat and sophisticated players will be more likely bound by more ambiguous forms of assent than will innocent ones.[62]

Thus, standard-form contract doctrine on the Web, while controversial, is largely stable. Courts relying on this doctrine give great weight to the specific language of the terms, often with little regard to other under-standings and representations that arise within relationships. Thus, these terms have great significance for user privacy.

PROBLEMS RELATED TO PRIVACY AND TERMS OF USE IN SOCIAL MEDIA

Privacy Policies

Seemingly every social media website has a privacy policy. Privacy policies explain how a website will use a visitor's personal information.[63] Allyson Haynes has found that these policies "have appeared all over the Internet both in response to increases in legislation requiring such disclosure, and as a voluntary measure by websites to appeal to consumers by emphasizing the care with which they treat consumer information."[64] These policies are perhaps most significant as tools by which the FTC can regulate unfair and deceptive trade practices.

While privacy policies, on their face, are often simply statements of a website's practices, many websites incorporate the policy into their terms of use as, according to Haynes, "binding upon visitors, using the language of contract and assent."[65] Most dictate that a user manifests assent to the policy by simply using the website, which is a form of a "browsewrap" contract. Haynes found that "the typical privacy policy includes, or incorporates by reference, a slew of terms both relating to privacy (and often allowing sharing and multiple uses of personal information) and relating to other rights of the consumer."[66] However, in some of the most prominent court decisions addressing breach of contract claims arising from privacy policies, courts have not enforced the privacy policy against the website owner.[67]

Pamela Samuelson found promise in the binding nature of privacy policies. She argues that:

> [a]s between the website and the user, a privacy policy bears all the earmarks of a contract, but perhaps one enforceable only at the option of the user. It is no stretch to regard the policy as an offer to treat information in specified ways, inviting a user's acceptance by using the site or submitting the information. The website's promise is sufficient consideration to support a contractual obligation, as is the user's use of the site and submission of personal data.[68]

However, Haynes argued that such binding policies can actually provide a liability shield for companies looking to take advantage of a user's failure to read by selling or sharing that user's personal information.[69]

As applied to most commercial websites, the existing legislation requires that a privacy policy be posted, and that the entity abide by that policy, but does not regulate the substance of that policy. No law prevents a website operator from sharing or selling personal information it has lawfully been given, although a website can be held liable for failing to notify its customers of its practice of selling or sharing such information. As long as they comply with the disclosure requirement, websites are free to state in their privacy policies that they will treat a visitor's personal information virtually any way they wish, arguably immunizing themselves from liability for such treatment.[70]

Others have noted that privacy policies and other online agreements included provisions that permitted websites to track and exploit user information.[71] Nancy Kim stated that "even those users that have some knowledge of website customer privacy practices may not have an accurate perception of the nature or extent of such practices. Websites may respond to customer ignorance by inserting increasingly more aggressive and intrusive terms in 'wrap contracts'."[72]

Thus, the true effect of privacy policies on an individual, like standard-form contracts in general, is dependent upon the drafter of the contract. A number of lawsuits have been filed by website users claiming breach of contract and promissory estoppel resulting from a website's violation of their privacy policy.[73] However, applying a strict standard-form contract analysis, a number of courts have denied any meaningful recovery for a website breaking promises it made in a privacy policy.[74]

Behavioral Restrictions

Many of the privacy threats created by the actions of other individuals are explicitly prohibited by online contracts. For example, in September 2007, a cheerleading coach at Pearl High School in Mississippi required the members of her cheerleading squad to reveal the usernames and passwords of their Facebook accounts.[75] With this information, school officials could access the private profiles of all of those students' "friends." However, as part of the registration process, Facebook requires a promise that "[y]ou will not share your password . . . let anyone else access your account, or do anything else that might jeopardize the security of your account."[76]

These requests for access to protected information are seemingly on the rise. The Florida Board of Bar Examiners and the city of Bozeman, Montana, have also implemented policies requesting an individual's username and

password for online services.[77] Indeed, the trend is not even limited to state action—employers have now begun to request access to their employees' profiles in order to access private content.[78] Terms of use, like those proposed by Facebook, often explicitly prohibit this activity. Yet it remains to be seen what effect that prohibition might have. Maryland has responded to these requests by passing legislation explicitly prohibiting the practice of employers asking current employees as well as job applicants for access to their social media accounts.[79]

Restrictions on behavior in terms of use could be beneficial to others using the same website. For example, the social network website Facebook encourages millions daily to share personal information as a part of the site. Unsurprisingly, its terms of use prohibit certain kinds of user activity that could deter the disclosure of information.[80] Users might not disclose information if they feel their privacy is threatened. These terms are representative of terms commonly found on social network sites,[81] and are useful examples of terms of use that specifically address privacy issues.

Information harvesting by third parties also threatens individuals' privacy,[82] and is typically governed via terms of use. A number of entities have employed "web scraper" software to systematically and automatically access and download ownership information of websites.

Facebook mandates that visitors "will not collect users' content or information, or otherwise access Facebook, using automated means (such as harvesting bots, robots, spiders, or scrapers) without our permission."[83] It goes on to state that "[i]f you collect information from users, you will: obtain their consent, make it clear you (and not Facebook) are the one collecting their information, and post a privacy policy explaining what information you collect and how you will use it."[84] Thus, terms of use can regulate both automated and non-automated collection of information from social media.

Behavior restrictions can be beneficial terms for website users. Typically, they attempt to keep an online community civil and relatively safe while protecting their users from abuse. Yet, under traditional contract analysis, the restrictions only indirectly benefit website users. Only the website, not the users, can enforce these restrictions. Could users ever invoke these terms in a cause of action against other users who violate the behavior restrictions?

Contracts and Reasonable Expectations of Privacy

Social media terms of use and privacy policies can also affect whether users have a reasonable expectation of privacy. The Fourth Amendment only protects individuals from a governmental search of information if society recognizes that an expectation of privacy in that information was reasonable. Orin Kerr stated "[t]he 'reasonable expectation of privacy' test governs

Fourth Amendment law, and it is up to the courts to determine when an expectation of privacy is 'reasonable'."[85] Regarding a determination of "reasonable," a number of courts have found that "the terms of service agreement or subscriber agreement . . . are relevant to characterizing objective privacy interests."[86]

Courts have typically found that terms of use can dispel an expectation of privacy regardless of whether the user actually read the terms.[87] In *United States v. Hart*,[88] the government sought and obtained personal information from an email the defendant allegedly used to commit a crime. As part of the email registration process, the defendant consented to terms of service that required the user to acknowledge that his personal information might be disclosed to comply with legal process.[89] The court found that given the defendant consented to the terms of use, "it is difficult to conclude that [the defendant] has an actual expectation of privacy in the contents of any communications sent or received with his Yahoo! accounts."[90]

Fourth Amendment cases are not the only ones to consider the effect of terms of use on a user's expectation of privacy.[91] Courts grappling with issues of anonymity and the public disclosure of private facts have tackled the issue, with results that—if not inconsistent—are highly dependent upon the terms of the contract.

Social Media Contracts and the Maintenance of Anonymity

Social media terms of use and privacy policies can also affect the anonymity of the user. The Supreme Court has repeatedly held that the First Amendment protects anonymous speech and expressive activity.[92] Yet anonymous speech can also cause harm that results in lawsuits that aim to expose the speaker's identity.[93] In order to balance the interest of the speaker with the interest of the harmed person or entity, courts often employ a balancing test. This determines whether a court will compel the exposure of an individual's identity. One of the factors a court considers when determining whether to compel identity disclosure is "the expectation of privacy held by the Doe defendants, as well as other innocent users who may be dragged into the case (for example, because they shared an IP address with an alleged infringer)."[94]

While a court's decision whether contract terms establish an expectation of privacy is naturally dependent upon the text of the agreement, interpretation of what a user should expect from the language varies. Some have interpreted the vague nature of online agreements to mean that users naturally expect privacy if the website offers general promises of confidentiality.

For example, in *McVicker v. King*,[95] the United States District Court for the Western District of Pennsylvania in 2010 considered whether to grant a motion to compel the disclosure of records that could identify seven anonymous users who commented on a website's message board. The website objected to the motion as an "attempt to strip anonymity from those who choose to engage in political discussion and debate on its website."[96]

The plaintiff asserted, among other things, that the terms of use of the blog did not create any expectation of privacy because they didn't explicitly provide that the identity of the user would be protected.[97]

The court disagreed. Instead, the court found that "[t]he Privacy Policy clearly reflects that Total Trib Media will disclose its users' personally identifiable information only in very limited situations. Thus, the Court finds that the terms of service of the blog create an expectation of privacy for any registered user."[98]

Other courts provide no such benefit to contract adherents. In *London-Sire Records v. Doe 1*,[99] record companies brought copyright infringement claims against several unnamed defendants using peer-to-peer file-sharing software to download music. The United States District Court for the District of Massachusetts attributed great importance to the ISP's (Boston University) terms of use agreement, stating the "agreement could conceivably make a substantial difference to the expectation of privacy a student has in his or her internet use."[100]

The court foreshadowed what it was seeking by requesting additional evidence of the terms of use agreement when it stated "many internet service providers require their users to acknowledge as a condition of service that they are forbidden from infringing copyright owners' rights, and that the ISP may be required to disclose their identity in litigation."[101]

Although it would later be reversed on other grounds, the United States District Court for the District of Columbia in *In re Verizon Internet Services*[102] had similar strong words for a plaintiff's expectation of privacy in light of terms of use:

> In the end, Verizon's customers should have little expectation of privacy (or anonymity) in infringing copyrights. Subscribers to Verizon's Internet services are put on clear notice that they cannot use Verizon's service or network to infringe copyrights. In fact, as part of its corporate policy, Verizon alerts its subscribers at the outset that it will "disclose individual customer information to an outside entity . . . when Verizon is served with valid legal process for customer information." And if an individual subscriber opens his computer to permit others, through peer-to-peer filesharing, to download materials from that computer, it is hard to understand just

what privacy expectation he or she has after essentially opening the computer to the world.[103]

Thus, terms of use can also be used as evidence to destroy a social media user's pseudonymity.[104]

Contracts and Unfair or Deceptive Trade Practices

The Federal Trade Commission (FTC) has recently taken a keen interest in the privacy practices of social media, particularly focusing on adherence and changes to social media privacy policies.[105] Social media could be found liable for a deceptive or unfair trade practice even if the website's terms of use and privacy policies purportedly gained the consent of their users for collection and use of their personal information.[106]

Susan Gindin noted that the

> FTC has long required that businesses clearly and conspicuously disclose material facts, and that an act or practice is deceptive and therefore a violation of the FTC Act if it is: likely to mislead consumers acting reasonably under the circumstances; and is "material"—that is, important to a consumer's decision to buy or use the product.[107]

However, Gindin noted that "while the FTC has become increasingly active in requiring that companies provide conspicuous notice of material terms, the courts have almost unanimously enforced online contracts against consumers—even those with so-called 'hidden terms.'"[108]

An excellent example of the role of the FTC in contractual privacy disputes is its 2009 action against Sears. Here, Sears distributed a software application that allowed Sears to track consumers' online behavior, as well as some offline activities.[109] Sears included a Privacy Statement and licensing agreement with the software that "described the Tracking Application in detail, and before a consumer agreed to have the Tracking Application installed, the consumer was required to check a box"[110] acknowledging those terms had been read. Yet, in a move that potentially renders the standard practices for obtaining consent ineffective, the FTC argued that the disclosures made by Sears were not adequate to avoid deceiving consumers.[111]

Some states have also acted under "mini-FTC" statutes to bring actions against entities that mislead consumers about the confidentiality of their personal information.[112]

Terms of Use and Liability as an Unauthorized Social Media User

Breaching a social media website's terms of use agreement could result in more than just contractual liability. A number of statutes that were designed to prevent computer fraud and misuse revolve around the concept of an "unauthorized user." If a user breaches the proposed terms of use, are they still authorized to use the website?

As previously discussed, restrictions on user behavior in online agreements can protect other user's privacy. These restrictions on behavior are common, so statutory penalties for breaching these contracts could be pervasive. Recall the Facebook prohibitions on soliciting login information, disclosing passwords, providing false personal information, and information harvesting.[113]

Some of the most recent relevant attempts to leverage terms of use violations have been through application of the Computer Fraud and Abuse Act (CFAA). The CFAA is a statute that criminalizes the unauthorized access, or use in excess of authorization of, a computer.[114] The CFAA permits a website owner in its terms of use to "spell out explicitly what is forbidden" or unauthorized on its site.[115] Breaches of these contracts can then be used to demonstrate a lack of authorization for site use under the CFAA.[116] The statute provides that "whoever . . . intentionally access[es] a computer without authorization or exceeds authorized access, and thereby obtains [. . .] information from any protected computer if the conduct involved an interstate or foreign communication" is in violation of the statute.[117]

In *United States v. Lori Drew*,[118] the prosecution relied upon the theory that Drew's cyberbullying of another user violated the MySpace terms of use. According to the prosecution, these violations negated MySpace's authorization for Drew to access MySpace's networked computers, thus violating the CFAA. However, U.S. District Court Judge Wu largely rejected this interpretation, stating

> if any conscious breach of a website's terms of service is held to be sufficient by itself to constitute intentionally accessing a computer without authorization or in excess of authorization, the result will be that section 1030(a)(2)(C) becomes a law 'that affords too much discretion to the police and too little notice to citizens who wish to use the [Internet].'[119]

This theory was also unsuccessful in *A. V. v. iParadigms*[120] and *Southwest Airlines Co. v. BoardFirst*[121] largely due to findings of insufficient damages alleged by the plaintiffs.

Yet the issue of whether violation of terms of use can be considered a violation of the CFAA is still a point of contention. Courts have relied upon terms of use violations to support liability under the CFAA in other contexts, most notably to enforce prohibitions on junk electronic communication.[122]

However, in *Facebook v. Power Ventures*,[123] the United States District Court for the Northern District of California ruled that merely violating a website's terms of use cannot constitute a violation of the CFAA.[124] Thus, the issue has not been definitively resolved. Given the availability of statutory damages and injunctive relief available under the CFAA,[125] this statute has emerged as a potential amplifier of the impact of contracts on privacy disputes stemming from the use of social media.

User Consent to Surveillance

Finally, social media terms of use agreements might even serve as consent to surveillance under a few statutes. Numerous electronic surveillance or privacy of commercial and personal data statutes deal with some form of "unauthorized" activity. The Stored Communications Act[126] (SCA) prohibits accessing without authorization or exceeding authorization digital or electronic technology to access an electronic communication.[127] The Wiretap Act as part of the Electronic Communications Privacy Act (ECPA) does not apply if one of the parties to an electronic communication consents to surveillance.[128]

Orin Kerr has questioned whether clicking through presented terms can constitute notice sufficient to satisfy the "consent" exceptions to these statutes. He discussed the use of "banners" or "messages that greet computer users when they log on to a network" informing them their communications might be monitored.[129] He noted that while banners can generate consent to monitoring, he questioned whether it was "sufficient if the notice of monitoring can be found somewhere in the Terms of Service or an employee manual."[130] While it is unclear exactly what constitutes consent under these statutes, it is possible that terms of use could play an important role.

WHAT DOES ALL OF THIS MEAN FOR PRIVACY?

Unfortunately, privacy in social media remains a vague and constantly evolving concept. Social norms and context play a large role in any such determination, thus standardized rules must be largely displaced with factually-specific determinations. To that end, the best strategy for social media users is to take a full stock of what context and cues are available when trying to determine whether to disclose personal information or determining if the disclosures of others are private.

Such context and cues can come primarily from three sources:

1. the terms of use;
2. technological protections such as privacy settings; and
3. the nature of the information itself in (and out) of context.

Because most social media websites mandate respect for the privacy of others and personal information in their terms of use, users must be aware that the information posted is likely not a free-for-all.

Instead, consider whether the user utilized privacy settings. If so, how restrictive are they? How many people were potentially privy to the same information? How sensitive is the information? Did the user hide his or her identity with a pseudonym, initials, or only his or her first name? Would the information make sense devoid of the context in which it was disclosed, or could extraction from context distort the message?

Also, while the terms of use might be dense and lengthy, they are also consequential. Although the enforceability of many of these terms is questionable, as is the viability of a breach of contract claim by Facebook for their violation, what is clear is that Facebook will rely on the violation of these terms to justify suspension or deletion of a user account. This is true even though most violations of these terms go unpunished because the violations are too vague or too numerous.

Ultimately, it is important to consider that while it may seem that another user's disclosure of personal information online is public, in many instances that user would disagree. Empirical research demonstrates that social media users regularly consider information disclosed on the website as private to some degree.[131] Only a careful consideration of context and cues will help you navigate the grey area of privacy within online communities.

FREQUENTLY ASKED QUESTIONS

1. If a social media user posts information to their profile, can I assume that it is not private information and thus free to use?

There is no categorically absolute answer to this question. Context, the nature of the information, the role of the user and your relationship with that user, the privacy settings, and any other implied or explicit terms of disclosure are all relevant in determining if information shared within a social network site can be appropriately shared or used elsewhere.

In any event, it is important to remember that all users are bound by both the terms of use and the other relevant duties such as those arising from tort law such as the duty to refrain from public disclosure of privacy facts and intentional infliction of emotional distress.

2. If someone posts an embarrassing picture of me on a social network site, what are my legal rights to remove it or collect damages?

Legal protection in these circumstances can vary. Your rights to have a photograph or piece of information about you removed or to collect damages are entirely dependent upon the context in which the photo was taken, the content of the photo, the extent of disclosure, the terms of use of the website, the technological allowances and dispute resolution procedures of the website, and your relationship to the poster of the photograph or piece of information.

Little *ex ante* advice can be given here, given the variables that can determine your rights. For example, was the photo taken in public? The term "public" itself has no fixed definition and is difficult to determine in practice. Additionally, a number of safeguards protect hosts and disclosers of information such as the First Amendment and Section 230 of the Communications Decency Act, which insulates websites from liability for hosting potentially harmful material that was posted by a third party.

Did you take the photo yourself? If so, you might be able to assert your copyright to take the photo down using the "notice and takedown" procedure provided for in the Digital Millennium Copyright Act. (See any social media website's terms of use for more information.)

The most efficient and low-cost method to have embarrassing photographs and information removed from social media is to utilize their internal technological controls or dispute resolution mechanisms. For example, Facebook and other social media provide users with the option of "tagging" certain photos as inappropriate, which could lead to their removal.

3. Am I bound by terms of use and privacy policies if I don't read them?

Yes. While not all terms of use agreements are enforceable, courts have almost uniformly rejected the "I didn't read or understand them" defense. This is known as "the objective theory of contracts."

4. Are all terms of use agreements enforceable? What about if I am just browsing a website?

It appears as though most courts are willing to enforce agreements where you "click" a button to indicate your agreement. Because most social media require such an action during the registration process, social media users with a registered profile are likely bound by the terms of use.

However, courts have been more reluctant to enforce agreements where the terms stipulate mere "use" (e.g., browsing) of the website constitutes acceptance of the terms. These so-called "browsewrap" agreements must be

prominent and clearly noticeable (e.g., not at the bottom of the page) to be enforceable.

5. Is each term within the agreement enforceable?

Even if a terms of use agreement is found to be binding, not every term in the agreement is automatically enforceable. While many of the standard terms, including many behavioral restrictions and user consent to common information practices have been found to be enforceable, some terms such as "we reserve the right to modify this agreement at any time without notice" have been ruled unenforceable.[132] Additionally, the doctrine of "unconscionability" limits the enforceability of some contractual terms such as some one-sided arbitration agreements.

Unconscionability is the main tool used by courts to reject some or all terms in standard-form contracts.[133] While "substantive unconscionability" supports the invalidation of fundamentally "unfair" or one-sided terms, procedural unconscionability focuses on deficiencies in the actual formation of the contract resulting from lack of knowledge of some or all of the terms or lack of voluntariness.[134] Thus, if a term stipulated that you promise to give up your kidney in exchange for use of a social media website, that term would likely not be enforceable because it was substantively unconscionable. Likewise, if a social media website tricked you into clicking "I Agree" by designing the "Cancel" button to indicate acceptance to the terms, then that agreement would likely be procedurally unconscionable.

NOTES

1 See, e.g., Daniel Solove, Understanding Privacy 1 (2008); see also Julie C. Innes, Privacy, Intimacy, and Isolation 3 (1992); Hyman Gross, The Concept of Privacy, 43 N.Y.U. L. Rev. 34, 35 (1967); Ruth Gavison, Privacy and the Limits of Law, 89 Yale L. J. 421 (1980); Alan Westin, Privacy and Freedom (1967); Daniel Solove, A Taxonomy of Privacy, 154 U. Penn. L. Rev. 477 (2006); Robert C. Post, Three Concepts of Privacy, Geo. L. Jour. 2087, 2087 (2001).

2 Solove, Understanding Privacy, supra note 1 at 1.

3 See, e.g., Neil Richards & Daniel Solove, Prosser's Privacy Law: A Mixed Legacy, 98 Cal. L. Rev. 1887 (2010); Daniel Solove, Conceptualizing Privacy, 90 Cal. L. Rev. 1087 (2002); Neil Richards, The Limits of Tort Privacy, 9 J. on Telecomm. & High Tech. L. 357 (2011).

4 See, e.g., Moreno v. Hanford Sentinel, 172 Cal. App. 4th 1125, 1128 (Cal. Ct. App. 2009); cf Pietrylo v. Hillstone Restaurant Group, 2008 WL 6085437 (D.N.J.).

5 See Patricia Sanchez Abril, A (My)Space of One's Own: On Privacy and Online Social Networks, 6 Nw. J. Tech. & Intell. Prop. 73, 77 (2007).

6 See Moreno v. Hanford Sentinel, 2009 WL 866795 (Cal. App. Ct. 2009); see also, Diane Zimmerman, Requiem for a Heavyweight: A Farewell to Warren and

Brandeis's Privacy Tort, 68 Cornell L. Rev. 291 (1983); Solveig Singleton, Privacy Versus the First Amendment: A Skeptical Approach, 11 Fordham Intell. Prop. Media & Ent. L.J. 97 (2000).

7   Eve Fairbanks, The Porn Identity, New Republic, February 6, 2006.

8   Emily Christofides, Amy Muise, & Desmarais Serge, Information Disclosure and Control on Facebook: Are They Two Sides of the Same Coin or Two Different Processes?, 12(3) CyberPsychology & Behavior 341 (2009); Zeynep Tufekci, Can You See Me Now? Audience and Disclosure Regulation in Online Social Network Sites, 28(1) Bulletin of Science, Technology & Society 20 (2008).

9   Christofides et al., supra note 8.

10 Jennifer Gibbs, Nicole Ellison, & Rebecca Heino, Self-Presentation in Online Personals: The Role of Anticipated Future Interaction, Self-Disclosure, and Perceived Success in Internet Dating, 33(2) Communication Research 152 (2006).

11 See, e.g., Alcoholics Anonymous, A.A. Guidelines – Internet, http://www.aa.org/en_pdfs/mg-18_internet.pdf.

12 See, e.g., Daniel Solove, The Digital Person (2004).

13 See, e.g., Solove, Taxonomy, supra note 1; M. Ryan Calo, The Boundaries of Privacy Harm, 86 Ind. L.J. 1131 (2011).

14 See, e.g., Electronic Communications Privacy Act of 1986, 18 U.S.C. §§ 2510–2522, 2701–2709 (2011).

15 See, e.g., Daniel Solove, Fourth Amendment Pragmatism, 51 B.C. L. Rev. 1511 (2010) (arguing that the "reasonable expectation of privacy" test should be abandoned).

16 See, e.g., Helen Nissenbaum, Privacy in Context (2009); Sharon Sandeen, Relative Privacy: What Privacy Advocates Can Learn from Trade Secret Law, 2006 Mich. St. L. Rev. 667, 694 (2006).

17 Restatement (Second) of Torts § 652 D.

18 See, e.g., Harry Klaven, Jr., Privacy in Tort Law – Were Warren and Brandeis Wrong?, 31 L. & Contemp. Probs. 326, 327 (1966).

19 Joseph Elford, Trafficking in Stolen Information: A "Hierarchy of Rights" Approach to the Private Facts Tort, 105 Yale L. J. 727 (1995).

20 491 U.S. 524 (1999).

21 491 U.S. at 533.

22 Andrew J. McClurg, Kiss and Tell: Protecting Intimate Relationship Privacy Through Implied Contracts of Confidentiality, 887 U. Cincinnati L. Rev. 877, 899 (2006).

23 Id. at 908.

24 Abril, supra note 5.

25 Id. at 3.

26 Id. at 10.

27 Id. at 10 (citing Albert W. Alschuler, Interpersonal Privacy and the Fourth Amendment, 4 N. Ill. U. L. Rev. 1, 8 n. 12 (1983)).

28 Zimmerman, supra note 6; Singleton, supra note 6.

29 Zimmerman, supra note 6 at 347.

30 Id. at 349.

31 Daniel Solove, The Slow Demise of Defamation and Privacy Torts, Huffington Post, October 12, 2010, http://www.huffingtonpost.com/daniel-j-solove/the-slow-

demise-of-defama_b_758570.html; Lauren Gelman, Privacy, Free Speech, and Blurry-Edged Social Networks, 50 B.C. L. Rev. 1315 (2009); James Grimmelmann, Saving Facebook, 94 Iowa L. Rev. 1137, 1197 (2009).

32 Lior J. Strahilevitz, A Social Networks Theory of Privacy, 72 U. Chi. L. Rev. 919, 920–921 (2005).

33 Id.

34 Samuel D. Warren & Louis D. Brandeis, The Right to Privacy, 4 Harv. L. Rev. 193 (1890).

35 Id. at 211.

36 See, Daniel Solove, The Future of Reputation (2007); Helen Nissenbaum, Privacy in Context (2009).

37 Black's Law Dictionary (8th ed. 2004).

38 74% of Americans Online, Pew Internet & American Life Project (2009), http://pewresearch.org/databank/dailynumber/?NumberID=948.

39 Friedrich Kessler, Contracts of Adhesion—Some Thoughts About Freedom of Contract, 43 Colum. L. Rev. 629, 640 (1943).

40 E. Allan Farnsworth, Farnsworth on Contracts § 1.1, at 4 (Little, Brown & Co. 1999); see also Restatement (Second) of Contracts § 1 (1981) (defining contracts as "A contract is a promise or a set of promises for the breach of which the law gives a remedy, or the performance of which the law in some way recognizes as a duty").

41 See, e.g., Pamela Samuelson, Privacy As Intellectual Property?, 52 Stan. L. Rev. 1125 (2000); Peter P. Swire & Robert E. Litan, None of Your Business: World Data Flows, Electronic Commerce, and the European Privacy Directive 8 (1998).

42 Juliet Moringiello, Signals, Assent and Internet Contracting, 57 Rutgers L. Rev. 1307, 1311 (2005).

43 Id.

44 Id.

45 See, e.g., Hotels.com v. Canales, 195 S.W.3d 147 (Tex. Ct. App. 2006).

46 Nancy Kim, Clicking and Cringing, 86 Or. L. Rev. 797, 799 (2007).

47 See Specht v. Netscape Comm. Corp., 306 F.3d 17 (2d Cir. 2002); Register.com, Inc. v. Verio, Inc., 356 F.3d 393 (2d Cir. 2004); Pollstar v. Gigmania Ltd., 170 F. Supp2d 974 (E.D. Cal. 2000).

48 Wayne Barnes, Toward a Fairer Model of Consumer Assent to Standard Form Contracts: In Defense of Restatement Section 211(3), 82 Wash. L. Rev. 227, 228 (2007).

49 Burcham v. Expedia, 2009 U.S. Dist. LEXIS 17104 (citing Feldman v. Google, Inc., 513 F. Supp. 2d 229, 236 (E.D. Pa. 2007); Specht v. Netscape Comm. Corp., 306 F.3d 17, 28-30 (2nd Cir. 2002)).

50 Id. at *8 (citing Register.com, Inc. v. Verio, Inc., 356 F.3d 393, 429 (2d Cir. 2004)).

51 See, e.g., Register.com, Inc. v. Verio, Inc., 356 F.3d 393, 429 (2d Cir. 2004).

52 Moringiello, supra note 42 at 1314.

53 Id.

54 Ian Rambarran & Robert Hunt, Are Browse-Wrap Agreements All They Are Wrapped Up To Be?, 9 Tul. J. Tech. & Intell. Prop. 173, 176 (2007).

55 Id.

56 Edith Warkentine, Beyond Unconscionability: The Case for Using "Knowing Assent" as the Basis for Analyzing Unbargained-For Terms in Standard Form Contracts, 31 Seattle U. L. Rev. 469, 475 (2008).

57 Id.

58 Id. at 476.

59 Id.

60 Id.

61 See Richard Craswell, Property Rules and Liability Rules in Unconscionability and Related Doctrines, 60 U. Chi. L. Rev. 1, 9–10 (1993).

62 Id.

63 Allyson Haynes, Online Privacy Policies: Contracting Away Control Over Personal Information?, 111 Penn St. L. Rev. 587, 594 (2007).

64 Id.

65 Id. at 598.

66 Id.

67 In re Northwest Airlines Privacy Litigation, 2004 WL 1278459 (D. Minn. 2004) (finding that the privacy statement did not constitute a unilateral contract and that plaintiff must have read the policy to rely on it); Dyer v. Northwest Airlines Corp., 334 F. Supp. 2d 1196 (D.N.D. 2004) (finding that plaintiffs failed to allege that they read, understood or relied upon the privacy policy and failed to allege contractual damages); In re Jet Blue Airways Corp. Privacy Litigation, 379 F. Supp. 2d 299 (E.D.N.Y. 2005).

68 Samuelson, supra note 41 at 1164–1165.

69 Haynes, supra note 63 at 594.

70 Id. (citations omitted).

71 Nancy S. Kim, Wrap Contracts and Privacy, Association for the Advancement of Artificial Intelligence Press Technical Report SS-10-05, 2010, at 1, http://papers. ssrn.com/sol3/papers.cfm?abstract_id=1580111.

72 Id. at 1.

73 Saffold v. Plain Dealer Publishing Co., CV 10 723512, Cuyahoga County Court of Common Pleas (filed April 7, 2010); McVicker v. King, No. 09-cv-436 (W.D. Pa. March 3, 2010); Sedersten v. Taylor, 2009 U.S. Dist. LEXIS 114525 (Case No. 09-3031-CV-S-GAF) (W.D. Mo. December 9, 2009).

74 In re Northwest Airlines Privacy Litigation, 2004 WL 1278459 (D. Minn. 2004) (finding that the privacy statement did not constitute a unilateral contract and that plaintiff must have read the policy to rely on it); Dyer v. Northwest Airlines Corp., 334 F. Supp. 2d 1196 (D.N.D. 2004) (finding that plaintiffs failed to allege that they read, understood, or relied upon the privacy policy and failed to allege contractual damages); In re Jet Blue Airways Corp. Privacy Litigation, 379 F. Supp. 2d 299 (E.D.N.Y. 2005).

75 Student Files Lawsuit After Coach Distributed Private Facebook Content, Student Press Law Center, July 22, 2009, http://www.splc.org/newsflash.asp?id=1938.

76 Statement of Rights and Responsibilities, Facebook, http://www.facebook. com/terms.php?ref=pf.

77 Andrew Moshirina, Florida Nukes the Fridge: Facebook, the Bar, and the Latest Entry in the Social Network Hijacking Saga, Citizen Media Law Project, September

2, 2009, http://www.citmedialaw.org/blog/2009/florida-nukes-fridge-facebook-bar-and-latest-entry-social-network-hijacking-saga; Molly McDonough, Town Requires Job Seekers to Reveal Social Media Passwords, ABA Journal Law News Now, June 19, 2009, http://www.abajournal.com/news/town_requires_job_seekers_to_reveal_social_media_passwords/. Bozeman quickly abolished its policy after public outcry.

78 Andrew Moshirina, Employee Privacy and Social Networks: The Case for a New Don't Ask Don't Tell, Citizen Media Law Project, July 2, 2009, http://www.citmedia law.org/blog/2009/employee-privacy-and-social-networks-case-new-don%E2%80%99t-ask-don%E2%80%99t-tell.

79 Emil Protalinski, Maryland Bans Employers Asking for Your Facebook Password, ZDNet, May 3, 2012, http://www.zdnet.com/blog/facebook/maryland-bans-employers-asking-for-your-facebook-password/12509.

80 Statement of Rights and Responsibilities, Facebook, supra note 76.

81 See, e.g. Myspace.com Terms of Use Agreement, MySpace, http://www.myspace.com/help/terms.

82 See Solove, supra note 12.

83 Statement of Rights and Responsibilities, Facebook, supra note 76.

84 Id.

85 Orin S. Kerr, The Fourth Amendment and New Technologies: Constitutional Myths and the Case for Caution, 102 Mich. L. Rev. 801, 802 (2004).

86 Lukowski v. County of Seneca, 2009 WL 467075 (W.D.N.Y. 2009) (finding that the "terms of service agreements between customers and businesses have been considered relevant to characterization of privacy interests"); United States v. Hart, 2009 WL 2552347 (W.D.Ky. 2009); Warshak v. United States, 532 F.3d 521 (6th Cir. 2008).

87 See, e.g., United States v. Hart, 2009 WL 2552347 (W.D.Ky. 2009); Warshak v. United States, 532 F.3d 521 (6th Cir. 2008); Lukowski v. County of Seneca, 2009 WL 467075 (W.D.N.Y. 2009).

88 2009 WL 2552347 (W.D.Ky. 2009).

89 Id.

90 Id. at *25.

91 See, e.g., Freedman v. America Online, 412 Supp. 174 (D. Conn. 2005) (finding AOL's privacy policy relevant in the scope of a user's Fourth Amendment rights).

92 London-Sire Records v. Doe, 542 F. Supp. 2d 153, 163 (D.Mass. 2008) (citing McIntyre v. Ohio Elections Comm'n, 514 U.S. 334 (1995); NAACP v. Alabama ex rel. Patterson, 357 U.S. 449 (1958)).

93 See Solove, supra note 36.

94 London-Sire Records v. Doe, 542 F. Supp. 2d 153, 179 (D.Mass. 2008).

95 No. 02:09-cv-00436 (W.D. Pa. 2010).

96 Id. at 7.

97 Id. at 9.

98 Id. at 10.

99 542 F. Supp. 2d 153 (D.Mass. 2008).

100 Id.

101 Id.

102 257 F. Supp. 244 (D.C.D.C. 2003), rev'd, Recording Industry Ass'n of America v. Verizon Internet Services, 351 F.3d 1229 (D.C. Cir. 2003).

103 Id. at 268.

104 See, Sony Music Entm't v. Does 1-40, 326 F. Supp. 2d 556 (S.D.N.Y. 2004) (finding there was only a minimal expectation of privacy under the ISP's terms of service).

105 See, e.g., FTC, Exploring Privacy: A Roundtable Series (2010), http://www.ftc. gov/bcp/workshops/privacyroundtables/index.shtml.

106 See, e.g., Susan Gindin, Nobody Reads Your Privacy Policy or Online Contract? Lessons Learned and Questions Raised by the FTC's Action Against Sears, 8 Nw. J. Tech. & Intell. Prop. 1 (2009), http://www.law.northwestern.edu/journals/ njtip/v8/n1/1/; Marcia Hofmann, The Federal Trade Commission's Enforcement of Privacy, in Proskauer on Privacy: A Guide to Privacy and Data Security Law in the Information Age (2010).

107 Id.

108 Id.

109 In the Matter of Sears Holdings Management Corp., FTC File No. 082 3099 (June 4, 2009) (available at http://www.ftc.gov/os/caselist/0823099/index.shtm). The final consent order was issued on September 9, 2009; FTC, Press Release, Sears Settles FTC Charges Regarding Tracking Software: Sears Failed to Disclose Adequately that Software Collected Consumers' Sensitive Personal Information, June 4, 2009, http://www.ftc.gov/opa/2009/06/sears.shtm.

110 Gindin, supra note 106 at 1.

111 Id.

112 Jonathan K. Sobel, et al., The Evolution of Data Protection as a Privacy Concern, and the Contract Law Dynamics Underlying It, in Anupam Chandler et al., eds., Securing Privacy in the Internet Age 56 (2008).

113 Statement of Rights and Responsibilities, Facebook, supra note 76.

114 18 U.S.C. §1030(a)(2) (2001); see, e.g., Orin Kerr, Computer Crime Law 478 (2nd ed. 2009).

115 EF Cultural Travel B.V. v. Zefer Corp., 318 F.3d 58, 63 (1st Cir. 2003).

116 United States v. Phillips, 477 F.3d 215, 220 (5th Cir. 2007).

117 18 U.S.C. §§1030(a)(2), (a)(2)(C).

118 U.S. v. Drew, 2009 WL 2872855 (C.D. Cal. 2009).

119 Id. at *17 (citing City of Chicago v. Morales, 527 U.S. 41, 60, 119 S.Ct. 1849, 144 L.Ed.2d 67 (1999)).

120 544 F. Supp. 2d 473, 486 (E.D.Va. 2008), aff'd in part, rev'd in part, 562 F.3d 630 (4th Cir. 2009) (remanded to determine actual amount of damages).

121 2007 U.S. Dist. LEXIS 96230, at *46 (N.D. Text. Sept. 12, 2007).

122 America Online v. LCGM, 46 F. Supp. 2d 444 (E.D. Va. 1998). Craigslist v. Naturemarket, 2010 WL 807446 (N.D. Cal. 2010).

123 NO. C 08-05780 JW (N.D. Cal. July 20, 2010).

124 Id. at 8–22.

125 18 U.S.C. §1030(e) (2001).

126 18 U.S.C. §§ 2701–2711 (2008). Similar to the Wiretap Act, The Stored Communication Act has a specific consent exception (§ 2702(b)).

127 18 U.S.C. § 2701 (2008).

128 18 U.S.C. § 2511(2)(c) (2008).

129 Kerr, supra note 114.

130 Id.

131 See, e.g., Frederic Stutzman and Woodrow Hartzog, Boundary Regulation in Social Media, ACM Conference on Computer Supported Cooperative Work (CSCW 2012); Robert Wilson, Samuel D. Gosling, & Lindsay T. Graham, A Review of Facebook Research in the Social Sciences, 7 Persp. Psychol. Sci. 203 (2012).

132 See, e.g., Harris v. Blockbuster, 622 F. Supp. 2d 396 (N.D. Tex. 2009).

133 Id.

134 Bank of Indiana, N.A. v. Holyfield, 476 F. Supp. 104, 109-10 (S.D. Miss. 1979).

Intellectual Property

Kathleen K. Olson

Lehigh University

ABSTRACT

The collaborative nature of social media challenges traditional notions of ownership of content online. This chapter summarizes the law of copyright, "hot news" and trademark as applied to social media and discusses current case law and legislative proposals. Copyright issues include fair use, linking and embedding video, Creative Commons licenses, liability for infringement by others and the "safe harbor" provisions of the Digital Millennium Copyright Act. The application of the hot news doctrine and trademark law to social media is examined, including liability for news aggregators and fake corporate and celebrity Twitter accounts.

Digital technology and the rise of social media have challenged the ability of existing legal rules to manage intellectual property online. Social media users engage with content in new ways: They create it, share it, curate it, remix it and collaborate with others to create new works from it. Questions about authorship and ownership arise that challenge traditional conceptions of intellectual property law and may require a re-examination of the law to determine ways to cope with these and future challenges.

For now, however, copyright and other intellectual property laws generally apply to content on social media sites in much the same way as other contexts, both with regard to original content and to the use of material that belongs to others. While the billions of pieces of content copied and distributed on sites such as Facebook, Twitter, Flickr, Pinterest and YouTube may make it impossible for copyright owners to fully enforce their rights, those rights are not forfeited. Because social media users are both creators and users of works, they need to understand both the rights and the limitations of intellectual property. This chapter discusses the basic rules of

copyright, "hot news" and trademark and describes the current state of the law governing content on social media platforms.

COPYRIGHT

Most content on social media sites is governed by copyright law. Copyright refers to ownership rights given to those who produce creative expression, whether it is text, photographs, video, music, software, works of art or other creative works. Among these ownership rights are the right to reproduce the work, prepare "derivative" works, distribute copies, and perform or display the work. Copyright protection begins as soon as the work is "fixed in a tangible medium of expression," which includes material posted online.

Copyright is governed exclusively by federal law and has as its source the Copyright Clause of the U.S. Constitution, which gives Congress the power to grant authors exclusive rights in their works, for a limited time, in order to "promote the progress of science and useful arts."[1] Copyright provides creators with a limited monopoly right in their works so they can profit economically from them. This helps promote the progress of science and the arts because it gives authors the incentive to create and disseminate political, social, and artistic expression that adds to the free flow of information and ideas. In return, their works will eventually become part of the public domain, free for others to use and build upon as material for new creative works.

Copyright protects original works of authorship created from an individual's own efforts and not by copying existing works, although originality requires only a minimal level of creativity. Facts are not copyrightable, however, so tweeting a piece of information from a news story is not infringement (although breaking news may be protected by the "hot news" doctrine, which is described in more detail later in this chapter). Recipes— a popular item on sites such as Pinterest—are not copyrightable if they consist mainly of a list of ingredients.

Copyright also does not protect ideas. The law limits property rights to the particular expression of an idea, but not the idea itself. In some cases, the idea and the expression can't be separated. Under the "merger doctrine," if an idea can be expressed only in a limited number of ways, the idea and its expression "merge" and the expression also will not be protected. Whether a post on a social media platform is protected by copyright depends, therefore, on the level of original expression it contains. Posts that consist of personal updates or other statements of fact or that express an opinion or idea without the level of creative expression necessary to escape the merger doctrine are not copyrightable and are free for others to copy and share.

The length of the post itself may determine its copyrightability, an issue that is especially relevant on microblogging sites such as Twitter. Because tweets are limited in length to 140 characters, they are generally not long enough to be entitled to copyright protection. The originality requirement means titles or short phrases or expressions are not protected (they may be protected by trademark if used commercially, however). Exceptions exist, of course: A haiku or other short work that is sufficiently expressive may be protected, but in general, the required level of creativity will not be found in something as short as a tweet. On the other hand, compilations of tweets—such as the 2010 *New York Times* bestseller *Sh*t My Dad Says*, derived from the popular Twitter account—are copyright-protected if there is creativity in the selection or arrangement of the tweets and if there is additional text that meets the originality requirements for copyrightability.

While the nature of social networking means many original posts are too short or non-creative to enjoy copyright protection, other types of user-generated content are protected. For example, as long as there is sufficient creative expression, written content is automatically protected by copyright as soon as it is "fixed" by being posted on a site. Creative works such as videos and photos retain their copyright when uploaded to a social media or photo-sharing site. While this may seem obvious, in 2010 Britain's *Daily Mail* published photos found on Twitpic without permission and then claimed in its defense that images on Twitpic are in the public domain. In 2011, the BBC made the same error, airing a blogger's photos of rioting in London without his permission and claiming that content on Twitter was not subject to copyright. Both later apologized for their error.[2] In January 2011, a federal judge in the Southern District of New York denied a motion to dismiss infringement claims brought by a professional photographer against the French wire service Agence France Press, Getty Images, CBS and CNN for using photos of the Haitian earthquake he had uploaded to Twitter and Twitpic. The media companies had argued that Twitter's terms of service granted third parties a license to use the site's content, but the judge ruled that any license extended only to Twitter and its partners, which did not include the parties involved in the lawsuit.[3]

To win a copyright infringement suit, the plaintiff must prove he owns a valid copyright in the work and that the defendant copied the original elements in the work without permission. If there is no direct proof that the defendant copied the work, the plaintiff must prove that the defendant had access to the work and that the two works are "substantially similar." Access may be proven by showing the defendant had a reasonable opportunity to see the original work—if it was posted on the Internet, that may be enough. The similarity standard is based on whether an average observer would see

the two works as similar enough to recognize that the alleged infringing work was copied from the original.

While copyright infringement may be prosecuted as a criminal offense, most cases are civil proceedings. Remedies in civil infringement lawsuits may include an injunction to stop the infringement, attorney's fees, and actual damages and profits. Statutory damages may also be available, and they can be as high as $30,000 per work for innocent infringement and $150,000 for willful infringement.[4] In the past decade, juries awarded substantial statutory damages in lawsuits brought by record companies against individuals who downloaded songs from file-sharing sites. In the case of a Minnesota woman who downloaded 24 songs on Kazaa, a jury in 2009 awarded the plaintiffs $80,000 per song, for a total damage award of $1.92 million. In another case involving Boston University graduate student Joel Tenenbaum, the jury awarded $22,500 per song, for a total of $675,000. Judges later reduced the damages for both defendants, but the original award was reinstated on appeal in Tenenbaum's case, and further proceedings were expected in both cases in 2012.[5]

Linking and Embedding Content

If copying without permission is infringement, what about linking to copyrighted material without permission? A simple hyperlink to content on another site does not generally raise intellectual property concerns. In the past, disputes have occurred over "deep linking," in which web pages inside a site are linked to directly, bypassing the site's homepage or other desired entry point, and "framing," in which content from one site is embedded on a second site and displayed through a scrollable window or frame. Many of these cases involved claims of unfair competition and trademark infringement or dilution because the defendant was attempting to "pass off" the imported content as its own or was otherwise damaging the plaintiff's business. In 1997, for example, news organizations including *The Washington Post* and CNN sued a website called TotalNews for its use of framing to embed stories from the plaintiffs' servers and display them surrounded by TotalNews advertising rather than that of the original news sites. The suit alleged unfair competition, trademark infringement and dilution, and copyright infringement, but the suit was settled before going to trial. Also in 1997, Ticketmaster sued Microsoft over deep links to the ticket seller's website from Microsoft's "Seattle Sidewalks" city guide site, alleging that the links diluted the Ticketmaster trademark and constituted unfair competition—but the parties settled that lawsuit out of court as well, leaving no established precedent in the case law on these issues.

The method used for framing content, "inline linking," is commonly used today to display images or embed videos on a site without having to copy the files. It allows a video to be played and viewed on a website while the actual video file remains on another server, such as YouTube. Visitors viewing the video on the website have no indication that it is not part of the site, but since no copying is involved—only linking—liability for copyright infringement is avoided.

That has been the general consensus, anyway, and the U.S. Court of Appeals for the Ninth Circuit adopted that position in a 2007 ruling. In *Perfect 10 v. Amazon.com*, Google was sued for copyright infringement over its visual search engine, which displayed images that matched search terms by using inline links, so that the actual image files remained on their original servers. The court ruled in favor of Google and adopted the "server test," which turned on whether the defendant's server housed an actual copy of the infringing content. If it did not and the site merely linked to the content on another site using inline linking, there was no infringement of the copyright owner's reproduction or display rights.[6]

The trial judge in a case that was considered on appeal in the Seventh Circuit in 2012 came to a different conclusion, however, and the outcome of the appeal has the potential to threaten the business model of sites, such as YouTube, that promote the ability to embed videos to its users. In *Flava Works v. Gunter*, an adult-entertainment video production company sued a "social video bookmarking site" called myVidster.com because some of its copyrighted videos had been embedded by users on the site. Since the videos were not copied onto myVidster.com's servers, the main issue was whether the site could be liable for contributory infringement for allowing its users to embed infringing videos. myVidster.com argued that there could be no contributory infringement because its users were not themselves liable for direct infringement under the Ninth Circuit's server test.

The district court judge rejected that test, however, and issued a preliminary injunction against the site, holding that "a website's servers need not actually store a copy of a work in order to 'display' it."[7] On appeal, the validity of the server test was one of the main issues, and YouTube and Facebook filed amicus curiae briefs urging the court to adopt the Ninth Circuit's test. If the Seventh Circuit or other courts follow the district court's reasoning that embedding content may qualify as infringement, it would have a significant impact on video hosting sites and other social media platforms that use inline links to import content, including curation sites such as Storify.

Limitations on Copyright Protection

Along with the threshold copyrightability requirements, other rules further the goals of copyright by putting limits on the monopoly copyright owners hold over their works. Copyright terms ensure that their monopoly does not last forever, for example, and the fair use doctrine ensures that their control over the use of their works is never absolute.

Because copyright terms limit the period during which a copyright owner has exclusive rights to the work, they foster the growth of the public domain by making material available for future authors to draw on to create new works. Congress has the power to give authors the exclusive right to their writings "for limited times," and this has been consistently interpreted to prohibit perpetual copyrights. In 1998, the Copyright Term Extension Act extended copyright terms by 20 years, so that today, the copyright term for a work of individual authorship is the life of the author plus 70 years, and for a work of corporate authorship, it is 120 years after its creation or 95 years after its publication, whichever is shorter.[8]

The fair use doctrine is one of the most important tools in copyright law to maintain the proper balance between an individual's property rights and the social benefits that come from a free flow of information. By allowing the use of material without the permission of the copyright owner, fair use helps resolve some of the potential conflicts that may arise between copyright and free speech. Fair use is an exception to the exclusive rights of a copyright owner; it allows creative works to be used by others for certain purposes that are socially beneficial. To determine fair use, courts examine and weigh four different factors, which are found in Section 107 of the 1976 Copyright Act. These are:

1. the purpose and character of the use, including whether such use is of a commercial nature or is for non-profit educational purposes;
2. the nature of the copyrighted work;
3. the amount and substantiality of the portion used in relation to the copyrighted work as a whole; and
4. the effect of the use upon the potential market for or value of the copyrighted work.[9]

The first factor requires an examination of the purpose of the secondary use. News reporting, comment, criticism, research, scholarship, and teaching are all listed in Section 107 as protected purposes under the fair use doctrine, although this is not an exclusive list. While non-profit uses are favored, a commercial use does not preclude a finding of fair use; the Supreme Court has said that other characteristics, such as "transformativeness," may be more

important. This factor is an important one for social media users, so it will be discussed in more detail below.

The second factor looks at whether the original work is highly creative or primarily factual; a factual work is given less copyright protection, while artistic works such as fiction or music have more protection. The third factor looks at how much of the original work was taken, and is measured in proportion to the entire work—secondary users should take only as much of the original as is needed for their purpose. Generally, only a small portion of the original work needs to be borrowed: When commenting on a news story, for example, excerpts may be quoted, but not the entire article. Sometimes using the entire work is necessary, however, as when commenting on a photograph or using a journal article for classroom use, and this will not prevent a finding of fair use.

The fourth factor, the effect of the use on the value of or potential market for the original work, is regarded by some as the most important factor. It measures the economic harm that may be caused by the secondary use of the work, which is often closely tied to the purpose of that use—if a secondary use serves mainly as a replacement for the original in the marketplace, for example, neither the first nor the fourth factor will weigh in favor of fair use. Secondary uses that go beyond merely substituting for the original work and instead create something new are less likely to harm the market for the original, and they also do more to further the goals of copyright. Because of this, the concept of "transformativeness" has come to have added weight in fair use analysis, particularly with regard to the first factor.

The Purpose and Character of the Use

While news reporting, comment, criticism, research, scholarship, and teaching are listed as protected purposes under the fair use doctrine, even they may not be fair use if a secondary work serves the same purpose as the original. Instead, the law favors a use that transforms the original or "adds something new, with a further purpose or different character, altering the first with new expression, meaning, or message."[10]

The protected categories found in Section 107 are often themselves transformative, however; examples include copying a short video clip for a movie review and quoting excerpts from a political speech in a scholarly biography or news story. Parody is generally considered transformative as a humorous form of comment or criticism. In one of the few Supreme Court cases involving fair use, the Court ruled that 2 Live Crew's song parodying Roy Orbison's 1964 hit "Oh, Pretty Woman" was transformative and that its commercial purpose did not disqualify it as fair use.[11] The Second Circuit

ruled in 2006 that incorporating part of a copyrighted fashion photograph from a magazine into an artistic collage was fair use because it was transformative: The artist, Jeff Koons, changed the look of the photo significantly and gave it an entirely new purpose and meaning as part of his "appropriation art."[12]

Even using a copyrighted work for a different purpose, without altering or adding to it to make it into something completely new, may be transformative. The Ninth Circuit ruled in two different cases that visual search engines that made thumbnail copies of images for indexing purposes were protected by fair use because the images were used for a different purpose—indexing the Web rather than for aesthetic purposes—and because that use benefitted the public.[13]

How does all of this apply to social media? While no bright-line rules apply, a variety of fair use defenses may be available for those who use the works of others. Material that is posted on social media sites is frequently done so for purposes of comment or criticism, whether it's a news story on a blog or the latest *Avengers* movie trailer on Facebook. Parodies, wikis and creative remixes of works, such as mashups and certain kinds of fan fiction, may be highly transformative. Compilations of photos or other copyrighted material on social curation sites like Pinterest and Storify may be protected by fair use, depending on the degree to which the aggregation of individual pieces of content transforms the material into something new or uses it for a different purpose, such as comment or criticism. Most social media uses are non-commercial, which weighs in favor of fair use.

At the same time, the other fair use factors may outweigh the first factor, even when the use is transformative. Fan fiction, for example, is more likely to be fair use if it borrows relatively little material and does not harm the market for the original. Posts that include comment or criticism of a work should copy only the amount of material needed to make the point. Copyrighted material should not be copied for the sole purpose of sharing it with others. Curating material just to compile it, without adding something extra that transforms it or otherwise gives it a new purpose, is not fair use.

Finally, practices such as attribution and linking back to the original source may be helpful to demonstrate good faith on the part of the secondary user. Although neither necessary nor sufficient for a finding of fair use, these practices may have some bearing on a judge's determination of the equities of the particular case. A lack of good faith on the part of a copyright plaintiff may also affect the outcome: Several district court judges in Nevada and Colorado sided with secondary users in infringement cases filed by the profit-driven "copyright troll" Righthaven LLC in 2010 and 2011, and the company's questionable business model and litigation tactics may have played

a role. After transferring the rights to content from clients such as the *Las Vegas Review-Journal* and the *Denver Post*, the company filed more than 200 infringement suits against bloggers and other non-profit websites for using the content without permission. The suits were filed without issuing the customary cease-and-desist letters or takedown notices, and maximum statutory damages were sought in each case.

While many of the suits were settled or dismissed for lack of standing, several judges ruled for the defendants based on fair use, in one case even when an entire article had been copied on a non-profit site.[14] Apart from the merits of the fair use argument, some judges made clear in their rulings their disapproval of Righthaven's aggressive legal strategy, which one opinion characterized as an "abuse" of the copyright law.[15] Righthaven's failures in court led to its insolvency, and in March 2012, its copyright registrations were transferred to a court-appointed receiver to be auctioned off to pay the company's creditors.[16]

Because fair use analysis accounts for the individual facts and equities of each case, specific guidelines for what is permissible are difficult to provide. The American University's Center for Social Media has created codes of best practices regarding fair use in different contexts, including one for online video, that may be helpful in some cases.[17] A use that is non-commercial, that transforms the original work or otherwise has some public benefit, that doesn't take more than is needed and that doesn't replace the original in the market has a plausible claim of fair use. Still, generalities such as these cannot predict the outcome in a particular case. The fair use doctrine, because it is meant to be flexible, can also be frustratingly unclear.

Fair use may provide a legal defense for some uses of copyrighted material on social media sites, but the fact is that many social media practices, even if infringing, are likely to be tolerated. In practice, most copyright disputes never make it to court, and an individual blogger or other social media user may at most receive a cease-and-desist letter from an attorney asking for infringing material to be removed. Social networking, because it has been used more for personal sharing than for commercial purposes, is a setting in which copyright owners have so far practiced a good deal of forbearance with regard to infringement.

Exceptions exist, of course. Media companies targeted file-sharing sites such as Grokster and LimeWire, and YouTube is currently defending a $1 billion infringement case, which is described in more detail in the next section. In the case of file-sharing sites, copyright owners also sued hundreds of individual users who downloaded music and asked for statutory damages that in some cases totaled more than $1 million. Facebook users have been spared that kind of draconian legal action, and there are some good reasons why. Most importantly, illegal file-sharing of digital music caused direct and

significant economic harm to the music industry in a way that most individual social media uses of copyrighted content do not. In addition, suing the moms who use Pinterest would be a public relations disaster to rival the record companies' ill-advised lawsuits against grandmothers and 12-year-olds in the last decade. Rather than trying to control social media, most copyright owners have realized they will be better off embracing it as a marketing and promotional tool.

As the use and sharing of content through social networking continues to grow, and as copyright owners continue to tolerate certain social uses of their material, standards will develop for acceptable practices in the social media context that may also shape what is permissible in other environments. The law, especially the fair use doctrine, reflects contemporary social norms. As social media becomes an integral part of the culture, the norms that govern it may begin to shape legal norms as well, especially for judges trying to make equitable decisions in fair use cases.

Liability for Infringement by Others

If an individual using a social media platform infringes copyright, the site itself may also be liable on the theory of contributory infringement, which may be found if the defendant has knowledge of the infringing activity and induces, causes or materially contributes to the infringement. Social media sites might protect themselves from such suits by monitoring for infringing activity and acting quickly to stop it, but the vast amount of material they host makes it impossible to do this effectively.

Instead, social media platforms receive statutory protection from secondary liability for content they do not control under the Digital Millennium Copyright Act of 1998 ("DMCA"), a federal statute that was aimed at addressing the unique copyright concerns of content online. The Act's primary purpose was to combat online piracy, and the statute raised the penalties for copyright infringement online and made it illegal to gain unauthorized access to a copyrighted work by circumventing anti-piracy protections.

For online service providers such as social media platforms, the DMCA provides protection against secondary liability for copyright infringement when they act simply as hosts of the content of others and do not play a role in determining its content. Section 512 of the statute provides a "safe harbor" for online service providers and other web-based hosts of content against liability for contributory infringement if they follow certain procedures to safeguard copyrights on their sites.

In order to be protected, an online service provider providing a forum for material to be posted at the direction of its users must not have "actual

knowledge" that the material is infringing or, in the absence of such know-ledge, must not be aware of "facts or circumstances from which infringing activity is apparent." The host site must also establish certain "notice and takedown" procedures, including designating an agent to receive notices of copyright infringement in order to remove infringing material when notified of its existence on the site by a copyright owner. While the DMCA does not require an online service provider to actively monitor its service for infringing activity, it must act "expeditiously" to remove or disable access to the material once it is made aware of it.[18]

Although the Act requires that a copyright owner provide a statement of a "good faith belief" that the material is infringing when it issues a takedown notice, critics contend that copyright owners can overreach by issuing takedown notices that are unwarranted or when the use of their content is fair use. One user fought back when YouTube, after receiving a takedown notice from Universal Music, removed a 30-second home video of her toddler dancing to the Prince song "Let's Go Crazy." Stephanie Lenz filed a counter-notification to challenge the removal, but then went further and sued the copyright owner in federal court for misrepresenting its claim of infringement under the Act. The court refused Universal's motion to dismiss Lenz's suit and held that copyright owners must make a good faith consideration of fair use before it issues a takedown notice or it may be held liable for damages.[19]

Litigation focusing on secondary liability under Section 512 has centered on what level of knowledge of infringing activity is sufficient for an online service provider to be disqualified from safe harbor protection. Courts have interpreted the awareness standard fairly narrowly under what Congress called a "red flag" test: The online service provider must be aware of facts and circumstances that raise a "red flag" that would indicate to a reasonable person that infringing activity is occurring on the site. The Ninth Circuit upheld that standard in December 2011, ruling that a video-sharing site did not lose its immunity under the safe harbor provision just because it may have had general knowledge that some of its users might use its services to infringe copyrights.[20]

In April 2012, the Second Circuit essentially agreed with this holding but added a theory of "willful blindness" that complicated the analysis. The court's ruling came in an appeal of a $1 billion lawsuit filed in 2007 by media giant Viacom against YouTube. Viacom accused YouTube of encouraging users to upload "The Daily Show" and other copyrighted content to the site. YouTube won at the district court level in 2010 when the court ruled that it qualified for protection under the safe harbor provision. The lower court found that YouTube quickly removed infringing material once it was notified of its existence by copyright owners, and that while YouTube may

have had a "general awareness" that users were posting videos that may be infringing, that awareness did not rise to the level of knowledge required to disqualify YouTube from safe harbor protection.

On appeal, however, the Second Circuit reversed the lower court's ruling and remanded the case for further proceedings. The court agreed that Section 512 requires not just general awareness but knowledge of specific instances of infringement. The court ruled, however, that in this case, a reasonable jury could find that YouTube did have actual knowledge of instances of specific infringing activity that would disqualify it from safe harbor protection. In addition, the court instructed the district court to examine whether YouTube had exercised "willful blindness" to avoid knowing about specific infringing clips on its site, which it suggested would jeopardize its immunity under the DMCA.[21]

Although both sides claimed partial victory, the ruling adds to the uncertainty of Section 512's knowledge requirements and will make it harder for online service providers to win safe harbor cases in the lower courts. In addition, the court's introduction of "willful blindness" to its analysis of the knowledge requirement may put a practical burden on such sites to be more proactive about possible infringement on their sites, even though the Act does not require such monitoring.

A "willful blindness" standard may be detrimental to Pinterest, the social curation site whose explosive growth has led to negative attention for its copyright practices. The site allows users to "pin" photos and other images onto their own virtual pinboards. Pinterest differs from other photo-sharing sites in some significant ways: Unlike Flickr or other photo host sites, on which a user must upload an image to her own account, on Pinterest a user can "re-pin" images from other sites on the Web by copying the image onto the Pinterest server, where it is stored. This is different from other social curation sites, such as Storify, as well. Storify avoids copying other sites' material by using inline links to embed and display content on its pages, although as has been described, the legality of that method has also come under fire.

Critics contend that Pinterest not only facilitates copying by its users, but seems to champion it. While Pinterest's terms of service require that users have the rights to any images they pin on the site, the company's business model is based on encouraging its users to collect material from other sites: "Pinterest lets you organize and share all the beautiful things you find on the web."[22] One commentator estimated that 99 percent of the pinned images on the site may infringe copyright.[23]

The company also drew criticism in 2012 over an additional provision in its terms of service that contained an indemnity clause holding Pinterest's corporate owner harmless from any claims against it arising from the use of

the site. Although other social media sites, including Tumblr and Twitpic, have similar clauses, Pinterest was attacked because of the perception that it actively encourages its users to infringe. In the face of the controversy, Pinterest added an opt-out option in the form of HTML code. Copyright owners who don't want their content pinned can include a "no pin" piece of code that will block a web page's content from being copied to Pinterest. The company also added a 500-character limit to image captions in order to prevent large-scale copying of blog posts and other copyrighted text onto the site.

Other online service providers have also implemented technological measures to supplement their notice and takedown procedures and limit their liability for user infringement. In 2007, YouTube began using Content ID, a content management tool that allows the site not only to identify copyrighted material but to take action, at the request of the copyright owner, to block it, track it and provide viewing statistics, or monetize it by linking to an official website or inserting advertising. Critics charge that the identifications are not always accurate, however, and that the system does not sufficiently protect fair use.

While technological tools that help sites monitor and prevent infringement may alleviate some of the uncertainty about the extent of safe harbor protection in the wake of the Second Circuit's *Viacom* ruling, they do not replace statutory protection. Without the promise of immunity from secondary liability, Web hosts would be forced to actively monitor their sites for possible infringement. Because of the expense and risk that entails, sites would simply bar or severely limit the ability of users to post content to their sites. Without the DMCA safe harbor protection, the explosion of social networking and user-generated content never would have occurred.

Creative Commons

Some copyright owners would like to voluntarily give up some or all of their property rights with regard to their creative works. In 2001, in order to promote "universal access to research, education and culture," Lawrence Lessig and other copyright activists founded Creative Commons, a non-profit organization that encourages the sharing of information online by providing "a free, public, and standardized infrastructure that creates a balance between the reality of the Internet and the reality of copyright laws."[24] Creative Commons sets up a "some rights reserved" system of licenses that allows copyright owners to permit certain uses of their work by others without forfeiting the entire bundle of rights that come with copyright.

The system lets copyright owners indicate up front whether they will permit others to use their works and for what purposes. Copyright owners can waive all of their rights and indicate that they have chosen to place the work in the public domain, or they can choose from a number of different licenses represented on their websites by symbols indicating different levels of permission. The most permissive license is an "Attribution" or "CC BY" license, which allows others to copy, distribute, remix or "tweak" the work, even for commercial purposes, as long as the original author is credited. The "Attribution-ShareAlike" (CC BY-SA) license adds the requirement that anyone who creates a derivative work by changing or building upon the original must make the new work available under the same licensing terms. This type of license is used by open source software projects and by Wikipedia and its affiliated Wikimedia sites.

Flickr, the online photo-sharing community, was one of the first social media sites to make Creative Commons licensing available as part of its user interface, and it is the single largest source of Creative Commons-licensed content on the Web, with more than 200 million images available. In 2011, YouTube added Creative Commons licensing as an option for users who upload video and created a library of CC BY-licensed videos from sources such as C-SPAN and Al Jazeera.

A Creative Commons license presumes, of course, that the licensor actually owns the copyright in the first place. Secondary works that are created from copyrighted works cannot be licensed under a Creative Commons license unless the permission of the original copyright owner is obtained, either expressly or through an existing Creative Commons license, unless the secondary work is protected by fair use.

The most restrictive license reserves all rights other than the right to download the work and to share it by copying, distributing, and transmitting it, with attribution and for non-commercial purposes only. Indicating even this level of permission is useful, however, because otherwise sharing it would most likely be infringement. The utility of the Creative Commons licensing system is that it eliminates the often-difficult task of identifying and contacting a copyright owner in order to ask permission and the uncertainty that comes with guessing if something is protected by fair use. It allows the free use of copyrighted works for everything from simple sharing on social media sites to incorporating images or music into new creative works without the fear of liability for infringement.

THE HOT NEWS DOCTRINE

Social media has become a significant source for news: When Osama bin Laden was killed in May 2011, more people learned about it through social networking than from a news site or blog.[25] What happens when breaking news is reported—do news organizations have a legal right to control access to their "scoop"? Since the facts of the news report are not copyrightable, any such right must come from another area of the law. The Supreme Court created such a right in 1918 and based it on the tort of unfair competition. Called "hot news misappropriation," it was developed to prevent competitors from free-riding on the time and effort required to report time-sensitive news and other information and preserve the economic incentive for companies to invest in those efforts.[26]

No one who tweeted the news of bin Laden's death was liable for repeating that fact, of course—the tort is available only in very limited circumstances. The public has the right to tell others about breaking news on Facebook or to live-tweet a basketball game. In some circumstances, however, if done repeatedly by a competitor for commercial advantage, those activities may be actionable.

The 1918 Supreme Court case that produced the hot news doctrine, *INS v. Associated Press*, featured a battle between competing wire services during World War I. The Associated Press sued the International News Service for rewriting AP dispatches and calling them their own. The Court granted the AP an injunction against this practice and created a limited quasi-property right in the news—in facts—based on a theory of unfair competition to protect the labor and expense required to gather and disseminate the news.[27]

Hot news misappropriation still exists, but only in the common law of a handful of states, and its scope was narrowed to avoid overlapping with and being pre-empted by federal copyright law. One important limitation is that the property right is strictly limited by time—the news must still be "hot" to be protected—in order to avoid First Amendment concerns. In 1997, the Second Circuit outlined the elements that are generally required in order for a hot news case to avoid copyright pre-emption. *NBA v. Motorola* centered on whether the transmission of "real-time" scores and statistics from NBA games via pagers constituted hot news misappropriation. The district court granted the NBA an injunction, but the Second Circuit reversed, holding that while the NBA and other sports leagues may own the copyright in the broadcast descriptions of their games, they do not own the underlying facts, which include statistical information and updated scores. The court held that, unlike INS, the pager service did not act as a substitute or direct competitor with the league's "product," which the court defined as the experience of watching the game in person or on TV. The pager service also did not free-ride on the effort required to provide the information because the service hired its own freelancers to watch the games and send out the score updates. The court set out some general guidelines for what would constitute an actionable hot news case. Although state laws differ to some degree, hot news appropriation has generally required that:

1. a plaintiff generates or gathers information at a cost;
2. the information is time-sensitive;
3. a defendant's use of the information constitutes free-riding on the plaintiff's efforts;
4. the defendant is in direct competition with a product or service offered by the plaintiffs; and
5. the ability of other parties to free-ride on the efforts of the plaintiff or others would so reduce the incentive to produce the product or service that its existence or quality would be substantially threatened.[28]

Using these guidelines, fans or even commercial ventures that live-tweet a sporting event would not be liable under the hot news doctrine if they are monitoring the games themselves and unless they pose direct competition sufficient to threaten the viability of the event itself. In the news context, the doctrine has undergone something of a revival as news organizations have fought aggregators, such as Google News, that reuse headlines and lead paragraphs or summaries on the Web. The Associated Press entered into a licensing agreement with Google in 2006, but it and other media companies continue to pursue hot news claims against other news aggregators.

In 2011, the Second Circuit affirmed the continuing survival of hot news claims but limited its future applicability in a case involving an online newsletter that regularly reported investment banks' time-sensitive analysis and stock recommendations. In *Barclays Capital v. TheFlyOnTheWall.com*, the court ruled the banks could not state a hot news claim because TheFly did not free-ride on the banks' efforts by making its own recommendations—it reported the banks' recommendations as news, not as its own product the way INS did. The court also indicated that the guidelines in the *NBA* case were not binding, and that future hot news claims would need to involve facts that closely parallel those in the *INS* case in order to be successful.[29] Twitter and other Internet companies submitted amicus briefs urging the court to throw out hot news as obsolete. Public interest groups urged the court to renounce the doctrine because it restricts free speech, but the court did not reach the First Amendment issue.

Calls by news organizations for federal hot news legislation have so far been unsuccessful. Any such legislation would have to be strictly limited to avoid limiting free speech, and it should retain most of the restrictive elements from the *NBA* case in order to limit claims to those that would have a direct and substantial anti-competitive effect and lead to long-term harm to the business of news- and information-gathering.

TRADEMARKS

A trademark can be a word, phrase, symbol or design, or a combination of words, phrases, symbols or designs that identifies and distinguishes the source of the goods of one party from those of others. The purpose of a trademark or a service mark, which protects services rather than goods, is to protect businesses from the unauthorized use of their corporate or product names, slogans or logos for commercial purposes.

Unlike copyright, which is exclusively federal law, trademarks may be governed by both the federal Lanham Act and state trademark laws. To qualify for protection, a trademark cannot be deceptive or confusingly similar to another mark and it must be distinctive—it must be capable of identifying the source of a particular good or service.

Infringement occurs when a trademark is used in a commercial context in a manner that is likely to cause consumer confusion as to the source of the product or service. Trademark "dilution" occurs when the distinctive quality of the mark is diminished, even though consumer confusion is not likely. A trademark may be diluted by "blurring," when it becomes identified with goods that are dissimilar to what made it famous, or by "tarnishment," when the mark is portrayed negatively, such as being associated with inferior or disreputable products or services. To bring a dilution claim under federal law, a trademark must be "famous"—one that is widely known, such as Xerox or Exxon.

As with copyright, free speech considerations require that a company's trademark may be used for descriptive purposes if necessary to accurately identify the product or service. As a result, a Facebook post that describes a celebrity's outfit at an awards ceremony using trademarks ("Zooey Deschanel wore Prada to the Golden Globes") infringes neither Prada's nor the Golden Globes' trademark. Parodies of trademarks are generally protected as critical commentary, although the degree to which the parody involves a commercial use of the mark may determine whether the use crosses the line into infringement or tarnishment. Editorial uses are favored over uses in commercial products such as posters or T-shirts, so a trademark parody posted on a social networking site would most likely be protected, although no bright-line rules apply.

On Twitter, the use of corporate trademarks for fake accounts has resulted in controversy, but not much litigation to date. Twitter allows users to sign up under another's name as long as the account profile makes clear that the account is an impersonation and they do not pretend to be someone else "in order to mislead or deceive"—if they do, their account will be suspended.[30] The guidelines also advise users to differentiate their account name from that of their parody subject; accounts such as "Google Brain," "AT&T Parody

Relations," and "The Fake CNN" make clear to consumers that the account is meant as an exercise in free speech, not commerce.

Fake accounts on social media sites may be actionable if they use trademarks for commercial purposes and if consumer confusion is likely to occur. Some have argued that confusion may be more likely on fast-moving and de-contextualized Twitter feeds than on a static website. The fake Twitter account @BPGlobalPR brought wide attention to the practice when it satirized the oil company's attempts at public relations after the massive 2010 Gulf Coast oil spill (example: "The ocean looks just a bit slimmer today. Dressing it in black really did the trick! #bpcares"). Although the account did not contain a disclaimer, a spokesman for the real BP indicated the company would not take legal action, saying, "People are entitled to their views on what we're doing and we have to live with those."[31]

In 2011, a viatical life insurance firm called Coventry First sued an anonymous Twitter user over a fake account that sent out tweets such as, "Praying to Jesus for an earthquake in the North Eastern US!!" The lawsuit included claims for trademark infringement and dilution. The account's user profile indicated it was meant as a parody, and the user subsequently changed the account name slightly to comply with Twitter's guidelines for parody accounts, which forbid use of the exact name of the parody's subject. The suit was eventually dropped.[32]

Celebrity Impersonation and Trademark

Impersonation is not limited to corporate identities on social media sites. In 2009, St. Louis Cardinals manager Tony La Russa sued Twitter over a fake account that used his name and image. Tweets were posted in his name that referred to team-related incidents such as the death of pitcher Josh Hancock and La Russa's own DUI arrest: "Lost 2 out of 3, but we made it out of Chicago without one drunk driving incident or dead pitcher," read one tweet. The only disclaimer was in the user profile, which stated, "Bio parodies are fun for everyone."

Although other celebrities had also had their names "twitterjacked," this was the first reported instance of a celebrity suing Twitter over a fake account. The complaint listed a number of claims against Twitter, including trademark infringement and dilution.[33]

The case is interesting for what it reveals about the limits federal law has put on plaintiffs hoping to hold online service providers responsible for harm caused by posts on social media sites. La Russa's real complaint about the fake account was that the tasteless statements in the tweets would be ascribed to him and would hurt his reputation. La Russa could not easily sue the actual impersonator because the person who set up the account was

unknown, and Twitter deleted the fake account the same day the suit was filed.

Although his harm had more to do with false light or defamation, he also would have been barred from suing Twitter on those claims, because the federal Communication Decency Act immunizes online service providers from liability for damages caused by offensive or harmful content posted by its users. Section 230 of the CDA gives sites like Twitter a safe harbor against secondary liability for a variety of state claims, which different courts have held to include defamation, misappropriation, obscenity, invasion of privacy, and state trademark dilution claims.[34]

Federal intellectual property claims are not included in the CDA's safe harbor provision but are covered by Section 512 of the DMCA and by a similar provision in the Lanham Act that protects online service providers from secondary liability for federal trademark infringement claims.[35] La Russa had little choice, then, but to sue Twitter for direct trademark infringement. He did so by claiming that the fake account falsely implied a personal endorsement of Twitter because of statements that said, "Tony La Russa is using Twitter" and "Join today to start receiving Tony La Russa's updates." To win, he would have had to show that the statements were likely to confuse consumers into thinking he had personally endorsed the site, and that as a result, he had been harmed. This may have been especially difficult to prove—according to news reports, the fake account had only four followers.[36]

In 2010, California passed an "e-personation" law that made online impersonation a crime. While its purpose was to combat fraud and cyber-bullying, critics charge that it undermines First Amendment rights and chills protected speech such as parody and satirical commentary.[37] Today, Twitter protects celebrity accounts with a verification policy that authenticates the identities of public figures and attaches a blue checkmark next to the profile name on verified accounts, although in at least one case it has authenticated the wrong account—due to a copy-editing error, an account spoofing Wendi Deng Murdoch, the wife of News Corp. CEO Rupert Murdoch, was authenticated instead of the real account.[38]

INTELLECTUAL PROPERTY: THE NEED FOR REFORM

Intellectual property is a complex issue and an increasingly important one in the digital age. The tension between protecting property rights in works and promoting creativity and the free flow of ideas is evident in the controversies and cases discussed in this chapter. Social networking highlights this tension, because traditional copyright rules, which emphasize exclusive

authorship and ownership, are not well suited to fostering a system based on collaborative and interactive creation.

While activists and copyright scholars have called for changes in the law to encourage this new means of creative production and reduce the uncertainty surrounding social media sharing, others have created their own guidelines. The Center for Social Media's development of fair use standards in their Codes of Best Practices is just one example of the kind of "bottom-up" rulemaking practiced by creative communities today. Self-regulation can be effective because it reflects pre-existing social norms and therefore has automatic moral authority and "buy-in" from the community, and because it can adapt to changes that occur in community practices and norms. At the same time, it risks tilting too much towards the interests of the community at the expense of copyright owners' property rights or the public interest.

Technology also provides a way for copyright owners to control their works online, as examples like Pinterest's "no pin" code and YouTube's Content ID system show. These tools also have the capability to create an imbalance of interests, however. In 1999, Lawrence Lessig contrasted the two types of "code" that regulate cyberspace: "East Coast Code," or the code that Congress enacts, and "West Coast Code," which is "the code that code writers 'enact' – the instructions imbedded in the software and hardware that make cyberspace work."[39] Lessig warned that as copyright owners increasingly turned to regulation by computer code—cheaper, more efficient and more flexible than East Coast Code—society must ensure that fundamental values like fair use are protected.

Finally, private ordering through contract can give social media sites the means to regulate their own sites with the flexibility needed to respond to changing circumstances—Twitter's terms of service, for example, give it the authority to regulate the use of its site and shut down a user's account without resorting to legal action. Here, too, however, default legal rules that try to strike a fair balance give way to whatever realignment of rights the private parties have bargained for. In the case of most terms of service agreements on social media sites, these rights are not truly bargained for and tend to favor the site rather than its users or the public interest, as the controversial indemnity provisions of Pinterest's terms of service demonstrate.

Legislation—East Coast Code—can be slow, cumbersome, and complex. At the same time, while private ordering through self-regulation, technology, or contract can fill in some of the gaps in the law, it can never completely replace it. When it comes to regulating the diverse and fast-changing social media environment, the challenge for Congress and the courts will be to strike the proper balance between private interests and public benefits so that intellectual property rights continue to be protected without limiting the future possibilities for expression that social networking represents.

FREQUENTLY ASKED QUESTIONS

1. Can I use a photo I find on Facebook?

It depends. The absence of a copyright notice does not mean the photo isn't copyrighted, and you should generally get permission unless you believe your use would be protected by the fair use doctrine. Non-commercial uses that are transformative or otherwise productive, such as comment, criticism, news reporting, research, scholarship, or teaching, may be fair use. Copying the photo for the same purpose as, or to substitute for, the original is not fair use. Attribution without permission ("Photo courtesy of CNN.com") is still infringement.

2. Can I embed a video from someone else's website on my Facebook page?

Probably. The Ninth Circuit has ruled that because embedding works by linking to a file that resides on another server, rather than by making a copy, it does not infringe copyright, and that seems to reflect the general view on the issue. In 2011, however, a federal district court judge in Chicago disagreed, ruling that copying isn't necessary to infringe a copyright owner's display right. The Seventh Circuit will hear the case on appeal later this year—if it affirms the lower court, it will reopen the question of embedding and infringement.

3. Can I be sued if someone posts a copyrighted photo on my blog?

You could be, but generally you will not be if you take the photo down when notified by the copyright owner. Because you host content on your blog that you do not control, you may be protected from secondary liability as an online service provider under Section 512 of the Digital Millennium Copyright Act. In order to take advantage of the safe harbor provision, you should include a notice to your readers not to post infringing content and file a form with the Copyright Office (http://www.copyright.gov/onlinesp/agent.pdf) to designate an agent for takedown notification.

4. Can I be sued for trademark infringement for creating a parody Twitter account?

Maybe, but you would most likely be protected by the First Amendment. In addition, trademark infringement requires commercial use of a trademark and the likelihood of consumer confusion. If you made clear your account was a parody, it would be hard for the subject of your parody to show it caused consumer confusion or that it caused any real harm to its trademark.

5. What is a Creative Commons license?

Creative Commons licenses give copyright owners a way to give permission in advance for certain uses of their content. Most of the licenses include some restrictions on use, such as requiring attribution or forbidding commercial use. Look for the CC logo on sites that use the licenses.

Notes

1   U.S. Const. art. I, § 8.
2   Olivier Laurent, Daily Mail Caught in Copyright Infringement Storm, British J. of Photography (May 26, 2010), http://www.bjp-online.com/british-journal-of-photography/news/1651087/daily-mail-caught-copyright-infringement-storm; Katie Poole & Olivier Laurent, BBC Caught in Twitter Copyright Row, British J. of Photography (August 15, 2011), http://www.bjp-online.com/british-journal-of-photography/news/2101942/bbc-caught-twitter-copyright-row.
3   Agence France Presse v. Morel, 769 F. Supp. 2d 295, 302–303 (S.D.N.Y. 2011).
4   17 U.S.C. §§ 502–506.
5   See Capitol Records v. Thomas-Rasset, 680 F. Supp. 2d 1045 (D. Minn. 2010); Sony BMG Music Entm't v. Tenenbaum, 721 F. Supp. 2d 85 (D. Mass. 2010).
6   Perfect 10, Inc. v. Amazon.com, Inc., 508 F.3d 1146, 1161–1162 (9th Cir. 2007).
7   Flava Works, Inc. v. Gunter, 2011 U.S. Dist. LEXIS 98451 (N.D. Ill., September 1, 2011).
8   17 U.S.C. § 302.
9   17 U.S.C. § 107.
10   Campbell v. Acuff-Rose Music, Inc., 510 U.S. 569, 579 (1994).
11   Id.
12   Blanch v. Koons, 467 F.3d 244 (2d Cir. 2006).
13   Kelly v. Arriba Soft Corp., 336 F.3d 811 (9th Cir. 2003); Perfect 10 v. Amazon.com, Inc., 508 F.3d 1146 (9th Cir. 2007).
14   Righthaven, LLC v. Jama, 2011 U.S. Dist. LEXIS 43952 (D. Nev. April 22, 2011).
15   Righthaven, LLC v. Wolf, 813 F. Supp. 2d 1265, 1273 (D. Colo. 2011).
16   For more on Righthaven, see Righthaven Stories, VegasInc (2012), http://www.vegasinc.com/news/legal/righthaven/.
17   Codes, Center for Social Media (2012), http://www.centerforsocialmedia.org/fair-use/related-materials/codes.
18   Digital Millennium Copyright Act, 17 U.S.C. § 512 (1998).
19   Lenz v. Universal Music Corp., 572 F. Supp. 2d 1150 (N.D. Cal. 2008).
20   UMG Recordings v. Shelter Capital Partners LLC, 667 F.3d 1022 (9th Cir. 2011).
21   Viacom Int'l., Inc. v. YouTube, Inc., No. 10-3270-cv, 2012 WL 1130851 (2d Cir. April 5, 2012).
22   What Is Pinterest? Pinterest, http://pinterest.com/about/ (last visited May 10, 2012).
23   Stephanie Medeiros, Websites Can Block Pinterest Pinning, Protect Content, Digital Journal, February 21, 2012, http://digitaljournal.com/article/319989.
24   About, Creative Commons, http://creativecommons.org/about (last visited May 7, 2012).

25 Public "Relieved" by bin Laden's Death, Obama's Job Approval Rises, Pew Research Center for the People & the Press, May 3, 2011, http://pewresearch.org/pubs/1978/poll-osama-bin-laden-death-reaction-obama-bush-military-cia-credit-first-heard-news.

26 See Victoria Smith Ekstrand, News Piracy and the Hot News Doctrine: Origins in Law and Implications for the Digital Age (2005).

27 Int'l News Serv. v. Associated Press, 248 U.S. 215, 236 (1918).

28 Nat'l Basketball Ass'n v. Motorola, Inc., 105 F.3d 841, 844–845 (2d Cir. 1997).

29 Barclays Capital, Inc. v. TheFlyOnTheWall.com, Inc., 650 F.3d 876 (2d Cir. 2011).

30 Impersonation Policy, Twitter, http://support.twitter.com/articles/18366-impersonation-policy# (last visited May 9, 2012).

31 Paulina Reso, Imposter BP Twitter Account That Parodies Oil Giant Left Untouched, N.Y. Daily News, May 27, 2010, http://articles.nydailynews.com/2010-05-27/news/27065593_1_bp-spokesman-toby-odone-gulf-oil-spill.

32 Complaint, Coventry First, LLC v. Does 1-10, No. 11-cv-03700-JS (E.D.Va. June 7, 2011); Jeff Roberts, Insurer Sues Twitter Imposter Who Cheers Death, Mayhem, Reuters, June 9, 2011, http://www.reuters.com/article/2011/06/09/us-coventry-idUSTRE7586ST20110609.

33 Complaint, La Russa v. Twitter, Inc., No. CGC09488101 (Cal. Sup. Ct. May 6, 2009).

34 Mark A. Lemley, Rationalizing Internet Safe Harbors, 6 J. on Telecomm. & High Tech. L. 101, 101 n. 2 (2007) (listing cases).

35 15 U.S.C. § 1114(2).

36 William McGeveran, Celebrity Impersonation and Section 230, Info/Law (June 25, 2009), http://blogs.law.harvard.edu/infolaw/2009/06/25/impersonation-and-230/.

37 Cal. Penal Code § 528.5 (West 2011).

38 Adam Clark Estes, How Twitter Accidentally Verified the Wrong Wendi Deng, The Atlantic Wire (January 4, 2012), http://www.theatlanticwire.com/technology/2012/01/how-twitter-accidentally-verified-wrong-wendi-deng/46991/.

39 Lawrence Lessig, Code and Other Laws of Cyberspace 53 (1999).

CHAPTER 5

Commercial Speech and Federal Regulations

Courtney Barclay

S.I. Newhouse School of Public Communications
Syracuse University

ABSTRACT

Online and mobile communications, including social media, provide new and valuable opportunities for interaction between an organization and its publics. The increased use of these media, however, presents unique concerns for consumer protection. Congress and key regulatory agencies—the Federal Trade Commission, the Food and Drug Administration, and the Securities and Exchange Commission—have worked to ensure consumers continue to be protected in the new media environment. These laws continue to focus on long-standing values of commercial speech regulation: truth, accurate disclosure, and fairness. This chapter discusses the legislative and regulatory developments essential to advertising and public relations professionals.

Historically, commercial speech—that speech which promotes financial transactions—received no protection under the First Amendment. However, this approach shifted in the 1970s, when the U.S. Supreme Court recognized that society "may have a strong interest in the free flow of commercial information."[1] The protection the Court recognized is limited, classifying commercial speech, such as advertising and public relations communications, as deserving lesser protection than other forms of protected expression.

In 1980, the Court established a four-part test for reviewing government restrictions on commercial speech.[2] In *Central Hudson Gas & Electric Corporation v. Public Service Commission*, the Court ruled that for a commercial speech regulation to be upheld, a court must first find that the speech is

eligible for First Amendment protection; false or misleading advertising, or the promotion of an illegal product or service, is not protected expression. If the speech is lawful and truthful commercial expression, the government must prove that there is a substantial government interest in restricting the speech and that the regulation directly advances that interest. Finally, the government must prove that the regulation is narrowly tailored, and thus not so broad as to prevent valuable speech.

This test demonstrates the lower status afforded commercial speech. Even truthful speech can be strongly regulated to serve an important government interest. A variety of federal agencies have been granted the authority to regulate commercial speech in an effort to protect consumers. In 1914, the federal government passed the Federal Trade Commission Act, which charges the Federal Trade Commission (FTC) to protect consumers from unfair and deceptive practices.[3] The FTC has exercised its authority on a variety of issues, including monopolistic practices, advertising directed to children, health-related claims, and consumer privacy.

While the FTC is the agency primarily responsible for regulating general business practices and advertising messages, other federal agencies focus on particular consumer products and practices. For example, the Food, Drug, and Cosmetic Act charges the Food and Drug Administration (FDA) with regulating the advertising and labeling of prescription drugs and medical devices.[4] The FDA has promulgated rules on the advertising of tobacco products, direct-to-consumer advertisements for prescription drugs, and off-label marketing of pharmaceuticals.

Another key agency in the regulation of commercial speech is the Securities and Exchange Commission, created by the Securities Exchange Act of 1934. The SEC ensures that investors receive truthful information about securities offered for sale.[5] For example, companies are required to accurately report, among other things, changes in the command structure of the company, changes in significant assets, and any bankruptcy filings.[6]

Much of the law enforced by these agencies is extended to online and mobile communications. However, the growth of online communications, including social media, has posed several new challenges for these regulatory agencies. This chapter will discuss key developments in the rules and regulatory actions of the Federal Trade Commission, the Food and Drug Administration, and the Securities and Exchange Commission that impact commercial speech.

DECEPTIVE AND UNFAIR PRACTICES

The Federal Trade Commission is the federal agency primarily responsible for protecting consumers from deceptive or misleading messages and unfair

business practices. In discharging this duty, the FTC has maintained advertisers must have a reasonable basis for all claims, either expressed or implied, for reasonable consumers.[7] The FTC works to ensure truthful information in advertising through the requirement of disclosures, substantiation, and enforcement actions. The FTC has applied these rules to online communications in the same way they have been applied to traditional media in print, radio, and television.

For example, in 2011, the FTC settled deceptive advertising charges with the marketers of AcneApp and Acne Pwner, mobile applications sold in the Apple iTunes store and Google Android Marketplace. The FTC charged the marketers with making unsubstantiated health claims, such as the ability for the smart phone apps to treat acne by emitting colored lights. In the complaint documents for both cases, the FTC relied on the requirement that advertisers have a reasonable basis to substantiate representations made to consumers. Such substantiation was lacking in these cases.

Although the FTC has held that online communications will be subjected to the same standards as traditional media, the development of new technologies, delivery methods, and user-generated content has pushed the FTC to focus on certain issues specific to protecting consumers online.

DISCLOSURE STATEMENTS

In 1975, the FTC issued the first Guides Concerning Use of Endorsements and Testimonials in Advertising, which set out rules for advertisements using testimonials and endorsements. Specifically, these Guides define endorsement relationships, require that certain standards are met in all endorsement communications, and mandate that all "material connections" between an advertiser and an endorser be disclosed to the public.

An endorsement is defined as "any advertising message that consumers are likely to believe reflects the opinions, beliefs, findings, or experiences of a party other than the sponsoring advertiser, even if the views expressed by that party are identical to those of the sponsoring advertiser." In general, the FTC Endorsement Guides require that endorsements "reflect the honest opinions, findings, beliefs, or experience of the endorser."[8] The Guides specifically address rules for endorsements by consumers, organizations, and experts. In all of these cases, the Guides require that where the audience would not reasonably expect it, any material connection between the endorser and the advertiser must be "fully disclosed."[9] The public generally expects that celebrity statements endorsing a product or service represent a relationship between the advertiser and the celebrity; no disclosure needs to be made in that instance. However, individuals unknown to the public would not raise similar expectations for the audience. In those situations, a clear

disclosure must be made regarding payment or other compensation received for the endorsement.

In 2009, the FTC revised these guidelines to include examples that specifically address these issues online. In one example provided in the Guides, the FTC considers a tennis player who provides information on her social networking site about the results of her laser eye surgery. In the post, the tennis player names the clinic where the surgery was performed. Because her followers on the social network may not realize that she is a paid endorser for the clinic, the relationship needs to be disclosed.[10]

In the revised Guides, the FTC was careful to include examples of online endorsements by consumers, as well. One such example discusses a college student blogger who posts a review of a video game and system he has received for free from the hardware manufacturer. The FTC states, "the blogger should clearly and conspicuously disclose that he received the gaming system free of charge." Further, the FTC requires that the manufacturer advise the blogger that the relationship be disclosed, and that the manufacturer monitor the blogger's posts for compliance.[11]

In the first regulatory action under these Guides, the FTC found that Reverb Communications, Inc., had engaged in misleading advertisements when it failed to disclose its relationships with reviewers.[12] Reverb provides marketing and public relations services to clients selling gaming applications via the Apple iTunes store. As part of these marketing efforts, employees of Reverb posted public reviews on iTunes with account names that did not disclose the relationship they had to the game developers. All of the reviews provided four- and five-star ratings as well as written accolades. The FTC found that these reviews misled consumers to believe independent users of the applications wrote them. Reverb was ordered to remove all reviews that violated the disclosure requirements.[13]

The FTC has also ruled that a contractual requirement for compliance is not enough to preclude an advertiser from being held responsible for the nondisclosures of its advertising affiliates. In 2011, the FTC fined Legacy Learning Systems $250,000 for failing to disclose material connections with online reviewers.[14] Legacy Learning Systems manufactures and sells instructional courses on DVD through a website. An affiliate program is the primary advertising method for these courses. Affiliates of the program work to direct traffic to Legacy's website and then receive between 20 and 45 percent commission for each course sold. Some of the affiliates are "Review Ad" affiliates, who place positive reviews in articles, blogs, and other online content. The reviews include hyperlinks to Legacy's website. Many of these reviews give the impression that they have been written by ordinary consumers. Although the contracts for the program mandated that the affiliates "comply with the FTC guidelines on disclosures," the FTC found

that Legacy had not instituted a compliance-monitoring program, resulting in consumers receiving deceptive and misleading information.

One step that advertisers can take to promote compliance with the FTC Guides is to develop an established social media policy that addresses under what circumstances disclosures must be made.[15] In 2011, the FTC determined not to pursue an enforcement action against Hyundai Motor America, in part due to the fact that such a policy was in place.[16] The FTC staff reviewed a blogging campaign executed in the lead up to the 2011 Super Bowl broadcast. Some of the bloggers were given gift certificates, but not all of them disclosed that information. The question was whether any of the bloggers were instructed to *not* disclose the gift certificates. The FTC staff determined that any such actions were the efforts of an individual working for a media firm hired by Hyundai to conduct the blogging campaign. Those actions conflicted with the social media policies at both Hyundai and the media firm, which specifically directed bloggers to disclose any compensation. Therefore, the FTC closed the investigation with no action against the media firm or Hyundai.[17]

A particular concern in social media has been the amount of space that may be required to make these disclosures. For example, the FTC Bureau of Consumer Protection (BCP) received questions about how to effectively make disclosures via the 140-character limit on Twitter's social media platform. The BCP has suggested that users may disclose an endorsement relationship by appending a hashtag identifier, such as #paid or #ad. This should provide readers sufficient information to evaluate the message.[18]

SPAMMING

"Spam" generally refers to unsolicited commercial emails.[19] Since the mid-1990s, the FTC has worked to protect consumers from spam-related unfair practices.[20] In 2003, the U.S. Congress granted the FTC special jurisdiction over spamming practices when it passed the Controlling the Assault of Non-Solicited Pornography and Marketing Act (CAN-SPAM Act). The CAN-SPAM Act places certain requirements on marketers to protect consumers against unfair practices. For example, marketers may not use deceptive subject lines, they must include a valid return address, and the messages must include a method for the recipient to opt-out of future messages.

The FTC has been particularly vigilant against spam that contains fraudulent content, malware, and links to phishing websites—a form of identity theft that uses emails to get consumers to provide personal and financial information.[21] In *FTC v. Hill*, Zachary Hill was charged—and pleaded guilty—to fraudulently acquiring credit card numbers and Internet account information through email ostensibly sent to users from AOL and PayPal.[22]

One of the difficulties of controlling spam and the related fraudulent practices is the constant development of new delivery methods. For example, botnets, or networks of hijacked computers, allow spammers to send bulk messages anonymously and remotely. The FTC continues to pursue these cases. In 2010, a district court judge permanently enjoined the operation of an Internet Service Provider that shielded and assisted botnet spammers.[23] The ISP, which the FTC estimated controlled nearly 5,000 malicious software programs, also was ordered to pay more than $1 million to the U.S. Treasury for disgorgement of ill-gotten gains.

In 2011, the FTC filed the first spam action for deceptive Short Message Service (SMS) ads sent to mobile phones.[24] In the complaint, the FTC charged Phil Flora, a California resident, with sending "at least 5 million unsolicited commercial electronic text messages." Many of the messages advertised mortgage and debt relief programs, referring recipients to a website, loanmod-gov.net. The inclusion of "gov" as part of the website address misled consumers to believe that these programs were government-sponsored. The FTC settled the case for a judgment of nearly $60,000. The settlement also includes a prohibition on Flora sending any unsolicited commercial text messages or making any misrepresentations that he, or anyone else, is affiliated with a government agency.[25] This case indicates that the FTC will regulate spam and other deceptive messages sent over wireless communications, a domain traditionally reserved for the Federal Communications Commission.

In addition to case-by-case enforcement, the FTC and Congress have explored preventative options to protect consumers on a larger scale. Most significantly, Congress charged the FTC with establishing a national Do-Not-Email Registry.[26] Upon investigation, the FTC reported that such a registry would be largely ineffective at reducing the incidence of spam. Rather, a registry of email addresses may pose privacy and security risks.[27] However, the FTC does work with a variety of federal agencies, industry associations and consumer groups to lead consumer education efforts through an interactive site launched in 2005.[28] OnGuardOnline.gov provides tips for consumers in the form of articles, games, and videos.[29] Additionally, the FTC hosts a spam-reporting service that allows consumers to forward unsolicited messages, including phishing scams, to be stored in a law enforcement database for further investigation. However, the FTC continues to urge the industry to develop technological solutions, such as authentication systems, to combat these issues.[30]

ONLINE BEHAVIORAL ADVERTISING

The Federal Trade Commission has also urged stringent self-regulation to address the consumer privacy concerns raised by behavioral advertising methods. These methods use tracking devices, such as cookies, to scan web activity in real time to assess a user's location, age, income, and, in some instances, medical conditions. The *Wall Street Journal*, in an investigative series on behavioral tracking, identified certain trackers that scanned the content of health-related pages on sites such as Encyclopedia Britannica that would allow companies to serve related ads to those users for diseases including bipolar disorder, bladder conditions, and depression.[31]

The use of these tracking methods, particularly for commercial purposes, has raised significant privacy concerns for consumers. Advertisers using behavioral tracking are able to analyze a person's web viewing habits "to predict user preferences or interests to deliver advertising to that computer or device based on the preferences or interests inferred from such Web viewing behaviors."[32] Approximately 80 percent of all online advertisements are served as a result of behavioral targeting.[33] Behavioral advertising revenues for 12 advertising networks were approximately $598 million.[34]

The FTC has recognized the serious concerns these practices raise for consumers, including loss of privacy, fraud, and deceptive marketing.[35] In 1996, the FTC staff recommended that the Commission continue to monitor issues of online privacy, but concluded that self-regulation and technological solutions may be sufficient to protect consumers' privacy in the marketplace.

However, in 2000, the FTC reported to Congress on online profiling and recommended that Congress legislate online profiling to mandate compliance with established fair information practices.[36] Although the FTC praised industry efforts at self-regulation, the Commission noted that not all advertisers and website owners were allied with the organizations issuing these guidelines.[37] Federal legislation would mandate compliance for all websites and advertising networks and provide an agency with the authority to enforce privacy protections.[38] Congress failed to pass any such law.

In 2009, the FTC released a statement supporting a policy of industry self-regulation, including proposed principles to guide the industry's efforts.[39] These principles focused on transparency, data security, changes in privacy policies, and sensitive data.[40] In response, the industry, represented by two key groups—the Network Advertising Initiative (NAI) and the Digital Advertising Alliance (DAA)—released a series of guidelines and tools to advance privacy protections for online consumers.[41] These guidelines have focused on improving the transparency and clarity of privacy notices, edu-

cating consumers about behavioral or interest-based advertising techniques, and providing consumers with user-friendly opt-out tools.[42]

The NAI completed compliance reviews of member companies in 2009 and 2010.[43] These reports indicate that member companies have improved their notices in various ways, including specific data retention period information, increasing visibility and readability of notices, using more prominent "privacy" or "opt-out" labels, and using an industry developed advertising option icon on served advertisements.[44]

However, in December 2010, the FTC issued a report stating that these efforts "have been too slow and up to now have failed to provide adequate and meaningful protection."[45] The report called for a Do–Not–Track mechanism that would allow consumers to opt out of data collection for ad targeting with one simple, easy-to-use tool.[46] Following this report, privacy issues became a hot commodity in Congress, with more than 10 privacy-related bills introduced to the 112th Congress in 2011. Among them was the Do Not Track Me Online Act to authorize the FTC to adopt regulations requiring companies to use an online opt-out tool.[47]

The FTC has engaged in enforcement actions against companies for failing to protect consumers' personal information.[48] For example, in 2011, the FTC settled complaints against social networking sites Facebook and Twitter that focused on the failure of those companies to protect users' personal information. A settlement against Google Buzz alleged inadequate privacy policies and ordered the company to implement a "comprehensive privacy policy." The settlement agreement also orders the company to submit to independent privacy audits for 20 years.

The agency also has pursued cases specifically dealing with behavioral targeting.[49] Chitika, an online advertising company, engages in behavioral tracking and reportedly delivers three billion ad impressions a month. In a complaint against the ad company, the FTC alleged that Chitika deceptively offered consumers an "opt-out" mechanism that only stored the consumer's preference to not be tracked for 10 days. After 10 days had passed, Chitika would begin tracking those consumers again until they opted out again. The settlement agreement requires that every targeted ad served by Chitika include a hyperlink to a clear opt-out tool that allows consumers to opt out of tracking for at least five years.[50]

CHILDREN'S PRIVACY ONLINE

Since Congress and the FTC began monitoring behavioral advertising, a key concern has been protecting information collected on minors using online services. In 1998, Congress passed the Children's Online Privacy Protection

Act (COPPA).[51] This delegated to the FTC the authority to regulate websites targeting children under the age of 13. COPPA requires that these websites limit collection to information that is necessary for the child to use the websites' functions. Additionally, these sites must notify parents about the type of information being collected from children and get consent from the parents before collection, use or disclosure begins. These sites must develop procedures to reasonably secure the personally identifiable data and allow parents access to any data collected about their children.

In 2012, the FTC was considering amendments to its COPPA rule to address key changes in the technologies.[52] Specifically, children's use of mobile devices has increased significantly, as well as the use of interactive video games and social networks. These platforms present new types of data, such as geolocation, and new challenges for meaningful notice and consent. The FTC has engaged in enforcement actions against smartphone app developers and social network sites for their deceptive practices in collecting information from children. For example, in 2011 the FTC settled with a mobile app developer for failing to provide notice and gain consent before collecting information from children using games such as Emily's Girl World, which included games and a journal for users to record "private" thoughts.[53] In response to children's increasing use of mobile technology and social networks, the FTC has proposed several key changes to the current COPPA rule, including expanding the definition of personal information to include IP addresses and geolocation information, as well as persistent identifiers placed on a computer for tracking purposes. This change would mean websites would need parental consent for these practices.

PHARMACEUTICAL ADVERTISING

Although the FTC is the agency that protects consumers in the general marketplace, the Food and Drug Administration polices the labeling, advertising, and public relations efforts for prescription medications and medical devices.[54] In addition to general requirements of truth and accuracy, the FDA requires that commercial messages for pharmaceuticals include the generic or "established" name of the drug, a detailed list of ingredients, and a summary of side effects and contraindications.[55] These mandates commonly are enforced through the use of notices of violation and warning letters sent to pharmaceutical companies, describing the offending conduct, asking for remediation, such as removal or corrective advertising, and threatening further legal action.

The FDA has moved to enforce existing mandates to new media, including pharmaceutical company websites, online videos, online advertising, and social media. Generally, the concerns expressed by the FDA in these letters

are that pharmaceutical companies either overstate the efficacy of a drug, or omit or minimize the risks associated with the drug.

Overstatement of Efficacy

The Food, Drug and Cosmetic Act requires that all prescription drug advertisements include a "true statement" of information relating to the drug's effectiveness.[56] FDA regulations require that this information include specific indications for the drug use being advertised.[57] In its enforcement actions, the FDA has consistently held that "promotional materials are misleading if they represent or suggest that a drug is more effective than has been demonstrated by substantial evidence or substantial clinical experience."[58] For example, in 2010, the FDA issued a Warning Letter to Axcan Pharma stating that the company's web page for Photofrin, a drug therapy for patients with certain kinds of lung and esophageal cancer, presented misleading information about the drug's efficacy. According to the FDA, patient and physician videos on the web page presented Photofrin as helping patients live symptom free, or even providing a cure. However, the studies on the efficacy of this drug therapy do not support these claims.[59] It is important that claims made by pharmaceutical companies are supported by "substantial" evidence or clinical experience.

Omission or Minimization of the Risk

The Food, Drug and Cosmetic Act requires that all prescription drug advertisements include a "true statement" of information relating to the drug's side effects.[60] FDA regulations require that advertisements broadcast through media like radio and television include the side effect information in the audio and video portions of the advertisements.[61] The information must disclose each specific side effect or other warning or contraindication. For example, in a 2009 Warning Letter, the FDA found that web pages for the drug Sotradecol were misleading to consumers because they failed to communicate the risks associated with the drug, as well as overstating the indication and efficacy of the drug.[62] The FDA did note that the pages included links for "further information . . . including its approved indication and possible side effects."[63] However, these links were "not sufficient to provide appropriate qualification." To meet this standard, the risk and indication information must appear within the main body of any promotional materials that communicate information on the effectiveness of a drug.[64]

In applying this standard to online videos, the FDA alleged that Pfizer had omitted risk information in a promotion for the drug Viagra.[65] The video,

which portrayed a group of men playing instruments and singing a song ending with "Viva Viagra," appeared on CNN's website as a video advertisement. Although the video included text at the beginning that directed viewers to "see important safety information on this page," the FDA noted that the page on cnn.com did not contain any such information.[66]

The FDA also requires that information relating to side effects be presented in "fair balance" with information about the drug's efficacy and benefits. Advertisements that fail to provide "sufficient emphasis" on side effect information or fail to present the side effect information with "prominence and readability reasonably comparable" to the information on efficacy will be found false or misleading.[67] In a seven-minute webcast video, Johnson & Johnson only devoted the last minute to including specific risk information about a drug that manages chronic pain. Additionally, the risk information was presented only in "rapidly scrolling text in small type font." The FDA found that the inclusion of risk and indication information presented in the text alone is not sufficient.[68]

Although the FDA has applied these requirements to a variety of new media, including web pages, online videos, and online sponsored advertisements, there is little guidance for advertisers online beyond this general application of existing rules. Most of the guidance documents—in the form of notices of violation and warning letters—have focused on product websites, rather than social media tools. There are a variety of notices of violation that address some of these tools. Specifically, the FDA has cited multiple online sponsored ad links as misleading. These links generally appear on search engine sites, such as Google.com. For example, one such sponsored link that the FDA noted as problematic was a sponsored link for Femara, a drug indicated for the treatment of postmenopausal women with early stage breast cancer. The link contained the following information:

Breast Cancer Information

Online Resource for Women with Breast Cancer. Review Treatments.
www.Femara.com

The FDA found that this did constitute a statement of efficacy for the drug because it communicated the main use of the drug.[69] The link information was then found misleading because it does not contain any mention of risks or side effects. The links to further information on the product web pages was "insufficient to mitigate the misleading omission of risk information" on the promotional material.[70]

Similarly, the FDA issued a Notice of Violation to Novartis Pharmaceuticals related to the company's use of Facebook Share widgets.[71] The widget

appeared on a variety of Novartis product web pages. Clicking on the widget allowed a user to share on his or her Facebook news feed customized information or comments about the drug. However, the user comments were accompanied by Novartis-created content about the drug, which the user could not edit. An example the FDA supplied in the Notice was a Facebook Share for the drug Tasigna, which is approved to treat certain chronic conditions in adults.

> **Treating Your PH+ CMP with Tasigna | Tasigna (nilotnib) 200-mg capsules**
>
> http://www.us.tasigna.com
>
> In addition to taking Tasigna (nilotnib) 200-mg capsules, talking to your doctor and receiving health tips can help you treat your CML.

Like the sponsored links, the FDA noted that the shared content linked to more in-depth product information, including side effects and other risks. However, this linking was again found "insufficient to mitigate the misleading omission of risk information."[72]

Guidance Documents for the Use of Online and Social Media Tools

The FDA has noted the "dramatic increases" in online users, including pharmaceutical companies, who look to the Internet as a new medium for disseminating product information.[73] Industry experts also have noted not only the increase in the use of online media by product manufacturers, but the increasingly significant role played by user-generated content in the online conversation surrounding health care, including drug treatments.[74]

Despite calls from the industry, the FDA has failed to provide drug advertisers with any specific, comprehensive guidance documents on the use of online and social media tools. In 2009, the FDA began holding public hearings to discuss the challenges and opportunities presented by online media.[75] However, the rules promised to follow were consistently delayed. In 2011, the FDA announced a study to investigate the function, form, and influence of various online media, including testimonial videos, interactive graphics, and linked risk information. The primary purpose of the study is to provide the FDA with more support in developing guidance for online direct-to-consumer advertising.[76]

Despite these delays, in addition to the warning letters and notices of violation, the FDA has issued subject-matter specific guidance documents that address some of the concerns surrounding the application of existing drug

promotion regulations to computer-mediated communications. These documents include information on how pharmaceutical companies can comply with the requirement to include the established drug name in all marketing materials, under which circumstances the companies must report adverse drug effects reported on the Internet, and how to respond to Internet-based requests for off-label information. These are each discussed below.

Product Name Promotion

The FDA requires that when promotions for a drug include the proprietary name—or trademark name—of the drug, the established name of the drug must also be presented.[77] In 2012, the FDA issued a guidance document providing more specific information on the placement, size, and prominence requirements for inclusion of the established name as related to the proprietary name.[78] For all media, the FDA mandated that the established name be

1. placed in "direct conjunction" with the proprietary name;
2. presented in the same text and font as the proprietary name when used in the body of the promotion;
3. be presented in text "at least half as large" as the proprietary name when used in a headline; and
4. be presented with "a prominence commensurate with the prominence of the proprietary name."[79]

Although the FDA applied consistent measures, regardless of media outlet, for the juxtaposition, size, and prominence of the established name, the required frequency of the established name was treated differently in online media than in traditional print and broadcast communications. The FDA recognized that online media might not be presented through traditional text pages. Therefore, the FDA recommended that if the proprietary name appears in a headline or other element outside the main body of text, the established name should appear each time the proprietary name appears. However, if the proprietary name appears in the main text of a website, for example, the established name need appear only at least once per screen span.[80]

This guidance seems to group all online communications for purposes of compliance with the required disclosure of the established name. The recommendations, though seemingly written from the perspective of the traditional web page format, would apply equally to shorter online messages, such as sponsored links and Twitter posts. This significantly restricts the information that can be distributed through those tools.

Reporting Adverse Drug Events

Pharmaceutical companies are required to report to the FDA any adverse drug events they receive, including information obtained from commercial marketing efforts.[81] In 2001, the FDA released a draft guidance further addressing this concern, but provided very little comment on online tools beyond traditional web pages. As more pharmaceutical companies began to take advantage of online and social media tools, industry professionals began to question to what extent pharmaceutical companies would be responsible for reporting adverse events reported via these formats.

The FDA requires that pharmaceutical companies monitor websites sponsored by the company.[82] Companies are not responsible for sites sponsored by third parties unless the company is notified of adverse event reports appearing on third-party sites. Companies must review the adverse drug experiences to determine whether they need to be submitted to the FDA. Events must be reported only if the pharmaceutical company can gather the basic information required for a safety report including an identifiable patient, an identifiable reporter, a suspect drug or biological product, and an adverse experience or fatal outcome suspected to be due to the suspect drug or biological product. This does not require that the patients be identifiable by name, only that there is specific enough information to "suspect that specific patients were involved." For example, the FDA suggests that a report that "an elderly woman had anaphylaxis" constitutes identifiable patient information.

Seemingly, pharmaceutical companies would be required to review and report information submitted via social media platforms for which the company has some ownership. For example, if a user comment made directly on the company's Facebook page recounts an adverse drug event, and contains the requisite information, that would be reportable.

User-Generated Off-Label Marketing

Pharmaceutical companies are prohibited from marketing any prescription drug for any purpose not approved by the FDA, or "off-label uses." However, the FDA has recognized that individuals may make unsolicited requests for off-label information, and that information may be helpful to certain individuals researching medical treatments.[83] Therefore, the FDA permits companies to respond to these requests "by providing truthful, balanced, non-misleading, and non-promotional scientific or medical information that is responsive to the specific request."[84] The response should only be provided to the initial requestor, regardless of whether the request was made in a non-public or public forum.

Special concerns arise when requests are made in a public forum. Online and social media platforms have potentially increased the visibility of such user-initiated, public requests for off-label information. The FDA noted that an area of concern is the broad audience and indefinite availability of any information that pharmaceutical companies may provide in response.[85] Therefore in 2011, the FDA provided specific recommendations for responding to unsolicited requests through online forums.

First, companies should only respond when a request "pertains specifically to its own named product." Second, public responses should not be promotional in any way. A public response should use an objective tone to inform the audience that the request refers to unapproved uses of the drug and provide easy access to FDA-approved information on the drug, such as labeling or other patient information. These links should not lead to product websites or any other promotional materials. The response also should provide direct contact information for interested individuals to seek follow-up information. Once a private request has been made, the company may respond with "truthful, balanced, non-misleading, and non-promotional scientific or medical information" in a one-on-one communication.

INVESTOR RELATIONS

Investors are increasingly turning to the Internet as a source of information. Brokerage firms such as TD Ameritrade and Charles Schwab are devoting resources to provide their clients with social media access and tools. As online communications have become increasingly important to investors, the Securities and Exchange Commission (SEC) has encouraged companies to use these new platforms, while underscoring the importance of compliance with existing securities regulations.

The SEC was established in 1934 to ensure the public received timely, complete and truthful information about publicly traded securities.[86] This is accomplished through the requirement for and oversight of specific financial filings, such as corporate registration forms, annual and quarterly filings, annual reports to shareholders and other corporate financial communications.[87] An industry self-regulatory agency—the Financial Industry Regulatory Authority (FINRA)—works both independently and in coordination with the SEC to offer guidance to securities firms on a variety of regulatory issues, and act to penalize firms that violate these regulations. Both the SEC and FINRA have released documents addressing the application of existing regulations to online communications.

Online Communications to the Public

Publicly traded companies are required to disclose to the public information relevant to investment decisions. Additionally, companies must ensure that the information disclosed is truthful and accurate.[88] The SEC has ruled that these disclosure requirements apply equally to any online disclosures as well as those made through traditional print and broadcast media.

In 2008, the SEC issued an interpretive release to provide guidance to companies on how to comply with SEC disclosure regulations when posting information to company websites.[89] The guidance provides that when a company's website is recognized by the public as a channel of information, posting material information on the site would satisfy the requirement of disclosing information to the public at large, as opposed to a more selective group.[90] This encourages companies to develop their websites in the marketplace. The 2008 interpretive release also addresses concerns with preventing fraudulent communications. For example, the SEC recommends carefully explaining the context of any link to third-party content that the company is not adopting. This will ensure that consumers do not rely on the information found at the linked page as information directly from the company.

The SEC also recognized the contribution that certain interactive features of a website, such as a blog, can make to the "robust use" of company websites. The SEC encourages the use of these technologies but cautions companies to educate any company representative using these blogs, or other forums, that they are acting "on behalf of the company." Companies should, therefore, develop procedures for monitoring these communications. The guidance provides that responsibility transfers to statements made on behalf of the company via third-party websites, as well. This indicates that companies should rely on the SEC recommendation for sponsored Twitter and Facebook accounts as well as traditional owned website content.

In 2010, FINRA released guidance more specific to social media. FINRA has categorized online communications tools as advertisements, correspondence, sales literature, and public appearance.[91] For example, information posted on publicly available websites and feeds, such as a Twitter profile, is considered an advertisement. However, password-protected websites and social media feeds are considered sales literature. Content posted in real-time that allows for consumer interaction, such as a chat or a Twitter post, is considered a public appearance. FINRA's 2010 guidance document addressed the recordkeeping and pre-approval requirements for these various communications to the public.[92]

Advertisements, or static content on social media sites, such as profile information, requires pre-approval by a principal in the company. Interactive

elements, or public appearances, do not require pre-approval, but companies should archive all communications through these media for record retention. This should be considered as the company determines which technologies and social networks to use for public communication. Additionally, companies must develop a method to supervise these communications to ensure content regulations are not violated.

FINRA has also addressed third-party statements. Generally, FINRA does not consider a post by a consumer to represent the company. Therefore, approval and recordkeeping rules would not apply. However, if a company republishes the comment through a Facebook Share or a retweet on Twitter, the company can be found to have endorsed the statement.

"Crowd Funding"

Social media tools also have enabled companies to raise funds in new ways. For example, "crowd funding" allows companies to solicit small investments from thousands of investors.[93] In 2011, the SEC settled with two entrepreneurs over an "experiment" to raise funds online to purchase Pabst Brewing Company. The SEC stated that the entrepreneurs violated securities law when they launched a website seeking pledges of money in exchange for ownership shares. This online offering triggered requirements for security registration and financial information disclosures.[94]

This case demonstrated the fundraising opportunities available for small companies via online communication tools. Other crowd-funding websites, such as Kickstarter, allow entrepreneurs to raise capital without triggering SEC investigation because the capital is considered a donation; investors do not receive an ownership share of the company. Pebble, a start-up company developing a digital watch that links to smartphones to run and control apps, has set a new record for money raised through Kickstarter. The company offered returns including exclusive updates, prototypes of the watch, and the opportunity to vote on the fourth color option for the watch. The company raised more than $10 million from more than 65,000 backers.

In 2012, the JOBS Act created an exception to traditional securities requirements for small companies going public via online offerings.[95] The JOBS Act exception would allow companies to raise up to $1 million within a 12-month period through the online issuance of stock shares. This law requires significant SEC rulemaking to protect online investors that will impact online disclosure requirements, including pre-approval statements, supervision, and recordkeeping. These changes will likely expand the ability of startups to raise money on websites like Kickstarter by allowing the exchange of ownership shares.

FREQUENTLY ASKED QUESTIONS

1. Can bloggers and Twitter users endorse products?

Yes. The FTC defines an endorsement as "Any advertising message . . . that consumers are likely to believe reflects the opinions, beliefs, findings, or experiences of a party other than the sponsoring advertiser, even if the views expressed by that party are identical to those of the sponsoring advertiser." Bloggers and social media users can endorse commercial products and services through online and social media posts. However, if the poster has any relationship to the company that offers the product or service for sale, that relationship must be disclosed in a clear and prominent way. For example, if a blogger receives a free gaming system to test, he or she must disclose in any blog post about the performance of that system that he or she received the product for free.

The FTC's Bureau of Consumer Protection has noted that such disclosures can be made via social media short cuts. For example, on Twitter, users were concerned that the limit of 140 characters to a post would make the required disclosures too difficult. The FTC Bureau of Consumer Protection has suggested that including such hashtags as #paidad or #paid or #ad may be sufficient to help consumers evaluate the usefulness of the sponsored statements.

2. Does engaging in behavioral targeting online run afoul of FTC regulations?

Currently, the only FTC documents on behavioral targeting are principles for self-regulation. These principles address the need to protect consumer privacy and data security. Companies collecting or maintaining consumer data should ensure reasonable data security measures are in place. Additionally, online consumers should receive adequate notice of the data collection and use, as well as a meaningful opportunity to opt out of targeting.

3. Are pharmaceutical companies liable for third-party comments on Facebook about off-label uses of drugs?

Pharmaceutical companies are not liable under FDA regulations for unsolicited comments regarding off-label uses of drugs. However, companies can respond to individual questions about these uses in a truthful and accurate way using one-on-one communications. Companies may also respond publicly by providing non-promotional materials that clarify the FDA-approved uses of a drug. For example, the company could post to a public forum a statement that the drug is not approved for the related use

with a link to the FDA-approved drug packaging or patient information sheet.

4. Do Twitter posts, and other interactive social media posts, trigger SEC scrutiny?

If the posts are on behalf of a publicly traded company, they are subject to securities law requirements. Companies must ensure that the communications are truthful and accurate. Additionally, companies should develop methods to archive these communications to the public under SEC record-keeping requirements.

5. Can companies use online website and social media platforms to seek investments for startup companies?

Yes, but these efforts are subject to securities regulations. In 2012, President Obama signed into the law the JOBS Act, which does allow companies to raise up to $1 million within a 12-month period through the online issuance of stocks without triggering many of the existing SEC requirements. However, the SEC has not yet drafted the required regulations for this provision. There may be additional requirements triggered by this practice. All investments exceeding $1 million per year trigger traditional SEC registration and disclosure requirements.

NOTES

1 Virginia State Board of Pharmacy v. Virginia Citizens Consumer Council, Inc., 425 U.S. 748, 764 (1976).
2 Central Hudson Gas & Elec. Corp. v. Public Serv. Comm'n, 447 U.S. 557, 564 (1980).
3 15 U.S.C. §§ 41 et seq.
4 21 U.SC. §§ 301 et seq.
5 15 U.S.C. 78d; 17 C.F.R. § 200.1.
6 17 C.F.R. § 240.13a-11.
7 Advertising Substantiation Policy Statement, appended to Thompson Med. Co., 104 F.T.C. 648, 839 (1984), aff'd, 791 F.2d 189 (D.C. Cir. 1986).
8 16 C.F.R. § 255.1.
9 16 C.F.R. 255.5.
10 Id. at Example 3.
11 Id. at Example 7.
12 In the Matter of Reverb Communications, Inc., FTC Docket No. C-4310 (November 22, 2010).
13 Id.
14 In the Matter of Legacy Learning Systems, Inc., FTC Docket No. C-4323 (June 1, 2011).

15 See, e.g., In re: Hyundai Motor America, FTC File No. 112-3110 (November 16, 2011); In re: AnnTaylor Stores Corp., FTC File No. 102-3147 (April 20, 2010).

16 Hyundai Motor America, FTC File No. 112-3110.

17 Id.

18 The FTC's Revised Endorsement Guides: What People are Asking, FTC Bureau of Consumer Protection (June 2010), http://business.ftc.gov/documents/bus71-ftcs-revised-endorsement-guideswhat-people-are-asking.

19 See Black's Law Dictionary 1430 (8th ed. 2004).

20 Spam Summit: The Next Generation of Threats and Solutions, Federal Trade Commission, Division of Marketing Practices (November 2007).

21 Id.

22 CV No. H 03-5537 (S.D. Tex. Filed December 3, 2003), http://www.ftc.gov/os/caselist/0323102/0323102zkhill.htm.

23 FTC v. Pricewert, No. C-09-CV-2407 (N.D. Cal. April 8, 2010).

24 FTC v. Flora, No. 11-CV-00299 (C.D. Cal. August 16, 2011).

25 Id.

26 15 U.S.C. § 7708.

27 Federal Trade Commission, National Do Not Email Registry, Report to Congress (June 2004).

28 Federal Trade Commission, Protecting Consumer Privacy in an Era of Rapid Change, Preliminary FTC Staff Report 14 note 32 (December 2010).

29 See generally, OnGuardOnline.gov.

30 Spam Summit, supra note 20 at 19.

31 Julia Angwin, The Web's New Gold Mine: Your Secrets, The Wall Street Journal, July 30, 2010.

32 American Association of Advertising Agencies, the Association of National Advertisers, the Better Business Bureau, the Direct Marketing Association, and the Interactive Advertising Bureau, Self-Regulatory Principles for Online Behavioral Advertising (July 2009) [hereinafter Coop Principles], http://www.iab.net/media/file/ven-principles-07-01-09.pdf.

33 IAB Tells Congress Privacy Bills May Harm Business and Consumers, Interactive Advertising Bureau, http://www.iab.net/public_policy/1296039 (last accessed March 28, 2011); see also Omar Tawakol, Forget Targeted Ads—I'd Rather Pay for Content, MediaPost.com, February 15, 2011, http://www.iab.net/public_policy/1296039.

34 Howard Beales, The Value of Behavioral Targeting, Network Advertising Initiative, March 24, 2011, http://www.networkadvertising.org/pdfs/Beales_NAI_Study.pdf. The report states that total ad revenues for the 12 companies equaled $3.32 billion; 17.9 percent of that was attributed to behavioral targeting.

35 Federal Trade Commission, Staff Report: Public Workshop on Consumer Privacy on the Global Information Infrastructure (Federal Trade Commission 1996).

36 Federal Trade Commission, Privacy Online: Fair Information Practices in the Electronic Marketplace: A Report to Congress (2000).

37 Id. at 35.

38 Id. at 36.

39 Online Behavioral Advertising: Moving the Discussion Forward to Possible Self-Regulatory Principles, FTC (December 2007), http://www.ftc.gov/os/2007/12/P859900stmt.pdf.

40   Id.

41   See generally NAI website, http://www.networkadvertising.org; The Self Regulatory Program for Online Behavioral Advertising, http://www.aboutads.info (last accessed March 2, 2012).

42   See, e.g., Understanding Online Advertising, Interactive Advertising Bureau, http://www.iab.net/privacymatters/; Self-Regulatory Principles for Online Behavioral Advertising, July 2009, http://www.aboutads.info/resource/down load/seven-principles-07-01-09.pdf; Self-Regulatory Principles for Online Behavioral Advertising Implementation Guide, October 2010, http://www. aboutads.info/resource/download/OBA%20Self-Reg%20Implementation%20 Guide%20-%20Full%20Text.pdf; NAI, Opt Out of Behavioral Advertising, http://www.networkadvertising.org/managing/opt_out.asp.

43   NAI 2009 Annual Compliance Report, December 30, 2009, http://www. networkadvertising.org/pdfs/2009_NAI_Compliance_Report_12-30-09.pdf; NAI 2010 Annual Compliance Report, February 18, 2011, http://www.network advertising.org/pdfs/2010_NAI_Compliance_Report.pdf.

44   NAI 2010 Annual Compliance Report, id. at 13–15. For more information on the icon, see Advertising Option Icon Application, http://www.aboutads.info/ participants/icon/.

45   Federal Trade Commission, Protecting Consumer Privacy in an Era of Rapid Change: A Proposed Framework for Businesses and Policymakers, Preliminary FTC Staff Report iii (December 2010).

46   Id. at 63.

47   H.R. 654, 112th Cong. (2011).

48   See Federal Trade Commission, supra note 45 at 39–68.

49   In the Matter of Chitika, Inc., FTC File No. 1023087 (Complaint filed March 14, 2011).

50   In the Matter of Chitika, Inc., FTC Docket No. C-4324 (June 7, 2011).

51   15 U.S.C. §§6501–6506.

52   76 Fed. Reg. 59804 (September 27, 2011).

53   U.S. v. W3 Innovations, CV11-03958 (N.D. Cal. 2011).

54   Food, Drug and Cosmetic Act, 21 U.S.C. §§ 352–353.

55   Prescription Drug Advertisements Rule, 21 CFR 202.1 (2008).

56   21 U.S.C. § 352(n).

57   21 CFR § 202.1(e3ii)

58   See, e.g., FDA Notice of Violation to Dow Pharmaceutical Sciences, Inc. (June 16, 2011); FDA Warning Letter to Hill Dermaceuticals, Inc. (December 3, 2010); FDA Warning Letter to Abbot Laboratories (July 14, 2009).

59   Id.

60   21 U.S.C. § 352(n).

61   21 C.F.R. § 202.1(e)(1).

62   FDA Warning Letter to Bioniche Pharma USA LLC (September 14, 2009). See also FDA Warning Letter to BioMarin Pharmaceutical, Inc. (October 11, 2006).

63   FDA Warning Letter to Bioniche Pharma, supra note 62.

64   Id. See also 21 C.F.R. §201.1(e)(3)(i)(2011).

65   FDA Warning Letter to Pfizer, Inc. (April 16, 2008). See also FDA Warning Letter to Warner Chilcott, LLC (May 5, 2011); FDA Warning Letter to Shire Dev., Inc. (September 25, 2008).

66   FDA Warning Letter to Pfizer, supra note 65.

67   21 C.F.R. § 202.1(e)(7).

68   FDA Warning Letter to Johnson & Johnson (May 12, 2009). See also FDA Notice of Violation to Cephalon, Inc. (June 21, 2011).

69   FDA Notice of Violation to Novartis Pharmaceuticals Corp. (March 26, 2009).

70   Id.

71   FDA Notice of Violation to Novartis Pharmaceuticals Corporation (July 29, 2010).

72   Id.

73   Promotion of FDA-Regulated Medical Products on the Internet; Notice of Public Meeting, 61 Fed. Reg. 48,707 (September 16, 1996).

74   Promotion of Food and Drug Administration-Regulated Medical Products Using the Internet and Social Media Tools, FDA Public Hearing (November 12, 2009) (statement of Tony Blank, Co-Chair, AdvaMed Advertising and Promotion Working Group). See also 74 Fed. Reg 48083 (September 21, 2009).

75   Promotion of Food and Drug Administration-Regulated Medical Products Using the Internet and Social Media Tools Notice of Public Hearing, 74 Fed. Reg 48083 (September 21, 2009).

76   FDA Notice, 76 Fed. Reg. 23821 (April 22, 2011).

77   21 C.F.R. § 202.1(b)(1).

78   FDA, Guidance for Industry: Product Name Placement, Size, and Prominence in Advertising and Promotional Labeling (January 2012).

79   Id.

80   Id.

81   Postmarketing Reporting of Adverse Drug Experiences, 21 C.F.R. § 314.80 (2009).

82   FDA, Guidance for Industry: Postmarketing Safety Reporting for Human Drug and Biological Products Including Vaccines (March 2001).

83   FDA, Guidance for Industry: Responding to Unsolicited Requests for Off-Label Information About Prescription Drugs and Medical Devices (December 2011).

84   Id.

85   Id.

86   15 U.S.C. § 78gg.

87   SEC, The Investor's Advocate: How the SEC Protects Investors, Maintains Market Integrity, and Facilitates Capital Formation, http://www.sec.gov/about/whatwedo.

88   17 C.F.R. § 240.10b-5.

89   Commission Guidance on the Use of Company Web Sites, 73 Fed. Reg. 45,862 (August 7, 2008), codified at 17 C.F.R. pt. 241 (2008).

90   Id.

91   FINRA, Guide to the Web for Registered Representatives, http://www.finra.org/industry/issues/advertising/p006118.

92   FINRA, Guidance on Blogs and Social Networking Web Sites, Reg. Notice 10-06 (2010).

93   Jean Easglesham & Jessica Holzer, SEC Boots Up for Internet Age, The Wall Street Journal, April 9, 2011 at B1.

94   Michael Migliozzi, II and Brian William Flatow, SEC No. 3-14415 (June 8, 2011).

95   Jumpstart Our Business Startups Act, Pub. L. No. 112-106 (2012).

Government Information and Leaks

David Cuillier

University of Arizona School of Journalism

ABSTRACT

Facebook, Twitter, and other social media platforms provide the opportunity for government to communicate quickly and freely with citizens, but at the same time the technology provides new temptations for officials to conduct the public's business in secret. This chapter examines the implications of social media in government and public record laws. Also, social media outlets, such as WikiLeaks, offer the potential of quickly disseminating records, including classified documents, that the government doesn't want out. The chapter ends with best practices for government and information seekers in dealing with social media and public records.

M ore and more, the government by the people, for the people, is moving online. People don't just vote for a candidate anymore; they "like" him or her. They don't just listen to long political stump speeches; they read electronic snippets of 140 characters or less. They don't drive to City Hall to sit in a four-hour council meeting; they tune into podcasts.

Integration of social media in government communication introduces new wrinkles in the public's ability to know what its government is up to. Officials might conduct important business via text, or on private smartphones, with limited ability for the public to see the messages. Cities post information on a Facebook page but might let the messages expire, or remove them, if they turn out to be embarrassing. WikiLeaks and other sites allow for fast and easy dissemination of public records to the world, with or without the consent of government officials. In an era of social media, it would seem that government would be more transparent. Or is it just the opposite?

This chapter examines issues emerging as social media and the Internet change the way government information is disseminated, and the ability for journalists and citizens to access that information. On the one hand, the use of social media provides new avenues for public officials to engage citizens through e-government, such as broadcasting city council meetings live online with chat rooms, or allowing officials to debate and inform through Facebook and Twitter. However, the new technology provides challenges for ensuring the public's business via social media stays the public's business and complies with public record and open meeting laws.

For example, Twitter feeds sent by a government official regarding his or her official duties, even if sent on a private cell phone, would likely be considered a public record, according to some states' court rulings and the fundamental principles of freedom of information. But how does an agency record these transmissions and provide them for journalists and others who request them later? And what about the international dissemination of public records, including classified records, via the Internet and social media (e.g., WikiLeaks)? Can the U.S. government punish a U.S. newspaper for spreading classified documents online? These and other issues will be discussed in this chapter to explain the application of freedom of information laws to government and social media.

FREEDOM OF INFORMATION 1.0

The public's right to know what the government is up to is a centuries-old concept that spans the globe. Long before Facebook and Twitter, government established policies, laws, and common practices of communicating with its public through less electronic means—mainly paper.

The first known public records law was adopted in 1766 by Sweden and Finland, called the Freedom-of-Press and the Right-of-Access to Public Records Act.[1] The law required government officials to provide documents to citizens immediately and for free, and also created the world's first public records ombudsman to help people access their government (something the United States didn't do until 2009[2]). Now, more than 90 countries have such laws.

Access to government information in the United States started simple but developed into a complicated web of statutes, case law, and common practices. Originally, it was based on common law, assuming that people should have access to government information that it made sense for them to have; there was no need for statutes or court rulings, although that changed over time. In 1813, Congress created the Federal Depository Program to make sure people could access federal records from designated university libraries. The salaries of federal employees became public starting

in 1816. Wisconsin adopted the first state law ensuring open records and meetings in 1849, and now every state has such laws. Congress enacted the Freedom of Information Act in 1966, and it continues to be updated every decade or so, including 1996 revisions requiring federal agencies to make certain records available electronically and online.[3] The Clery Act requires universities to post crime data,[4] and the Government in the Sunshine Act of 1976[5] requires some federal agencies to meet in public.

The basic premise of freedom of information laws, often called sunshine laws because they shed light on government, is that people need to know what their officials are doing in order to self-govern. Citizens want to know how their taxes are being spent. They want to make sure services and duties are carried out fairly, effectively, and honestly. They want to see how decisions are made by elected leaders so they can decide whether to re-elect them or find someone better. Access to public records and meetings is essential for democracy,[6] and some international courts are even ruling that access to government information is a fundamental human right.[7]

Under most of these laws, citizens have a right to look at any government records, including paper, audio, video, or electronic files, that show what the government is up to. In general, the government may keep some records, or parts of records, secret if the material contains information that would cause harm to the government or individuals. With paper records, the process has been relatively straightforward: Person walks up to counter, asks for record, clerk scuttles to filing cabinet, comes back to counter, shows record to person. Maybe the requester asks for a photocopy, pays 10 cents per page, and leaves. Sometimes the requester and official haggle over what should be public and what should be kept secret, blotting out the secret information with a Sharpie. Rarely are there hitches caused by the physical nature of a paper public record.

No longer is access that simple. The electronic nature of government records today—in databases and online—have created whole new issues. The U.S. Supreme Court has been reluctant to take on some of these matters, instead allowing lower courts to sort it out as technology develops. That's probably a good thing. When the nation's high court decides to take a case pertaining to electronic government records and technology, the outcomes are sometimes puzzling. For example, in the 1989 case *U.S. Department of Justice v. Reporters Committee*, the court decided that if a person wants to get criminal court records about someone, he or she can drive to various court houses and look up the paper files, but that person should not have access to the same information in one database because that would make it too easy.[8] Similarly, in the 2000 case *Reno v. Condon*, regarding states' rights, the justices viewed department of motor vehicle data as an "article of commerce," of little public-interest value and something to be bought and sold, like

lumber.[9] Given the way the court understands electronic information and technology, it's probably best the law of social media and public information be hashed out at the state level to resolve disputes organically. As it turns out, that is exactly what is happening.

TEXTS AND EMAILS AS PUBLIC RECORDS

When email emerged as a useful communication device in the early 1990s, government officials found they could easily exchange information in secret without worrying about anyone seeing what they were writing. After all, emails aren't "written," right? They just disappear in some computer that no citizens can access, or flitter into cyberspace. Poof!

But eventually, state courts and legislatures made it clear that emails and text messages sent by public officials regarding public business must be made available to citizens just as if they were written on a piece of paper. Today, most state public record laws require that officials' work emails, texts, and other electronic communications be made available to citizens. This information has helped journalists expose problems in government. In 2008, for example, the *Detroit Free Press* and *Detroit News* sued for the text messages of then-Mayor Kwame Kilpatrick, and the resulting stories exposed corruption and perjury that resulted in Kilpatrick being sent to prison.

But even today, decades after the emergence of electronic messages, it's not simple or settled. Some government agencies have found several ways to avoid public scrutiny.

Deletion

Some government officials have simply avoided disclosure with the "delete" key. Former President George W. Bush deleted millions of official White House emails from 2003 through 2005.[10] In 2008, Texas Gov. Rick Perry developed a system to automatically delete emails every seven days, even though correspondence via paper had been kept for at least one year. Such deletions are flagrant violations of public record laws, or at least the intent of the laws, and can get public officials in hot water. Public records should be retained for a suitable amount of time, at least six months to a year depending on the nature of the record, and agencies should follow their retention policies.

Personal Devices

Some government officials have attempted to skirt the law by conducting work business on private computers or cell phones, instead of their work

devices. The George W. Bush White House used email accounts through the Republican Party to conduct business.[11] When Sarah Palin was governor of Alaska, she used Yahoo accounts for state business to avoid scrutiny,[12] and governors in North Carolina, Iowa, Colorado, and other states followed suit.

The courts have sometimes allowed for such practices, reasoning that the government agencies don't have possession of the messages so they can't be expected to cough them up. For example, in 2006, *The Dallas Morning News* had requested personal emails from city officials, including the mayor, relevant to a federal corruption investigation involving Dallas employees. The city refused to provide the emails, saying the messages didn't meet the definition of public records because the emails were sent on the mayor's personal BlackBerry. An appeals court ruled in favor of the city.[13]

However, the tide is turning, and a majority of state-level courts are realizing that the mode or ownership of the message isn't what matters; it's the content. In states such as Florida, Illinois, and Arkansas, if a public official sends an email or text message regarding public business on a personal smartphone or computer, then that message is subject to disclosure. Likewise, courts in Arizona, Wisconsin, and elsewhere have acknowledged that messages that are purely personal can be kept secret, regardless of what type of device they are sent on, or the physical nature of the record. That makes sense. Public business is the public's business, and personal business can be kept secret.

Avoidance

Many government officials have simply instructed their employees to avoid using email for anything that could be embarrassing. In 2011, Florida Gov. Rick Scott told his staff to talk to him by phone instead of emailing. Unless the calls are recorded, those conversations can indeed be kept secret. Of course, it's not good management practice to conduct important business verbally without records. There are good reasons why humans learned to document their thoughts and communications.

Technical Barriers

Perhaps the most challenging barrier in accessing electronic messages, particularly tweets and texts, is how to physically archive and provide them to citizens. Is every public employee to download his or her texts daily, pick out the ones pertaining to public business, and save them to a central database for the public to see? As technology keeps changing, access gets more challenging. One solution is to require public employees do their agency business on work devices, which can be accessed more easily, and

prohibit work communications on their personal equipment. Also, agencies will need to invest in technical solutions to archive tweets and messages, not to mention the online material that is linked from those messages.

Because Twitter itself does not provide a public archive of tweets, people seeking them may have to look elsewhere. In 2011, Twitter reached an agreement to provide full archives of public tweets to the Library of Congress, and federal agencies have been encouraged to retain their own social media postings through the National Archives and Records Administration.[14]

GOVERNMENT FACEBOOK AND TWEETS

Perhaps no politician knows the power of Twitter and Facebook more than Texas Gov. Rick Perry. While running for president in 2011–12, Perry used social media effectively, including having his son, Griffin, tweet like a hurricane, tossing out 140-character zingers about the other Republican nominees. Yet, the social media world is fickle, and volatile. In fall 2011, Perry blocked journalists he didn't like from his Twitter account. His spokesperson justified it by saying the account, with 35,000 followers, is personal and his to run how he wishes. In spring 2012, after Perry made a decision to cut funding for women's health programs, his Facebook page was deluged with more than 4,000 posts from women sarcastically seeking advice on their menstrual periods. The posts were removed.

Just how personal are these social media records, regarding a person who wanted to become president of the United States and sought the attention of all Americans? Government agencies are grappling with those issues and the legal terrain is still taking shape, but the same principles governing emails and other records apply: If it's the public's business then it should be public, regardless of the medium, and often regardless of where it is posted.

In 2009, the U.S. General Services Administration provided social media recommendations for federal agencies, making it clear that anything posted online is fair game for public scrutiny, particularly for those people in leadership positions. "Assume your thoughts are in the public domain and can be published or discussed in all forms of media. Have no expectation of privacy."[15] That is good advice for anyone, public official or not.

Many states have begun adopting social media policies. Washington state, for example, created guidelines in 2010 for social media use, making it clear that government officials should consider anything they write online regarding agency business to be subject to the state public records law.[16] The guidelines also state that it is the agency's responsibility to capture electronic copies of its social media records, using third-party tools to do so (e.g., TwInbox, Tweetake, SocialSafe, and Cloudpreservation).

North Carolina's agency guidelines for social media go a little further, recommending that public employees be wary of posting opinions, discussing areas outside of one's expertise, and committing the agency to an action. The guidelines make it clear that anything posted online in any forum may not be able to be "taken back" and that all are subject to the public' records laws, including responses posted by citizens in response to an agency post. All privacy settings on social media sites are to be set to "public."[17]

It is unclear how moderating government social media sites will evolve, particularly regarding content issues and records retention. When a city employee deletes a comment deemed inappropriate on an agency Facebook page, that is essentially destroying a public record, or part of the record, before its time. The City of Seattle's social media policy, for example, states nine reasons for why the government can remove a post on its Facebook page—essentially censoring speech of citizens in a public forum.[18] Reasons include profanity, sexual content, advertisements, encouragement of illegal activity, content that promotes discrimination, comments not on topic, and comments supporting or opposing a political campaign. It is easy to see that discussions about medicinal marijuana, race, or city politics could lead to disagreement and potential suppression of protected speech and destruction of a public record.

So far, the case law regarding social media and public records is undeveloped. Only now are government agencies, journalists, and citizens beginning to realize that agency Facebook pages and tweets are public records. Most people don't even realize they are legally entitled to see such communications, but once they figure it out, litigation will ensue. As access disputes erupt and rulings are issued, no doubt the first place we will find out about it is in a status update.

WIKILEAKS: SPREADING DOCUMENTS ONLINE

In 2010, U.S. Army Private Bradley Manning made available to the public more than 250,000 classified documents regarding U.S. diplomatic relations with world leaders, the largest leak of top-secret material in history, dubbed "Cablegate" by some. He didn't need a box or U-Haul to transfer the records to WikiLeaks, the website that published the material. All he used was a rewritable CD labeled "Lady Gaga" while listening to her song "Telephone."

The fact that an Army private in Iraq could have unrestricted access to millions of classified government records and download them easily brought to light the new realities of electronic information dissemination. Despite worries from government officials, the information release resulted only in embarrassment of U.S. diplomats and no deaths of informants. Some people say the online information, spread via social media, actually helped spur

revolution in the Arab world in 2011.[19] But nevertheless, if one person could do this, what could be released in the future that would cause harm?

This wasn't the first time a government insider copied classified records and got them out to the public. In 1969, Daniel Ellsberg photocopied 7,000 pages of classified "Pentagon Papers" documents regarding the Vietnam War and provided them to the *New York Times*. Cablegate was different, though, in several respects. First, the volume of Cablegate records was enormous, equaling about 300 million words, compared to two million words in the Pentagon Papers. Second, the electronic nature of the records allowed fast worldwide dissemination to anyone with access to a computer. The Pentagon Papers were published in a newspaper and reprinted in a book.

Today, anyone can get a government document or database and pop it on the Internet for instant reading. Social media allows it to be spread quickly, from friend to friend, network to network. Following Cablegate, government officials expressed extreme concern about the potential danger of classified documents being easily spread online. Some called for the criminal prosecution of WikiLeaks founder Julian Assange and of the *New York Times* for printing some of the information, based on the Espionage Act of 1917.[20] Senator Joseph Lieberman said:

> I certainly believe that WikiLeaks has violated the Espionage Act, but then what about the news organizations—including *The Times*—that accepted it and distributed it? To me, *The New York Times* has committed at least an act of bad citizenship, and whether they have committed a crime, I think that bears a very intensive inquiry by the Justice Department.[21]

While the government might have a case against the leaker, Manning, it is unlikely the Department of Justice could successfully prosecute Assange or editors of the *New York Times*. True, despite the First Amendment, the government does have some limited authority over publication, but to do so it must apply strict scrutiny, which means that a content-based restriction is OK only if it promotes a compelling interest and is the least restrictive means to further the interest. Certainly, protecting civilians and soldiers from enemies is a compelling interest. But the burden is on the government to make a strong case that publication would cause immediate harm.[22] In the case of Cablegate, nobody was killed or harmed, at least that has been reported. Because of that burden to show immediate harm from publication, no journalist has been prosecuted under the Espionage Act.

Because of the constitutional difficulty in prosecuting journalists, the government has instead focused its efforts on punishing leakers. In 2012, the Obama administration pursued the prosecution of six government leakers

under the Espionage Act, more than any other president in U.S. history. Lucy Dalglish, former director of the Reporters Committee for Freedom of the Press, discussed the issue at an Aspen Institute summit with national security officials in 2011. The officials told her that Cablegate caused the government to institute a zero-tolerance policy on leaking information. If they couldn't stop journalists from printing information, or force reporters to reveal their anonymous sources, then they could scare government employees from giving it out. As one national security representative said: "We're not going to subpoena reporters in the future. We don't need to. We know who you're talking to."[23]

CONCLUSION: MODEL PRACTICES IN PUBLIC SOCIAL MEDIA

Social media provide exciting opportunities for the public to engage with its government, and politicians with their voters. As technology evolves and changes, so will the information dissemination practices of government agencies and information collection practices of journalists. Regardless of the technology or platform—Facebook, MySpace, Twitter, Tumblr, Second Life, LinkedIn, or whatever new gizmo is invented—the same basic principles of transparency and accountability apply to government uses of social media.

Government Practices

Government agencies have an obligation to follow public record laws, even in cyberspace. But it can be tricky. Here are some best practices for making it work:

1. Assume anything posted online by a government employee regarding agency business could be subject to public record laws, whether it's on an official agency Facebook page, personal page, tweet or email, and whether it's sent from an agency-issued device or a personal device. Make that clear to all employees and the public. Government employees should not use personal cell phones or computers for their work communications. Avoid commingling public and personal conversations by using separate personal email accounts, Facebook pages, and cell phones for purely personal information.
2. Utilize software to collect and archive in real-time Facebook pages, email, tweets, and other social media records. Make the electronic files easily searchable, preferably online, and capture the materials linked from the agency communications—similar to saving the paper attachments referred to in a memo.

3. Social media records should be retained for a suitable amount of time, at least six months to a year depending on the nature of the record, and agencies should follow their retention policies by not prematurely deleting records.

4. Develop social media policies that clearly explain to employees and the public that the agency's social media communications, including posts by citizens, are considered public records and can be copied and shared with others.

5. If citizens are encouraged to share their thoughts on agency social media platforms, then agency moderators should be careful to remove only those writings that would be considered unprotected speech (advocating violence, obscenity, etc.). Removal of posts because they are unpopular or embarrassing to the agency could be considered a form of prior restraint.

6. High-ranking elected leaders should consider their Twitter accounts, Facebook pages, and other social media outlets available and open to all. Blocking specific journalists or other "undesirables" appears shady.

7. Governing bodies, such as city councils, should not use email, Twitter, or other online forums to discuss official matters without providing those messages to the public. Even when conversations are one-on-one, if a majority of the members are involved in such discussions, the communications can be construed as "serial meetings" and a violation of state open meeting laws.

Information-Gathering Practices

Journalists and citizens who want to keep an eye on government today need to do so with fingers on a keypad. Here are some suggestions for accessing government in the age of social media:

1. Encourage, nay, demand, that public agencies adopt the practices and policies listed above. Resources are tight in many government agencies, so urge elected leaders to dedicate more money toward social media and records retention.

2. If government agencies don't archive their social media posts, save them yourself. Record the mayor's tweets. Save Facebook posts, especially if they are removed later. Remember that sunshine laws do not apply to private organizations such as Twitter and Facebook, which are not obligated to provide public archives, so if you don't do the archiving, your only source may be the government agency.

3. When asking for government officials' emails, texts, or social media records, ask that they be provided electronically rather than paper printouts. It will save you copy fees and allow for easier keyword searching.

4. Learn the law of electronic public records. A great guide is provided by the Reporters Committee for Freedom of the Press at http://www.rcfp.org/access-electronic-communications.

5. When gathering information from government social media sites, be upfront about your identity. Don't hide behind pseudonyms. Disclose in your reports the source of the information you gather, and be careful who you friend. Apply the same ethical standards to social media as in any other information gathering.

6. Know that any communications you have with government could be considered a public record. Assume anything you post or type could be revealed publicly, so take appropriate precautions when communicating sensitive or potentially libelous information.

7. Carefully vet any information or documents leaked to you before disseminating them. That's what the *New York Times* did with the WikiLeaks Cablegate documents. They verified the information, and checked to make sure nobody would get hurt.

Social media will continue to evolve, with new platforms and exciting opportunities for people to communicate and discuss issues and events that affect their lives and communities. Regardless of the technology, the same basic principles should apply: Public business is the public's business. Any communications by government employees discussing what the government is up to, no matter the forum or machinery it is communicated upon, should be subject to public record laws. Online technologies have the potential of making government more transparent and accessible to the average person. That is what James Madison, the author of the Bill of Rights, would applaud, once he could figure out how to operate an iPad: "Knowledge will forever govern ignorance: And a people who mean to be their own Governors, must arm themselves with the power which knowledge gives."[24]

FREQUENTLY ASKED QUESTIONS

1. Are citizens entitled to see text messages and emails sent by public officials?

In general, yes, if the messages pertain to public business. In most states, any electronic messages created by or possessed by a public employee regarding public business are subject to disclosure under public record laws. That usually includes messages sent on personal computers or smartphones, but it depends on the state. If a message is purely personal, though, the information is unlikely to be required to be made public, and public record laws allow for material to be kept hidden if it would harm national security or impede in some other government function.

2. Are government Facebook pages and their posts subject to public record laws and required to be made public?

In most cases, yes. If the purpose of the page or message is to convey what government is up to, and it is produced by government employees, then most state courts would consider them subject to public record laws. That would include any comments posted by citizens, and any videos or other materials incorporated in the page. It is likely that work-related comments posted on a high-ranking leader's *personal* Facebook page also might be subject to public record laws. Government agencies should develop systems to capture and archive their social media content, including the materials that are linked to from the page.

3. How does a journalist or citizen get to see text messages, emails, or Facebook posts written by government officials?

With much persistence. Emails on agency-provided accounts are relatively easy to get because most government agencies save them to a central server. However, email messages sent on personal Yahoo or Gmail accounts can be more difficult to produce. That's why government employees shouldn't do government business on personal email accounts. Text messages, also, can be tricky. Ultimately, it is the responsibility, by law, of the government agency to figure out a way to archive these government communications and provide a way for citizens to see them or get copies. Put the onus on the agency to follow the law.

4. Are *my* emails, texts, and Facebook posts subject to public record laws?

Generally, no. What you communicate in your own time as a private citizen is your own business. You might make it "public" by posting something on a blog or Facebook page, but public records laws do not apply. There are exceptions, however. For example, if you communicate with a public official via email, text, or a post on his or her Facebook page, those communications might be subject to public record laws. Some jurisdictions, including federal agencies, blot out identities of people communicating with officials, but some don't. It's a good idea to assume that anything you write online could end up in the public sphere.

5. Can the government prosecute a journalist or anyone else for posting classified documents online?

The Espionage Act of 1917 suggests that unauthorized publication of classified documents could result in a fine, up to 10 years in prison, or both. However, no journalist has been prosecuted for publishing classified

documents, and it is unlikely to happen unless the information is certain to cause immediate harm. If the government can make a strong case that the information will cause harm, then prior restraint or punishment might be allowed. Because it is difficult to show that, the government instead would likely go after the government employee who leaked the documents.

NOTES

1   For a brief history of the creation of this law, see Stephen Lamble, Freedom of Information, a Finnish Clergyman's Gift to Democracy, Freedom of Information Review, 97, 2–8 (2002). Also, find more information at the Anders Chydenius Foundation website, www.chydenius.net.
2   The Office of Government Information Services was created in 2009 through the Open Government Act. The agency, contained in the National Archives, assists citizens who seek public records from federal agencies, and mediates disputes between requesters and agencies. See https://ogis.archives.gov.
3   Electronic Freedom of Information Act of 1996 ("E-FOIA"), 5 U.S.C. § 552(a)(2)(A)–(E), 5 U.S.C. § 552(e)(2)(1996).
4   20 U.S.C. § 1092(f).
5   5 U.S.C. § 552b.
6   See Vincent Blasi, The Checking Value in First Amendment Theory, 2 Law & Soc. Inquiry 521, 609–610 (1977) (arguing that "the First Amendment may require that journalists have access as a general matter to some records"). See also Harold L. Cross, The People's Right to Know: Legal Access to Public Records and Proceedings (1953); Alexander Meiklejohn, Free Speech and its Relation to Self-Government (1948); Aimee C. Quinn, Keeping the Citizenry Informed: Early Congressional Printing and 21st Century Information Policy, 20 Gov't Info. Q. 281 (2003).
7   See Cheryl Ann Bishop, Access to Information as a Human Right (2012) (discusses rulings by the European Court of Human Rights and the Inter-American Court on Human Rights enunciating that access to government information is a human right based on the need to have information to express oneself).
8   U.S. Department of Justice v. Reporters Committee for Freedom of the Press, 489 U.S. 749, 780 (1989).
9   Reno v. Condon, 528 U.S. 141, 120S. Ct. 666, 145 L. Ed. 2d 587 (2000).
10 See the report, Citizens for Responsibility and Ethics in Washington, Without a Trace: The Story Behind the Missing White House E-Mails and the Violations of the Presidential Records Act (2010), http://www.scribd.com/doc/48889149/Untold-Story-of-the-Bush-White-House-Emails (the documentation was a result of a settlement of two consolidated lawsuits, Nat'l Sec. Archive v. Executive Office of the President (D.D.C.), filed September 5, 2007, and CREW v. Executive Office of the President (D.D.C.), filed September 25, 2007).
11 CREW, Without a Trace.
12 Lisa Demer, Governor's Two E-mail Accounts Questioned, Anchorage Daily News, October 21, 2008.
13 City of Dallas v. Dallas Morning News, LP, 281 S.W.3d 708 (Tex. App. – Dallas 2009).

14   Emily Kopp & Jack Moore, Agencies Have 120 Days to Start Getting E-records in Shape, FederalNewsRadio.com, November 29, 2011, http://www.federal newsradio.com/?nid=85&sid=2648774.

15   General Services Administration, GSA Social Media Policy, CIO 2106.1 (2009), p. 2.

16   Office of the Governor in Coordination with Multiple State Agencies and Contributors, Guidelines and Best Practices for Social Media Use in Washington State (2010).

17   North Carolina Office of the Governor, Best Practices for Social Media Usage in North Carolina (2009).

18   See City of Seattle, Social Media Use Policy, http://www.seattle.gov/pan/ SocialMediaPolicy.htm.

19   See Bill Keller, Wikileaks, a Postscript, N.Y. Times, February 19, 2012, p. A19. Also, see Robert Mackey, Qaddafi Sees WikiLeaks Plot in Tunisia, N.Y. Times, January 17, 2011 (Colonel Qaddafi blames WikiLeaks for the uprisings in the Middle East).

20   18 U.S.C. § 793 (2005).

21   Charlie Savage, U.S. Prosecutors Study WikiLeaks Prosecution, N.Y. Times, December 7, 2010, p. A-10.

22   See, e.g., New York Times Co. v. United States, 403 U.S. 713, 725 (1971) (Brennan, J., concurring) (rejecting as insufficient government's assertions that publication of Pentagon Papers "could," "might," or "may" prejudice the national interest); also, the Supreme Court has indicated that journalists can't be punished for publishing information that was provided to them, even if illegally obtained by a third party, see Bartnicki v. Vopper, 532 U.S. 514 (2001). For further discussion of this issue, see Congressional Research Service report 7-5700, Criminal Prohibitions on the Publication of Classified Defense Information, October 18, 2010, by Jennifer K. Elsea.

23   Lucy Dalglish, Lessons from Wye River, News Media & The Law, p. 1.

24   James Madison, Letter to William T. Barry, August 4, 1822. In James Madison: Writings (1999).

Student Speech

Dan V. Kozlowski

Department of Communication
Saint Louis University

ABSTRACT

Social media now pervade the lives of students. This chapter explores existing cases and developing issues as the legal and school communities wrestle with how to handle students' social media speech, which is often created off campus but may have impact on campus. Confusion and uncertainty about social media and students' rights prevail, as the law has failed to catch up to the technology around it. Rather than outlawing social media use by students, educators are advised to encourage responsible, constructive uses.

Nearly three-fourths of wired American teens use social networking sites such as Facebook and MySpace, according to one recent study.[1] Another study found that young people who visit those sites spend an average of almost an hour a day there.[2] Social media no doubt pervade the lives of students. And while these media give students the power to turn a performance at a school's sixth-grade music festival into fame and a viral video phenomenon (see Greyson Chance, whose cover of Lady Gaga's "Paparazzi" drew almost 50 million YouTube page views), social media also represent, in the words of one commentator, a school's "new bathroom wall"—a place where a student's "online postings . . . can destroy reputations, end relationships and intensify negative feelings."[3] School officials' attempts to regulate that virtual "bathroom wall" and to punish students for publishing on it constitute the all-important but still-unresolved quandary now facing student speech law: How far does school authority reach? Can schools constitutionally punish students for speech they create and post online, even if they do so from off school grounds (which is typically the case)? Because

the U.S. Supreme Court has not answered the question directly, lower courts have issued an array of often inconsistent, incongruent rulings. And, as one legal scholar has written, school authorities have filled the "judicial vacuum"[4] by seizing the opportunity for censorship, punishing students for Facebook posts, for example, or banning social media use by athletes entirely.

Indeed, instances of schools doling out discipline for social media speech occur constantly. School officials barred a high school senior in Florida from attending his graduation ceremony because a song that he recorded and uploaded to MySpace included "profanity, sexual innuendo and threats of violence"—and "school officials said they had jurisdiction because some students had listened to the song at school on iPods."[5] An Indiana high school senior was expelled from school for a tweet he posted while at home, in the middle of the night, that opined on the myriad ways the F-word could be employed. The student insisted he posted using his personal computer, but he said the superintendent told him that, even if he did, when he later logged into Twitter with his school-issued laptop, the post could show up with a school IP address in the school's system that monitors tweets.[6] And in just one more recent example, a Louisiana high school student sued his school after he was removed from an honors society and suspended from school for a Facebook post that criticized a teacher.[7]

The list of examples could go on—and on, which is why scholars such as Clay Calvert have called the issue of how to treat students' online speech a "pervasive and pernicious First Amendment problem."[8] This chapter will trace existing cases and developing issues as the legal and school communities both wrestle with how to handle student speech in a culture that is defined by its always-evolving technology and media use.

STUDENT SPEECH AND THE U.S. SUPREME COURT

The U.S. Supreme Court has decided four cases that govern the First Amendment rights of public school students,[9] all within the last 50 years. In its first ruling, the 1969 case *Tinker v. Des Moines Independent Community School District*, the Court broadly supported student expression, famously declaring that "it can hardly be argued that either students or teachers shed their constitutional rights to freedom of speech or expression at the schoolhouse gate."[10] In the case, school officials suspended three students for wearing armbands in school to protest the Vietnam War. The Court ruled that students' speech could not be punished unless school officials reasonably conclude that the speech did, or would, "materially and substantially disrupt the work and discipline of the school."[11] And the Court indicated that standard should be interpreted stringently—even though the armbands caused "comments, warnings by other students, the poking of fun at [the

students]," and even though a teacher said his lesson was "practically wrecked"[12] that day, the Court said the disruption caused by the armbands was not enough to justify censorship.

The Court's three subsequent student speech cases scaled back *Tinker's* protections. In *Bethel School District v. Fraser*, the Court upheld the suspension of a high school student who gave a "lewd"[13] speech laced with "pervasive sexual innuendo"[14] at a school assembly. Emphasizing that "schools must teach by example the shared values of a civilized social order,"[15] the Court sided with the school, concluding that the "First Amendment does not prevent the school officials from determining that to permit a vulgar and lewd speech such as [the student's] would undermine the school's basic educational mission."[16] Two years later, the Court held *Tinker* was inapplicable again, this time in a case involving a school-sponsored student newspaper. In the 1988 case *Hazelwood School District v. Kuhlmeier*, the Court ruled that educators could regulate school-sponsored student speech—curricular speech that bears "the imprimatur of the school"[17]—so long as their actions are "reasonably related to legitimate pedagogical concerns."[18]

In 2007, in *Morse v. Frederick*, the Court carved out another exception to *Tinker*: speech that school officials "reasonably regard as promoting illegal drug use."[19] The Court in *Morse* acknowledged that "there is some uncertainty at the outer boundaries as to when courts should apply school-speech precedents."[20] But the Court did nothing to resolve that uncertainty in *Morse*. Instead, the Court ruled that, even though the student in the case was across the street from the school, off school grounds, he was participating in a "school-sanctioned and school-supervised event"[21] when he held up his controversial BONG HiTS 4 JESUS banner as the Olympic Torch Relay passed in front of his high school. None of the Court's student speech cases have involved what it considered off-campus speech, then, and—with that lack of guidance from the Court—lower courts have offered differing rulings in cases interpreting how far administrators' arms can reach.

CONFUSION IN THE LOWER COURTS

The dilemma over whether schools can punish students for online speech they create off campus isn't new. The first federal court opinion to deal with the issue was decided back in 1998.[22] But the rise and ubiquity of social media have escalated both the number of disciplinary sanctions for such speech and the number of legal cases challenging punishment. Students, of course, have badmouthed teachers or school officials or other students for generations. Whereas before, though, students might have kept a diary or shared conversations involving those topics on the bus or over landline phones or at the shopping mall, now students can use social media tools to

reach a wide audience rapidly.[23] And lower courts have struggled with how to respond.

Tracing the path of one recent case nicely illustrates the degree of confusion. In *J. S. v. Blue Mountain School District*, a middle school student and her friend—on a weekend and on a home computer—created a fake MySpace profile as a parody of their principal. It included his photograph as well as "profanity-laced statements insinuating that he was a sex addict and pedophile."[24] In the words of the en banc Third Circuit Court of Appeals, "The profile contained crude content and vulgar language, ranging from nonsense and juvenile humor to profanity and shameful personal attacks aimed at the principal and his family."[25] The profile initially was accessible to anyone, but, the day after they created it, one of the students, known in the court proceedings as J.S., set the profile to "private" and limited access to about 20 students to whom she had granted "friend" status. The school's computers blocked access to MySpace, so no student ever viewed the profile while at school. Another student, however, told the principal about the profile and who had created it, and—at the principal's request—that student printed out a copy of the profile and brought it to him. The principal then suspended J.S. and her friend for 10 days.

J.S. sued, sending the case on a meandering journey through the federal courts. At the district court level, she lost. U.S. District Judge James Munley ruled that, even though the profile arguably did not cause any *Tinker*-level disruption, it was "vulgar, lewd, and potentially illegal speech that had an effect on campus."[26] The judge relied on *Fraser* and *Morse* and said that J.S. could be punished. In February 2010, a panel of the Third Circuit agreed—but for different reasons. The Third Circuit panel said that *Tinker* did govern the case and that the suspension was constitutional because the school could *forecast* disruption. "We hold that off-campus speech that causes or reasonably threatens to cause a substantial disruption of or material interference with a school need not satisfy any geographical technicality in order to be regulated pursuant to *Tinker*," Judge D. Michael Fisher wrote for the court. Because the profile accused the principal of having "interest or engagement in sexually inappropriate behavior and illegal conduct,"[27] the court said it was foreseeable that the profile would disrupt his work as principal and encourage others to question his demeanor and conduct.

Two months later, however, the Third Circuit vacated the panel opinion and ordered en banc review. And in June 2011, a divided en banc court of Third Circuit ruled in favor of J.S. This time, an eight-judge majority ruled that it did not need to decide definitively if *Tinker* controlled the case because, even if it did, the profile caused no actual disruption, nor could the school reasonably forecast disruption. Although the court acknowledged that the profile was "indisputably vulgar," it ultimately ruled the speech "was so

juvenile and nonsensical that no reasonable person could take its content seriously, and the record clearly demonstrates that no one did."[28] The court also categorically ruled that *Fraser* does not apply to off-campus speech. Five judges concurred in the case and wanted to go much further, though. The concurrence argued that *Tinker* should not apply to students' off-campus speech at all because "the First Amendment protects students engaging in off-campus speech to the same extent it protects speech by citizens in the community at large."[29]

Judge Fisher wrote in dissent this time, joined by five other judges. He argued again that *Tinker* applied and that disruption from the profile was reasonably foreseeable. Moreover, he chided the majority for adopting a rule that he thought was unworkable for schools. "[W]ith near-constant student access to social networking sites on and off campus, when offensive and malicious speech is directed at school officials and disseminated online to the student body, it is reasonable to anticipate an impact on the classroom environment," he argued.[30]

J.S. thus perfectly exemplifies disagreements the judiciary has had over when school authority begins, what standard to apply, and how to apply it. Judges, first, have differed about how, or when, speech even becomes eligible for on-campus punishment. Some courts confronting the issue have used what Mary-Rose Papandrea has called a "territorial approach"[31]—asking whether a student either used school computers or servers to create, share, or view the speech in question or whether someone actually brought hard copies of the speech to school.[32] Other courts, on the other hand, have said that schools have jurisdiction to regulate off-campus speech if it is "reasonably foreseeable"[33] that the speech will come to the attention of school officials, whether because the speech is directed or targeted at students or school officials or because it is about school generally.

Still other courts, though, have generally skipped over the threshold question of whether speech amounts to on-campus or off-campus expression and instead have just directly applied the Court's school speech precedents.[34] Courts have been especially willing to apply *Tinker* in cases involving off-campus, social media speech, with outcomes hinging on whether schools can persuade courts that speech either did, or would, create a material and substantial disruption at school. And different courts have seemingly required different levels of disruption, similar to what occurred in *J.S.*: a panel of the Third Circuit said that disruption was reasonably foreseeable, while the en banc majority disagreed. Social media obviously allow speech to spread fast, to a wide audience, at virtually any time, making the speech both easier for school officials to monitor than traditional oral or written speech and also easier for a whistleblower student to find and bring in.[35] "[W]ireless internet access, smart phones, tablet computers, social

networking services like Facebook, and stream-of-consciousness communications via Twitter give an omnipresence to speech," one federal judge has written.[36] School officials argue that, given that "omnipresence," online speech inevitably finds its way to school and can thus be punished under *Tinker* because school officials can forecast disruption. Some courts also have loosely interpreted what amounts to an actual disruption at school. Those courts that have interpreted *Tinker's* standard so leniently have thus made it easy for school officials to extend their reach off campus.

That was arguably the case in *Doninger v. Niehoff*, a Second Circuit decision involving a student blog post that disparaged school officials and encouraged readers to contact the superintendent in order "to piss her off more."[37] The student who wrote the blog, Avery Doninger, was frustrated about the scheduling of a band contest at school known as "Jamfest." Her blog post, which she wrote from home, called school administrators "douchebags" for canceling the event and encouraged students to contact the superintendent.[38] When the principal discovered the post, two weeks after it was written, she punished Doninger by barring her from running for senior class secretary. Doninger sued, seeking an injunction that prevented her discipline.

A panel of the Second Circuit held that *Tinker* applied and that the post created a risk of substantial disruption. The court first said that the language Doninger used in her post was "not only plainly offensive, but also potentially disruptive of efforts to resolve the ongoing controversy."[39] The school, moreover, argued that the post was misleading because school officials had informed Doninger that the event would be rescheduled rather than canceled. The Second Circuit thus said that Doninger used "at best misleading and at worst false" information in an effort to solicit more calls and emails.[40] And because rumors were already swirling at school about the status of the event when Doninger wrote on her blog, the court deferred to the school and concluded that "it was foreseeable in this context that school operations might well be disrupted further by the need to correct misinformation as a consequence of [the] post."[41]

Courts have been especially likely to rule against students when applying *Tinker* in cases involving threatening speech.[42] In *Bell v. Itawamba County School Board*,[43] for instance, a high school student posted to Facebook and YouTube a rap song he recorded that alleged two coaches at his school had improper contact with female students. The song included the lyrics "looking down girls' shirts/drool running down your mouth/messing with wrong one/going to get a pistol down your mouth" and "middle fingers up if you can't stand that nigga/middle fingers up if you want to cap that nigga."[44] The student insisted the allegations about inappropriate behavior were true, but school officials said the song constituted "harassment and

intimidation of teachers and possible threats against teachers," and they thus suspended the student for seven days and transferred him to an alternative school for the remaining five weeks of the period.[45]

The student sued. U.S. District Judge Neal Biggers said that because the student intended for his song to reach school, *Tinker* applied. "[The student] clearly intended to publish to the public the content of the song as evidenced by his posting of the song on Facebook.com with at least 1,300 'friends,' many of whom were fellow students, and to an unlimited, world-wide audience on YouTube.com," Biggers wrote.[46] And the judge ruled that the punishment was constitutional because the song both caused an actual disruption and that school officials could reasonably forecast disruption. In terms of actual disruption, the court was persuaded by the coaches' testimony that one of them was "angered" by the song and the other "felt threatened" by it and that both coaches said their teaching styles were affected because students became wary of them.[47] Biggers also ruled that further disruption was reasonably foreseeable given the wide reach of the song on social media.

In July 2011, the Fourth Circuit Court of Appeals faced a case involving speech not about, nor directed at, a teacher or school official—instead the incident at issue resulted from student speech targeting another student, amounting to what the court said was impermissible cyberbullying on MySpace.[48] In the case, high school senior Kara Kowalski created a discussion group on MySpace titled "S.A.S.H.," which she claimed was an acronym for "Students Against Sluts Herpes." The comments and pictures posted to the group, though, targeted one student, named Shay N., and one of the nearly two dozen students who joined the group at Kowalski's invitation said S.A.S.H. was actually an acronym for "Students Against Shay's Herpes."[49] Shay and her parents went to school officials the next day to report the site and file a harassment complaint. For creating a "hate website" in violation of a school policy against bullying, Kowalski received out-of-school suspension for five days and a 90-day social suspension, which prevented her from attending school events in which she was not a direct participant.[50]

The Fourth Circuit upheld the punishment. The court said Kowalski knew talk about the MySpace group would reach school and that thus the "nexus of Kowalski's speech to [the school's] pedagogical interests was sufficiently strong to justify" the school's actions under *Tinker*.[51] "Given the targeted, defamatory nature of Kowalski's speech, aimed at a fellow classmate, it created 'actual or nascent' substantial disorder and disruption in the school," Judge Paul Niemeyer wrote for the court.[52] He pointed out that Shay missed school in order to avoid further abuse. Moreover, the court ruled, "had the school not intervened, the potential for continuing and more

serious harassment of Shay N. as well as other students was real."[53] The court said that "harassment and bullying is inappropriate" and that the First Amendment does not "hinder school administrators' good faith efforts to address the problem" of bullying generally.[54]

Not all students who have faced punishment for social media speech have lost their cases under *Tinker*, however. *J.S.*, of course, offers one example. In another case, a U.S. magistrate judge refused to dismiss a student's lawsuit against her school after she was punished for creating a Facebook group titled "Ms. Sarah Phelps is the worst teacher I've ever met."[55] The student deleted the group two days after it was created when three commenters on the page showed support for Phelps. The teacher herself never saw the group. Nevertheless, the principal learned of the group after it had been deleted, and he suspended the student for three days. U.S. Magistrate Judge Barry Garber said the student's lawsuit challenging the punishment could go forward because, under *Tinker*, there was no indication "that a well founded expectation of disruption was present."[56] In December 2010, the school settled with the student by agreeing to remove any record of her suspension and to pay her attorney's fees.[57]

And in *T.V. v. Smith-Green Community School*,[58] a district court ruled in favor of two high school students who were barred from participating in a quarter of their fall extracurricular activities—including volleyball games and a show choir performance—as punishment for posting pictures of themselves simulating sex acts with phallic-shaped lollipops. The students took the pictures during a slumber party over the summer and posted them on MySpace, Facebook, and Photobucket. A parent brought printouts of the pictures to the school superintendent and said they were causing "divisiveness" among the girls on the volleyball team.[59] The principal subsequently said the students violated a code of conduct that forbade students participating in extracurricular activities from bringing "discredit or dishonor upon yourself or your school."[60]

The students sued, and U.S. District Judge Philip Simon struck down the punishment. He assumed without deciding that *Tinker* controlled but ruled that the actual disruption in the case did not "come close" to meeting *Tinker*'s standard.[61] "In sum, at most, this case involved two complaints from parents and some petty sniping among a group of 15 and 16 year olds. This can't be what the Supreme Court had in mind when it enunciated the 'substantial disruption' standard in *Tinker*," Simon wrote.[62] He concluded that the school also did not demonstrate any factual basis to justify that officials reasonably forecast disruption. Even though the speech at issue in the case amounted to "crass foolishness,"[63] Simon said the First Amendment forbids any attempt at line drawing between worthy and unworthy speech.

Moreover, Simon also ruled that the school's code of conduct was unconstitutionally vague and overbroad. A school's code cannot nullify students' First Amendment rights, and Simon said that the code at issue here poorly defined the subjective terms "discredit" and "dishonor," and the code was overbroad because it potentially could be applied to a variety of constitutionally protected out-of-school student conduct.[64]

SOCIAL MEDIA AND COLLEGE STUDENTS

The cases discussed so far have all involved middle or high school students, but college students also have found themselves embroiled in legal disputes over their social media speech. In *Yoder v. University of Louisville*,[65] for instance, a federal judge ruled that a former nursing student, Nina Yoder, effectively waived her First Amendment rights when she signed a consent form as part of a childbearing course that required her to follow a mother through the birthing process. The form, which was signed by both Yoder and the mother she followed, provided that any information shared with the student "will be presented in written or oral form to the student's instructor only."[66] After Yoder witnessed the mother's labor and delivery, though, she wrote a blog post on her MySpace page about the experience. Although she did not reveal any information that specifically identified the mother or her family, Yoder's post described, "in intimate detail," what took place, including "medical treatment the birth-mother received, such as an epidural," along with other health-related issues.[67] One of Yoder's classmates told the course's instructor about the post, and the instructor then told School of Nursing administrators, who decided to dismiss Yoder from school. U.S. District Judge Charles Simpson III upheld the punishment, ruling that the school had legitimate reasons for having patients and students sign the consent form, and "because Yoder herself agreed not to publicly disseminate the information she posted on the internet, she is not entitled to now claim that she had a constitutional right to do so."[68]

In another example, in a much-publicized case two Minnesota courts ruled that a college student could be punished for her Facebook posts. In *Tatro v. University of Minnesota*, Amanda Tatro, a student in the mortuary science department, was punished for a series of Facebook posts she made to her wall over two months in late 2009. In one post, she wrote that she "gets to play, I mean dissect, Bernie today"—which was the name she had given to the donated cadaver on which she was working.[69] In another post, she wrote that she wanted to use an embalming tool "to stab a certain someone in the throat . . . [P]erhaps I will spend the evening updating my 'Death List #5' and making friends with the crematory guy."[70] The

comments concerned a fellow mortuary science student, who reported them to university officials. The officials notified university police, who conducted an investigation but determined no crime had been committed and Tatro could return to class. The university, though, instead filed a formal complaint against Tatro, alleging she violated the school's student conduct code by engaging in "threatening, harassing, or assaultive conduct" and by engaging in conduct "contrary to university rules related to the mortuary-science program."[71] A panel of the campus committee on student behavior agreed that Tatro violated the code. As punishment, she was given a failing grade in the course and required to enroll in an ethics course, write a letter of apology, and complete a psychiatric evaluation. She also was placed on academic probation for the remainder of her undergraduate career.

Tatro's attorney argued that *Tinker* should not apply to a university student at all, particularly in a case involving off-campus speech. The Minnesota Court of Appeals disagreed, though. Citing a recent Third Circuit decision that applied *Tinker* in the university setting, the Minnesota court reasoned that *Tinker* controlled the case but "what constitutes a substantial disruption in a primary school may look very different in a university."[72] The court nevertheless arguably leniently applied *Tinker* and sided with the school. Tatro said she jokingly was referring to her ex-boyfriend when she wrote about stabbing someone, and police determined that she posed no threat. Even so, the court said "the fact that the university's concerns were later assuaged does not diminish the substantial nature of the disruption that Tatro's conduct caused or the university's need to respond to the disruptive expression."[73] Moreover, the court emphasized that media attention to the situation had spread word about Tatro's posts to funeral directors and also to families who had donated cadavers to the mortuary science program. In June 2012, however, the Minnesota Supreme Court upheld Tatro's punishment on a different ground: The court concluded that Tatro's posts violated the rules for her mortuary science program and she could thus be punished.[74]

Tinker protected a college student from discipline for his online speech in *Murakowski v. University of Delaware*, however. There, a student's "sophomoric, immature, crude and highly offensive" essays—some of which referenced violence and sexual abuse—that he posted on a website he created led to his suspension.[75] The website, maintained on the university's server, came to the attention of school authorities after two students complained about the student and said they had visited his website and felt "uneasy and fearful around him."[76] U.S. Magistrate Judge Mary Pat Thynge ruled that, although the writings contained "graphic descriptions of violent behavior," they did not "evidence a serious expression of intent to inflict harm" to specific individuals.[77] The court also ruled that the complaints did

not amount to a substantial disruption, nor had the university presented evidence that demonstrated it reasonably could forecast disruption. The suspension was thus unconstitutional.

PRIVACY AND SOCIAL MEDIA

An emerging, though still largely unlitigated, area of controversy involves student privacy on social media. Issues surrounding the monitoring of student athletes have been especially visible. In one high-profile incident, for instance, a top high school football player saw an elite university withdraw its scholarship offer to him after the school discovered the student had used racial and sexual slurs in his tweets.[78] Schools say such offensive speech risks damaging both students' reputations and the school's image, so to curb any controversy some colleges have adopted policies that, among other things, require their student athletes to "friend" either a coach or a compliance officer. For example, a recently implemented University of North Carolina social media policy requires that "each team must identify at least one coach or administrator who is responsible for having access to and regularly monitoring the content of team members' social networking sites and postings."[79] The policy emphasizes to students that playing for the school "is a privilege, not a right."[80] The university adopted the policy, in part, in response to an NCAA investigation of the school that found a former UNC football player had tweeted about expensive purchases, revealing improper contact with an agent.[81]

Other schools have started relying on software packages—offered by companies such as Varsity Monitor, UDiligence, and Centrix Social—that automate the monitoring of athletes' social media use. The *St. Louis Post-Dispatch* reported that, as of February 2012, about three dozen colleges were using UDiligence's program, including the University of Missouri's football team.[82] According to the *Post-Dispatch*, the program "searches for key words in tweets, blogs, comments on Facebook and photo captions that could be considered objectionable or raise a red flag."[83] UDiligence provides each school with a list of words, from which schools can add or subtract. Players then download an app to each of their social media accounts, giving UDiligence permission to monitor them—which involves a daily scan of the accounts and an email sent to the student and a school administrator if any of the key words appear. The company charges $1,500 a team or $8,000 a school. "It's not a gotcha tool, it's a mentoring tool," the CEO of the company told the *Post-Dispatch*.[84] Privacy advocates have decried the programs, however, as violating the privacy rights of both student athletes and the athletes' "friends" on social media.[85]

Also alarming student speech advocates, some college coaches have instituted outright bans on social media use—banning social media generally or focusing specifically on Twitter. In recent seasons, coaches at Boise State, Mississippi State, Texas Tech, New Mexico State, Kansas, and South Carolina, among other places, have barred student athletes from using Twitter.[86] The bans have frequently involved football or men's basketball programs, but in January 2012, UNC women's basketball coach Sylvia Hatchell also instituted a Twitter ban for her players.[87] To date, none of the bans has been challenged in court. Commentators, though, have questioned their legality.[88] Rather than punishing students for specific tweets—critical comments about the coaching staff, for instance, which the coach might argue could cause a disruption[89]—the outright bans impose a blanket prior restraint that extends into the athletes' private lives, encompassing speech about their activities and interests off the field and away from school. The bans also necessarily prevent student athletes from using social media to discuss political or social issues, and protecting political speech has long represented a core concern of the First Amendment.

Issues other than those surrounding college athletes have also raised privacy concerns. For example, in March 2012, a sixth-grade student in Minnesota sued her school district, claiming, among other things, that her Fourth Amendment rights were violated when school officials demanded that she give them her Facebook password and they then searched her account—without a warrant—while she was in the room.[90] In that same month, a school district investigation revealed that a Florida high school teacher undertook a series of questionable actions aimed to determine whether students had made disparaging comments about her on Facebook. The teacher reportedly called a student to the front of the classroom and told her to sign into her Facebook account on the teacher's personal cell phone.[91] According to news coverage of the incident, the teacher also "gave a small group of students a list with red marks next to the names of those suspected of making comments. She asked them to review Facebook accounts and write 'ok' next to those who did not write anything negative."[92] The school superintendent found the teacher's behavior "very troubling" and suspended her.[93]

Another privacy controversy involves attempts to regulate social media interactions between students and teachers. School officials and legislators have insisted guidelines and restrictions serve to keep students safe from educators who misuse social media. Although administrators recognize that the vast majority of teachers use social media properly, examples do exist of teachers engaging in inappropriate contact that blurs teacher–student boundaries.[94] And in extreme cases, educators have been arrested for sexual misconduct—for relationships that law enforcement officials say began with online communication.[95]

But strict regulations banning social media interactions entirely have faced pushback from teachers. Missouri, for instance, passed a state law in 2011 that provided, in part, "No teacher shall establish, maintain, or use a nonwork-related Internet site which allows exclusive access with a current or former student."[96] The law, among other things, presumably would have thus forbidden teachers from "friending" students on Facebook. Teachers criticized the law, saying they used social media as a valuable pedagogical tool and to engage students. The state teachers union sued, and in August 2011 a judge issued an injunction that barred the law from going into effect. The judge said the breadth of the prohibition was "staggering" and that it would have "a chilling effect on speech."[97] On the heels of the injunction, legislators dropped the ban and instead ordered school districts to develop their own policies.

GUIDANCE AND BEST PRACTICES

Confusion and uncertainty about social media and students' rights obviously prevail, as the law has failed to catch up to the technology around it. Absent a Supreme Court decision providing clarity, educators would be wise not to be so quick to censor and punish. Such overreactions invite negative attention and miss an opportunity to teach—about free speech, about tolerance, and about civility.

In November 2011, for instance, a Kansas high school senior on a field trip to the state capitol tweeted: "Just made mean comments at gov. brownback and told him he sucked, in person #heblowsalot." The student, Emma Sullivan, was frustrated at Brownback, the Kansas governor, for cutting arts funding in schools, but the tweet was untrue—she had not actually spoken to him. Members of the governor's social media staff saw the tweet and alerted program managers leading the Youth in Government trip Sullivan was on. The program mangers then told the student's principal, who demanded that she apologize. Sullivan refused, and the incident quickly became a national story. Her Twitter account had around 60 followers at the time of the controversial tweet; once the story attracted national attention, her followers rocketed to more than 11,000.[98] Within a week, the principal backed off the demand that she apologize. As Ken Paulson of the First Amendment Center wrote at the time, "[E]fforts to punish her for her free expression backfired on every adult involved."[99] Brownback even issued a statement, apologizing for his staff's overreaction. "Freedom of speech is among our most treasured freedoms," he said.[100]

Sullivan's tweet itself—occurring at an off-campus, school-sanctioned event—certainly did not cause any *Tinker*-level disruption. The controversy

that ensued instead was brought on by the social media staff's monitoring, and then by the principal's readiness to punish a student for criticizing her governor. That temptation to monitor and punish is hard for school officials to resist. Western Kentucky University, for instance, recently attracted media attention for its aggressive monitoring of social media.[101] The school persuaded Twitter to briefly shut down an account parodying the university, and the university's president has used Facebook to scold students for social media etiquette, telling them that employers "can and will track ways in which prospective employees have used social media. We, at WKU, track such things as well."[102] One student who said school officials have rebuked her friends for their social media posts told a reporter, "I don't ever criticize the school on Twitter because I don't want an ordeal made."[103]

But discouraging criticism of government and encouraging self-censorship rather than voicing complaints are not lessons we want schools to embrace. School officials instead should handle off-campus, social media speech with the legal remedies already available for off-campus speech generally: If the speech is libelous, for instance, school officials can sue. If the speech communicates a serious intent to commit violence against a particular person or group, it can be punished as a true threat. If a school becomes aware of cyberbullying that is "sufficiently severe, pervasive, or persistent as to interfere with or limit a student's ability to participate in or benefit from the services, activities or opportunities offered by a school," the speech may constitute harassment.[104] But if the speech is criticism or parody or inflammatory in general—whether crude or sophisticated, juvenile or mature— schools are better off resisting punishment. Obviously no school officials will be thrilled at discovering a vulgar social media profile parodying them. Arguably the best approach to social media, though, is not to punish or ban, but instead to educate, to teach social media literacy, talking with students— and students' parents—about the positives and negatives of social media and about the possible consequences and impact of social media speech (for students and for those whom they write about). Schools, in other words, can emphasize the importance of civility, of treating others—even those with whom we disagree—respectfully, and of using social media, and First Amendment rights, responsibly.[105]

Fear of social media instead has led school officials to impulsively punish students (backed by lenient applications of *Tinker* by some lower courts), to monitor their social media use, and to ban social media entirely inside many K-12 schools. When used appropriately, though, social media tools can help educators reach students on their own terms. Armed with that perspective, in April 2012 a coalition of education and technology advocates put forth a series of recommendations "aimed at rebooting school technology policies."[106] The recommendations, in part, called for K-12 schools to move

away from blanket bans on cell phones and social networking sites inside schools and instead to adopt a "responsible-use policy . . . that emphasizes education and treats the student as a person responsible for ethical and healthy use of the Internet and mobile devices."[107]

Student Media

Given social media's popularity for students, student media advisers, at both the high school and college level, should encourage their staffs to embrace social media as a reporting tool. Courts have yet to grapple with cases generated from social media use by student journalists working for school-affiliated media. Presumably how school officials could regulate a Facebook page created as a way for a high school student newspaper to distribute news, for instance, or a tweet by a student reporter breaking news for that publication, would depend on the legal categorization of the student media outlet. School-sponsored media are governed by *Hazelwood* and can be censored if school officials point to a legitimate pedagogical concern. Student media designated—either by policy or practice—as public forums for student expression, where student editors make their own content decisions, are instead governed by *Tinker*. It remains an open question whether *Hazelwood* applies at all to college media. A controversial 2005 Seventh Circuit decision said it did,[108] but other courts have ruled that college media are free from *Hazelwood*'s constraints. No matter the outlet, advisers should push their staffs to consider developing social media guidelines that encourage responsible use and professionalism when using social media to represent their publication.[109]

Research conducted by the Knight Foundation has shown that students who work on student media are more aware and more supportive of First Amendment rights. That research has also now found that as students' social media use grows generally, so too does their support for free expression.[110] By championing social media, then, schools are better preparing students for civic life.

FREQUENTLY ASKED QUESTIONS

1. Can K-12 public schools ban students' social media use at school?

Yes. Although outright bans on cell phones and all social media use during the school day might not be the best pedagogical policy, schools can constitutionally bar students from accessing social media while at school. The bans, schools say, are reasonable content-neutral policies put in place to protect the learning environment from distractions.

2. Can schools punish students for speech they create using social media off campus, away from school?

Right now it depends—on the court, on the standard the court applies, on how the court applies that standard, and on the speech at issue. The Supreme Court has not answered the question, and confusion thus pervades the lower courts. Many of those lower courts have applied *Tinker* and have seemingly required different levels of disruption. The *J.S.* case offers striking evidence of the confusion: The district court said a student's MySpace parody profile could be punished under *Fraser* and *Morse*; a panel of the Third Circuit instead said that *Tinker* applied and that the student could be punished because the school could reasonably forecast disruption; while the en banc Third Circuit ruled that, even if *Tinker* did apply, no disruption occurred, nor could the school forecast disruption. Three decisions involving the same case, with three different rationales.

3. Is a college student's off-campus, social media speech treated with a different legal standard than speech from a middle or high school student?

Not necessarily, according to some recent court decisions. Although the Supreme Court ruled in 1972 that the First Amendment applies with "[no] less force on college campuses than in the community at large,"[111] lower courts have applied *Tinker* to cases involving college students' social media speech. And in *Yoder*, a federal judge ruled that a college student effectively waived her First Amendment rights when she signed a consent form as part of a childbearing course, which meant that she could thus be dismissed from school for her MySpace blog that described the labor and delivery she witnessed.

4. Can schools ban student athletes from using social media entirely?

That's unresolved. Coaches have instituted social media bans, particularly bans on using Twitter, at several universities in recent years. None of the bans has been challenged in court. In a 1995 case involving student athletes' privacy, the Supreme Court did say that students "who voluntarily participate in school athletics have reason to expect intrusions upon normal rights and privileges."[112] The outright bans on social media use, though, impose a blanket prior restraint that extends far into the athletes' private lives.

5. What will it take to resolve the confusion and uncertainty?

A Supreme Court ruling. The Court so far has denied cert when it has been asked to hear student speech cases involving social media. But given the inconsistencies in the lower courts, and given how frequently social media cases now arise, the Court will likely weigh in soon.

NOTES

1 Amanda Lenhart, Kristen Purcell, Aaron Smith, & Kathryn Zickuhr, Pew Internet & American Life Project, Social Media and Young Adults (2010), http://www.pewinternet.org/Reports/2010/Social-Media-and-Young-Adults.aspx.

2 Kaiser Family Foundation Study, Generation M2: Media in the Lives of 8- to 18-Year-Olds (2010), http://www.kff.org/entmedia/upload/8010.pdf.

3 Evie Blad, Networking Web Sites Enable New Generation of Bullies, Ark. Democrat-Gazette, April 6, 2008, at A1.

4 Clay Calvert, Punishing Public School Students for Bashing Principals, Teachers and Classmates in Cyberspace: The Speech Issue the Supreme Court Must Now Resolve, 7 First Amend. L. Rev. 210, 219 (2009).

5 Id. at 219–220 (internal quotations and citations omitted).

6 See Emily Summars, Ind. Senior Says He was Expelled for Tweeting Profanity at Home, Student Press L. Ctr., March 29, 2012, http://www.splc.org/news/newsflash.asp?id=2358.

7 See Nicole Hill, La. Student Sues After Being Punished for Facebook Status, Student Press L. Ctr., October 26, 2011, http://www.splc.org/news/newsflash.asp?id=2288.

8 Calvert, supra note 4 at 211.

9 The First Amendment does not apply to private schools because they are not government agencies. Private school students could possibly find relief, though, either in state constitutions or state laws or in claiming school censorship amounts to a breach of the guidelines or rules established by the private school itself—if those guidelines or rules promise protections for free speech. See generally Legal Guide for the Private School Press, Student Press L. Ctr., http://www.splc.org/knowyourrights/legalresearch.asp?id=52.

10 393 U.S. 503, 506 (1969).

11 Id. at 513.

12 Id. at 517 (Black, J., dissenting).

13 478 U.S. 675, 677 (1986).

14 Id. at 683.

15 Id.

16 Id. at 685.

17 484 U.S. 260, 271 (1988).

18 Id. at 273.

19 551 U.S. 393, 408 (2007).

20 Id. at 401.

21 Id. at 396.

22 See Beussink v. Woodland R-IV Sch. Dist., 30 F. Supp. 2d 1175 (E.D. Mo. 1998).

23 See generally Mary-Rose Papandrea, Student Speech Rights in the Digital Age, 60 Fla. L. Rev. 1027, 1036–1037 (2008).

24 593 F.3d 286, 290 (3rd Cir. 2010), rev'd en banc, 650 F.3d 915 (3rd Cir. 2011).

25 650 F.3d 915, 920 (3rd Cir. 2011).

26 2008 U.S. Dist. LEXIS 72685, 18 (M.D. Pa. 2008).

27 593 F.3d 286, 308 (3rd Cir. 2010), rev'd en banc, 650 F.3d 915 (3rd Cir. 2011).

28 650 F.3d 915, 929 (3rd Cir. 2011).

29 Id. at 936 (Smith, J., concurring).

30 Id. at 950–951 (Fisher, J., dissenting).

31 Papandrea, supra note 23 at 1056.

32 See, e.g., J.S. v. Bethlehem Area Sch. Dist., 569 Pa. 638, 668 (Pa. 2002) ("We hold that where speech that is aimed at a specific school and/or its personnel is brought onto the school campus or accessed at school by its originator, the speech will be considered on-campus speech").

33 Wisniewski v. Weedsport Cent. Sch. Dist., 494 F.3d 34, 39 (2nd Cir. 2007) ("[I]t was reasonably foreseeable that the IM icon would come to the attention of school authorities and the teacher whom the icon depicted being shot"). See also D.J.M. v. Hannibal Pub. Sch. Dist., 647 F.3d 754, 766 (8th Cir. 2011) ("[I]t was reasonably foreseeable that D.J.M.'s threats about shooting specific students in school would be brought to the attention of school authorities and create a risk of substantial disruption within the school environment"); J.C. v. Beverly Hills Unified Sch. Dist., 711 F. Supp. 2d 1094, 1108 (C.D. Cal. 2010) ("Several cases have applied Tinker where speech published or transmitted via the Internet subsequently comes to the attention of school administrators, even where there is no evidence that students accessed the speech while at school").

34 Papandrea, supra note 23 at 1064.

35 See Calvert, supra note 4 at 235.

36 Layshock v. Hermitage Sch. Dist., 650 F.3d 205, 220–221 (3rd Cir. 2011) (Jordan, J., concurring). The judge continued, "Modern communications technology, for all its positive applications, can be a potent tool for distraction and fomenting disruption." Id. at 222.

37 Doninger v. Niehoff, 527 F.3d 41, 45 (2nd Cir. 2008).

38 Id.

39 Id. at 50–51.

40 Id. at 51.

41 Id. After being denied the injunction, Doninger continued her case in court and argued that she deserved monetary damages because she was denied her First Amendment right to criticize school officials. In 2011 a different Second Circuit panel ruled that it did not need to decide whether her punishment in fact violated the First Amendment because the law surrounding off-campus speech is so unsettled that the school officials were entitled to qualified immunity. See Doninger v. Niehoff, 642 F.3d 334 (2nd Cir. 2011).

42 This is generally true in all student speech cases, not just those involving social media. See generally Calvert, supra note 4 at 243–244.

43 2012 U.S. Dist. LEXIS 34839 (N.D. Miss. 2012).

44 Id. at 2.

45 Id. at 3.

46 Id. at 7.

47 Id. at 15. See also O.Z. v. Bd. of Tr. of the Long Beach Unified Sch. Dist., 2008 U.S. Dist. LEXIS 110409, 11 (C.D. Cal. 2008) (upholding the transfer of a student as punishment for a slide show she posted to YouTube that depicted the killing of her English teacher because "although O.Z. created the slide show off-campus, it created a foreseeable risk of disruption within the school").

48 Kowalski v. Berkeley County Sch., 652 F.3d 565 (4th Cir. 2011). In extreme instances in recent years, students have committed suicide as a result of bullying from their peers, some of which occurred online. See, e.g., Martin Finucane, DA Defends

Light Sentences in Phoebe Prince Case, Boston Globe, May 5, 2011, http://www. boston.com/news/local/breaking_news/2011/05/two_more_teens.html.

49 For example, one student uploaded a picture of himself and a friend holding their noses while displaying a sign that read "Shay Has Herpes." 652 F.3d at 568.

50 Id. at 568–569.

51 Id. at 573.

52 Id. at 574 (internal quotations and citations omitted).

53 Id.

54 Id. at 577. But see J.C. v. Beverly Hills Unified Sch. Dist., 711 F. Supp. 2d 1094, 1122 (C.D. Cal. 2010) (striking down a student's punishment for posting a video to YouTube that demeaned another student because the court "cannot uphold school discipline of student speech simply because young persons are unpredictable or immature, or because, in general, teenagers are emotionally fragile and may often fight over hurtful comments").

55 Evans v. Bayer, 684 F. Supp. 2d 1365, 1367 (S.D. Fla. 2010).

56 Id. at 1373.

57 See David L. Hudson, School Learns Lesson in Facebook Case, First Amendment Ctr., December 29, 2010, http://www.firstamendmentcenter.org/school-learns-lesson-in-facebook-case.

58 807 F. Supp. 2d 767 (N.D. Ind. 2011).

59 Id. at 5.

60 Id. at 7.

61 Id. at 35.

62 Id. at 38.

63 Id. at 41.

64 Id. at 51–56.

65 2012 U.S. Dist. LEXIS 45264 (W.D. Ky. 2012).

66 Id. at 3.

67 Id. at 17.

68 Id. See also Snyder v. Millersville University, where a judge upheld the removal of a university student, Stacey Snyder, from a student teaching placement at a local high school. The punishment kept her from obtaining teacher certification. The judge ruled that Snyder was more akin to a teacher—a public employee—than a student given that she did not take university classes during the placement and instead was responsible for curriculum planning, grading, and attending faculty meetings at the high school. She could thus be punished, in part, for her MySpace postings that referenced the school and her students and for a picture that showed her drinking since the posts did not discuss matters of public concern but instead "raised only personal matters." 2008 U.S. Dist. LEXIS 97943, 42 (E.D. Pa. 2008).

69 800 N.W.2d 811, 814 (Minn. Ct. App. 2011).

70 Id.

71 Id. at 815.

72 Id. at 821. The court cited DeJohn v. Temple University, 537 F.3d 301 (3rd Cir. 2008)

73 800 N.W.2d at 822.

74 See Tatro v. Univ. of Minnesota, 816 N.W.2d 509, 521 (Minn. 2012).

75 575 F. Supp. 2d 571, 590 (D. Del. 2008).

76 Id. at 578.

77 Id. at 590.

78 See Nick Glunt, Expulsion Over Raunchy Tweets May Cost High School Football Star His College Dream, Student Press L. Ctr., January 23, 2012, http://www. splc.org/wordpress/?p=3109. The student subsequently accepted a scholarship offer from the University of Colorado.

79 The University of North Carolina at Chapel Hill, Department of Athletics, Policy on Student-Athlete Social Networking and Media Use (2011), http://grfx. cstv.com/photos/schools/unc/genrel/auto_pdf/2011-12/misc_non_event/Social NetworkingPolicy.pdf.

80 Id.

81 See Bob Sullivan, Govt. Agencies, Colleges Demand Applicants' Facebook Passwords, The Redtape Chronicles (March 6, 2012), http://redtape.msnbc.msn. com/_news/2012/03/06/10585353-govt-agencies-colleges-demand-applicants-facebook-passwords.

82 See Kathleen Nelson, Services Monitor Athletes on Facebook, Other Sites, St. Louis Post-Dispatch, February 1, 2012, http://www.stltoday.com/sports/college/mizzou/ services-monitor-athletes-on-facebook-other-sites/article_8e6517ba-e78d-5dfe-83ba-30d673042dfb.html. Although the monitoring programs presumably could be applied broadly to a range of students, to this point schools have limited their use to student athletes.

83 Id.

84 Id.

85 The state of Maryland is currently considering legislation that would forbid colleges from forcing students to hand over their social media account information. The proposed law would prevent "an institution of postsecondary education from requiring a student or an applicant for admission to disclose any user name, account name, password, or other means for accessing specified accounts or services through an electronic communications device." See S.B. 434, Reg. Sess. (Md. 2012).

86 See generally Eric Robinson, Intentional Grounding: Can Public Colleges Limit Athletes' Tweets? Citizen Media Law Project (November 9, 2010), http://www. citmedialaw.org/blog/2010/intentional-grounding-can-public-colleges-limit-athletes-tweets.

87 See Michael Lananna, Sylvia Hatchell Bans UNC Women's Basketball Team's Twitter Use, The Daily Tar Heel, January 27, 2012, http://www.dailytarheel.com/ index.php/article/2012/01/sylvia_hatchell_bans_womens_teams_twitter_use.

88 See, e.g., Robinson, supra note 89. But see Mary Margaret "Meg" Penrose, Free Speech Versus Free Education, 1 Miss. Sports L. Rev. 1, 94 (2011) (arguing that "athletic departments should feel confident in regulating or banning their student-athletes' use of social media").

89 See, e.g., Terry Hutchens, IU DB Andre Kates now suspended indefinitely, Indystar.com (October 31, 2010), http://blogs.indystar.com/hoosiersinsider/2010/ 10/31/iu-db-andre-kates-now-suspended-indefinitely/ (Indiana University football player suspended for tweets critical of the coaching staff). In the high school setting, courts have upheld punishment of athletes under Tinker for speech that criticized coaches and sought to undermine their authority. See, e.g., Lowery v. Euverard, 497 F.3d 584 (6th Cir. 2007).

90 See Emily Summars, Lawsuit Claims Minn. School Officials Demanded Sixth-grader's Facebook Password, Student Press L. Ctr., March 7, 2012, http://www.splc.org/news/newsflash.asp?id=2344.

91 See Jeffrey Solochek, Pasco Teacher Accused of Policing Students' Facebook Comments, Tampa Bay Times, March 22, 2012, http://www.tampabay.com/news/education/k12/pasco-teacher-accused-of-policing-students-facebook-comments/1221093.

92 Id.

93 Id.

94 See Jennifer Preston, Rules to Stop Pupil and Teacher From Getting Too Social Online, N.Y. Times, December 17, 2011, http://www.nytimes.com/2011/12/18/business/media/rules-to-limit-how-teachers-and-students-interact-online.html.

95 Id. ("In Sacramento, a 37-year-old high school band director pleaded guilty to sexual misconduct stemming from his relationship with a 16-year-old female student; her Facebook page had more than 1,200 private messages from him, some about massages").

96 S.B. 54, 96th General Assembly, 1st Regular Sess. (Mo. 2011).

97 Mo. State Teachers Ass'n v. Mo., No. 11AC-CC00553 (Cir. Ct. Cole County Aug. 2011).

98 See Nicole Hill, School District Won't Make Kan. Student Apologize for Tweet Against Governor, Student Press L. Ctr., November 28, 2011, http://www.splc.org/news/newsflash.asp?id=2302.

99 Ken Paulson, Tweet Backlash: Kan. Officials Learn Lesson About Free Speech, First Amendment Ctr., November 28, 2011, http://www.firstamendmentcenter.org/tweet-backlash-kan-officials-learn-lesson-about-free-speech.

100 Id.

101 See, e.g., Ky. School Aggressively Fights Twitter Criticism, Fox News.com (February 27, 2012), http://www.foxnews.com/us/2012/02/27/ky-school-aggressively-fights-twitter-criticism/.

102 Id.

103 Id.

104 See Department of Education, "Dear Colleague" Letter Re Bullying (October 26, 2010), http://www.nacua.org/documents/DearColleagueLetter_Bullying.pdf.

105 See, e.g., Denielle Burl, From Tinker to Twitter: Managing Student Speech on Social Media, 9 NACUA Notes (2011), http://www.studentaffairs.uconn.edu/docs/risk_mgt/nacua5.pdf (advising that the best way to prevent student misuse of social media is to "fight speech with speech"); Neal Hutchens, You Can't Post That . . . Or Can You? Legal Issues Related to College and University Students' Online Speech, 49 J. of Student Aff. Res. and Prac. 1, 13 (2012) (arguing that "colleges and universities should engage students more broadly and deeply regarding issues related to their online expression"); Papandrea, supra note 23 at 1098 (arguing that "the primary approach that schools should take to most digital speech is not to punish their students, but to educate their students about how to use digital media responsibly").

106 Frank LoMonte, In "Making Progress" Report, Education Leaders Call for a Reboot of Schools' Restrictive Technology Policies, Student Press L. Ctr., April 11, 2012, http://www.splc.org/wordpress/?p=3508.

107 Making Progress: Rethinking State and School District Policies Concerning Mobile Technologies and Social Media (2012), http://www.splc.org/pdf/making_progress_2012.pdf.

108 Hosty v. Carter, 412 F.3d 731 (7th Cir. 2005).

109 See, e.g., Nick Dean, Living Social: College Newsrooms Revisiting Ethics Policies for the Twitter Generation, 32 Student Press L. Ctr. Rep. 30 (2011), http://www.splc.org/news/report_detail.asp?id=1611&edition=56.

110 Knight Foundation, Future of the First Amendment (2011), http://www.knightfoundation.org/media/uploads/article_pdfs/Future-of-the-First-Amendment-2011-full.pdf.

111 Healy v. James, 408 U.S. 169, 180 (1972).

112 Vernonia Sch. Dist. v. Acton, 515 U.S. 646, 657 (1995).

CHAPTER 8

Obscenity, Sexting, and Cyberbullying

Amy Kristin Sanders

University of Minnesota School of Journalism and Mass Communication

ABSTRACT

The rise of the Internet brought about new challenges in the regulation of undesirable sexually explicit content in the United States. At the core of these challenges is our nation's fundamental belief in the protection of expression under the First Amendment. Increased use of electronic communication devices and social media, however, transformed these challenges into everyday concerns for employers, parents, and communicators—looking to limit the exchange and receipt of sexual photos, text messages, and other content. This chapter examines the legal implications of instantaneous communication in this context, including cyberbullying, sexting, and exchange of indecent and obscene images and text.

Police sergeant Jeff Quon wasn't really all that different from many Americans who use technology owned by their employers to engage in personal communication[1]—except for the fact that his actions gave rise to a U.S. Supreme Court case after his employer disciplined him.[2] Quon's employer, the City of Ontario, California, relying on its Computer Usage, Internet and E-Mail Policy, audited his text usage after he acquired multiple overages. In doing so, the city found a number of messages to be personal, including some that were of a sexually explicit nature. Ruling 9-0 in favor of the City of Ontario, the U.S. Supreme Court ruled that Quon's right to privacy had not been violated when his employer audited his text messages. Those actions, the Court held, amounted to a reasonable search under the Fourth Amendment given they were motivated by a legitimate work-related purpose.

The development of electronic communication technology and social media tools opens the door for criminal and civil litigation in a variety of areas including defamation, privacy, and intellectual property, as this book has suggested. But, many of the earliest areas of legal concern relate to the availability and regulation of sexually explicit content on the Internet. In 2004, one researcher testified before Congress, likening Internet pornography to illegal drugs:

> The [I]nternet is a perfect drug delivery system because you are anonymous, aroused and have role models for these behaviors. To have [a] drug pumped into your house 24/7, free, and children know how to use it better than grown-ups know how to use it. [I]t's a perfect delivery system if we want to have a whole generation of young addicts who will never have the drug out of their mind.[3]

Congressional interest in regulating sexually explicit content—including obscenity and pornography—on the Internet pre-dates the development of social media and even the aforementioned 2004 legislative hearing.[4] However, those efforts largely inform current attempts to proscribe cyberbullying and the transmission of sexually explicit content resulting from the use of social media.

After a basic introduction to the regulation of obscenity and indecency, this chapter provides an overview of early legislation to stem the tide of sexually explicit content on the Internet. Particular attention will be paid to early legislative efforts that resulted in litigation culminating at the U.S. Supreme Court. Next, the regulation of sexting, or the practice of sending sexually explicit messages or photos using electronic communication, is explored. The discussion focuses on several prominent cases and the resulting legal action. The chapter then addresses cyberbullying, including the evaluation of legislative efforts designed to curtail the practice. Finally, the chapter concludes by highlighting related areas of legal concern that are likely to develop as the popularity of social media tools continues to grow.

REGULATING SEXUALLY EXPLICIT SPEECH OFFLINE AND ONLINE

The U.S. Supreme Court set the stage for the regulation of obscene and indecent expression long before the Internet arrived in our homes. More than 55 years ago in *Roth v. United States*,[5] Justice William Brennan, writing for a six-justice majority, clearly enunciated the Court's belief that obscene speech fell outside the protection of the First Amendment:

> The dispositive question is whether obscenity is utterance within the area of protected speech and press. Although this is the first time the question has been squarely presented to this Court, either under the First Amendment or under the Fourteenth Amendment, expressions found in numerous opinions indicate that this Court has always assumed that obscenity is not protected by the freedoms of speech and press.[6]

He went on, noting that as far back as 1942, the Court acknowledged in *Chaplinsky v. New Hampshire* the permissible regulation of sexually explicit speech rising to the level of obscenity.[7]

Shortly after the *Roth* decision, however, consensus broke down on the Court as to what standard should be used to determine whether speech was obscene. It was during this time period that Justice Potter Stewart, when describing obscenity, made his oft-repeated remark:

> I shall not today attempt further to define the kinds of material I understand to be embraced within that shorthand description; and perhaps I could never succeed in intelligibly doing so. But I know it when I see it, and the motion picture involved in this case is not that.[8]

Obscenity law remained in a state of disarray, with the Court deciding cases on an almost ad-hoc basis until 1973.[9]

In that year, a 5-4 majority in *Miller v. California* agreed upon the standard currently used to determine whether expression should be considered obscene and outside the scope of First Amendment protection.[10] The Supreme Court vacated a California criminal conviction under the state's obscenity statute, ruling that the First Amendment required a three-part showing for speech to be considered obscene:

> (a) whether the average person, applying contemporary community standards would find that the work, taken as a whole, appeals to the prurient interest; (b) whether the work depicts or describes, in a patently offensive way, sexual conduct specifically defined by the applicable state law; and (c) whether the work, taken as a whole, lacks serious literary, artistic, political, or scientific value.[11]

The ruling served to cement the Court's approach to obscenity regulation, and the *Miller* test has returned to the forefront as Congress has attempted to legislate expression occurring on the Internet and via social media.

Legislative efforts to regulate sexually explicit expression on the Internet have not solely been based on obscenity's status outside the scope of First Amendment protection. In fact, a number of legislative attempts have tried to curtail indecent speech and pornography as well. Such a regulatory approach would have limited the rights of Internet speakers in much the same way the Court limited the rights of broadcasters in its 1978 ruling in *FCC v. Pacifica*.[12] There, a majority of the Court upheld the FCC's right to sanction broadcasters for airing indecent content, in part based on the notion that broadcast television and radio were pervasive and uniquely accessible to children.[13] As a result, the FCC has the authority to fine broadcasters who air indecent content outside the Safe Harbor hours of 10 p.m. to 6 a.m.

Indecency, however, remained a concept reserved solely for broadcast media throughout much of the 1980s and 1990s. Print publishers and cable operators were not subject to the FCC's regulations, which prohibited the broadcast of "language that describes, in terms patently offensive as measured by contemporary community standards for the broadcast medium, sexual or excretory activities and organs, at times of the day when there is a reasonable risk that children may be in the audience."[14] However, that changed when President Bill Clinton signed the Telecommunications Act of 1996[15] into law.

The Telecommunications Act of 1996 represented the first comprehensive overhaul of telecommunication policy since the 1934 Communications Act, and it attempted to solidify the Internet's place within the FCC's regulatory authority.[16] Contained within the Act's 128 pages was Title V, targeting obscenity and violence in various telecommunication media, including the Internet. Title V, also known as the Communications Decency Act, was of particular interest to those concerned about freedom of expression because Section 223 criminalized the knowing transmission of obscene or indecent material to recipients under 18.[17]

On the day President Clinton signed the law, the American Civil Liberties Union and 19 additional plaintiffs challenged Section 223 of the Communications Decency Act in federal court,[18] laying the groundwork for the U.S. Supreme Court's first decision[19] in the area of cyberspace law. In the case, the ACLU argued that two of the CDA's provisions designed to protect minors from harmful material on the Internet were unconstitutional.[20] After the issuance of a temporary restraining order, a three-judge panel in U.S. District Court made a lengthy finding of fact before issuing a preliminary injunction that prevented the government from enforcing the provisions against material claimed to be indecent under §223(a)(1)(B) or any material under §223(d). Based on a special provision in the statute, the government appealed the District Court decision directly to the U.S. Supreme Court.

Justice Stevens, writing for the majority in *ACLU v. Reno*, penned an opinion that laid the foundation for the Court's subsequent jurisprudence in the realm of cyberspace and electronic communication. Observing that the rules of traditional media should not automatically be applied to the Internet, Justice Stevens opined:

> Neither before nor after the enactment of the CDA have the vast democratic fora of the Internet been subject to the type of government supervision and regulation that has attended the broadcast industry. Moreover, the Internet is not as "invasive" as radio or television.[21]

Distinguishing the Internet from the regulations permitted in broadcast, Justice Stevens noted that the Court need not be bound by the *Pacifica* ruling.[22] Section 223(a)(1)(B), the opinion asserted, was more akin to regulations the Court had struck down in a 1989 case involving the prohibition of sexually oriented commercial telephone messages.[23] In *Sable Communications*, the Court ruled that a provision in the Communications Act that prohibited the transmission of both obscene and indecent dial-a-porn messages was unconstitutional as to the indecent content, which was entitled to some First Amendment protection.[24] Relying heavily on *Pacifica*'s reasoning that broadcast is uniquely pervasive, the Court distinguished commercial messages transmitted via the telephone:

> In contrast to public displays, unsolicited mailings and other means of expression which the recipient has no meaningful opportunity to avoid, the dial-it medium requires the listener to take affirmative steps to receive the communication. There is no "captive audience" problem here; callers will generally not be unwilling listeners . . . Unlike an unexpected outburst on a radio broadcast, the message received by one who places a call to a dial-a-porn service is not so invasive or surprising that it prevents an unwilling listener from avoiding exposure to it.[25]

Justice Stevens also observed that the scarcity rationale used by Congress to justify the regulation of broadcast and embraced by the Court in *Red Lion Broadcasting v. FCC*[26] simply did not apply in the Internet context.[27] In all reality, the Court likened the Internet more to the print medium, establishing a jurisprudential approach that would make content regulation extremely difficult.[28]

In addition to the hands-off regulatory approach that seemed to be embraced by the Court in *Reno*, the majority took issue with the breadth of

the CDA's restrictions on speech. Foreshadowed by Justice Stevens' discussion of *Sable*, the majority held both provisions to be unconstitutionally overbroad. The majority found troubling the statute's restriction on "indecent" content as well as its prohibition on "patently offensive" material—neither of which were defined in the legislation. Both terms, Justice Stevens wrote, could be interpreted to include within their sweep content that adults possessed a First Amendment right to access:

> We are persuaded that the CDA lacks the precision that the First Amendment requires when a statute regulates the content of speech. In order to deny minors access to potentially harmful speech, the CDA effectively suppresses a large amount of speech that adults have a constitutional right to receive and to address to one another. That burden on adult speech is unacceptable if less restrictive alternatives would be at least as effective in achieving the legitimate purpose that the statute was enacted to serve.[29]

The Court further noted the breadth of application of the CDA's provisions.[30] As written, the statute applied to all transmissions of material harmful to minors—commercial or otherwise. No exceptions were made for non-profit entities, individuals, or educational institutions, leaving within the provisions' scope non-pornographic materials that may have educational or other social value.

On the heels of the loss in *Reno*, legislators returned to the drawing board in an attempt to craft a new statute that could address the Court's concerns. As a result, the Child Online Protection Act[31] (COPA) was enacted in October 1998.[32] It prohibited:

> any person from "knowingly and with knowledge of the character of the material, in interstate or foreign commerce by means of the World Wide Web, mak[ing] any communication for commercial purposes that is available to any minor and that includes any material that is harmful to minors."[33]

Taking cue from the Court's decision in *Reno*, legislators attempted to draft COPA in a more narrow fashion, making three distinct changes. First, the new provision applied only to World Wide Web content whereas the CDA provisions applied to all expression via the Internet, including email.[34] Second, COPA was limited to communication for commercial purposes, meaning educational or other non-profit communication would be exempted from its criminal penalties. Finally, lawmakers reworked the CDA prohibition on "indecent" and "patently offensive" speech—terms that had

doomed the legislation in the Supreme Court—by substituting in the phrase "material harmful to minors" which was drawn from a previous Supreme Court case, *New York v. Ferber*[35] and defining the term using a test similar to the *Miller* test.

One month prior to COPA taking effect, free speech advocates, including the ACLU, challenged the legislation in court, claiming it violated the First Amendment.[36] After winning an initial injunction against COPA, the ACLU was victorious when the Third Circuit ruled the use of "community standards" to define "material harmful to minors" was overbroad.[37] However, the U.S. Supreme Court in 2002 rejected this reasoning, and the case returned to the Third Circuit.[38] Hearing the case a second time, the Third Circuit once again struck down the law as unconstitutional, finding it limited adults' rights to access content to which they had a constitutional right.[39] In 2004, the U.S. Supreme Court again heard *Ashcroft v. ACLU*, ruling this time that the law was likely to be unconstitutional and noting the ability of filtering software to serve as an alternative to more harsh restrictions.[40] After a re-hearing at the District Court, where a permanent injunction was issued, the Third Circuit upheld that decision, effectively killing COPA.[41]

After the ACLU's victories in both cases, it seemed the government was at a loss to regulate sexually explicit content on the Internet, adding support to the colloquial references to the Internet as the Wild West. On the heels of the government's early losses in *Reno* and *Ashcroft*, Congress was busy drafting additional legislation aimed to protect children from sexually explicit Internet content. The Children's Internet Protection Act (CIPA), signed into law in 2000, took a different approach than its predecessors. Instead of tackling all Internet use, CIPA focused on two key providers of Internet access to children: schools and libraries. Although Congress could not force all school and library boards to require the use of filtering software on their Internet stations, it could condition funding through its E-Rate program on their installation. Given the large number of schools and libraries that were dependent on the funding, the legislation swept broadly across the country.

In response, the American Library Association sued, claiming CIPA required librarians to violate patrons' constitutional rights by blocking access to protected speech. In 2002, a three-judge panel in U.S. District Court agreed with the librarians group, ruling that less restrictive means—including supervision by librarians—would better achieve the government's objective without infringing on patrons' First Amendment rights. The U.S. Supreme Court, in a 6-3 vote, overruled the lower court decision, characterizing CIPA not as a speech restriction but instead as a condition of participating in a government funding program—which libraries were not required to do.[42]

The government's victory in *U.S. v. American Library Association* empowered lawmakers, who have introduced numerous pieces of legislation involving minors and sexually explicit speech on the Internet since the Court's 2003 decision. Legislation that would require schools and libraries to protect children from sexual predators when using social networking and chat sites has been introduced in Congress a number of times—though never being passed by both chambers. Known as the Deleting Online Predators Act (DOPA), the legislation would have limited access to a wide range of websites based on its broad definition of "social networking site."[43]

Several states, including Georgia, North Carolina, and Illinois, have attempted to take similar actions to protect children using the Internet. Typically, these laws take one of two forms. The first group of laws—similar to the proposed Illinois Social Networking Prohibition Act—impose restrictions on libraries and schools, mandating limitations on what students can access or prohibiting the access of certain sites altogether. The second type—more akin to the North Carolina Protect Children From Sexual Predators Act enacted in 2008[44]—place the onus on social networking sites by punishing those that allow minors to create profiles without parental consent and requiring the site allow parents full ability to monitor their children's profiles.

The constitutionality of these types of laws is questionable. In early 2012, a U.S. District Court in Louisiana struck down a recently enacted state law that prohibited registered sex offenders whose crimes involved children from using or accessing social networking sites, chat rooms, and peer-to-peer networks.[45] In the decision, the court noted the statute was both unconstitutionally overbroad and vague:

> Although the Act is intended to promote the legitimate and compelling state interest of protecting minors from [I]nternet predators, the near total ban on [I]nternet access imposed by the Act unreasonably restricts many ordinary activities that have become important to everyday life in today's world. The sweeping restrictions on the use of the [I]nternet for purposes completely unrelated to the activities sought to be banned by the Act impose severe and unwarranted restraints on constitutionally protected speech.

Cases dealing with similar restrictions have been heard in several states, including Nebraska, where a federal court held that three sections of the state's sex offender registration law that dealt with restrictions on Internet usage appeared to be unconstitutional, which suggests lawmakers will have a hard time legislating in this area.[46]

Shortly after Facebook's Initial Public Offering in May 2012, news outlets, including the *Sunday Times* in the U.K. and CNET, circulated stories that suggested Facebook would lift its ban on children under the age of 13 using the social networking site. These articles seemed to coincide with earlier statements by Facebook CEO Mark Zuckerberg, who has been quoted as saying children should be allowed on Facebook because of the site's educational value. The articles made mention of the prospect of keeping minors safe from inappropriate content and the reality of trying to block children from accessing explicit text and photos. Further, Facebook's under-13 ban is largely guided by the Children's Online Privacy Protection Act (COPPA), which took effect in the U.S. in 1998. COPPA wouldn't impact under-13s in other countries such as the U.K., but some countries, such as Spain, have their own laws limiting Facebook access by children under a certain age. Not long after the headlines appeared, other media—including the *Telegraph* and FOX News—reported that Facebook denied the plans. The statements, which Facebook claims were taken out of context—related more to Facebook seeking to work with the industry on ways to make social networking and the Internet safer for minors.

TLK 2 ME DURTY—STEMMING THE TIDE OF SEXTING

A Pennsylvania high school math teacher made headlines after he was charged with sending a teenage student sexually explicit pictures followed by a video of himself performing a sex act. What started out as a Facebook friendship between a 26-year-old teacher and 17-year-old student resulted in the teacher facing charges of sending sexual materials to a minor and corruption of a minor, both misdemeanors. Court records revealed a history of two-way contact, and the student admitted to sending sexually explicit nude photos to the teacher after receiving some from him. As a result of his actions, the teacher was suspended from teaching while he faced trial, but could be allowed back in the classroom if acquitted of the charges.

The case in Pennsylvania represents only the tip of the sexting iceberg—albeit one of the most concerning types of sexting situations. With the increased availability of sexually explicit content available on the Internet, it should come as no surprise that individuals quickly began sending and receiving pornographic emails, text messages, chats, and photos using their computers and smartphones. Four distinct situations emerge within the law in relation to sexting: sexting between consenting adults, sexting between two adults where one does not consent, sexting between an adult and a minor child, and sexting between two minor children.

Traditionally, prosecutors have used a number of existing laws to address sexting where one adult sends another unwilling adult pornographic or nude

messages. These could include harassment, stalking, and similar criminal statutes. In a most interesting development, attorneys and legal scholars are divided about whether criminal statutes could be used to prosecute a person who records the audio of his neighbors engaged in sexual relations and then posts the sound file to the Internet. A post to the user-generated news site Reddit drew significant attention after the poster mentioned a friend had recorded his neighbors' noisy encounter and uploaded the audio to SoundCloud.[47] Prosecutors looking to bring a case might be able to turn to the Electronic Communications Privacy Act (ECPA), a federal law that is designed to protect the transfer of information through wire, radio, electromagnetic, photoelectric or photooptical communications systems. Although the chance of a successful federal prosecution is slim, it isn't clear it wouldn't be possible. Even withstanding ECPA, a number of state laws, which vary from state to state, could apply. These would include wiretapping laws, communication privacy statutes similar to ECPA and possibly any statutory privacy protections. To further complicate the issue, the aggrieved couple might be able to sue civilly based on the state's common law privacy torts or a trespass if the recorder entered onto private property. Whether a court would allow the use of these existing statutes and common law torts in this way is unclear.

Courts have been willing to use existing statutes to deal with sexting that occurs between an adult and a minor child—whether the child consented or not. Often these might include prostitution, child sexual abuse, or misconduct statutes.

More disturbing than sexual indiscretions involving adults is the rise in the practice of sexting among "consenting" minors—a practice the law has seemed unequipped to combat. A 2008 study done by The National Campaign to Prevent Teen Pregnancy found that 48 percent of teens had received sexually explicit text messages, and a 2009 study by the Pew Internet and American Life project found that 15 percent of cell-phone owners ages 12 to 17 had received nude or partially nude photos from someone. A 2009 survey by Cox Communications found that nearly half of teens surveyed believed that sexting with photos should be illegal for those under 18.

Not surprisingly, lawmakers across the nation have responded to media reports about the rise of sexting, often by attempting to pass legislation prohibiting its various forms. The National Conference of State Legislatures began tracking sexting legislation in 2009, and at least 16 states and Guam have enacted laws aimed to curtail teen sexting. In 2012 alone, at least 13 additional states had bills under consideration. Two states, Indiana and Rhode Island, have previously created commissions to study the issue.

Although most legislation aims to prohibit the sending of sexually explicit, nude or partially nude text and photos messages, two states have

taken a different approach. In Arizona, SB 1219 would require cellular providers to offer parents the right to view their children's text messages when issuing new contracts. At the time of publication, it remained in committee. In South Carolina, HB 4555 would give parents the right to review messages sent or received with the minor's device, and it would not allow minors to have access to text services without providing consent for parents and guardians to review the messages. At the time of publication, it remained in committee.

If school districts or other employers try to restrict personal communication among employees and other consenting adults, other challenges would likely arise. Given the emphasis on freedom of speech in the United States, courts are likely to find policies that prohibit communication completely to be unconstitutional, even for teachers who deal with minors. Policies related to texting and other social media will have a better chance of withstanding judicial scrutiny if they are limited in scope—addressing only sexually explicit communication, for example. Further, policies that attempt to restrict communication between parties over the age of 18 will no doubt face higher scrutiny. Employers who attempt to block access during working hours are likely to have more success with their policies than those who attempt a blanket prohibition that would include employees' personal time. Regardless of the effort taken by employers, any social media policy put in place by a government body will face significant obstacles based on its potential to chill speech.

BANISHING THE BULLY FROM THE BEDROOM

The fact pattern has become all too familiar. A young person—often a pre-teen or teenager—commits suicide after being the target of online harassment. Cyberbullying—the name for online harassment most often used when minors are the victims—rose to the public purview in a 2006 case involving a mother, Lori Drew, whom prosecutors alleged created a MySpace profile impersonating "Josh Evans" in order to befriend one of her daughter's female classmates.[48] After deceiving 13-year-old Megan Meier into believing Evans liked her, prosecutors argued that Drew (acting under her cyberpersona) then told her the world would be a better place without her. Afterward, Meier hanged herself in her bedroom. Although state prosecutors wanted to charge Drew with a crime, there was no federal cyberbullying statute to rely on. After being charged with four felony counts of unauthorized computer access under the federal Computer Fraud and Abuse Act (CFAA), a jury found Drew guilty of three lesser charges. In July 2009, a federal judge overturned the jury verdict, acquitting Drew of all charges.

Although teasing and other forms of bullying have been around as long as there have been schoolyards for the bullies to occupy, cyberbullying cases like the one involving Lori Drew present an entirely new set of challenges. Initially, one of the most difficult challenges posed is a definitional one. Even if lawmakers were to come to a consensus as to what constituted cyberbullying, regulating expressive activities without violating the First Amendment presents a further challenge. Add to that the complex nature of regulating on-campus/off-campus activities and the plot thickens. Finally, even with laws in place, cyberbullying that goes unreported cannot be prohibited. All of these factors combine to create an environment in which most of the undesirable behavior goes unpunished.

Child psychologists and educators in the United States often have little difficulty defining cyberbullying, and even though they may not all agree on the exact terms of a single definition, the similarities are striking. One of the first definitions of cyberbullying is attributed to Canadian teacher Bill Belsey, who started Bullying.org. Belsey defines it as "the use of information and communication technologies to support deliberate, repeated, and hostile behaviour by an individual or group, that is intended to harm others." Most definitions include a number of these requirements, including the desire to harm, the use of technology to communicate, and deliberate contact. Other organizations limit cyberbullying to cases involving victims who are minors. StopCyberbullying.Org has one of the narrowest definitions of cyber-bullying:

> Cyberbullying is when a child, preteen or teen is tormented, threatened, harassed, humiliated, embarrassed or otherwise targeted by another child, preteen or teen using the Internet, interactive and digital technologies or mobile phones. It has to have a minor on both sides, or at least have been instigated by a minor against another minor.

Although there may be minor differences in the various definitions, those in education and healthcare largely agree on the primary characteristics of the behavior.

Despite the nearly universal agreement as to the types of undesirable behavior that constitutes cyberbullying among health and education professionals, a larger disagreement results among lawmakers, who are tasked with defining the type of conduct a state desires to punish. Given the expressive nature of the conduct at issue, lawmakers have a particularly difficult task at hand. This is because the First Amendment to the U.S. Constitution provides a certain amount of protection for expression—and even children attending school are not completely without these protections.[49] Thus, when

drafting statutes to curtail cyberbullying, lawmakers must walk the fine line between prohibiting the conduct they seek to regulate and running afoul of the First Amendment.

The constitutional challenges have not stopped lawmakers in their efforts. As of April 2012, 49 states have laws in place to address bullying, but only 14 of those include cyberbullying, according to the Cyberbullying Research Center. In addition, as of June 2012, six states have proposed legislation to specifically address cyberbullying. More than 80 percent of the current laws do include prohibitions on electronic harassment, which depending on how each state defined the term, could include both sexting and cyberbullying. Of the laws in place, only 20 percent provide for a criminal penalty while the majority allow the school to sanction the students instead.

The protections in the various states run the gamut—from Montana's hands-off approach to Arkansas' attempt to restrict an enormous amount of student activity. Montana represents the outlier—the one state that doesn't even have a bullying law in place let alone a cyberbullying prohibition. Arkansas and several other states, including Louisiana, South Dakota, and Massachusetts, represent the other end of the spectrum. Each of these four states have laws that address bullying, cyberbullying, and electronic harassment. Their laws require school policies, allow for school sanctions and even reach off-campus activity. Arkansas and Louisiana provide for criminal penalties.

Most states, however, fall somewhere in between. Nearly all states require the school district to establish a policy but also allow the school district to sanction students. Far fewer allow the regulation of off-campus activity or criminal penalties. Nearly all of the states have enacted or updated their laws in the past five years, and they will not come without legal challenges.

In addition to state laws, legislation has been proposed at the federal level. At the time of publication, though, no federal law specifically prohibited cyberbullying. In 2009, lawmakers introduced the Megan Meier Cyberbullying Prevention Act (HR 1966), which would have criminalized "any communication, with the intent to coerce, intimidate, harass, or cause substantial emotional distress to a person, using electronic means to support severe, repeated, and hostile behavior" that was transmitted between states. Under the bill, violators faced up to two years in prison or a fine. Although subcommittee hearings were held in late 2009, the bill never made it to the House floor.

Similar legislation—the Tyler Clementi Higher Education Anti-Harassment Act—was introduced in 2011 after Rutgers University freshman Tyler Clementi committed suicide after being harassed online by another college student. The legislation (HR 1048) mandated that universities who receive federal funds must implement a policy that prohibits harassment

of students based on race, color, national origin, sex, disability, sexual orientation, gender identity, or religion. Although the bill was referred to committee in 2011, it never made it to the House floor.

To date, most legal challenges have resulted when school districts have attempted to sanction students for assaultive speech aimed at teachers and administrators. In those cases, courts are less likely to consider the conduct cyberbullying or harassment and often uphold the students' free speech rights to maintain their websites or make their online postings.

REPLY HAZY, TRY AGAIN: PREDICTING THE FUTURE OF LIABILITY

As Internet communication and social networking proliferate as a part of our daily lives, so too will the legal challenges resulting from electronic communication and online conduct. Most courts are struggling to decide whether to apply traditional laws to new forms of communication or wait for lawmakers to create new laws addressing social media and other technology. In general, the most successful prosecutions have occurred using traditional laws that target conduct instead of expression, but that hasn't stopped legislatures from attempting to craft bills that address sexting, cyberbulling, and other activities that many people view as undesirable. Particularly when the harms involve children, members of the public initially seem more willing to curtail constitutional free speech rights in the name of protecting minors. However, the calculus grows more complicated when restrictions target consenting adults or create sweeping prohibitions on all forms of online communication.

Additionally, the relationship between employers and employees appears to be changing along with notions of what a person can do in his or her "private life." One only needs to open the newspaper to unearth examples of employees—teachers, in particular—who have been reprimanded as a result of electronic communication or social media usage, suggesting Jeff Quon's situation is no longer that unique. The law is murky—at best—with regard to the action employers can and cannot take, and a number of factors complicate the inquiry. Should it matter whether the employer issued the communication device? What about if the employee used a personal device while at the employer's place of business? Does it matter if it was after hours? Should some employees—teachers, for example—be held to a higher standard because they are viewed as role models and interact with children? One thing is clear: Judges and lawmakers face an uphill battle addressing these important issues.

Whether and how to regulate electronic communication and social media use in the workplace and schools also raises a number of constitutional issues,

including the First Amendment. As Congress' history of regulation in the area of sexually explicit speech on the Internet suggests, legislation will likely result in significant scrutiny from the courts and must be drafted with the utmost care to be found constitutional. Based on the Court's opinion in *Reno*, it seems unlikely the justices will be willing to constrain speech online any more than they would offline.

What is clear is that social media policies dealing with sexually explicit communication or bullying/harassment must be tightly worded to clearly define the types of conduct to be regulated. The policies should differentiate between conduct involving minors and conduct involving adults given that courts would be more likely—though not guaranteed—to support incidental restrictions on speech aimed at protecting minors. Policies aimed at adults should clearly address professional versus personal conduct, including appropriate use of employer-provided communication devices. Enforcement of these types of policies should be done uniformly and with a high level of documentation. When possible, action should be taken under existing laws aimed to curtail undesirable conduct—stalking, harassment, and sexual misconduct statutes—that have already withstood constitutional scrutiny.

Not only must Congress and employers worry about outcomes in the court of law, they also must be concerned with an even more unpredictable jury: the court of public opinion. As news stories surface of employers spying on employees and inappropriately using social media to screen applicants, employers must be cautious about the effects of the publicity on the next generation of employees and consumers. Policies made by executives who came of age in the pre-Internet era are likely to strike prospective Millennial generation employees as antiquated and overbearing.

Further, the gaps in law surrounding social media and its uses suggest it is incumbent upon sites like Facebook, Flickr, and Twitter to set their own standards of conduct. Many of these sites have attempted to do so through Terms of Service and Privacy Policy agreements. But, as many users know, the language in those agreements is often obscure and tedious for the non-legal mind. Some improvements have been made, including Facebook's Community Standards, which tries to spell out in lay terms what kind of conduct will be permitted on the social media site. The challenge for all of these sites is not only to lay out what is impermissible in concrete enough terms that users can understand but to also do so in a manner that creates a policy that is adaptable as the technology and its uses change.

This challenge is not a particularly novel one. The same task was expected of CompuServe and Prodigy when the Internet was in its youth. In fact, the example serves to remind us that multiple paths are possible. Prodigy, for example, set out to become the family friendly portal—policing its site for offensive content to encourage parents to allow their children to use its

services. Today, the law specifically allows social media sites the flexibility to choose whether to filter out "offensive" content—sexually explicit photos or profanity-laden posts—without fear of legal retribution by the posters. Google+ might choose to carve out a niche by following the trail Prodigy attempted to blaze in the 1990s, for example. YouTube could create family specific channels, where parents could allow their children to watch without fear of what linked videos may appear.

It is the users themselves, however, who wield the most influential card in the deck. Public outcry has caused a number of businesses to rethink certain policies or practices, and social media companies are not immune to the court of public opinion. In this case, users truly vote with their clicks of the mouse—choosing to accept Terms of Service and Privacy Policy language when they log in. Evidence suggests that social media sites are listening—at least when the outrage is large enough—and making changes with regard to their services in some instances.

FREQUENTLY ASKED QUESTIONS

1. Can I get in trouble for posting sexually explicit photographs on a social media site?

Facebook—like most social media sites—expressly prohibits the sharing of content it labels "pornographic." In its Community Standards section, you will find language that suggests users can have their content removed or be blocked from using the service if they violate the standards, which include posting pornographic content and violating copyright terms, among other things. Further, because Facebook is not a government entity, the First Amendment will not protect your right to post content to the site—pornographic or otherwise. The law does not require Facebook to allow you to use its site to post any or all of the content you wish. In addition, any sexually explicit content that rises to the level of obscenity, as defined by state law, could be regulated because obscene speech falls outside the scope of First Amendment protection.

2. Does the First Amendment protect use of foul language on Twitter?

Like Facebook, Twitter also need not follow the First Amendment. Therefore, it has the legal right to make rules about permissible content on its site. Interestingly, although Twitter's Rules make mention of a number of restricted areas, including threats, copyright, trademark, and pornography, they make no mention of profane language—suggesting that your taste in language is for you to decide.

3. Can my employer examine my mobile device or email for indecent or obscene materials?

In light of the *Quon* case, it would seem that employers have the right to examine employer-issued devices, including cell phones and laptops—particularly if they are doing so with probable cause or in accordance with a standard procedure. A smart employee should think twice about using an employer-issued device to engage in any conduct that would violate the employer's rules. Although it might seem extreme, employees would be wise to act as though they have no right to privacy with regard to employer-provided devices, email, and landline phone service. Similarly, an employer would be wise to establish rules and regulations for acceptable use of technology both at, and away from, the workplace to inform their employees as to what is permissible.

4. If a user makes an offensive post about me or tags me in an inappropriate photograph on Facebook, can I demand that the post or photograph be removed?

Under Section 230 of the Communications Decency Act, you are unlikely to be able to demand that Facebook remove unwanted content about you. However, you may well have a cause of action against the specific user who posted the content—if it defamatory or violated your privacy, for example. Even if you succeed in getting the content removed from one site, there is no guarantee that it has not been archived or may re-appear on another site. The soundest course of action is often simply to ask the poster to remove the offending content.

5. What kinds of social media activities are most likely to lead to criminal charges?

Users of social media sites can face criminal charges for their expression, particularly if the speech is not protected by the First Amendment. In most states, this means that speech that amounts to a true threat, fighting words, obscenity, or false advertising can likely be punished if there are applicable criminal sanctions in place. Further, users in states that have criminal defamation statutes may find themselves in legal trouble if they post defamatory statements about others using their social media accounts. Although most of these activities are unlikely to constitute felonies that carry lengthy prison terms, it is important to be cautious when posting these types of speech.

NOTES

1   Nearly one quarter of employees surveyed reported using instant-messaging tools at work to share jokes, gossip, rumors, and disparaging remarks while 10 percent reported engaging in sexual, romantic, or pornographic chat using IM tools in the workplace, according to a 2006 survey. AMA/ePolicy Institute, 2006 Workplace E-Mail, Instant Messaging and Blogging Survey, http://www.epolicyinstitute.com/survey.asp.
2   City of Ontario v. Quon, 560 U.S. ___ (2010).
3   The Science Behind Pornography Addiction: Hearing Before the Subcommittee on Science, Technology and Space of the S. Comm. on Commerce, 108th Cong. (2004) (statement of Mary Anne Layden, co-director of the Sexual Trauma and Psychopathology Program at the University of Pennsylvania's Center for Cognitive Therapy).
4   See Communications Decency Act of 1996, 47 U.S.C. §223 (1997).
5   354 U.S. 476 (1957).
6   Id. at 481.
7   Id. at 485 (quoting Chaplinsky v. State of New Hampshire, 315 U.S. 568, 571–572 (1942)).
8   Jacobellis v. Ohio, 378 U.S. 184, 197 (1964) (Stewart, J., concurring).
9   See, e.g., Jacobellis, 378 U.S. at 184; Memoirs v. Massachusetts, 383 U.S. 413 (1966); Interstate Circuit v. Dallas, 390 U.S. 676 (1968).
10 413 U.S. 15 (1973).
11 Id.
12 438 U.S. 726 (1978).
13 Id. at 748–749.
14 Id. at 732 (quoting 56 F. C. C. 2d, at 98).
15 P.L. No. 104-104, 110 Stat. 56 (1996).
16 For more information on the Telecommunications Act of 1996, see Telecommunications Act of 1996, http://transition.fcc.gov/telecom.html.
17 47 U.S.C. §223(1)(a).
18 929 F. Supp. 824 (E.D. Pa. 1996).
19 Reno v. ACLU, 521 U.S. 844 (1997).
20 The lawsuit specifically challenged §223(a)(1)(B), which criminalizes the "knowing" transmission of "obscene or indecent" messages to any recipient under 18 years of age and §223(d) prohibits the "knowin[g]" sending or displaying to a person under 18 of any message "that, in context, depicts or describes, in terms patently offensive as measured by contemporary community standards, sexual or excretory activities or organs."
21 Reno, 521 U.S. at 868–869.
22 Id.
23 Sable Communications of Cal., Inc. v. FCC, 492 U.S. 115 (1989).
24 Id. at 128.
25 Id.
26 Red Lion Broadcasting v. FCC, 397 U.S. 367 (1969).
27 Reno, 581 U.S. at 866–867.
28 Id.
29 Id.

30   Id.

31   Pub. L. No. 105-277, 112 Stat. 2681-736 (1998).

32   Child Online Protection Act, 47 U.S. §231.

33   47 U.S. §231(a)(1). "Whoever knowingly and with knowledge of the character of the material, in interstate or foreign commerce by means of the World Wide Web, makes any communication for commercial purposes that is available to any minor and that includes any material that is harmful to minors shall be fined not more than $50,000, imprisoned not more than 6 months, or both."

34   Id.

35   458 U.S. 747 (1982).

36   American Civil Liberties Union v. Reno, 31 F. Supp. 2d 473 (E.D. Pa. 1999).

37   American Civil Liberties Union v. Reno, 217 F.3d 162 (3d. Cir. 2000).

38   Ashcroft v. American Civil Liberties Union, 535 U.S. 564 (2002).

39   American Civil Liberties Union v. Ashcroft, 322 F.3d 240 (3d. Cir. 2003).

40   Ashcroft v. American Civil Liberties Union, 542 U.S. 656 (2004).

41   American Civil Liberties Union v. Mukasey, 534 F.3d 181 (3d. Cir. 2008).

42   U.S. v. American Library Ass'n, Inc., 539 U.S. 194 (2003).

43   Deleting Online Predators Act of 2006, H.R. 5319.

44   Senate Bill 132 / S.L. 2008-218 (signed in law August 16, 2008).

45   Doe v. Jindal, 2012 U.S. Dist. LEXIS 19841 (M.D. La. 2012).

46   Doe v. Nebraska, 734 F. Supp. 2d 882 (D. Neb. 2010).

47   Helen A.S. Popkin, Is It Illegal to Record and Post Noisy Neighbors Having Sex?, MSNBC.com, May 19, 2012.

48   Kim Zetter, Judge Acquits Lori Drew in Cyberbullying Case, Overrules Jury, Wired.com, July 2, 2009.

49   Tinker v. Des Moines Indep. Sch. Dist., 393 U.S. 503, 506 (1969).

Social Media Use in Courtrooms

Cathy Packer

University of North Carolina at Chapel Hill
School of Journalism and Mass Communication

ABSTRACT

News reporters want to blog and tweet from courtrooms. Jurors are blogging and tweeting about cases and searching the Internet for information about cases they sit on, including the applicable laws and the parties involved. This chapter examines how the rules governing the use of cameras in the courtroom apply to computers and smartphones; how courts are handling juror issues; the implications of federal, state, and local rules on courtroom technology use; and what rights journalists have to use social media to cover trials.

The recent explosion of social media use, combined with the pro-liferation of smartphones, tablets, and other small computers, is present-ing new challenges to state and federal court judges whose duty it is to ensure the fairness of court proceedings. Americans now go everywhere with phones in hand, including to court, and they are accustomed to constantly communicating with family, friends, and colleagues. Therefore, courts must grapple with issues such as whether reporters should be permitted to blog or tweet news and commentary from the courtroom and whether a juror—or even an attorney or a judge—who comments about a case on her Facebook page or uses Google to conduct a bit of independent research has deprived a defendant of a fair trial.

This chapter outlines the major case precedents on access to courtrooms and then surveys the current state of the law on reporters' use of social media

in federal and state courts, the law on juror use of social media, and the problems that arise when judges and attorneys use social media.

ACCESS TO COURTROOMS

Some of the strongest First Amendment opinions ever written by the U.S. Supreme Court established the rights of journalists and citizens to attend judicial proceedings and to report on those proceedings. Most famously, Chief Justice Warren E. Burger wrote for the Court in *Richmond Newspapers Inc. v. Virginia* (1980):

> We hold that the right to attend criminal trials is implicit in the guarantees of the First Amendment; without the freedom to attend such trials, which people have exercised for centuries, important aspects of freedom of speech and "of the press could be eviscerated."[1]

The Court held that criminal trials in state and federal courts are presumptively open, and, in subsequent cases, the Supreme Court or lower courts ruled that most criminal and civil judicial proceedings could be closed only upon the showing of a compelling government interest and that any closure had to be "narrowly tailored to serve that interest."[2] Four years earlier, in *Nebraska Press Association v. Stuart*, the Supreme Court had ruled that prior restraints on media coverage of judicial proceedings are allowed only as a last resort to ensure the fair trial guaranteed to criminal defendants by the Sixth Amendment.[3]

In those cases, the Supreme Court clearly articulated how courtroom access serves the public interest. The Court said open courts promote confidence in the fair administration of justice and have a "significant community therapeutic value . . . providing an outlet for community concern, hostility, and emotion."[4] Access to courtrooms also serves as a check on government power, helping to ensure that defendants receive fair trials.[5] The Court observed that the public receives most of its information about the judicial process from reporters. The media "contribute to public understanding of the rule of law and to comprehension of the functioning of the entire criminal justice system," the Court said.[6]

Today journalists have the right to attend trials and most other judicial proceedings and to report on what they see and hear in courtrooms. There are only a few exceptions, including grand jury proceedings, some juvenile proceedings, and involuntary commitment and adoption proceedings. However, the Supreme Court has had very little to say about what technology journalists can use in courtrooms. In the absence of guidance from

the Supreme Court, the *Richmond Newspapers* decision recognizing a right of access to criminal trials has been interpreted by lower courts as guaranteeing a right to bring to court only the most rudimentary and unobtrusive newsgathering tools—a notebook or sketchbook, pencil or pen. Several federal courts have ruled explicitly that the media's First Amendment right to attend criminal trials does not include a right to record or televise those trials.[7]

Television was once a new technology that raised difficult questions about its use in courtrooms. In the 1930s, when television was new, the Supreme Court began hearing cases in which criminal defendants claimed to have been denied their Sixth Amendment rights to a fair trial because the presence of television reporters and their equipment in the courtroom caused physical and psychological disruptions.[8] In several high-profile cases, the Court granted the defendants new trials.[9] In those cases, the Court decried courtrooms with multiple, large cameras; microphones on the judge's bench and aimed at the jury box and counsel tables; and cables snaking across the floor. All of that deprived criminal defendants of "that judicial serenity and calm to which [they are] entitled."[10]

By the mid-1970s, only two states allowed cameras in their courtrooms, and there were no cameras in federal courts. However, communication technology continued to change, with bulky television cameras being replaced by smaller, less obtrusive cameras. Consequently, the rules governing the use of communication technology in courtrooms changed, too. In *Chandler v. Florida* (1981), the Court ruled that the presence of cameras in courtrooms does not automatically violate criminal defendants' Sixth Amendment rights to a trial by an impartial jury and that states were free to experiment with allowing cameras in court.[11] Today, all states allow cameras in at least some of their courtrooms. The federal courts have been more resistant, and currently cameras are allowed only in two federal circuits and in some federal district courts on an experimental basis.

Federal and state courts are just beginning to figure out how, if at all, these legal rules apply to reporters and others who want to use smartphones, tablets, and laptop computers to report on courtroom proceedings. The Reporters Committee on Freedom of the Press reported in 2011: "Tweeting from the courtroom is *de rigueur* nowadays among courts reporters. It's a fast growing trend, especially in competitive markets."[12] In the 2012 trial of Dr. Conrad Murray concerning the death of Michael Jackson, for example, tweeting was permitted in court, and one local news station sent out nearly 1,900 tweets to 3,000 followers.[13] However, the Reporters Committee article noted that the rules governing tweeting and blogging in court vary from court to court and even from trial to trial.

Jurors' use of smartphones, computers, and the Internet creates a some-what different legal problem. The problem is that jurors are supposed to arrive at a verdict based solely on the evidence presented in court—not based on a Google search performed on a smartphone or a Facebook discussion. Jurors' independent research or communication related to a case can result in a defendant being denied his Sixth Amendment right to trial by an impartial jury and result in a mistrial—what some call a "Google mistrial"[14] or a "digital misadventure."[15] This has put pressure on judges to find a way to control jurors' use of smartphones and other devices that link them to the Internet.

When judges and attorneys use social media to communicate about cases, they also risk interfering with the fair administration of justice. They risk running afoul of their professional codes of ethics, too.

In 1965, the Supreme Court predicted that "[t]he ever-advancing tech-niques of public communication and the adjustment of the public to its presence may bring about a change in the effect of telecasting upon the fairness of criminal trials."[16] How judges are dealing with the very latest techniques of public communication is the subject of the subsequent sections of this chapter.

SOCIAL MEDIA IN FEDERAL COURTS

In 2009, a federal court judge for the first time specifically granted permission for a journalist to use a smartphone to report on a trial from the courtroom.[17] The order, which enabled a *Wichita* (Kan.) *Eagle* reporter to tweet updates on a racketeering trial, was based on Federal Rule of Criminal Procedure 57(b). That rule says a judge may regulate his courtroom in any manner consistent with federal law and judicial rules, giving federal judges broad discretion to regulate courtroom affairs. The judge in this case reasoned that allowing reporters to tweet about the case would open the judicial process to the public, which would lead to greater public understanding of the judicial process.[18]

That same year, another U.S. district court judge denied a request from a reporter for the *Columbus* (Ga.) *Ledger-Enquirer* to be allowed to use a smartphone to tweet during a criminal trial.[19] The judge ruled that Rule 53 of the Federal Rules of Criminal Procedure—the rule that bans photog-raphy and broadcasting in most federal courtrooms—also prohibits tweeting from the courtroom.[20]

As these two cases suggest, federal judges differ in their views on whether reporters should be allowed to use smartphones, tablets, or other small computers in federal court. Overall, however, most federal courts remain opposed to allowing social media—or any form of photography or audio recording—in the courtroom, especially in criminal courts. Federal courts

often ban reporters and other spectators from bringing phones, tablets, or other small computers into their courthouses, not just into their court-rooms.[21] However, there are exceptions. One federal judge banned the use of computers and cell phones in the courtroom but allowed reporters to step outside the courtroom to tweet or blog in the hallway.[22] Another judge allowed a reporter covering a fraud trial to tweet from the back of the courtroom where her typing would not be distracting.[23]

The conflicting federal rules and practices raise several intriguing ques-tions. What are the rules that currently govern reporters' use of smartphones, tablets, and other small computers in federal courtrooms? Do the use of smartphones, tablets, and other small computers in courtrooms serve the values the U.S. Supreme Court said it was protecting when it granted media and public access to courtrooms? Or do these new technologies create physical and psychological disruptions similar to those that have been the bases for banning cameras from courtrooms for decades? First, it is helpful to review the federal rules governing this topic.

Federal Criminal Courts and Rule 53

Rule 53 has kept most cameras, smartphones, tablets, and other small computers out of the hands of reporters in federal criminal courtrooms. Rule 53 says in part, "[T]he court must not permit the taking of photographs in the courtroom during judicial proceedings or the broadcasting of judicial proceedings from the courtroom." The judge who did not allow a reporter to tweet in a U.S. district court in Georgia used a dictionary definition of broadcasting to determine that tweeting was a form of broadcasting. The judge observed that the definition of broadcasting "includes 'casting or scattering in all directions' and 'the act of making widely known.' . . . It cannot be reasonably disputed that 'twittering,' as previously described, would result in casting to the general public and thus making widely known the trial proceedings."[24]

The district court judge also ruled that, as previously established by federal courts, Rule 53 did not violate the media's First Amendment right of access to attend criminal trials. He explained:

> The press certainly has a right of access to observe criminal trials,
> just as members of the public have the right to attend criminal trials.
> In this case, the press will be able to attend, listen and report on the
> proceedings. No restriction is being placed upon their legitimate
> right of access to the proceedings.[25]

Tweeting, however, was out of the question.

The Federal Rules of Criminal Procedure are written by the Judicial Conference of the United States. The Judicial Conference is a body of federal court judges responsible for making policy regarding the administration of the federal courts. Rule 53 was enacted in 1946. It was rewritten in 2002 to remove a reference to "radio" but leave the word "broadcasting." The Judicial Conference's Advisory Committee on Rules of Criminal Procedure said it viewed the change as "one that accords with judicial interpretation applying the current rule to other forms of broadcasting and functionally equivalent means."[26] This suggests the question for the federal judges is whether tweeting or blogging are "functionally equivalent" to broadcasting. In practice, it means judges have broad discretion over how or whether to regulate the use of new media technologies in their courtrooms.

Federal Civil Courts

Reporters and the public have a strong right of access to federal civil courts, just as they do to criminal courts. Furthermore, there is no federal civil court equivalent to Rule 53 to bar the broadcasting of civil proceedings. In practice, camera access to federal civil courts remains very limited, although there is a steadily increasing number of reports of federal judges allowing reporters to tweet and blog during civil court proceedings.

Since 1996, Judicial Conference policy has been to allow circuit courts to determine when cameras are permitted in their civil courtrooms. As a result, cameras are allowed during oral arguments in the U.S. Courts of Appeals for the Second and Ninth Circuits. The Conference also has conducted several experiments with cameras in courtrooms. In 2011, for example, the Judicial Conference began a three-year project to evaluate the effects of cameras on civil trials in 14 federal districts.[27] However, the project allows video recordings, which will be posted online, to be made only by the court, not by any other party.

While these forays into televising court proceedings dealt only with cameras—not with smartphones, tablets, or other small computers—they do suggest that federal courts' interest in allowing communication technologies to be used in their courtrooms is growing.

Local Federal Court Rules and Their Application

The Judicial Conference has left it to individual courts to decide how to implement the Conference's rules on technology in the courtroom. Each federal court posts its local rules online,[28] and those rules vary in ways that are both interesting and significant. For example, the rule adopted by the U.S. District Court for the Middle District of North Carolina says,

"Photographic, recording or transmitting devices are prohibited in all court-houses. Prohibited devices include, but are not limited to, laptop computers, wireless microphones, recorders, cameras, 2-way radios, push to talk cellphones and cellphones with cameras. (Exceptions may be made by the Court or its designee.)"[29] In that district, lawyers need special permission—a laptop authorization card—to bring a computer into the courthouse.[30]

The U.S. District Court for the Middle District of Alabama has a somewhat more lenient local rule that says cell phones and laptop computers "without photographic, video or audio recording capabilities" may be possessed in the courtroom by members of the press, court personnel, and attorneys. Laptop computers can be used in the courtroom, but cell phones must be turned off. Cell phones can be used outside the courtroom.[31]

The U.S. District Court for the District of Connecticut has a local rule on laptops and another on cell phones, but both speak only to whether phones and laptops can be brought into the courthouse—not whether they can be used in court.[32] The laptop rule is that laptops are prohibited in the courthouse except for use by attorneys, court personnel, and "[o]ther individuals permitted by the Court." The cell phone policy is similar, allowing attorneys, police, jurors, and court personnel—and "[o]ther individuals permitted by the Court"—to bring cell phones into the courthouse. Other people have their cell phones collected by the U.S. Marshals Service as they enter the courthouse.

Clearly some courts are resistant to the mere presence of smartphones and computers in the courthouse. Other courts tolerate the presence of the devices in the courtroom but not their use. And there is growing anecdotal evidence that some courts are allowing them to be used. Federal court judges who view blogging and tweeting as forms of broadcasting logically will be more resistant to allowing smartphones and laptops to be used in the courtroom. Judges who see the newer technologies as smaller and quieter than television cameras, and thus less physically and psychologically disruptive, might allow their use while continuing to ban traditional broadcasting of court proceedings. However, it is difficult for an outside observer to assess how federal court rules actually are applied and why or how often reporters are allowed to tweet and blog from court. Judges' decisions on these matters most often do not result in written court opinions. Instead the evidence is largely anecdotal and based on news reports.

One recent federal court case that illustrates the confusion in the federal courts created by the new communication technologies involved the U.S. district court trial on the challenge to Proposition 8, California's constitutional amendment outlawing same-sex marriages in the state. In 2010, the U.S. Supreme Court ruled that the district court could not allow the broadcasting of the courtroom proceedings as part of a pilot project because the court had failed to give proper public notice and opportunity for comment on the pilot program.[33] Meanwhile, the proceedings were covered live by hundreds of news companies using Twitter, Facebook, and blogs from the courtroom gallery.[34] The Supreme Court did not comment on that.

Congress on Access to Federal Courts

Beginning in 2005, members of the U.S. Congress repeatedly have introduced bills that would let federal court judges decide whether to allow cameras and other electronic media in their courtrooms. The law would invalidate federal Rule 53, the rule that has kept cameras out of most federal criminal courtrooms. However, while the Senate and House judiciary committees both have passed versions of these "Sunshine in the Courtroom" bills, the bills never have come up for a vote of the full House or Senate.

Two recent bills—one in the House and one in the Senate—are both called the Sunshine in the Courtroom Act of 2011. The name of the proposed legislation is a reference to former U.S. Supreme Court Justice Louis Brandeis' statement that "sunlight is said to be the best of disinfectants."[35] The bills say, in part, that a presiding federal court judge "may, at the discretion of that judge, permit the photographing, electronic recording, broadcasting, or televising to the public of any court proceeding over which that judge presides."[36] The bills also provide that some facets of judicial proceedings, such as the faces of jurors, cannot be photographed.

Is it not clear what effect, if any, such a law would have on activities such as blogging and tweeting from the courtroom. However, it is interesting to note that during a 2007 House Judiciary Committee hearing on one of the Sunshine in the Courtroom bills, a U.S. attorney from Oklahoma expressed concern that "broadcasts now in the modern world do not just include major networks or Court TV or C-SPAN, but also include, of course, bloggers and all kinds of Web sites and all kinds of unique other delivery mechanisms."[37] Whether tweeting and other social networking posts are, in fact, forms of broadcasting is a question that might have to be addressed by Congress as well as by the courts.

SOCIAL MEDIA IN STATE COURTS

Since the U.S. Supreme Court paved the way for the opening of courtroom doors to cameras and recordings devices in 1981, each state has adopted its own rules governing cameras in courtrooms. Some states allow cameras only in their appellate courts, some allow cameras only with the consent of the parties involved in the judicial proceeding, most limit the number of cameras allowed in the courtroom at one time, and most allow broad judicial

discretion. A few states have updated their rules to clarify whether the use of smartphones and laptop computers is permitted, but most have not.[38] Therefore, like their federal counterparts, state judges have little guidance when deciding whether to allow new technologies to be used in their courtrooms. A complete list of the state court rules on the use of television cameras, still cameras, audio-recording devices and, in some cases, smartphones and laptop computers, is available on the website of the Radio Television Digital News Association.[39] Also, the Reporters Committee on Freedom of the Press has a website that indicates most states have no rules regarding social media in courtrooms.[40] But the lack of rules does not mean reporters and others will not be allowed to tweet or blog from court. It means those activities are allowed at the discretion of the presiding judge.

A 2011 study of how Wisconsin judges are applying their camera-in-the-courtroom guidelines to online media observed that some of the debate in state courts across the nation focuses not on what recording devices should be allowed in the courtroom but on who should be allowed to use them.[41] For example, in 2010 an independent blogger was not allowed to photograph and audio record a public divorce proceeding in an Ohio courtroom because the judge determined the blogger was not a member of the media—unlike Channel 5 News, the judge said. The blogger said her work would be published on the Internet, but the judge was not persuaded.[42]

Another issue that has arisen in state courts is how rules that limit the number of cameras or recording devices that can be used in a courtroom at one time apply when dozens of people want to use their smartphones or laptops at the same time. For example, in 2010 a Florida judge banned blogging in the courtroom during a murder trial. He first explained that Florida's 1979 cameras-in-the-courtroom rule did not address laptop communication. After his order was quickly reversed by an appeals court, the judge said a photographer for one news outlet and a blogger for another could be in the courtroom at the same time but they could not use their equipment—a camera and a laptop computer—at the same time. A video camera already was in the courtroom, and only two devices were allowed.[43]

The author of the Wisconsin study also noted that most television stations pool their video feeds, so restrictions on the numbers of cameras allowed in a courtroom are not problematic for them. However, the author expressed concern that "[a] blogger who simply wishes to record on a handheld device . . . may lack the tools and know-how to contribute to or partake from the established media pool."[44]

The study of the Wisconsin courts also found that judges were most concerned that nothing disrupted the court proceedings—including the sound of typing on a laptop.[45] For example, the judge presiding over the 2012 trial of the man accused of killing the family of singer/actress Jennifer

Hudson told reporters they could not tweet or post on Facebook from inside the courtroom. According to a court spokesman, the judge "didn't want constant typing on cell phones to distract jurors and other courtroom participants."[46]

Other judges seem to think the use of new technology is not distracting. For example, a U.S. district court judge in Kansas has been quoted as saying that he did not "see any difference between this and a journalist sitting there taking notes."[47] And scholars commonly note that typing on a smartphone or laptop computer is less distracting that having reporters repeatedly leaving the courtroom to post the news.

In at least one case, a reporter's tweet from a courtroom has resulted in a mistrial. In a 2012 case in Kansas, a judge ordered a mistrial in a murder case after a reporter tweeted a courtroom photo that included the profile of a juror. That photo violated a Kansas Supreme Court rule that prohibited the photographing of individual jurors—a common rule in state courts. The publisher of the *Topeka Capital-Journal* apologized for his reporter's tweet, and the murder trial was to be rescheduled.[48]

Prior Restraints

In a couple of state court cases involving blogging and tweeting reporters, the legal issue was not access to courtrooms but prior restraint on media coverage of judicial proceedings. Prior restraints on the media are considered by the U.S. Supreme Court to be "the most serious and least tolerable infringement on First Amendment Rights"[49] and thus rarely are allowed to be used to control media coverage of judicial proceedings.

In early 2012, a Texas trial court judge ordered the media covering a capital murder trial not to report on any court proceedings that occurred in open court when the jury was not present. The court order, which listed 19 rules to be followed, led the newspaper to remove a number of blog posts and tweets that already had been published. Those blog posts and tweets reported on testimony given outside the jury's presence, the judge's ruling on motions from the prosecution and defense, and an informal admonishment by the judge of two attorneys in the case. The order said the restrictions were put in place "to ensure due and proper administration of justice."[50] The order was quickly revised on appeal to allow the media to report everything that happened in open court regardless of whether the jury was present. The posts that had been removed then were republished.[51]

In 2010, a *Pittsburgh Press-Gazette* reporter posted more than 1,000 tweets while covering a criminal case involving a former state representative and several other state employees. She tweeted about the atmosphere in the courtroom and witness testimony, among other topics.[52] The criminal

defendants had moved to ban that reporter and others in the courtroom from "using any and all social networking systems to electronically publish testimony during trial." The defendants argued that tweeting violated a state judicial rule that prohibited "advanced communication technology" transmissions from the courtroom and would have informed sequestered witnesses about events in the courtroom. The court denied the motion, in part because it would have constituted an unconstitutional prior restraint on the media. The court did not address the meaning of the state judicial rule in question.[53]

JURORS AND THEIR DIGITAL MISADVENTURES

Googling and tweeting jurors have received much more attention—and criticism—than tweeting courtroom news reporters. The scholarly and popular media contain many reports of jurors conducting their own research or tweeting or posting messages on Facebook about the cases they are deciding. Such activities can result in the dismissal of a juror or a mistrial.[54]

For example, in April 2012, the jury foreman in a second-degree murder trial in California used Wikipedia and nolo.com to research the difference between second-degree murder and manslaughter. A deputy sheriff cleaning the jury room at the end of the trial found printouts from those websites and reported his findings to the judge. The judge said the jury foreman disobeyed instructions not to conduct independent research. Declaring a mistrial, the judge said, "We tell jurors time and time again not to go to the internet and this case is a textbook example of why. The internet is a morass of misinformation. And it is wrong."[55]

In addition to sometimes being wrong, information jurors find on their own can be incomplete or outdated. It also might be information that has been purposely excluded from a case, such a record of a criminal defendant's prior convictions.[56]

Judges declare mistrials when they determine that the trial was not fair. In the American criminal justice system, defendants' right to a fair trial is firmly rooted in their Sixth Amendment right to a trial by an impartial jury. An impartial jury is one that reaches a verdict based solely on the evidence presented in court, not on evidence jurors gather from other jurors or from outside the courtroom. In both criminal and civil cases, each piece of evidence and all testimony are evaluated by the parties to the case. Only evidence that meets the standards established by the rules of evidence is presented to the jury.[57] Sometimes the evidence presented to the jury is unclear or incomplete. Even in those cases, jurors are instructed to decide the case based only on the evidence presented. They can make reasonable inferences, but they are not allowed to do research.

Jurors' use of social media and other Internet services can jeopardize a fair trial when a juror conducts independent research either before being selected for a jury or during a trial. When a judge discovers a juror has engaged in such research, the judge decides whether the activity was prejudicial. When juror research is directly related to an issue of fact in a trial, is shared with other jurors, and causes a jury to vote differently than it would have without the information, a mistrial is likely.[58] For example, the Oklahoma Court of Appeals ruled that a mistrial was warranted in a medical negligence case in which a juror conducted Internet and other research. The juror used the Internet to research a medical procedure, medications taken by the plaintiff, and a court case similar to the one being tried. The juror, who was a nurse, said she also consulted nursing care plans she possessed. The juror said she communicated some but not all of that information to the other jurors.[59] The court affirmed the decision to order a mistrial because, it said, "there is no doubt" that the information about the similar court case "had a direct bearing upon a key issue in plaintiffs' theory and proof of negligence."[60]

The case law clearly suggests that not all juror research is prejudicial, however. It generally is not prejudicial if the research is not shared with the other jurors.[61] For example, in a 2002 civil case in a California state court, a juror used the Internet to research the meaning of the word "negligence." The state appeals court ruled that research was not prejudicial. The court found no evidence that the juror's research either confused the jury as a whole or prejudiced the jury in favor of one party or the other.[62]

Problems also arise when jurors use social media to share information and opinions about cases on which they are serving with other jurors, parties to the case, or others. For example, in 2011, a Texas juror tried to "friend" the defendant in the civil car-accident case on which he was serving, and he discussed the case on his Facebook page. The defendant in the case reported the friend request to her lawyer. As a result, the juror was dismissed from the jury, and the trial continued with 11 jurors. The juror was charged with and pleaded guilty to four counts of contempt of court, for which he was sentenced to two days of community service. The juror's lawyer said:

> It is a reflection of the times. Most everyone has smartphones now. They can hop on at almost anytime. And there's a lot of down time in jury duty, so what most people do is hop on their phone. But the rules are there for a reason.[63]

The state of Texas recently had added new rules barring jurors from discussing cases on social networking sites.[64]

There is some disagreement about how many jurors are conducting online research about cases or using social media to communicate about

cases. In 2011, the Federal Judicial Center surveyed federal district court judges about their experiences with jurors using social media during trials and deliberations.[65] Of the 508 judges who responded to the survey, only 30 judges—6 percent—reported having detected jurors using social media. Most of those judges had detected social media use only once or twice. According to the survey results, nine judges who learned of jurors using social media removed the juror from the jury, eight cautioned but did not remove the juror, and four declared mistrials. The vast majority of the judges surveyed said they had taken some precautionary steps to ensure that jurors did not use social media in their courtrooms. Those steps included using social media jury instructions, confiscating phones and other electronic devices, reminding jurors repeatedly throughout the trial not to use social media, and requiring jurors to sign a written pledge agreeing to refrain from social media use while serving on the jury.

In contrast to the 2011 Federal Judicial Center survey results, others have observed that one can search online and find countless tweets posted by jurors. Almost all of them are inconsequential observations or complaints like "There was a run on salads and yogurt at the cafeteria. I ended up with a dry chicken sandwich. #juryduty" or "Day 4. Hour 5. Captain's Log: We sat through a heartbreaking testimony by a 9 year old. It is SO real on these streets. I'm spent. #JuryDuty" or "I don't know why I'm always so disappointed in courtrooms #JuryDuty is just not like TV."[66] Judges generally have found that a juror who posts online comments about a case like these but does not receive information about the case from others does not prejudice the trial.[67]

Long before the Internet, judges had to control juror use of newspapers, television, and radio to ensure jurors did not read, view, or hear about the case they were charged with deciding. They also worked to discourage jurors from talking about their cases with each other before deliberations began or with other people before the trial was concluded. Jury instructions have been the most common methods of dealing with these problems. Jury instructions are the oral instructions a judge gives to members of the jury at any point during the trial but most commonly at the beginning of the trial and at the beginning of deliberations.

Since 2009, scholars have been calling for judges to update their jury instructions to specifically address juror use of computers for Internet research and communication through social media sites such as Twitter and Facebook. They encourage judges to deal with today's jurors by writing instructions that specify which technologies jurors are prohibited from using and when. Most courts allow jurors to bring their mobile devices to court for use during breaks, and today's jurors, in their lives outside court, are

accustomed to immediately researching the answer to any question that comes to mind and to sharing their thoughts online throughout the day.

In 2010, a federal Judicial Conference committee issued a memorandum encouraging federal district court judges to consider using a new set of jury instructions to help prevent the improper use of cell phones and Internet during trials. The memorandum said, "The Committee believes that more explicit mention in jury instructions of the various methods and modes of electronic communication and research would help jurors better understand and adhere to the scope of the prohibition against the use of these devices."[68] The memorandum suggested one set of instructions before a trial and another at the close of the case. It also suggested making specific reference to cell phones, smartphones, and instant messaging services, for example, and to specific web services such as Twitter, Facebook, and YouTube. The memorandum said the specific references to technologies and web services were needed because some jurors did not understand that those were forms of communication.

Two-thirds of the states also have rewritten their jury instructions to specifically restrict Internet research.[69] Some states have dealt with the Googling and tweeting jurors by forbidding jurors from bringing their cell phones to court.[70]

SOCIAL MEDIA USE BY JUDGES AND ATTORNEYS

Judges increasingly use social media to communicate with friends and family and, in states in which they are elected, as a campaign tool.[71] Attorneys conduct online research for their cases and often have websites on which they advertise their legal practices. There even are jury-selection apps for smartphones, tablets, and computers that help lawyers organize information about prospective jurors for use during jury selection.[72] While such uses of social media generally do not interfere with the judicial process, social media use by judges and attorneys sometimes does interfere with a fair trial or detract from the dignity of the court.

The federal courts and most state courts adhere to rules of judicial and attorney behavior based on the American Bar Association's Model Code of Judicial Conduct[73] and Model Rules of Professional Conduct.[74] Both sets of rules have provisions that, while not specifically addressing social media use, clearly govern such activities. The Code of Judicial Conduct, for example, provides that a judge must disqualify himself from presiding over any proceeding in which his impartiality "might reasonably be questioned," including instances in which the judge has made a public statement outside of court that "commits or appears to commit the judge to reach a particular result or rule in a particular way in the proceeding or controversy."[75] Those

public statements would include tweets and Facebook posts. A dozen of the rules governing attorneys similarly can be applied to their use of social media.[76]

Some states have begun offering guidelines for judges' social media use. Ohio's guidelines, for example, instruct judges to maintain dignity in every online posting, not to post online comments about any case before the judge or before any other judge, not to view the social networking sites of those who are parties to a case or who are witnesses, and not to offer legal advice online.[77]

State judicial ethics boards can investigate and recommend punishment for judges who violate judicial ethics codes.[78] For example, in 2009 a North Carolina trial court judge was reprimanded by the state Judicial Standards Commission for having an inappropriate Facebook relationship with an attorney and the attorney's client in a child-custody case before his court. The judge posted on his Facebook page the opinion that he had "two good parents to choose from" and used Google to find information about the mother. He found poems on the mother's website, and he read one of the poems in court. He said the poem gave him "hope for the kids" and convinced him the mother "was not as bitter as he first thought." The Judicial Standards Commission ruled that the judge's behavior "constitute[d] conduct prejudicial to the administration of justice that brings the judicial office into disrepute." The Commission specifically objected to the judge's *ex parte* (outside the courtroom) communications with an attorney in a case before the court and to the fact the judge had been influenced by his own online research, which was not entered into evidence.[79]

LOOKING FORWARD

Social media use in courtrooms is a new and rapidly developing area of the law. Professional communicators and others are advised to pay close attention to developments in their local courts, including the possible adoption of new court rules governing social media and judicial decisions regarding whether smartphones, tablets, and computers can be brought into the courthouse or the courtroom, and, if they are, when they can be used.

Journalists are encouraged to make their voices heard as courts decide how to deal with social media use. Judges who still are uncomfortable with television cameras in court cannot be expected to quickly embrace social media. However, if judges can be convinced that smartphones, tablets, and laptop computers are not as physically and psychologically disruptive as traditional television cameras, they very well might agree that those new technologies can be used in court. Also, professional communicators can argue that social media serve the values that have prompted judges to keep

most courtrooms open to the public throughout U.S. history. Social media are the twenty-first century means of ensuring that justice is administered fairly, that the public has confidence in the courts, that the public understands the workings of the judicial system, and that communities have outlets for their emotions.

Journalists should report and editorialize on these issues. They also should attempt to become part of the decision-making process by, whenever possible, discussing with judges the use of social media to report from courtrooms. These discussions should be in both formal and informal settings, individually and with journalistic and judicial professional organizations.

An important issue that apparently has not been addressed is whether citizens will have the same rights to blog or tweet from court as traditional journalists. Who is a reporter in this age of citizen journalism? Professional communicators should weigh in on this issue.

Meanwhile, journalists and others must take responsibility for learning the rules that govern social media use in the courts they cover.

FREQUENTLY ASKED QUESTIONS

1. Can judges forbid citizens or journalists from bringing smartphones or computers into courthouses or courtrooms? If people are allowed to bring their communication devices into the courtroom, does that mean they can use them there?

Courts can and often do forbid people from bringing smartphones or computers into the courthouse. Some courts allow the devices to be brought into the courtroom but do not allow them to be used there. Other courts allow the use of social networking sites such as Twitter in the courtroom. The rules on what technology you can bring to court and whether you can use it there vary from court to court and even from trial to trial. Judges have the authority to decide these matters.

Even if you are allowed to bring a smartphone into a courthouse, though, you may not be able to use it—or to use social networking sites such as Twitter—depending on the judge's rules for such usage.

2. Don't these restrictions violate the First Amendment?

No, because while you do have a strong First Amendment right to be in the courtroom, that right does not include the right to use cameras or recording equipment—or smartphones, tablets, or laptop computers. Many courts have found the use of cameras or recording equipment in the courtroom to be physically and psychologically disruptive, jeopardizing the fair administration of justice.

3. Is "friending" a juror on Facebook during a trial a good newsgathering strategy?

No. This could result in the dismissal of the juror or a mistrial. Judges routinely admonish jurors that they are not to discuss the case with anyone while the case is under way.

4. Can I tweet from my smartphone if the judge can't see me?

No. That's at least unethical and might well be illegal. You could be found in contempt of court. However, once you have posted a tweet, a judge probably cannot make you delete the post without running afoul of the very strong legal rules against prior restraints on the press.

5. Then what should I do?

Ask court officials what media use is allowed, and, if you don't like the answer, try to reason with the judge. Find out what spaces may be fair game, such as courthouse halls or just outside the building, for social networking communications. Also, work with your local professional organizations to encourage your local courts to adopt rules that allow you to use social media to report on courtroom proceedings.

NOTES

1   448 U.S. 555, 580 (1980) (quoting Branzburg v. Hayes, 408 U.S. 665, 681 (1972)).
2   Globe Newspaper Co. v. Superior Court, 457 U.S. 596, 607 (1982); see also Press-Enterprise Co. v. Riverside Cnty. Superior Court, 464 U.S. 501 (1984); Publicker Indus. v. Cohen, 733 F.2d 1059 (3d Cir. 1984).
3   Nebraska Press Ass'n v. Stuart, 427 U.S. 539 (1976).
4   Richmond Newspapers, 448 U.S. at 570–571.
5   Id. at 595–596 (Brennan, J., concurring).
6   Nebraska Press Ass'n, 427 U.S. at 587 (Brennan, J., concurring).
7   See, e.g., United States v. Moussaoui, 205 F.R.D. 183 (E.D.Va. 2002); United States v. Hastings, 695 F.2d 1278 (11th Cir. 1983).
8   Estes v. Texas, 381 U.S. 532, 541 (1965).
9   See, e.g., id.; Sheppard v. Maxwell, 384 U.S. 333 (1966).
10   Estes, 381 U.S. at 536.
11   449 U.S. 560 (1981).
12   Nicole Lozare, More Reporters Tweeting from Courtroom: High-profile Trials can Increase Reporters' Followers by Thousands, News Media & The Law, Fall 2011, at 6.
13   Bruce Carton, Is Tweeting From the Courtroom by Reporters Too Distracting for Jurors?, Legal Blog Watch, April 6, 2012, http://legalblogwatch.typepad.com/legal_blog_watch/2012/04/is-tweeting-from-the-courtroom-by-reporters-too-distracting-for-jurors.html.

14   John Schwartz, As Jurors Turn to Web, Mistrials are Popping Up, N.Y. Times, March 17, 2009, http://www.nytimes.com/2009/03/18/us/18juries.html?page wantedall. This might be the first time the term was used.

15   Hilary Hylton, Tweeting in the Jury Box: A Danger to Fair Trials?, Time Online, December 29, 2009, http://www.time.com/time/nation/article/0,8599,1948971, 00.html.

16   Estes, 381 U.S. at 551–552.

17   Ahnalese Rushman, Courtroom Coverage in 140 Characters, News Media & The Law, Spring 2009, at 28.

18   Id.

19   United States v. Shelnutt, No. 4:09-CR-14, 2009 WL 3681827 (M.D. Ga. Nov 2, 2009).

20   Id. at *1.

21   Rushman, supra note 17.

22   Id.

23   Id.; see also, Lozare, supra note 12.

24   Shelnutt, 2009 WL 3681827 at *1.

25   Id. at *2.

26   Fed. R. Crim. P. 53 advisory committee's note to 2002 amendment.

27   Rosemary Lane, Lights, Camera and Some Action: The Movement to Expand Cameras into Federal Courtrooms Gets a Few Boosts, News Media & The Law, Fall 2010, at 33.

28   See Court Websites, http://www.uscourts.gov/Court_Locator/CourtWebsites. aspx (last visited October 5, 2012).

29   Electronic Device Notice (U.S. Dist. Ct. for M.D.N.C.), http://www.ncmd. uscourts.gov/electronic-device-notice.

30   Local Rule 83.7 (U.S. Dist. Ct. for M.D.N.C.), http://www.ncmd.uscourts.gov/ laptop-permission-requests.

31   Photography, Broadcasting, Recording and Electronic Devices (U.S. Dist. Ct. for M.D. Ala.), http://www.almd.uscourts.gov/getSearch.cfm.

32   Laptop Computer Policy and Cell Phone Policy (U.S. Dist. Ct. for D.Conn), http://www.ctd.uscourts.gov/policies.html.

33   Hollingsworth v. Perry, 130 S.Ct. 705 (2010).

34   Matthew E. Feinberg, The Prop 8 Decision and Courtroom Drama in the YouTube Age: Why Camera Use Should be Permitted in Courtrooms During High Profile Cases, 17 Cardozo J.L. & Gender 33, 61 (2010) (citing Hollingsworth, 130 S.Ct. at 719).

35   Louis D. Brandeis, What Publicity Can Do, Harper's Weekly, December 20, 1913, available at http://www.law.louisville.edu/library/collections/brandeis/node/196.

36   Sunshine in the Courtroom Act, H.R. 2802, 112th Cong. § 2(b)(1)(A) (2011); Sunshine in the Courtroom Act, S.410, 112th Cong. § 2(b)(1)(A) (2011).

37   Sunshine in the Courtroom Act of 2007: Hearing on H.R. 2128 Before the H. Comm. on the Judiciary, 110th Cong. 125 (2007) (testimony of John C. Richter, U.S. Att'y).

38   See, e.g., Md. Rules, Rule 16-110, Cell Phones; Other Electronic Devices; Cameras (Thomson Reuters 2012) (ordering that cell phones must be turned off in the courtroom); Ark. Amin. Order 6(d)(7), Broadcasting, Recording, or Photographing in the Courtroom (2010) (ordering that "[e]lectronic devices shall not be used in

the courtroom to broadcast, record, photograph, e-mail, blog, tweet, text, post, or transmit by any other means except as may be allowed by the court"), http://courts.arkansas.gov/rules/admin_orders_sc/index.cfm.

39   Radio Television Digital News Association, Cameras in the Court: A State-By-State Guide, http://www.rtdna.org/pages/media_items/cameras-in-the-court-a-state-by-state-guide55.php (last visited April 16, 2012.).

40   Reporters Committee for Freedom of the Press, Open Court Compendium, http://www.rcfp.org/open-courts-compendium (last visited April 16, 2012).

41   Stacy Blasiola, Say "Cheese!" Cameras and Bloggers in Wisconsin's Courtrooms, 1 Reynolds Courts & Media L.J. 197 (2011).

42   Id. at 197 (citing Ohio ex. rel. Macfarlane v. Common Court of Pleas, No. 10-1771 (Ohio order December 15, 2010)).

43   Id. at 197, 203; see also, Steve Patterson, Appeals Court Tosses Court-Blogging Order Against Jacksonville.com, Jacksonville.com (January 20, 2010), http://jacksonville.com/news/metro/2010-01-20/story/appeals_court_tosses_court_blogging_order_against_jacksonvillecom#ixzz1s2mn8jCO.

44   Id. at 209.

45   Id. at 207.

46   Carton, supra note 13.

47   Adriana C. Cervantes, Note, Will Twitter Be Following You in the Courtroom? Why Reporters Should Be Allowed to Broadcast During Courtroom Proceedings, 33 Hastings Comm/Ent L.J. 133, 148 (2010) (citing Lynn Marek, What is that Reporter Doing in Court? "Twittering", The National Law Journal March 16, 2009, http://www.law.com/jsp/nlj/PubArticleNLJ.jsp?id=1202428987661&Whats_that_reporter_doing_in_court_Twittering&slreturn=20120907093052 (last visited October 5, 2012).

48   Rachel Bunn, Reporter's Tweeted Photo of Juror Leads Judge to Declare Mistrial in Murder Prosecution, Reporters Committee for Freedom of the Press (April 16, 2012), http://www.rcfp.org/browse-media-law-resources/news/reporters-tweeted-photo-juror-leads-judge-declare-mistrial-murder-pr.

49   Nebraska Press Ass'n v. Stuart, 427 U. S. 539, 559 (1976).

50   Dianna Hunt, Judge Restricts Reporting on Capital Murder Trial in Fort Worth, Fort Worth Star-Telegram (January 6, 2012), http://www.startelegram.com/2012/01/06/3640977/judge-restricts-reporting-on-capital.html#storylink=cpy.

51   Rachel Bunn, Texas Judge Limits Media Coverage of Murder Trial (January 10, 2012), http://www.rcfp.org/browse-media-law-resources/news/texas-judge-limits-media-coverage-murder-trial.

52   Mark L. Tamburri, Thomas M. Pohl, & M. Patrick Yingling, A Little Bird Told Me About the Trial: Revising Court Rules to Allow Reporting from the Courtroom Via Twitter, 15 BNA Electronic Com. & L. Rep. 1415 (September 15, 2010), available at http://papers.ssrn.com/sol3/papers.cfm?abstract_id=1888025.

53   Id. (citing Pa. R. Crim. P. 112; Order Denying Joint Motion To Bar The Use Of Advanced Technology [Twitter] From Trial, Commonwealth v. Veon, No. CP-22-CR-4656-2008 (Pa. C.P. Dauphin January 25, 2010)).

54   Fed. R. Evid. 606(b) (mandating a new trial if the jury has uncovered prejudicial information on its own. The judge determines whether there is a "reasonable possibility" that the outside research altered the verdict).

55   Sontaya Rose, Juror Misconduct in Fresno County Led to a Mistrial, abc30.com (April 20, 2012), http://abclocal.go.com/kfsn/story?section=news/local&id= 8630153.

56   Timothy J. Fallon, Mistrial in 140 Characters or Less? How the Internet and Social Networking are Undermining the American Jury System and What Can Be Done to Fix It, 38 Hofstra L. Rev. 935, 939 (2010).

57   Judge Dennis M. Sweeney (Ret.), Worlds Collide: The Digital Native Enters the Jury Box, 1 Reynolds Courts & Media L.J. 121, 129 (2011).

58   Id. at 174, 175.

59   Thompson v. Krantz, 137 P.3d 693, 697 (Okla. Civ. App. 2006).

60   Id. at 698.

61   Gareth S. Lacy, Untangling the Web: How Courts Should Respond to Juries Using the Internet for Research, 1 Reynolds Courts & Media L.J. 169, 175 (2011).

62   Id. (citing Real v. Wal Mart Stores, Inc., No. B145819, 2002 WL 80664 (Cal. App. Dist. January 22, 2002)).

63   Eva-Marie Ayala, Tarrant County Juror Sentenced to Community Service for Trying to "Friend" Defendant on Facebook, Fort Worth Star-Telegram.com (August 28, 2011), http://www.star-telegram.com/2011/08/28/3319796/juror-sentenced-to-community-service.html.

64   Id.

65   Meghan Dunn, Jurors' Use of Social Media During Trials and Deliberations: A Report to the Judicial Conference Committee on Court Administration and Case Management, Federal Judicial Center (November 22, 2011), http://www.fjc.gov/library/fjc_catalog.nsf.

66   Joe Palazzolo, Law Blog: Court Tweets: Volume One, Wall St. J. (January 26, 2012), http://blogs.wsj.com/law/2012/01/26/court-tweets-volume-one/.

67   See, e.g., United States v. Fumo, CR No. 06-319, 2009 WL 1688482 (E.D. Pa. June 17, 2009) (finding a juror's postings on Twitter and Facebook during a trial were innocuous and not grounds for a mistrial).

68   Memorandum from Judge Julie A. Robinson, Chair, Judicial Conference Committee on Court Administration and Case Management regarding Juror Use of Electronic Communications Technologies 2 (January 28, 2010), http://www.wired.com/images_blogs/threatlevel/2010/02/juryinstructions.pdf.

69   Lacy, supra note 61 at 176.

70   See, e.g., Tresa Baldas, For Jurors in Michigan, No Tweeting (or Texting, or Googling) Allowed, Nat'l L.J. Online (July 1, 2009), http://www.law.com/jsp/nlj/PubArticleNLJ.jsp?id=1202431952628&slreturn=1; Anita Ramasastry, FindLaw.com Legal Commentary: Why Courts Need to Ban Jurors' Electronic Communications Devices (August 11, 2009), http://writ.news.findlaw.com/ramasastry/20090811.html.

71   See Conf. of Ct. Public Info. Officers, New Media and the Courts: The Current Status and a Look at the Future 9 (2010), http://www.ccpio.org/documents/newmediaproject/New-Media-and-the-Courts-Report.pdf (indicating that 40 percent of state court judges used social media, especially Facebook, in 2010. That is about the same percentage as for the general population).

72   See, e.g., Ken Broda-Brahm, Is It Time for the iPad to Replace Paper Notes in Voir Dire?, The Jury Expert (March 30, 2011), http://www.thejuryexpert.com/2011/03/is-it-time-for-the-ipad-to-replace-paper-notes-in-voir-dire/ (reviewing iJuror and Jury Duty, two jury-selection apps for the iPad).

73   See Genelle I. Belmas, That's What "Friend" Is For? Judges, Social Networks and Standards for Recusal, 1 Reynolds Courts & Media L.J. 147, 155 (2011) (discussing Model Code of Jud. Conduct R. 2.11 (2007)).

74   Model Rules of Prof'l Conduct (2011).

75   Model Code of Jud. Conduct R. 2.11 (2007).

76   See Angela O'Brien, Note, Are Attorneys and Judges One Tweet, Blog or Friend Request Away from Facing a Disciplinary Committee?, 11 Loy. J. Pub. Int. L. 511 (2010).

77   Ohio B. Commr's of Grievances & Discip. Opinion 2010-7 (December 3, 2010), available at www.supremecourt.ohio.gov/Boards/BOC/Advisory_Opinions/2010/Op_10-007.doc.

78   For example, the North Carolina Judicial Standards Commission receives written complaints about judicial behavior from citizens, investigates those complaints, and, where appropriate, recommends to the state Supreme Court that the judge be disciplined. See The North Carolina Court System, Judicial Standards Commission, http://www.nccourts.org/Courts/CRS/Councils/JudicialStandards/Default.asp (last visited April 10, 2012).

79   Public Reprimand B. Carlton Terry Jr. District Court Judge, Inquiry No. 08-234, N.C. Jud. Stds. Comm. (April 1, 2009), http://www.aoc.state.nc.us/www/public/coa/jsc/publicreprimands/jsc08-234.pdf; see also, Belmas, supra note 73 at 156–157.

Social Media Policies for Journalists

Daxton R. "Chip" Stewart

Schieffer School of Journalism
Texas Christian University

ABSTRACT

As social media tools have become prevalent ways for people to share and connect, journalists have increasingly incorporated these tools into their daily practice. However, few professional codes of ethics have been updated, and those that have been updated have been heavily criticized as too restrictive to engage the audience effectively. This chapter reviews social media policies of several print, online, and broadcast journalism institutions to find common themes and concerns. Major issues addressed in this chapter include transparency, balancing the personal and the professional, maintaining confidentiality, rules for "friending," intellectual property matters, and breaking news on social media.

The president was in what he thought was an off-the-record discussion with a pool of White House reporters. Less than a week before, Kanye West had famously interrupted country music star Taylor Swift's speech during the Video Music Awards, and a reporter from CNBC casually asked what President Obama thought about West's outburst. An ABC employee, listening on a shared live feed of the discussion, circulated Obama's slightly crude response, and soon after, Nightline co-anchor Terry Moran sent out the following on Twitter: "Pres. Obama just called Kanye West a 'jackass' for his outburst at VMAs when Taylor Swift won. Now THAT's presidential."

Before ABC officials could respond or make a decision regarding whether this should be published, the damage was done. Moran had more than one million followers on Twitter, the microblog site created in 2006 that allows

users to share information through "tweets" 140 characters or less in length. Even though Moran later deleted the tweet, the word was out. ABC was widely condemned for its lack of professionalism in the matter, and the network soon issued an apology, noting that its "employees prematurely tweeted a portion of (Obama's) remarks that turned out to be from an off-the-record portion of the interview. This was done before our editorial process had been completed. That was wrong."[1]

Social media tools present great opportunities for communicators, including news media professionals, to engage with the audience in ways impossible just a decade ago. However, the benefits social media allow communicators are tempered by the risks inherent in tools that allow messages to be sent immediately and spread rapidly. Further, laws and professional ethics policies drafted with a twentieth-century understanding of mass media may not be in tune with communication tools that emerge, develop, spread, and change constantly.

In the aforementioned situation involving the rogue tweet of a Nightline co-anchor, the statement by ABC News concluded with the following: "We apologize to the White House and CNBC and are taking steps to ensure that it will not happen again."[2] But what steps can media organizations take to prevent embarrassing, unprofessional, or even illegal behavior when its employees use social media tools?

Several news media organizations have developed guidelines and policies for employee use of social media. These have been catalogued and discussed by professionals,[3] and there is no shortage of blog posts about social media risks and best practices warehoused at sites such as socialmediagovernance. com. However, social media policies have not yet been subjected to any greater academic scrutiny in light of the legal and ethical demands of the journalism field. The purpose of this chapter is to build understanding of social media policies in this context, cataloguing the chief concerns of journalists and outlining best practices in developing such policies.

Despite such risks, journalists cannot avoid engaging their audiences through social media. News media companies have incorporated social media into their plans, trying to build online followings as print circulation and broadcast audiences have dwindled. The *Chicago Tribune* built a following on Facebook and its own site by creating the humorous Col. Tribune, a character inspired by Tribune founder Col. Robert McCormick and used to share links and engage younger readers with some success.[4] Major news media had also created social media editor positions, including National Public Radio, *USA Today*, and the *New York Times*. The *Times* ultimately eliminated the position because the growing importance of social media demanded more attention and transitioned oversight of social media to a 10-person "interactive news team."[5]

As Twitter use has grown among American adults, news media institutions have developed large followings on the site as well. A look at the Twitter pages in June 2012 showed that the *New York Times* had more than 5.2 million followers, ABC News had more than 1.7 million followers, CBS News had more than 2 million followers, ESPN had more than 4.1 million followers, and Fox News had more than 1.5 million followers. Following these feeds allows users to get updates about major headlines, with links back to full stories and video on the websites of the news companies.

However, despite the emergence of Web 2.0 in the past decade and the widespread use of sites such as Facebook, Flickr, YouTube, and Twitter, use of social media has not been specifically incorporated into the most visible codes of ethics in the mass communication field. The Society of Professional Journalists (SPJ) Code of Ethics provides guidance to journalists through language that reaches across publication platforms, and SPJ provides a blog handling current issues in the field. However, the code itself was last revised in 1996. Two other major professional groups—the Radio Television Digital News Association (RTDNA) and the American Society of News Editors (ASNE)—have issued guidelines for social media use. However, these have come under fire from several critics who have worked to build community engagement for news media.

For this chapter, the author identified 12 policies of news media companies and organizations to examine their definitions and descriptions of social media tools, the main topics the policies addressed, and themes regarding the way these organizations advised practitioners to handle the particular challenges of social media. The views of critics who have found these policies to be too restrictive are also presented. The chapter concludes with best practices for designing social media policies for journalists in light of the policies discussed and the previous chapters of this book.

DEFINITIONS AND DESCRIPTIONS OF SOCIAL MEDIA

To provide a foundation for designing best practices for journalists using social media, the way journalism organizations define and describe social media was examined first.

Ten journalism organizations (ASNE, the *Austin American-Statesman*, the *New York Times*, the Associated Press, the *Los Angeles Times*, Reuters, the *Roanoke Times*, National Public Radio, Politico, and the Radio Television Digital News Association) listed specific tools in their social media policies. Each included Facebook and Twitter. Four others included MySpace, and one—the *New York Times*—specifically mentioned LinkedIn, a SNS aimed at connecting professionals. Politico, the political news website, was a bit broader, mentioning location-based application Foursquare, Digg, and Yahoo Buzz as well.

The tone of the policies and guidelines was generally accepting of the fact that social media had emerged and should be dealt with according to usual newsroom standards. When the Associated Press updated its guidelines in 2011, it moved away from a more restrictive policy to one that encourages all of its journalists to have accounts on social media sites because they have become "an essential tool for AP reporters to gather news and share links to our published work."[6]

The necessity of dealing with social media issues is perhaps best summarized with the following opening passage from the RTDNA guidelines:

> Social media and blogs are important elements of journalism. They narrow the distance between journalists and the public. They encourage lively, immediate and spirited discussion. They can be vital news-gathering and news-delivery tools. As a journalist you should uphold the same professional and ethical standards of fairness, accuracy, truthfulness, transparency and independence when using social media as you do on air and on all digital news platforms.[7]

MAJOR THEMES FROM JOURNALISM SOCIAL MEDIA POLICIES

The most comprehensive effort to date to build a social media policy for news organizations was completed by ASNE in 2011, when its Ethics and Values Committee issued its "10 Best Practices for Social Media." The guide includes references to 18 other social media policies from news organizations, and included the following 10 guidelines:

1. Traditional ethics rules still apply online.
2. Assume everything you write online will become public.
3. Use social media to engage with readers, but professionally.
4. Break news on your website, not Twitter.
5. Beware of perceptions.
6. Independently authenticate anything found on a social networking site.
7. Always identify yourself as a journalist.
8. Social networks are tools, not toys.
9. Be transparent and admit when you're wrong online.
10. Keep internal deliberations confidential.[8]

Embedded in these 10 guidelines are several themes common to other social media policies for journalists. These themes include transparency, friending matters, clearance and review, sourcing, balancing personal and

private matters, confidentiality, and intellectual property concerns. Each is discussed briefly below.

Transparency

The SPJ Code of Ethics calls for journalists to identify sources when possible and to "avoid undercover or other surreptitious methods of gathering information" in most situations.[9] This call for openness in reporting methods is reflected in the social media policies as well, most of which demand that journalists identify themselves as journalists in two particular circumstances. First, they should always identify themselves as journalists who are representing a particular organization before posting comments or updates on social media sites, blogs, or while commenting on other news stories. As National Public Radio notes:

> Just as we do in the "real" world, we identify ourselves as NPR journalists when we are working online. So, if as part of our work we are posting comments, asking questions, tweeting, retweeting, blogging, Facebooking or doing anything on social media or other online forums, we clearly identify ourselves and that we work for NPR. We do not use pseudonyms when doing such work.[10]

The RTDNA extends this to avatars and forbids anonymous blogging, and Reuters extends it to chat rooms.

Second, journalists should also be transparent about who they are when they contact potential sources for reporting purposes. The *Wall Street Journal* requires that its employees never "us(e) a false name when you're acting on behalf of your Dow Jones publication or service" and always self-identify as a reporter for the *Journal* when gathering information for a story.[11]

Friending

Journalists are called to "act independently" under the SPJ Code of Ethics, in particular by avoiding conflicts of interest, "real or perceived." This concern is at the heart of statements in nearly every news organization social media policy reviewed in this study, reflected by specific guidelines for who can be added to a list of "friends" or what organizations or movements journalists can become a "fan" or "follower" of. Journalists are warned to be careful in who they associate with online for fear of compromising their appearance of independence and neutrality.

First, becoming a "friend" of a source or subject of coverage invites risk. The *New York Times* 2009 policy asked, for example, if reporters can write about someone who is a friend on a SNS before concluding:

> In general, being a "friend" of someone on Facebook is almost meaningless and does not signify the kind of relationship that could pose a conflict of interest for a reporter or editor writing about that person. But if a "friend" is really a personal friend, it would.[12]

The *Wall Street Journal* requires approval by an editor before a source who may demand confidentiality can be added as a friend. "Openly 'friending' sources is akin to publicly publishing your Rolodex,"[13] according to the *Journal*'s policy. Issues can also arise in newsrooms between managers and employees who may be "friends" in social media. The AP says that managers "should not issue friend requests to subordinates, since that could be awkward for employees. It's fine if employees want to initiate the friend process with their bosses."[14]

Second, becoming a friend of a person involved in a controversial issue, or becoming a fan of a movement, may present issues. Reuters notes that its duty to be "responsible, fair and impartial" may be compromised when journalists "'like' a post or adopt a 'badge' or join a 'cause,'" though it defers to the judgment of individual journalists to handle this as circumstances dictate.[15] NPR forbids its reporters from advocating "for political or other polarizing issues online," a policy that extends to using social media "to express personal views . . . that you could not write for the air or post on NPR.org."[16] The *Roanoke Times*, however, is more flexible, advising caution and consistency:

> Either avoid them entirely, or sign up for lots of groups. If you become a fan of a political party, become a fan of the other parties as well . . . Manage your friends carefully. Having one source on your friends list but not another is easily construed as bias. As above, be consistent. Accept no sources or people you cover as friends, or welcome them all.[17]

Clearance and Review

News organizations generally require journalists to receive clearance from editors or managers before engaging in social media or releasing news items publicly. While most policies were less formal—as NPR advises, "when in doubt, consult with your editor"—others required specific clearances.[18]

The Associated Press, for example, requires anything that could potentially be "breaking news" to be cleared by a manager in advance.[19] Similarly, the *Roanoke Times* requires employees who blog to "notify their immediate supervisor that they have a blog and talk through any potential conflicts of interest or complications." However, this is not a policy to forbid blogs—rather, the paper encourages blogging, but wants to make sure that reporters are "build(ing) off our institutional voice."[20]

Sourcing

The SPJ Code of Ethics requires journalists to "test the accuracy of information from all sources," a demand that can be challenging when reporters use social media tools to engage with sources. A healthy skepticism of sources contacted or uncovered through social media tools is built into many of the news organizations' social media policies.

The RTDNA treats information found on social media sites as similar to "scanner traffic or phone tips,"[21] which must be confirmed independently. Similarly, the *Roanoke Times* notes that "Facebook and MySpace are not a substitute for actual interviews by phone or in person, or other means of information gathering, and should not be solely relied upon," instead requiring offline confirmation and verification of claims made through these sites.[22]

The Associated Press and the *Los Angeles Times* specifically extended requirements of verification and authentication to retweeting items found on Twitter. As the AP notes: "Sources discovered (on social networks) must be vetted in the same way as a source found by any other means."[23]

Personal vs. Professional

The primary concern expressed in social media policies of news organizations was blurring of the line between a journalist's personal life and his or her professional life. Several policies, such as those of the *Los Angeles Times* and NPR, suggest that journalists assume that there is no divide between one's professional life and one's personal life. "(E)verything you write or receive on a social media site is public," as NPR notes.[24]

NPR and the *New York Times* extend this caution to reporters expressing personal opinions, in a similar manner to concerns about following or becoming a "fan" of a political person or movement mentioned above. As the *Times* notes, "Anything you post online can and might be publicly disseminated, and can be twisted to be used against you by those who wish you or *The Times* ill—whether it's text, photographs, or video."[25] The AP notes that expressions of opinion "may damage the AP's reputation as an

unbiased source of news" and thus employees should avoid "declaring their views on contentious public issues in any public forum" such as social media.[26]

Reuters says its policy is "not to muzzle anyone," but it recommends that employees should "identify ourselves as Reuters journalists and declare that we speak for ourselves, not for Reuters."[27] The *Roanoke Times* is similarly less restrictive, instead suggesting that social media posts "be crafted with concern for how they might reflect on our news products or our reputation for fairness and professionalism."[28]

Confidentiality

Several social media policies demand that journalists avoid revealing confidential information. The AP forbids "(p)osting AP proprietary or confidential material,"[29] while the *Wall Street Journal* advises journalists to avoid discussing "articles that haven't been published, meetings you've attended or plan to attend with staff or sources, or interviews that you've conducted."[30]

Intellectual Property

While a concern about intellectual property rights was not common in these social media policies, they were noted in different ways in a few policies. The *Roanoke Times* and NPR both made it clear that the company owned copyrights on the materials created by its employees and that employees should not violate those rights on social media. As NPR notes, linking to stories on NPR.org is fine, but employees

> may not repost NPR copyrighted material to social networks without prior permission. For example, it is o.k. to link from your blog or Facebook profile to a story of yours on the NPR site, but you should not copy the full text or audio onto a personal site or Web page.[31]

The BBC expressed similar concerns about using creative works elsewhere on the web, encouraging its employees to make sure the BBC has the "necessary rights to any content we put on a third-party site" and that the company is "aware of, and comfortable with, the site's own terms and conditions," which may limit uses to personal or non-commercial purposes.[32]

CRITIQUES OF JOURNALISM SOCIAL MEDIA POLICIES

After the ASNE issued its guidelines—which largely include the themes discussed above—the response from the digital journalism community

was swift and hardly complimentary. Steve Buttry, director of community engagement and social media for the Journal Register Company and a widely-respected news editor, said the ASNE guidelines reflected a fear of social media—"Their need to control remains an impediment to innovation"—and called the underlying policies used as sources "far more fearful and restrictive than they should be."[33] Joy Mayer, a professor at the University of Missouri School of Journalism and former fellow of the Reynolds Journalism Institute who specializes in community engagement, noted that there were some good things in the guidelines, but that it also included some "real missteps."[34]

The major critiques of the aforementioned policies particularly targeted two topics: Friending policies and handling breaking news.

Who's a Friend?

The ASNE guidelines caution journalists about whom they follow on Twitter and whom they select as friends on Facebook. This warning came under the heading "Beware of Perceptions," which Buttry said was overly cautious. "The tone of fear and restriction here and in the lengthy discussion of 'friends' is unnecessary," Buttry wrote. "I don't think journalists need more here than simple advice to consider appearances when sharing links and using social media to connect with sources."[35]

Similarly, Mayer expressed concern that such a policy would restrict experimentation among editors. Further, she said that in the discussion of this guideline the ASNE suggests that journalists who friend sources and should then hide their friend lists contradicted another important tenet—transparency.

Breaking News

The most controversial of the ASNE best practices was the call to "break news on your website, not on Twitter." The ASNE policy calls for balance between "getting the information out" and "waiting for a story to move through the editorial pipeline," but it favors holding back breaking news from Twitter because it may damage the "main value" of social media—driving traffic to the news organization's website.[36] This practice was mirrored later in the year when ESPN announced similar guidelines for its employees.[37]

Mayer said she was "horrified" when she first read of the ASNE's policy because it undercut journalists' ability to be "a relevant, quick part of ongoing conversations."[38] Buttry said this guidance was "as foolish as the silly old newspaper fear of 'scooping ourselves' by publishing stories online before they have been in print."[39]

While both Buttry and Mayer said some caution is warranted in breaking news situations, particularly when there are details that need to checked for accuracy, they thought this policy would make it more difficult for journalists to take advantage of the positive aspects of social media—using it as a tool for community engagement, crowdsourcing, and verifying information gleaned from social media users. Buttry offered the example of NPR's Andy Carvin, who would often retweet unconfirmed information from sources during times of strife in the Middle East, but would raise questions and ask his Twitter followers "to help verify and refute" facts streaming in from his various sources.[40]

BEST PRACTICES FOR DEVELOPING SOCIAL MEDIA POLICIES

John Paton, CEO of Digital First Media, once stated his three employee rules for using social media as follows:

"1.
2.
3."[41]

This minimalist approach—one that trusts journalists to make responsible decisions while using social media—is the antithesis of the reality for news organizations. In general, news media social media guidelines for employees seem to be quite restrictive, both in terms of what kinds of social media tools are typically used and how they should be used. Critics have rightly assailed these policies as damaging to the essential nature of social media tools. However, the policies from both perspectives so far seem to avoid addressing the legal challenges presented by these tools.

Journalism organizations mostly focused on Facebook and Twitter, and the policies about these seem largely concerned with protecting the organization's status as an objective, neutral reporter of the news. This is to be expected considering the ethical demands of the field. However, it can also be unnecessarily limiting. One of the great benefits of social media tools is enhancing interconnectivity with the audience, and the journalism organization policies seem to inhibit the ability of journalists to engage the audience in this manner. When organizations such as the *New York Times* and NPR do not allow journalists besides those in the business of providing opinions to blog about personal or political matters, it limits how the audience understands who journalists are and what they do. This policy may detract from, rather than enhance, transparency. If journalists cannot publicly

"friend" some people or become fans or followers of their organizations, the audience may be left in the dark as to their motivations and affiliations.

Beyond transparency matters, the social media policies for journalists reviewed in this chapter have several weaknesses. For one, they do not specifically address several very important concerns of professionals. For journalism organizations, the rogue tweet of President Obama's off-the-record aside still seems likely to occur. While the policies mention using social media posts as sources of information and seeking clearances for breaking news, handling informal comments and items perhaps not suited for publication may fall in between the cracks of these policies. Further, journalism organizations should approach social media in a more expansive and inclusive manner, recognizing sites beyond Facebook and Twitter.

Location-based applications (such as Foursquare) and review sites (such as Yelp) were rarely mentioned in the policies, suggesting that journalists have either found little use for these tools or are unsure of dealing with any possible dangers they present. As social media tools develop, the social media policies should adapt to handle them. Broad statements of principles that guide engagement through social media tools can help practitioners, but specific advice for different sites is of value as well. These policies should be constantly updated.

Overall, the social media policy debate amongst journalists shows that while individual news organizations have developed social media policies that provide guidance to practitioners, there is much more work to be done to ensure that communicators understand the benefits and risks of the broad array of social media tools. Professional organizations such as the Society of Professional Journalists should follow the lead of the Radio Television Digital News Association and the ASNE to develop social media guidelines to serve as best practices for their fields. These could be incorporated into existing codes of ethics or drafted as addenda that can be updated online as new tools and situations arise.

FREQUENTLY ASKED QUESTIONS

What Are the Five Things Every Social Media Policy for Journalists Should Address?

1. Transparency

Transparency is a hallmark of journalism. Professional standards require journalists to be honest about who they are and their methods, and deception is strongly discouraged. As such, journalism organizations should require employees to use their real names and to disclose their affiliations when using

social media for work purposes. For example, a Twitter account used by J. Jonah Jameson for the *Daily Bugle* should be something along the lines of "JJJameson_DB" or should otherwise include a note that Jameson works for the *Bugle* in his profile information. He should not skulk about using pseudonyms, either on Twitter or while commenting on stories on Facebook or elsewhere.

One of the great strengths of social tools is that they allow interaction with citizens. While citizens may hide behind false profiles or comment anonymously, journalists should not respond in kind, instead promoting honest communication and accountability to the public.

2. Friending and Following

Journalism organizations should make clear what the rules are for journalists who use social media accounts, both in their professional and in their private activities. However, such guidelines should provide some flexibility for journalists to maintain a private life in which they can participate meaningfully in democracy, culture, and relationships.

While fairness and objectivity are noted professional standards for journalists, these concepts have flaws, as noted by Bill Kovach and Tom Rosenstiel in their manifesto, *Elements of Journalism*.[42] More important, they argue, is independence from faction and avoiding conflict of interests. As such, journalists should be able to friend or follow whoever they wish, as long as they remain independent from those friends or causes and are transparent about any connections they may have. One possible policy would be urging journalists to maintain separate professional and private accounts— one for business, one for personal connections. However, even then, skeptical members of the public or subjects of coverage may uncover the journalist's private account, leading to potential embarrassment for his or her organization.

To avoid the appearance of conflict of interest or bias, once a journalist follows or friends one side of a cause, he or she should look to follow/friend other sides as well. And, perhaps most essentially, journalists should make clear in their profiles that personal statements are their own and not representative of their employer's thoughts.

3. Intellectual Property

Intellectual property matters—particularly copyright—present some of the greatest challenges for journalists using social tools. Journalism organizations should ensure that employees are of the mindset that anything not created by the organization needs permission from the copyright holder before it can be republished.

This means that hosting photographs, YouTube videos, and text from sites other than your own are all potentially dangerous. True, news reporting is one of the categories protected by the fair use doctrine (see Chapter 4), but because news is a commercial use, and because photographs and videos are typically used in full, there is a strong likelihood that republishing them for news purposes does not qualify as fair use. Using trademarks is another matter—logos and such used for news reporting purposes has stronger protection under the Federal Trademark Anti-Dilution Act—but still, journalism organizations should be cautious of such uses without permission.

Therefore, journalism organizations should get in the habit of asking permission to use the works of others. Social media guidelines should establish a process for seeking permission and confirming that it has been granted. And when in doubt, journalists should seek the aid of their attorneys before publishing something that could cost the organization damages for infringement.

4. Sharing and Retweeting

The culture of social media is one of sharing, and journalists should recognize this for effective use of social tools. However, the culture of sharing does not automatically mean sharing has strong legal protections.

First, before posting the video, audio, or words of another person, journalists should consider potential intellectual property and copyright issues (see Intellectual Property, above and in Chapter 4). Then, journalists should provide proper attribution for the source of the shared material. If a reporter hears a news tip or breaking story from another organization, he or she should note the source in the social media post—for example, by using the HT ("hat tip") notation in Twitter.

The easiest and most widely accepted form of acknowledgment is the hyperlink. Journalism organizations should take advantage of linking to provide both background to their stories and credit where it is due.

Another very easy way to share information gathered by or stated by others on Twitter is the retweet, which has caused headaches for several news organizations such as the Associated Press, which generally discourages retweeting as a form of reporting. Retweeting is Twitter's form of sharing—either a link, a photo, a video, or even a tip or snippet of information provided by citizens. The culture of social media makes it clear that retweeting is not an endorsement, or even a statement that the underlying information is truthful. It's more of a "heads up" to the audience—though if a journalist has doubts about the veracity of a statement, or if it is yet to be independently confirmed, the journalist certainly should make this clear in the process of sharing.

Nothing in the law makes retweeting particularly dangerous for news organizations—Section 230 of the Communications Decency Act provides a robust shield against defamation and other tort actions for republishing the posts of others online (see Chapter 2). The greater concerns are accuracy and timeliness, both of which can be handled through proper use of social tools.

5. Breaking News

There is simply no legal justification for the notion that journalists should avoid breaking news via social media. If a journalist is confident in the facts and sourcing enough to publish, the consequences for error will likely be the same for publication online as it would be if the statement were made in broadcast or print.

While caution may be urged—for example, contentious issues or factual discrepancies should be cleared by an editor or lawyer before publishing on Twitter—journalists should feel comfortable publishing on a social platform. Twitter and Facebook are tools for publishing, not their own publications. News organizations may very well have strategic or financial considerations in mind when establishing a "no breaking news on Twitter" rule, but the law should be no more barrier for publishing online than it is offline.

Further, publications via social media have the opportunity to be corrected in real time. Previous social media posts can be deleted, though this may interfere with the goal of transparency. Instead, social media posts can include updates and corrections to steer the audience to accurate, updated information.

In short, if a news organization isn't comfortable publishing something, it shouldn't. The platform for publishing makes very little difference in the eyes of the law.

NOTES

1   Clint Hendler, Pinning Down the "Jackass" Tale, Columbia Journalism Rev., September 18, 2009, http://www.cjr.org/transparency/pinning_down_the_jackass_tale.php.
2   Id.
3   Pamela J. Podger, The Limits of Control, Am. Journalism Rev., August/September 2009, 32.
4   Bill Adee, Digging Into Social Media to Build a Newspaper Audience, Nieman Reports, Winter 2008, http://www.nieman.harvard.edu/reports/article/100697/Digging-Into-Social-Media-to-Build-a-Newspaper-Audience.aspx.
5   Mallary J. Tenore, Why The New York Times Eliminated its Social Media Editor Position, Poynter.org, December 10, 2010, http://www.poynter.org/latest-news/top-stories/110111/why-the-new-york-times-eliminated-its-social-media-editor-position/.

6   Associated Press, Social Media Guidelines for AP Employees 1 (January 2012), http://www.ap.org/Images/SocialMediaGuidelinesforAPEmployees-Revised January2012_tcm28-4699.pdf.

7   Radio Television Digital News Association, Ethics: Social Media and Blogging Guidelines (2012), http://www.rtdna.org/pages/media_items/social-media-and-blogging-guidelines1915.php.

8   James Hohmann & the 2010-2011 ASNE Ethics and Values Committee, 10 Best Practices for Social Media: Helpful Guidelines for News Organizations 3 (May 2011), http://asne.org/portals/0/publications/public/10_best_practices_for_social_media.pdf.

9   Society of Professional Journalists, SPJ Code of Ethics (1996), http://www.spj.org/ethicscode.asp.

10   National Public Radio, NPR Ethics Handbook: Social Media (2012), http://ethics.npr.org/tag/social-media/.

11   J.D. Lasica, Wall Street Journal's Social Media Policy, SocialMedia.biz, May 14, 2009, http://www.socialmedia.biz/social-media-policies/wall-street-journals-social-media-policy/.

12   The *New York Times* policy was an internal memo circulated by standards editor Craig Whitney and sent to Poynter.org in 2009. J.D. Lasica, New York Times Social Media Policy, SocialMedia.biz, January 19, 2009, http://www.socialmedia.biz/social-media-policies/new-york-times-social-media-policy/. It is unclear whether the *Times* still employs this policy; in 2011, Liz Heron, the *Times'* social media editor, said the company's policy was basically "use common sense and don't be stupid." Noah Davis, The New York Times Social Media Strategy Boils Down To "Don't Be Stupid," Business Insider, May 23, 2011, http://articles.businessinsider.com/2011-05-23/entertainment/29997911_1_facebook-chat-code-common-sense.

13   Lasica, supra note 11.

14   Associated Press, supra note 6 at 3.

15   Reuters Handbook of Journalism, Reporting from the Internet and Using Social Media (2012), http://handbook.reuters.com/index.php/Reporting_From_the_Internet_And_Using_Social_Media.

16   National Public Radio, supra note 10.

17   The Roanoke Times, News Standards and Policies (2009), http://www.roanoke.com/newsservices/wb/xp-59614#48.

18   National Public Radio, supra note 10.

19   Associated Press, supra note 6 at 4.

20   Roanoke Times, supra note 17.

21   Radio Television Digital News Association, supra note 7.

22   Roanoke Times, supra note 17.

23   Associated Press, supra note 6 at 5.

24   National Public Radio, supra note 10.

25   Lasica, supra note 12.

26   Associated Press, supra note 6 at 1.

27   Reuters, supra note 15.

28   Roanoke Times, supra note 17.

29   Associated Press, supra note 6 at 1.

30   Lasica, supra note 11.

31   National Public Radio, supra note 10.

32   British Broadcasting Company, Social Networking, Microblogs and other Third Party Websites: BBC Use (2012), http://www.bbc.co.uk/editorialguidelines/page/guidance-blogs-bbc-full#social-media-representatives.

33   Steve Buttry, ASNE Offers Good Advice on Social Media, But Too Much Fear and Not Really "Best Practices," The Buttry Diary, May 12, 2011, http://stevebuttry.wordpress.com/2011/05/12/asne-offers-good-advice-on-social-media-but-too-much-fear-and-not-really-best-practices/.

34   Joy Mayer, Good advice interspersed with real missteps in ASNE's social media best practices, Donald W. Reynolds Journalism Institute, May 12, 2011, http://www.thankthis.com/r/Q606Fq6aT02bsRvwnIATaQ:3g_zM1ILVq4ae7L6eEAi_vBmsk W_D5s7sIp-cNxZRsA.

35   Buttry, supra note 33.

36   Hohmann, supra note 8 at 8.

37   ESPN, Social Networking for Talent and Reporters (August 2011), http://frontrow.espn.go.com/wp-content/uploads/2011/08/social-networking-v2-2011.pdf.

38   Mayer, supra note 34.

39   Buttry, supra note 33.

40   Id.

41   John Paton, JRC Employee Rules for Using Social Media, Digital First, April 30, 2011, http://jxpaton.wordpress.com/2011/04/30/jrc-employee-rules-for-using-social-media/.

42   See Bill Kovach & Tom Rosenstiel, Elements of Journalism (2007).

CHAPTER 11

Social Media Policies for Advertising and Public Relations

Holly Kathleen Hall

Arkansas State University

ABSTRACT

The increasing use of social media strategies and tactics in advertising and public relations leave some feeling a loss of control—leaders and managers are losing some control over what employees, consumers, and others say about their organization. But all control is not lost. After a number of brand-damaging incidents, more and more public relations practitioners are recommending and drafting policies and guidelines for the appropriate use of social media. Particular areas of attention include the importance of transparency and the need to disclose any conflicts of interest in order to avoid deception or manipulation of relationships with consumers and respecting privacy.

Organizations are increasingly discovering they need to be utilizing social media strategies and tactics in their public relations plans and campaigns. With the definition of social media comprising "a group of Internet-based applications that . . . allow the creation and exchange of user-generated content," many companies are feeling some loss of control over the conversation and grappling with the power shift to the consumer.[1] However, all power is not lost. After a number of brand-damaging incidents, more and more organizations are drafting policies and guidelines for the appropriate use of social media.

While many companies already have general communication policies in place, such as how to handle media interviews, social media presents some unique challenges. Particular areas of attention include the importance of

transparency and the need to disclose any conflicts of interest in order to avoid deception or manipulation of relationships with consumers, as well as issues regarding privacy and the boundaries of labor laws. This chapter will address those concerns as well as examine successful and unsuccessful policies, and provide a framework for drafting effective and dynamic social media guidelines. Every company and campaign is unique and will differ on what is appropriate, in some respects. Yet, there are some standard principles that can be applied universally.

USES OF SOCIAL MEDIA IN THE PUBLIC RELATIONS INDUSTRY

The appeal of social media in public relations is multifaceted. Social media can provide instantaneous feedback from consumers or potential consumers and an unparalleled level of engagement with audiences. Social media is less about selling products and more about helping solve consumers' problems, whereby the organization's brand and reputation is enhanced and the organization positions itself as the trusted expert in their particular area. This new communication dynamic also means a lot of the power and access to data has transferred from the organization (or the mass media) to the consumer. Alex Bogusky, formerly of Crispin Porter + Bogusky and now founder of FearLess Cottage, a consumer advocacy group, likened the shift to the once powerful notion of secret ingredients: "I think of the obsolete notion of secret ingredients in food. Remember secret ingredients? Secret ingredients point to the old power. The new power is in transparency."[2]

When social media programs are executed well, the benefits to the brand can be exponential. When implemented incorrectly, the consequences range from no translation to the bottom line to big time losses and a brand that is irreparably damaged; from the loss of one or two customers to thousands of customers; from the loss of one or two ill-thinking employees to a major lawsuit against the entire organization. And that means money damages and attorneys' fees in addition to a tarnished reputation. With so much at stake, it is easy to see why many organizations have hesitated to dip their toes into the social media ocean. Unfortunately, even fewer organizations have actually taken the step of crafting policies educating employees on the boundaries of social media usage.

We're Losing Control!

"On the one hand, there's a lot of demand for the business to be out on social media, and there's a lot of need to be out there—but on the other hand, you don't want to do anything to destroy the reputation or change it

in ways you really can't control," said Doug Chia, assistant general counsel for Johnson & Johnson. "Once you're out on social media, the expectations for transparency are much higher than they otherwise are."[3]

One of the issues associated with the loss of control is that some people feel too comfortable being extremely transparent. As chief counsel for the Pennsylvania School Boards Association puts it, "The thing about social media that seems to lead to difficulties . . . is that people tend to say and reveal things about themselves . . . that years ago, they wouldn't say in a roomful of friends, and yet they feel comfortable writing about it online."[4]

Hence, there is a litany of social media mishaps that provide solid proof of the need for social media policies. Take, for example, the Domino's Pizza employees who weren't afraid to video themselves and post the video on YouTube displaying numerous health code violations while preparing food in the most lewd manner possible.[5] Other instances of over-sharing tend to deal with disgruntled employees who air their grievances on a social medium and, many times, face the consequences from a slap on the wrist to being fired. Often, because of the novelty of the first few social media–legal cases, there is much publicity and it usually does not reflect positively on the organization.

Despite the lessons of recent years, the statistics showing how many companies actually have social media policies are dismal. One study from 2010 showed 29 percent of American companies have drafted some formal guidelines for their employees.[6] Peter Vogel, a Dallas attorney and Internet expert, gave speeches to chief information officers in Atlanta, Boston, and Philadelphia in 2010 in which he asked how many of the companies represented had social media policies. The estimate of the response was in the range of 10 to 15 percent.[7] Another study from eMarketer noted the rate of companies without social media policies in early 2010 was at 69 percent.[8] Whatever the true number is, the fact remains that countless organizations remain unprotected and are at risk. While many people continue to envision the Internet as a great unenforced marketplace or Wild West where all kinds of misbehavior is perfectly acceptable, the medium is actually developing "certain customs, ethical standards and unspoken social interactions."[9]

The inability to control the message in the marketplace is the major reason cited as to why some organizations outright forbid their employees from using social media altogether. This is an impractical approach for companies who need the level of engagement and the data that social media can provide. Instead, strategic communicators should draft social media policies that, as Lansons head of digital Simon Sanders noted, "set the boundaries of what can be said and offer guidelines on how it can be said. As much as they restrict, they also enable and empower, giving freedom within a framework."[10]

Without that framework, some kind of harm is very probable. We need only look to a few examples to see the kind of damage a single tweet can do. In March 2011, an employee of New Media Strategies, the agency responsible for Chrysler's consumer-facing Twitter account, tweeted, "I find it ironic that Detroit is known as the #motorcity and yet no one here knows how to f***ing drive." Chrysler dropped the agency, fearing the resulting firestorm from the tweet would impair their relationship with the Motor City.[11] Around the same time, attention turned to the aftermath of the earthquake and tsunami in Japan. Gilbert Gottfried, the voice of the Aflac duck, posted a stream of jokes on his Twitter feed related to the tragedy. In addition to displaying incredible insensitivity, Gottfried's actions had the potential to destroy 75 percent of Aflac's revenue, which came from Japan. The company soon announced the duck would be voiced by a new actor.[12]

And what of the companies who actually have policies in place? A 2010 survey of 261 companies revealed 20 percent of them took action against an employee for policy violations.[13] However, companies actually have to monitor social media and be aware of their policies. In a 2010 poll conducted by Deloitte, one-fifth of respondents claimed their organization does not monitor their social media. If the organization is not monitoring and is involved later with a lawsuit dealing with social media, it can be problematic in terms of finding and handing over data during the discovery process.

So, policy or no policy, how do you know if you are at risk? As far back as 2007, Michael Wiley, head of digital strategy at Edelman, cautioned organizations to "adapt or die" and that "those who fail to stay abreast of change in today's 'conversation society' do so at their own risk." He offered a list of questions to ask yourself to gauge whether your organization is at risk or missing the social media boat:

> "Who is telling our story?" and "What is the narrative?" The days of monolithic message ownership are long gone . . . Do you have a digital and/or social media newsroom? Are your websites RSS-enabled? . . . Do you have a search engine optimization strategy? Do you have an employee-centric social media policy? If your answer to any of these questions is "no", you are missing opportunities and taking unnecessary risks.[14]

So, are you at risk? What is the likelihood of a Domino's, Chrysler, or Aflac-type incident in your organization? The key is to participate in the social media conversation. Provide employees the opportunity to contribute in those spaces. Give them the freedom. But, provide them with the tools and principles to guide them in this new environment.

LEGAL CASES AND CONSIDERATIONS

One of the aspects making social media policy development so challenging is that many times the drafters feel compelled to touch on every aspect of laws or regulations that might be implicated. This is, obviously, an impossible task. Some of the most pressing areas of the law that should be considered in the policy development phase include intellectual property considerations, labor/union issues, defamation, harassment, privacy, and obscenity.

One of the most interesting legal issues to watch in recent years is how the U.S. courts have dealt with privacy (see Chapter 3). Three cases in particular are viewed as groundbreaking. In *Pietrylo v. Hillstone Restaurant Group*, a federal district court in New Jersey found the restaurant group liable for violating the Stored Communications Act.[15] Two employees of the restaurant group developed a password-protected MySpace page in which they aired their grievances about their employment. A manager learned of the site and asked for the log-in ID and password. One of the employees provided the information and the two creators of the site were fired "for damaging employee morale and for violating the restaurant's 'core values.'"[16] During the trial, the employee stated she felt she had been coerced into providing the ID and password. The court felt the restaurant group was at fault; that the managers had not been authorized to view the site. Had this been a non-password protected site, the outcome might have been different.

In *Stengart v. Loving Care Agency*, a home health employee used her company-provided laptop to access her Yahoo! mail account to communicate with her attorney regarding issues with her work situation.[17] Again, this was a personal, password-protected site and the court felt this employee had a certain expectation of privacy in emails to her attorney. This case also incorporated the aspect of attorney–client privilege. So, does this mean companies cannot monitor workplace computers? Not necessarily. The New Jersey Supreme Court opinion stated:

> Our conclusion that Stengart had an expectation of privacy in e-mails with her lawyer does not mean that employers cannot monitor or regulate the use of workplace computers. Companies can adopt and enforce lawful policies relating to computer use to protect the assets, reputation, and productivity of a business and to ensure compliance with legitimate corporate policies . . . But employers have no need or basis to read specific contents of personal, privileged, attorney-client communications in order to enforce corporate policy.[18]

Perhaps the most fascinating decision was in *City of Ontario v. Quon*. In this case, the city of Ontario, California, combed through an employee's text

messages from his city-issued pager to see how many messages were personal or work-related due to overage fees that were being assessed to the city. The legal issue at hand was whether this search violated the Fourth Amendment. The Supreme Court refused to decide whether or not Mr. Quon had a reasonable expectation of privacy. While the Court held the city did not violate Mr. Quon's privacy, the justices acted with an abundance of restraint regarding privacy expectations and new technologies, urging prudence regarding emerging technology and stating:

> Cell phone and text message communications are so pervasive that some persons may consider them to be essential means or necessary instruments for self-expression, even self-identification. That might strengthen the case for an expectation of privacy. On the other hand, the ubiquity of those devices has made them generally affordable, so one could counter that employees who need cell phones . . . could purchase and pay for their own. And employer policies concerning communications will of course shape the reasonable expectations of their employees, especially to the extent that such policies are clearly communicated.[19]

While the absence of a sudden and perhaps inflexible decision from the court was welcome, the case also leaves many questions unanswered for employers and employees alike. The key takeaway from these privacy cases seems to be: Employers need to have a policy in place that specifically and clearly outlines the level of privacy employees can expect in their workplace. And any employer searches conducted of employee sites or content should be done for legitimate business reasons. When courts are determining if an employee had a reasonable expectation of privacy, any employer policy or terms of service-type document will likely be examined to assist in characterizing what is reasonable.[20]

Somewhere in the middle, the right of the employer to protect his or her enterprise collides with the right of an employee to exercise speech that might very well be protected by the National Labor Relations Act, which applies to union and non-union employees. Under the act, employees should be allowed to discuss online "wages, hours, or terms or conditions of employment."[21] So, employers have to determine the fine line between working condition discussions, for example, and disparaging the company's leaders.

The first groundbreaking case relating to workers and social media dealt with an employee of a Connecticut ambulance service who criticized her employer on Facebook, using several vulgarities in ridiculing her supervisor. Regardless, the National Labor Relations Board (NLRB) labeled her speech

under the "working conditions" discussion category.[22] In February 2011, the parties settled, leaving the question open as to the range of speech allowed to employees in social media policies. The company did agree to revise its rules, recognizing they were too broad. The case does demonstrate, however, that the NLRB is willing to fight for employees' rights in this area, despite the vulgarities and mocking that may be involved in an employees' postings.[23]

In April 2011, the NLRB filed a complaint against Reuters news service after a Reuters reporter, Deborah Zabarenko, sent a Tweet stating, "One way to make this the best place to work is to deal honestly with Guild members." She was verbally scolded over what she considered to be free speech. Reuters did have a policy in place, which it believed to be clear and understandable. Reuters decided to settle and changed its social media policy, recognizing the right of its employees to engage in online discussions about workplace issues.[24]

In May 2011, the NLRB sided with a BMW employee who posted criticisms of his employer on Facebook. The employee was asked and agreed to remove the postings, yet was subsequently let go. The NLRB maintained the discussions qualified as "protected concerted activity."[25] In September 2011, an administrative law judge for the NLRB agreed with the NLRB's position and said BMW had "an overly broad policy about employee speech."[26]

One conclusion we can draw about social media and labor issues is that employers simply cannot have a blanket policy stating employees cannot talk about their organizations. Companies have to be specific about the type of speech that is and is not protected. Speech that has as its purpose improving working conditions including critique of supervisors, should be protected to be in compliance with labor laws, including the National Labor Relations Act (NLRA), and any federal and state laws such as Sarbanes Oxley and whistleblower statutes which would protect employees who complain about working conditions or bring potential fraud to light. Speech that simply defames or insults supervisors would most likely not be protected.

ETHICAL CONSIDERATIONS

The instantaneous, sometimes brutally honest feedback and high level of engagement from consumers stems from organizations that are open and transparent in their social media efforts. What is transparency in the context of social media? Sharlyn Lauby, president of Internal Talent Management defines it like this: "Transparency is about being open, honest, and accountable. It's about responsibility. People are listening to you and making evaluations and decisions based upon what you say."[27] Andy Sernovitz, organizer

of BlogWell events, believes transparency is vital: "The number one issue around ethics comes down to disclosure – being honest about your true identity . . . Almost every social media scandal involving brands boils down to a lack of disclosure. The blogosphere expects to know your motivations."[28] The disclosure statement can be shockingly simple. Sernovitz recommends this statement to help disconnect the company views from the individual: "I work for X, and this is my personal opinion."[29]

Sometimes it is not that a person is trying to dupe someone into believing he or she is someone else, rather they omit information that then leaves a false impression. For example, during one of the points at which Facebook revised their terms of service, but barely communicated the change, suspicion and doubt among Facebook users rose.[30] The lesson: even if you aren't purposefully trying to deceive, a less-than-high level of disclosure and transparency can be just as damaging.

Due to those instances, however, when consumers did not know, for example, that someone was being paid by a company to blog about their products, the Federal Trade Commission (FTC) enacted new guides in 2009 prompting disclosure of any such arrangements (see Chapter 5). The same level of transparency should be in effect for situations where a company has hired a third party to produce social media content, such as blogs, on their behalf. Though that kind of disclosure is not yet required, one could argue that the failure to disclose the true author of those materials is misleading. Without that disclosure, won't consumers think they are truly interacting with someone at the company; not the company's advertising or public relations agency? The FTC is responsible for protecting consumers from misleading or deceptive information, including omissions. While their general philosophy maintains that online communications are subject to the same regulations and principles as traditional media, the FTC finds itself having to step in and carve out specific policies and recommendations for online commercial speech. In addition to the FTC, there are also many groups actively self-regulating.

The Word of Mouth Marketing Association (WOMMA) is a well-respected trade organization that represents the social media industry. WOMMA's code of conduct attempts to guide appropriate behavior in the social media sphere. Of the eight listed standards in the code, the first five are all about disclosure: disclosure of relationships, identity, compensation, being honest in communications, and being compliant with the FTC guides mentioned previously.[31]

A group called SocialMedia.org provides a "Disclosure Best Practices Toolkit" to help organizations "learn the appropriate and transparent ways to interact with blogs, bloggers, and the people who interact with them."[32] The first checklist echoes WOMMA's suggestions, encouraging disclosure of

identity, relationships, and compliance with appropriate laws. In addition, it recommends clear disclosure of involvement on all blogs produced by their company or agencies and specifically prohibits the use of pseudonyms or unclear aliases.

Another subject area within transparency is the level of honesty organizations allow within their own ranks. How much dissent and criticism does your company allow without an individual facing discipline or being fired? Consumer advocate Alex Bogusky supports a kind of radical transparency: "When you allow people to be transparent within the company construct, then the company gets a soul. It's not the company's soul. It's the soul of every individual that works there. They no longer have to check who they are at the door and reclaim themselves on the way home."[33] It's a philosophy that may not be readily embraced by many organizations, but some healthy organizations welcome some of that rebellious spirit and conflict in order to take the brutal feedback and use it to strengthen the company.

Companies continue to struggle to find the appropriate balance. As Edelman director of strategy Stefan Stern described the considerations, "If social media are to have any energy or vitality to them, employees should feel free to speak openly about their work and experiences . . . But they should always remember that they are employees, and anything they say could be taken as a semi-official company statement."[34] So, how do you encourage, but caution employees without chilling speech? It begins with employees being confident and knowing what the boundaries are. Vogel recommends beginning the process with your existing employee handbook—many of the foundational elements will most likely already be there such as conflict of interest, trade secrets, and anti-harassment policies. They all should apply to the social media realm. Keep the verbiage simple and clear. And proactively encourage social media use by employees, but provide training and guidance.

Lessons can be learned from organizations that began with too restrictive social media policies. The ambulance company case previously discussed involved a company policy that prohibited employees from discussing practically anything about the organization online. There is a high likelihood that such a policy would run afoul of the First Amendment. A union representing teachers in Santa Rosa County, Florida, threatened a lawsuit over the county's "overly restrictive social media policy" in 2010.[35] The policy was a classic illustration of the "thou shalt not" litany. Far from encouraging social media use, it listed with great legal flair all the risks and liabilities associated with social media and email use.

The assumed standard-bearer for an association to guide best practices in public relations social media use, the Public Relations Society of America (PRSA) offers a rather unwieldy 25-page policy for PRSA social media use.

While comprehensive, the sheer size of the policy discourages a basic under-standing of PRSA's social media use philosophy or beliefs. This demonstrates again the need for conciseness, which in turn leads to understanding. The policy includes sections dealing with communicating via social media, the "rules" of participation, information on measurement, and a specific policy on blogging. Specific legal areas of concern such as copyright, antitrust, and trademark are mentioned. Ethics are alluded to briefly via a referral to the overall PRSA Code of Ethics, which does include provisions such as transparency and disclosure of information.[36]

Organizations who have "done it right" provide some guidance in drafting social media policies. Generally well-regarded policies include those from Kodak, Coca-Cola, Kaiser Permanente, GM, Best Buy, Ogilvy PR, Hill and Knowlton, the British Broadcasting Corporation (BBC), and IBM. The strength of Kodak's policy is in its ability to briefly educate employees on the purpose of different platforms to guide them in their decision as to which format will be of the greatest engagement benefit. Likewise, Coca-Cola aims to educate its employees on the Coca-Cola brand, ensuring that messages stay brand-consistent.[37] As an antithesis to the 25-page PRSA policy, Best Buy offers its no-nonsense, one-page "Be smart. Be respectful. Be human" guidelines.[38] The simplicity and clarity of Best Buy's policy should be emulated by others. The beauty of the BBC policy is in its attempt to foster "conver-sations" instead of "broadcasting messages," and IBM urges users to "try to add value" by providing "worthwhile information and perspective."[39] General Motors' strength is hardwiring the need for transparency into its policy.[40]

These are examples of some of the principles that can be universally incorporated into any social media policy. Every organization is unique and will have to decide what kind of social media usage will be appropriate and effective. Organizations can begin the policy formulation process by bring-ing the right team together to set the stage. Mario Sundar of LinkedIn advocates bringing in "your most active social media employees to collab-orate," which accomplishes two objectives: you have the knowledge base of these social media savvy employees and you have a set of social media evan-gelists to encourage appropriate social media use.[41] Think about including people from representative areas such as human resources, technology, public relations, and marketing. Once the actual content-crafting begins, consider the can–dos rather than the thou–shalt–nots in order to nurture social media practices. If further clarifications are needed on acceptable use, provide brief illustrations and examples of what is appropriate, rather than tacking on additional "don'ts" or augmenting the policy with legalese.

Suggested content areas can include transparency/disclosure, tone, level of engagement, and liabilities. Some would advise that policies need to "stress the potential reach and impact of information sent over the Internet" as a

caution and even require employees to sign forms stating their awareness of workplace equipment monitoring.[42]

While PRSA's own social media policy is lengthy, their toolkit for building a social media policy is a helpful and concise four pages. One particularly valuable piece of advice notes that policies surrounding social media "should morph and grow as social media use and tools evolve, and as an organization forges ahead in the social media landscape and interacts with stakeholders in new ways." PRSA recommends taking a new look at social media policies on an annual basis. In this ever-changing world of social media, it is important to not back the organization into a corner with the policy.

Recognize that social media can also be a powerful and effective tool during a crisis. However, policies and guidelines are needed here, too. If social media is mishandled, it can compound the crisis. Nestlé in 2010 provides an example of how social media made a crisis situation go from bad to worse. Greenpeace called out Nestlé for its use of palm oil, which Greenpeace claimed was obtained in such a way that it harmed rainforests. Consumers began to voice their discontent with this finding through social media. Nestlé was present and engaged. They were monitoring what was being said and they began to respond. So far, so good. Unfortunately, Nestlé's reactions "became problematic when responses lost professionalism and instead became defensive and, at times, juvenile."[43] The lesson learned? Make sure, especially in a crisis, to get the tone right and, like any good crisis communication situation, have a plan. Make sure the employee(s) responding on social media channels know the appropriate framework, tenor, and boundaries.

CONCLUSION

In the end, we are left with this question: Has social media really changed the landscape, or are we just reiterating and expanding existing policies to fit a new medium? As Johnson & Johnson's Doug Chia said, "Social media hasn't changed anything . . . People are blabbing insider information when they're not supposed to. They have been for years."[44] As an HR consultant put it, "It's no different than parents saying to their teenager, 'The stuff you put on Facebook will come back to haunt you in 10 years when you're looking or a job.' You wouldn't scream expletives about your boss, so don't post it."[45] It does seem, however, that there is a singular and unprecedented emphasis on disclosure, transparency, and privacy in social media use and policy development and that courts are still grappling with the unique labor-free speech issues social media presents. Solid policies will be dynamic, touch on transparency and expected privacy levels and do so in a clear, concise, comprehensible way.

No matter the policy or its content, it is worthless if an organization does not adequately train and educate its staff and seek numerous opportunities to communicate the policy's substance. The policy needs to be highly visible, dynamic, understandable, and employee-centric. Laws in this area will continue to evolve; so will social media policies. Is there risk for an organization that uses social media? Yes. Is there potential liability? Yes. Will a good social media policy protect an organization from every possible harm? No. Social media policies are not a cure-all. They are, however, essential. And they need to be well-constructed and administered. Every organization will differ on what they believe is appropriate. But, all organizations should have guidelines, principles, goals, or statements—something that provides a framework, but also freedom.

FREQUENTLY ASKED QUESTIONS

What Are the Five Things Every Social Media Policy for Strategic Communication Should Address?

1. Transparency

Every policy needs to address certain facets of the transparency principle: That you are who you say you are and that the content you write is your opinion. Use the simple statement "I work for X and this is my personal opinion." It is also a necessity that you clearly disclose if you are being given any money, products, or services by an organization you may choose to write about. The statement can be as straightforward as "Company X gave me this product to try."

2. Privacy

Employers can monitor employee social media use—to a degree. Employees will have an expectation of privacy in passwords and areas such as their communications with their attorney. It is vital that employers specifically and clearly state the level of privacy employees can expect in their workplace and as they are working with clients. Something as simple as a Foursquare check-in for a meeting at a client's workplace could be in contradiction to the "Safeguarding Confidences" provision of the PRSA Code of Ethics by revealing the name of a client who may wish to remain private.

3. Employee Control

The National Labor Relations Board seems very willing and eager to step in and fight for an employee's right to express themselves freely on

social media sites if the speech relates to working conditions and terms of employment. It is important for employers to realize their policies should not overly-restrict speech, such as including a blanket statement asking employees not to post content about their work, or else they potentially run afoul of the NLRA, Sarbanes-Oxley and other federal and state laws. With this freedom also comes the need for employer responsibility and employee expectations in any monitoring of the conversations taking place. Define the hours and the depth of monitoring taking place.

4. Intellectual Property

While materials are increasingly available and simple to copy online, it is important to give credit where it is due and to ask permission before using someone else's content such as photographs, videos, and logos. Strategic Communicators working for a specific client should also actively monitor the web for suspicious uses of the client's brand for nefarious purposes, such as online impersonation or setting up fake accounts (see Chapter 4).

5. Tone

When the actual policy-crafting begins, approach the discussion with a "here's what we can do" viewpoint rather than creating a catalog of "thou-shalt-nots" to cultivate appropriate social media practices. Provide illustrations to demonstrate acceptable online behavior and discourage negative tone-of-voice and online battles or fights, which can be brand-damaging.

NOTES

1   Andreas M. Kaplan & Michael Haenlein, Users of the World, Unite! 61 Business Horizons (2010).

2   Nutrition Business Journal, Corporations, You Could Be Losing Your Power, Jan. 1, 2011, http://newhope360.com/managing-your-business/bogusky-corporations-could-be-losing-their-power.

3   Melissa Klein Aguilar, Experts Speak on Using Social Media for Good, Compliance Week, June 20, 2010, http://www.complianceweek.com/pages/login.aspx?returl=/experts-speak-on-using-social-media-for-good/article/186783/&pagetypeid=28&articleid=186783&accesslevel=2&expireddays=0&accessAndPrice=0.

4   Adrienne Lu, How Far Can Schools Go in Regulating Teachers' Social Media Use?, Philadelphia Inquirer, March 14, 2011.

5   See Stephanie Clifford, Video Prank at Domino's Taints Brand, N.Y. Times, April 16, 2009, http://www.nytimes.com/2009/04/16/business/media/16dominos.html.

6   Dallas Lawrence, Six Terrific Examples of Social Media Policies for Employees; Smart Companies Stress Education, Transparency, Legal Liability, and Company Goals and Values, Ragan's Report, May 2010, http://www.ragan.com/Main/Articles/6_terrific_examples_of_social_media_policies_for_e_40774.aspx.

7   Cheryl Hall, Don't Have Social Media Guidelines? Get Some. Dallas Morning News, November 21, 2010, http://www.dallasnews.com/business/columnists/cheryl-hall/20101121-cheryl-hall-don_t-have-social-media-guidelines-for-company-then-get-some.ece.

8   Jason Falls, What Every Company Should Know About Social Media Policy, Social Media Explorer, February 3, 2010, http://www.socialmediaexplorer.com/social-media-marketing/what-every-company-should-know-about-social-media-policy/.

9   J.D. Lasica, Ethical Guidelines for Talking with Your Customers, SocialMedia.biz, February 16, 2010, http://www.socialmedia.biz/2010/02/16/ethical-guidelines-for-talking-with-your-customers/.

10 PR Week UK, Social Media – What's Your Policy?, November 19, 2010, http://www.prweek.com/uk/features/1041541/.

11 Stuart Elliot, When the Marketing Reach of Social Media Backfires, N.Y. Times, March 16, 2011, http://www.nytimes.com/2011/03/16/business/media/16adco.html.

12 Id.

13 Rita Pyrillis, Companies Grapple with Viral Vents, 89 Workforce Management 6, 6–8 (December 15, 2010).

14 Michael Wiley, Edelman – Beyond the Buzz: Adapt or Die, PR Week UK, December 7, 2007, http://www.prweek.com/uk/news/772522/Digital-Essays-Edelman—-Beyond-buzz-adapt-die/?DCMP=ILC-SEARCH.

15 Pietrylo v. Hillstone Restaurant Group d/b/a Houston's, United States District Court, District of New Jersey, Civil Case No. 2:06-cv-5754-FSH-PS.

16 Brian Hall, Court Upholds Jury Verdict in Pietrylo v. Hillstone Restaurant Group, Employer Law Report, October 19, 2009, http://www.employerlawreport.com/2009/10/articles/workplace-privacy/court-upholds-jury-verdict-in-pietrylo-v-hillstone-restaurant-group/#axzz24I04aHO1.

17 Stengart v. Loving Care Agency, Inc., 990 A.2d 650 (2010).

18 Id.

19 City of Ontario v. Quon, 560 U.S. ___ (2010).

20 Lukowski v. County of Seneca, 2009 WL 467075 (W.D.N.Y. 2009) (finding that the "terms of service agreements between customers and businesses have been considered relevant to characterization of privacy interests").

21 323 N.L.R.B. 244, 1997.

22 Steven Greenhouse, Company Accused of Firing Over Facebook Post, N.Y. Times, November 8, 2010, http://www.nytimes.com/2010/11/09/business/09facebook.html.

23 Philip L. Gordon, Settlement in NLRB's AMR/Facebook Case Contains Message for Employers about Social Media Policies, Workplace Privacy Counsel, February 8, 2011, http://privacyblog.littler.com/2011/02/articles/social-networking-1/settlement-in-nlrbs-amrfacebook-case-contains-message-for-employers-about-social-media-policies/.

24 Michael Grubbs & Patrick Scully, Back and Forth with the NLRB on Social Media, September 1, 2011, ShermanHoward.com, http://shermanhoward.com/NewsAndEvents/View/1B3CC7DE-5056-9125-63F98B49F10AF963/.

25 See Karl Knauz Motors, Inc., N.L.R.B.A.L.J. No. 13-CA-46452 (2011).

26 Ameet Sachdev, Judge Backs Car Dealer that Fired Employee over Facebook Post, Chicago Trib., October 1, 2011, http://articles.chicagotribune.com/2011-10-

01/business/ct-biz-1001-nlrb-20111001_1_facebook-post-karl-knauz-bmw-dealership.

27   Sharlyn Lauby, 5 Ways to Make Your Business More Transparent, Mashable, September 30, 2009, http://mashable.com/2009/09/30/business-transparency/.

28   Lasica, supra note 9.

29   Id.

30   Grubbs & Scully, supra note 24.

31   Word of Mouth Marketing Association, Code of Ethics and Standards of Conduct for the Word of Mouth Marketing Association (2009), http://womma.org/ethics/code/.

32   Disclosure Best Practices Toolkit (2012), http://www.socialmedia.org/disclosure/.

33   Nutrition Business Journal, supra note 2.

34   Supra at note 10.

35   Sarah Evans, Restrictive Nine-Page Social Media Policy Leads to Lawsuit. Employment Law in the Digital Age, August 30, 2010, http://www.lawhed.com/social-media/nine-page-social-media-policy-leads-lawsuit/.

36   PRSA Social Media Policy (2012), http://www.prsa.org/AboutPRSA/Guidelines Logos/SocialMediaPolicy/.

37   Supra at note 6.

38   Best Buy Social Media Policy (2012), http://forums.bestbuy.com/t5/Welcome-News/Best-Buy-Social-Media-Policy/td-p/20492.

39   Chris Lake, 16 Social Media Guidelines Used by Real Companies, EConsultancy.com, December 2, 2009, http://econsultancy.com/us/blog/5049-16-social-media-guidelines-used-by-real-companies.

40   Lawrence, supra note 6.

41   Tiffany Black, How to Write a Social Media Policy, Inc., May 27, 2010, http://www.inc.com/guides/2010/05/writing-a-social-media-policy.html.

42   Keisha-Ann G. Gray, Responding to Criticism on the Web, HREOnline.com, November 2, 2009, http://www.hreonline.com/HRE/story.jsp?storyId=282114288.

43   PR Week UK, supra note 10.

44   Aguilar, supra note 3.

45   Pyrillis, supra note 13.

Contributors

Courtney Barclay, Ph.D., J.D., is an assistant professor at Syracuse University's S.I. Newhouse School of Public Communication. She teaches courses in advertising and public relations law and researches developing legal policies regarding consumer protections in the online and mobile environments. In 2010, she published an article in *Media Law and Policy* that discussed the gaps in consumer protection against advertising practices based on behavioral tracking.

David Cuillier, Ph.D., is an associate professor at the University of Arizona School of Journalism and is the Freedom of Information Committee chairman for the Society of Professional Journalists. He is a former newspaper reporter and editor, teaches courses in access to public records, conducts research in freedom of information, and is co-author of *The Art of Access: Strategies for Acquiring Public Records*.

Holly Kathleen Hall, J.D., is an assistant professor of journalism at Arkansas State University teaching classes in media law and ethics, public relations, advertising, and social media. She has published in *Visual Communications Quarterly* and contributed to the book *Social Media: Usage and Impact*. Prior to joining the faculty at ASU, Hall worked in public relations for 10 years and is Accredited in Public Relations by the Public Relations Society of America.

Woodrow Hartzog, Ph.D., LL.M., J.D., is an assistant professor at the Cumberland School of Law at Samford University. His research on privacy, online communication, and electronic agreements has appeared in numerous law reviews and peer-reviewed publications such as the *American University Law Review* and *Communication Law and Policy*. He previously worked as an attorney in private practice and at the United States Patent and Trademark Office. He also served as a clerk for the Electronic Privacy Information Center.

Jennifer Jacobs Henderson, Ph.D., is an associate professor and chair of the Department of Communication at Trinity University in San Antonio, Texas. She specializes in issues of media law, the ethics of media, and the use of participatory cultures for political and social action. For more than a decade, she has been researching how voices outside of American mainstream discourse have pressured the government to expand free speech protections. Dr. Henderson is the author of *Defending the Good News: The Jehovah's Witnesses and Their Plan to Expand the First Amendment*, and co-editor of the 2012 *Routledge Handbook of Participatory Cultures*.

Dan V. Kozlowski, Ph.D., is an assistant professor in the Department of Communication at Saint Louis University. He has twice won the Laurence R. Campbell Research Award, which the Scholastic Journalism Division gives to the top faculty paper presented at the annual Association for Education in Journalism and Mass Communication conference. He is also co-author of the student speech chapter in the widely used media law textbook *Communication and the Law*.

Kathleen K. Olson, J.D., Ph.D., is an associate professor at Lehigh University in Bethlehem, Pennsylvania. She has worked as an attorney and copy editor and helped create the online version of the *Austin American-Statesman* in Austin, Texas. Her research focuses on intellectual property issues, including copyright and the right of publicity, and she is the co-author of *Mass Communication Law in Pennsylvania*.

Cathy Packer, Ph.D., is the W. Horace Carter Distinguished Professor in the School of Journalism and Mass Communication at the University of North Carolina at Chapel Hill. She is co-director of the UNC Center for Media Law and Policy and co-editor of the *N.C. Media Law Handbook*. A former newspaper reporter, she teaches courses in media law and Internet law to undergraduate and graduate students.

Amy Kristin Sanders, J.D., Ph.D., is an assistant professor of mass communication and law at the University of Minnesota as well as a licensed attorney in Missouri and Florida. Dr. Sanders' research focuses on the intersection of mass communication law and new technology, and she is a co-author on the law school casebook *The First Amendment and the Fourth Estate*. She worked as a copy editor and page designer for a New York Times Company newspaper before becoming a professor.

Derigan Silver, Ph.D., is an assistant professor in the Department of Media, Film and Journalism Studies at the University of Denver, where he is the director of the joint MA/J.D. dual degree program. He teaches graduate and undergraduate courses on the First Amendment, media law, Internet

law, and political communication. He has published scholarly articles on originalism, defamation law, social architecture theory, access to terrorism trials, national security law, and student expression. His first book, *National Security in the Courts: The Need for Secrecy v. the Requirements of Transparency*, was published in 2010. He is also the author of a chapter in the widely used media law textbook, *Communication and the Law*.

Daxton R. "Chip" Stewart, Ph.D,. J.D., LL.M., is an associate professor at the Schieffer School of Journalism at Texas Christian University. He has more than 15 years of professional experience in news media and public relations and has been a licensed attorney since 1998. Dr. Stewart's master's and doctorate in journalism are from the University of Missouri, where he focused on media law while working as an editor and columnist at the *Columbia Missourian*. He has served as the editor-in-chief of *Dispute Resolution Magazine*, the quarterly publication of the American Bar Association's Section of Dispute Resolution, since 2007. He is also one of the founding editors of *Community Journalism*, an online, peer-reviewed academic journal that is currently considering manuscripts for its inaugural issue in 2012.

Index